1980

Milton's Biblical and Classical Imagery

by John M. Steadman

Duquesne University Press
Pittsburgh, PA

Published in the United States of America
by Duquesne University Press,
600 Forbes Avenue, Pittsburgh, PA 15282

Distributed by
Humanities Press, Inc.
Atlantic Highlands, NJ 07716

First Edition

Library of Congress Cataloging in Publications Data

Steadman, John M.
  Milton's Biblical and classical imagery

  (Duquesne studies. Language and literature series; v. 5)
  Includes bibliographical references and index.
  1. Milton, John, 1608–1674—Style.   2. Milton, John, 1608–1674—
Religion and ethics.   3. Milton, John, 1608–1674—Knowledge and
learning.   4. Bible in literature.   5. Mythology, Classical, in
literature.   6. Theology in literature.   7. Classical literature—
History and criticism.   I. Title.   II. Series.
PR3594.S7   1984   821'.4   84–1667

For Thomas H. English
with gratitude and admiration

Contents

Acknowledgments

I am indebted to the editors of the following journals for permission to reprint (with revisions) material that has appeared earlier in their pages:

Chapter 3 first appeared in *Neuphilologische Mitteilungen,* vol. 44 (1963), pp. 209-232.

Chapter 4 was originally published in *Neophilologus,* vol. 47 (1963), pp. 61-74.

Chapter 5 originally appeared in *Archiv f. d. Studium d. neueren Sprachen u. Literaturen,* vol. 200 (1963), pp. 353-357.

Chapter 6 was originally printed in a slightly different form as "Milton and Patristic Tradition: The Quality of Hell-Fire," *Anglia,* vol. 76 (1958), pp. 116-128.

Chapter 7 first appeared in *Harvard Theological Review,* vol. 56 (1963), pp. 159-167. Copyright 1963 by the President and Fellows of Harvard College. Reprinted by permission.

Chapter 8 was originally printed in slightly different form as "Milton's Haemony: Etymology and Allegory," *PMLA,* Vol. 77 (1962), pp. 200-207. Reprinted by permission of the Modern Language Association of America. The Appendix to Chapter 8 was originally published in slightly different form as "Haemony and Christian Moly." Reprinted from *History of Ideas News Letter,* vol. 4 (1958), pp. 61-74.

Chapter 9 was first published in slightly different form, as "Dalila, the Ulysses Myth, and Renaissance Allegorical Tradition." Reprinted from *The Modern Language Review,* vol. 57 (1962), pp. 560-565.

Chapter 10 originally appeared in slightly different form, as "Eve's Dream and the Conventions of Witchcraft." Reprinted from *Journal of the History of Ideas,* vol. 26 (1965), pp. 159-167.

Chapter 11 was originally published as "Milton's *Paradise Lost* and the Apotheosis Tradition." Reprinted from *Antike und Abendland: Beiträge zum Verständnis der Griechen und Römer und ihres Nachlebens,* vol. 20, No. 2 (Walter de Gruyter & Co.: Berlin and New York, 1974), pp. 110-134.

Preface

The essays in this volume re-examine certain Biblical and classical images and motifs in Milton's poetry against their background in late classical, medieval, or Renaissance commentary and exegesis. Milton's allusions to the darkness of hell-fire exploit a commonplace of Christian eschatology, already elaborated by patristic and scholastic theologians and still familiar to seventeenth-century Englishmen. A metaphor like the eyelids of the morning evokes both classical and Biblical analogues. His invocations to the Muse of his sacred epics deliberately pit Biblical against pagan sources of inspiration, while paradoxically exploiting both Greek and Hebrew etymologies. In portraying Eve's demonic dream he draws on medieval and Renaissance controversies over the delusions of witchcraft and the illusions of flight. In function as in meaning, the herb Haemony in his masque at Ludlow counterpoints the herb Moly in the Circe-Odysseus myth; their differences as well as their analogies can be illuminated through the etymological associations of the word *haemony* and through the exegetical tradition associated with Homer's moly. In the encounter between Dalila and Samson Milton again turns to Homeric epic for a central image, likening the Philistine temptress to Circe and the Sirens and implicitly underlining the contrast between Odysseus' wisdom and Samson's uxorious folly.

The first chapter of this study, a general introduction, re-examines the interaction of classical and Scriptural motifs in Milton's poetry as a whole. The following chapters, on the other hand, are focused on particular images in his major and minor poetry and involve a more detailed scrutiny of their context in the Renaissance intellectual tradition: a context that includes patristic and medieval exegesis as well as Renaissance Biblical and classical scholarship. I have not attempted to re-examine images drawn from other literary sources, however, or drawn from nature and the visual arts; nor have I endeavored to analyze Milton's rhetorical exploitation of classical or Scriptural motifs in his prose.

I am grateful to friends and colleagues at the Henry E. Huntington

Library and at the University of California, Riverside for encourage-
ment in planning and revising this book, and to the editors of the
journals in which most of these essays originally appeared, for advice
and permission to reprint them. Research for the earlier studies was
conducted partly at the Taylorian Institute, the British Library, and
the Bodleian Library; and most of the research for the later essays
took place at the Huntington Library. I should like to express my
gratitude to the staffs of all four of these institutions. To Professor
Daniel Fineman I am indebted for valuable advice and help in trans-
literating the Hebrew words and quotations printed in the original
versions of several of these essays. A Fellowship from the John Simon
Guggenheim Memorial Foundation, and subsequently a sabbatical
leave from the University of California at Riverside, were helpful in
enabling me to evolve the plan and organization of this volume, along
with those of other and related projects.

CHAPTER ONE

Sion and Helicon

> . . . 'tis not vain or fabulous, . . .
> What the sage Poets taught by th' heav'nly Muse,
> Storied of old in high immortal vers
> Of Dire *Chimera's* and inchanted Iles,
> And rifted Rocks whose entrance leads to hell,
> For such there be, but unbelief is blind.
>
> > (*A Mask*, lines 513–519)

> . . . of the style and uniformitie, and that commonly called
> the Plot. . . ; they only will best judge who are not unacquainted
> with *AEschulus*, *Sophocles*, and *Euripides*, the three Tragic
> Poets unequalled yet by any, and the best rule to all who
> endeavour to write Tragedy.
>
> > ("Of that sort of Dramatic Poem which is call'd Tragedy")

> All our Law and Story strew'd
> With Hymns, our Psalms with artful terms inscrib'd,
> Our Hebrew Songs and Harps in *Babylon*,
> That pleas'd so well our Victors ear, declare
> That rather *Greece* from us these Arts deriv'd;
> Ill imitated, while they loudest sing
> The vices of thir Deities, and thir own
> In Fable, Hymn, or Song, so personating
> Thir Gods ridiculous and themselves past shame.*
>
> > (*PR* IV, lines 334–342)

As a *poeta doctus* — a learned poet, skilled in both Biblical and classical traditions — Milton could draw freely on either or both, limited only by his sense of decorum or the demands of his argument. In different contexts he might employ them to illustrate the same point, emphasizing the analogies between them and treating the classical as a figurative commentary or quasi-typological gloss on the Scriptural. Alternatively, instead of assimilating them to each other and underplaying their differences, he might heighten the contrasts between them, exploiting them rather as antithetical or contradictory than as parallel.

The problem that Milton faced — the relationship between Scriptural and Hellenic tradition, sacred and profane learning — had been a

---

The Poetical Works of John Milton, ed. H.C. Beeching (New York, 1935)

central concern of European Christian civilization since patristic times; but it did not (we should remind ourselves) always appear in the same form, and in Milton's own poetry it could assume quite different aspects.[1] In his elegies and other early Latin poems, he often relies heavily on classical allusions and ornaments, and references to the Christian Heaven and its Deity are usually disguised or assimilated to the prevailing classical imagery. He can on occasion treat his learning sportively, even though he does not always wear it lightly. The garment of Latin style, heavily brocaded with classical allusions, sometimes hampers the movement of thought. He appears at times, like Machiavelli, to have put on formal dress for special colloquy with the ancients. At times he seems, like the precocious schoolboy he is, to be merely "showing off."

The tensions between classical and Scriptural elements, which characterize the work of other Renaissance writers, are also present in Milton's poetry. Nevertheless the ways in which these tensions are brought into intelligible and dramatic relationship often vary not only with the particular poet but with the particular work. The basic issues that he may choose to emphasize in elaborating these tensions are themselves variable: historical fact versus poetic myth, or perhaps sacred versus secular history; contrasts between the moral philosophy and religion of ancient Greece and Rome and those of the Judaeo-Christian tradition. Or the points at issue may be more specifically (and narrowly) literary: an alliance between classical form and Biblical content, or the choice of a Scriptural model for poetry as well as a Scriptural theme. Milton himself had once considered the Book of Job as a model for the brief epic, and he had extolled the Psalms and the Apocalypse as examples of lyric and tragedy.

Yet perhaps the essential, the inevitable issue centered on the nature of the poetic image itself: an appearance of reality rather than reality itself.

There are, in fact, inherent contradictions in the poetics that Milton shared with his contemporaries, which threaten the integrity of the poem either as a "counterfeit" reality or as a mirror of the truth. In employing fiction as the garment of history, or types and shadows as the image of the real — in utilizing metaphors and allegories to convey the inexpressible, and symbols to communicate the unthinkable — in assimilating the true to the false and the real to the unreal, the poet runs the risk of blurring distinctions between fiction and fact. The rational, the sensible, the supersensible all are presented through sensuous values. False things and true things are combined, like colors on a canvas, for the sake of the "verisimilar" appearance: the fictional likeness of truth.

In resurveying briefly the interaction of classical and Biblical images and motifs in Milton's poetry, I shall not attempt in this chapter the

detailed exploration into the background of a particular image that I
have tried to achieve in the following chapters. Emphasizing the more
general aspects of the problem, I shall consider in order (though not in
chronological sequence) his Latin verse, his secular English poetry, and
(finally) his "divine" poetry in English.[2]

[I]

In his Latin epicedia—memorial verses for personal friends, Anglican bishops, university officials—and even in an elegiac epistle addressed to his Puritan tutor, now a pastor in Hamburg, he combines
classical and Scriptural images and themes. In the ode on Dr. John
Gostlin, the Vice/Chancellor's own death is attributed to the wrath
of Persephone, who has been offended because the dead physician's
medical skill has robbed Death itself of so many victims; the poem
concludes with allusions to Aeacus, Proserpina, and the Elysian fields.
The elegy on the death of Lancelot Andrewes, Bishop of Winchester,
combines classical allusions with references to the angelic chorus and
echoes of the Apocalypse (Revelation xiv. 2, 13).[3] In his verses on the
death of Nicholas Felton, Bishop of Ely, Milton echoes the Hesiodic
genealogy of the Hours from Zeus and Themis, refers to the moon as a
"triform goddess," and alludes to Hell as Tartarus and Heaven as
Olympus. On the other hand, he explicitly repudiates certain classical
genealogies of Death as false: as Chaos-born, or as the daughter of
Night, of Erebus, or of the Furies (Erinnyes). Instead he gives her a
celestial origin: she has been "sent from the starry sky to reap God's
harvest everywhere."[4] The spirit of the deceased bishop compares his
ascent to the heavens with that of the biblical Elijah. In *Epitaphium
Damonis*, Milton's pastoral elegy for his friend Charles Diodati, he combines allusions to the Apocalypse (Revelation vii. 9; xiv. 4; xix. 7) with
the imagery of the classical apotheosis and the Dionysian orgy:
"Among the souls of heroes and the immortal gods he drinks the
draughts of heaven. . . . [Y]ou shall enact your part eternally in the
immortal marriage where song and the sound of the lyre are mingled
in ecstasy with blessed dances, and where the festal orgies rage under
the heavenly thyrsus."[5]

The Fourth Elegy, addressed to Thomas Young, begins with numerous echoes of classical myth and history, introduces an allusion to Germanic legend in connection with the etymology of Hamburg, and proceeds gradually to imagery drawn from the Old and New Testaments.
The poet professes his intention of offering "prayers to the glaucous
deities and to Aeolus, . . . and to caerulian Doris, escorted by her
nymphs" to grant his letter a safe passage across the North Sea to
Germany. He exhorts his letter to commandeer Medea's team of

winged dragons, or else the chariot of Ceres and Triptolemus, in order to arrive more swiftly. At this point he introduces a direct reference to the Christian pastor who will receive the letter: "antiquae clarus pietatis honore/Praesul, Christicolas pascere doctus oves"), but returns immediately to his classical imagery and allusions. Thomas Young is dearer to the young Milton than Socrates to Alciabides, or Aristotle to Alexander the Great. After comparing him to Phoenix and Chiron, the legendary tutors of Achilles, Milton alludes, still in mythological terms, to the classical literature in which Young had instructed him: under Young's guidance he had first 'visited the Aonian retreats and the sacred lawns of the twin-peaked mountain," drunk "the Pierian waters" and "by the favour of Clio" moistened his lips with "Castalian wine." After picturing his former tutor "turning over the mighty volumes of the old Fathers or the Holy Scriptures of the true God, or watering tender souls with the dew of heaven," Milton introduces a series of classical allusions (to Penelope, to Thracian spearmen, to Enyo and Mars, to "Stygian darkness"), concluding with a sequence of images derived from Scripture: the rebuffs experienced by Elijah and Saint Paul and Christ. For the motif of divine protection Milton proceeds, by way of a mixed image ("Dei . . . sub aegide tutus"—a Christian adaptation of a pagan mythological motif) to an allusion to the divine rout of Ben Hadad's army. Into this account of how God had "wiped out so many Assyrian soldiers in a silent night under the walls of Zion," Milton inserts (as Professor Merritt Y. Hughes has observed) a patent imitation of Virgil (Aeneid VIII, line 596): "Cornea pulvereum dum verberat ungula campum, Currus arenosam dum quatit actus humum . . .").[6]

In *Naturam Non Pati Senium* the thesis "that nature is not subject to old age" is developed largely through an accumulation of classical allusions: first branding the contrary viewpoint as a human error, then elaborating the motif of nature's decay and the triumph of time in a series of rhetorical questions and mythological references, and finally asserting the continuity of natural order. Although Milton's allusions to Christian doctrine — to providential control over nature and fate, to the final destruction of the universe by fire, to the folly of measuring the ways of God by those of mankind — are central and essential to his argument, they do not violate classical decorum. Many of them have analogues in classical philosophy as well as in classical poetry. A possible echo of Isaiah lv. 8 is phrased in terms of "the gods" and linked with an allusion to the blindness of Oedipus. Again, a possible echo of II Peter iii. 10 is expressed in terms that could fit either Christian or classical doctrines concerning universal conflagration. (The essential difference is that the "final fire" which will destroy the world is absolutely final — "ultima" — for Christian theology, in contrast to the

periodic and cyclical pattern of world-destruction in classical philosophy.) By using the phrase "pater omnipotens" in asserting the providential government of the universe, Milton alludes directly to the
Christian God, while employing a terminology that could also fit the
classical Zeus.[7]

In one of his epigrams on the Gunpowder Plot Milton mixes an
allusion to Elijah with a reference to the classical Fates, or Parcae. His
brief mock-epic or epyllion on the same theme, *In Quintum Novembris*,
describes Satan in biblical terms as "the Deceiver, the Serpent" (cf.
Revelation xii. 9 and xx. 2), but also through classical allusions. Compared to the god Summanus and the Titan Typhoeus, the devil is
further described as the tyrant of Acheron, "the father of the
Eumenides," the outcast from Olympus, the inhabitant of Lethe ("in-
fandam, regnum illaetabile, Lethen"). In the same poem, Fame is depicted in Virgilian and Ovidian imagery, but also represented as the
minister and agent of the Christian Deity. The latter is introduced very
briefly; and, like the God of *Paradise Lost*, he combines classical and
Biblical features: the divine laughter of Psalm ii. 4 and the thunderbolt
associated traditionally with both Jehovah and Jove.[8]

In *Ad Patrem* Milton refers to both celestial and infernal gods and
combines the imagery of classical myth with that of the Apocalypse in
his account of the afterlife in "our native Olympus," where "we shall
walk, crowned with gold," singing to the accompaniment of the harp.[9]
In *Mansus* he hails his Neapolitan host in the name of Clio and Phoebus,
concluding with an anticipation of his own afterlife in the homes of the
celestial gods "on eternal Olympus."[10] The complimentary verses addressed to the Roman poet Salzilli during his illness accommodate
classical imagery to Milton's verse-form (scazontes or "limping" verse),
to Salzilli's vocation as poet and to his illness, and finally to the Roman
setting and the curative effects of the Italian countryside. The motif of
"limping" verse suggests a comparison between Vulcan's gait and "the
graceful ankles of blond Deiope dancing before the golden couch of
Juno. . . ." After invoking the goddess Salus (health) as sister of Hebe,
Milton calls on Apollo as Phoebus or Paean, god of healing as well as
poetic inspiration, reminding him that Salzilli is his priest: "hic tuus
sacerdos est." The final sequence of classical allusions, accommodated
to the topography of Rome and its environs, includes references to
Faunus, to the "gentle Evander" of Virgil's *Aeneid*, to Numa and Egeria,
to the Tiber and "the salt realms of curving Portumnus."[11]

There is a similar aptness in the graceful compliment that Milton
pays to the singer Leonora Baroni, written at about the same time.
Centering the central conceit of his epigram on her Neapolitan origins,
he figuratively identifies her with the Siren Parthenope, who has quit-
ted Posilippo for the Tiber. In another epigram he bases his compli-

ment on Christian rather than classical imagery; Baroni is compared to a guardian angel, and her voice "bespeaks the presence of God."[12]

[II]

Influenced by the humanist practice of literary imitation — in particular, the imitation of the ancients — these Latin poems lend themselves readily to classical imagery and allusion. An analogous reliance on classical imagery, or on a mixture of biblical and classical references,[13] is apparent in much of Milton's minor poetry in English. Some of this verse is occasional poetry: elegies commemorating a deceased friend or relative or "great person"; celebratory verse composed for a particular entertainment; devotional poetry apparently correlated with the Anglican liturgical calendar.[14] Milton's early poem on the death of his infant niece (the "fair infant" who has died of a cough) develops its central conceit — that Winter, enamoured of her beauty, had kissed her and thus unintentionally killed her)—on the analogy of well-known classical fables: the myth of the north wind Boreas and the princess Orithyia, and the myth of Apollo and Hyacinth. Milton then takes up the consolatory motif of immortality, introducing a series of variations on the theme of the child's inherent divinity and her return to the heavens. Does she now dwell above the primum mobile or "in the Elysian fields (if such there were.)"? Was she in actuality a fallen star which "careful *Jove*" has restored to the heavens? A fugitive goddess, who had fled to earth to escape the giants' war against Heaven? Astraea, goddess of Justice? Or perhaps Truth?[15] Or possibly an angel, one of "the golden-winged host"? After these fanciful conjectures (based largely on classical themes) the author concludes his poem on a Christian note. The dead child, with her "heav'n-lov'd innocence," can best perform the office of intercession between God and sinful mankind in Heaven, where she now is. The final stanza of the poem — addressed directly to the mother rather than to the soul of the dead girl — centers on the Christian theme of patience. Exhorting the bereaved (Milton's sister Anne) to cease her lamentation for this "false imagin'd loss" and to render God's gift back to him patiently, he predicts that the Deity will grant her another "off-spring" — a child who will perpetuate her name until Doomsday.[16]

In this juvenile work (written at the age of seventeen) Milton has transformed a family tragedy into a pseudo-classical myth. Writing in the tradition of his master Spenser, and of Spenser's master Ovid — freely, sometimes fancifully, adapting and altering various classical motifs much as Spenser and his followers had done — he transmutes the child's death into a love-story between an aged and childless seasonal deity and a child-bride. He converts a familiar topic of

consolation — the assurance that the dead person now enjoys eternal
life in Heaven — into a sequence of quasi-mythological questions about
her actual identity. As in his later elegies — the English *Lycidas*, the Latin
Epitaphium Damonis — the ultimate consolation lies in the assurance of
eternal life. In this apprentice-piece the play of fancy — the mythopoeic
fictions, the inventions and conceits, the paradoxes — has freer rein
and scope than in the later master-works; the classical images belong
more patently, for the most part, to the Spenserian tradition. Yet this
work shares with the later poems the element of consciously, sometimes
brilliantly achieved artificiality. Despite an allusion to a recent
epidemic of the plague, this poem communicates little sense of the
London setting and little sense of the personality or appearance or
feelings of the dead child and her parents. Instead we find ourselves in
a very different milieu — a milieu that is deliberately made different
and that calls attention to its differences: the consciously constructed
world of a mythological tapestry or Venetian painting, the world of the
Renaissance Ovid and his Spenserian imitators. Yet the transition from
pseudo-pagan to Christian themes and images is gradual. After query-
ing the reality of the Elysian fields, Milton proceeds from mythological
allusions (Jove, the Gigantomachia, Astraea) to an overt personification (Truth) and thence to the image of the child as incarnate angel and
to her present role as intercessor with God.

The epitaph on Lady Jane Paulet, Marchioness of Winchester, belongs to the Jonsonian rather than to the Spenserian tradition. The
classical allusions and the mythopoeic element are less exuberantly, less
fantastically, more soberly and chastely presented: the cypress bud in
Hymen's garland, the advent of Atropos instead of Lucina. The poet
can, without seeming indecorum, couple Helicon with the banks of the
river Cam, and pass from classical imagery to Biblical. Now a "new
welcome Saint" and newly-crowned queen, Jane Paulet sits next to
Rachel, thie "fair *Syrian* Sheperdess" who had similarly died in giving
birth to her second child.

In *Lycidas* the pastoral and classical tradition provides not only a
model but also a frame of reference for organizing and transforming
the specifically British and Christian elements in the poet's experience
and in the life of the Cambridge fellow whose death he is mourning.[17]
Professor Merritt Hughes has observed that "Milton's setting is really a
conventional Italian landscape rather than the drenched plains which
surround Cambridge."[18] Besides the echoes of Greek and Latin
pastoral, the basic metaphor associated with the pastoral genre — the
fiction that Cambridge University is a pasture, that its academic duties
are pastoral duties, that its students are Doric shepherds who bear
names like Thyrsis and Lycidas and pipe for the amusement of fauns
and satyrs, that the learned Milton (the *poeta doctus*) is himself an

"uncouth Swain"—tends to assimilate the milieu of seventeenth-century England to the antique, but virtually timeless, world of Virgil and Theocritus. Because this highly artificial world is both traditional and symbolic, it can include a wide variety of diverse and sometimes inconsistent motifs; and on occasion it can suffer violence—sudden interventions which temporarily shatter the prevailing pastoral decorum. Yet it can also survive these assaults, reestablishing (but also transforming, "transvaluing," and transcending) the pastoral order. The evocation of the nymphs of the classical tradition—echoing both Theocritus and Virgil—leads immediately to a specifically British setting: the vicinity of Edward King's death. These are the same muses who had inspired the Druidic bards of ancient Britain and the poets of ancient Greece. In the distant past—though not now—they have been associated with Anglesea (Mona) and the river Dee (Deva), just as they had once been identified with the hills and streams of Boeotia and Thessaly and Thrace. King's own close association with the Muses, their former association with places near the scene of his death, their absence at the time of his death inevitably bring to mind the analogy with Orpheus.[19]

Into this framework Milton can introduce figures as diverse as Apollo and the river Cam, Neptune and Saint Peter ("The Pilot of the *Galilean* lake"). In the same poem he can apostrophize Saint Michael the Archangel and invoke the rivers Alpheus and Mincius, the fountain Arethusa and the Sicilian Muse; insist that true fame is to be found in Heaven alone, in the eyes of "all judging *Jove*" and denounce the "corrupted Clergy" of the Anglican Church; scatter English flowers on an imaginary bier and visualize the actual fate of the drowned man's corpse, weltering in the savage seas off Cornwall and Scotland.[20] In this final allusion to King's body the focus has shifted (once again) to a British rather than a classical setting—to the stormy Hebrides, to Land's End and "the fable of *Bellerus* old," and to St. Michael's Mount. Milton ends this section of the poem by juxtaposing a prayer to the Archangel for pity with a classical motif reminiscent of the myth of Arion: "And, O ye *Dolphins*, waft the hapless youth."

For the motif of King's afterlife (Lycidas' apotheosis) Milton exploits both classical and Christian imagery. Besides an oblique reference to Matthew xiv. 26 ("the dear might of him that walk'd the waves"), there are echoes of the joys of the blessed as set forth in the Apocalypse (Revelation vii. 17; xxi. 4; xxii. 2). With these Biblical allusions Milton combines the classical apotheosis; henceforth *Lycidas* will be "the Genius of the shore," a beneficent guardian to "all that wander in that perilous flood."[21]

In *Lycidas* the movement from an artifically recreated classical world to a British setting, and from traditional pagan to Christian values, is momentarily broken by seeming violations of pastoral decorum and the intrusion of loftier strains, strains "of a higher mood. . . ." Similarly, there are deliberate inconsistencies in Milton's use of pagan and Christian, or classical and British motifs. At one moment Cambridge may be transformed into a Sicilian countryside. At a later point in the poem the Celtic fringes of Great Britain will be explicitly associated with the same Muses who had inspired the classical poets and whom the singer Thyrsis has previously invoked; but the singer's emphasis falls now on their absence from their British haunts at the time of King's death, and on the helplessness of Calliope herself to protect her son from violent death. When the British setting is once again evoked, still later in the poem, it is in the context of the failure of a pastoral convention when confronted with the uncertainties about the fate of the dead man's corpse. This incertitude concerning the location and destination of his body counterpoints, in turn, the certitude the poet now expresses concerning the destination and fate of the soul.

In the procession of mourners classical and Christian motifs are sharply contrasted. The pastoral imagery in Saint Peter's speech — based as it is on Scriptural tradition — stands in striking contrast with that of the pagan pastoral tradition. The streams of Sicily and Arcadia dare not mingle with those of the Christian oracles. On the other hand, classical and Biblical motifs are combined in the scene of Lycidas' apotheosis.

[III]

In Milton's masques — the fragmentary entertainment at Harefield and A *Mask Presented at Ludlow Castle*, which we know as *Comus* — the adaptation of classical imagery to a British setting, to a particular occasion, and to living persons (persons who were not only present at the performance but took an active part in the spectacle) raises further problems in poetic decorum. The one brings Arcadian shepherds to Harefield; the other celebrates the Earl of Bridgewater's installation as Lord President of Wales through an allegorical fable centered on the theme of spiritual combat and exhibiting the merits of the education (both musical and moral) that the Earl and his lady have given their three children.[22]

Arcades hinges on the conceit that certain nymphs and shepherds have forsaken their native Arcadia in quest of the Lady Alice Spencer—Dowager Countess of Derby and now the widow of Lord Ellesmere and step-mother of the first Earl of Bridgewater.[23] As these "Noble persons of Her Family," dressed in "pastoral habit," approach her "seat of State," they preserve the decorum of pagan antiquity, praising her as a goddess and comparing her to Latona, Cybele, and

Juno. Met by the Genius of the Wood (apparently played by Henry Lawes),[24] they follow him to the chair of state, where the Dowager Countess sits "Clad in splendor as befits/Her deity." Finally, alluding to the myth of Pan and Syrinx, the Genius urges them to renounce Arcadia to "serve the Lady of this place"; for "Such a rural Queen/All *Arcadia* hath not seen." The classical world has been transferred, both literally and metaphorically, to the English countryside. Comparison to Juno would be an appropriate compliment to the wife of the former Lord Chancellor; and allusions to the mother-goddesses who had rejoiced in their off-spring would compliment most of the participants in the masque — the disguised shepherds and nymphs as well as the Countess.

Although a central theme in this "entertainment" is the superiority of Harefield to the classical Arcadia ("A better soil shall give ye thanks") and the Dowager Countess's superiority to Arcadia's rural queens and even to Syrinx herself ("Your *Pan's* mistress"), the imagery of the verses contains little that suggests a distinctively English setting. Milton gives us a tutelary sylvan, "the pow'r/ Of this fair Wood" who holds this office "by lot from *Jove*," defends its vegetation from harm, and passes the night listening to the music of the spheres ("the celestial *Sirens'* harmony").[25] By a judicious use of Platonic myth and Pythagorean doctrine Milton seems to have combined an encomium of the power of music with an indirect compliment to Henry Lawes; the allusion to Nature's "law" in line 70 is characteristic, in fact, of contemporary puns on his name.[26] The gentlemen of the Bridgewater family ("gentle Swains") are complimented by an imaginary genealogy from the river Alpheus. The ladies are lauded as "Nymphs" and "breathing Roses of the Wood." The Countess is extolled as a goddess, and the beauty of Harefield itself heightened by analogy with Arcadia. Instead of introducing specifically English details to emphasize the superiority of this English country estate and its owner, Milton exploits the classical allusions themselves — the legendary associations of Arcadian place-names like Ladon and Lycaeus, Erymanth, Cyllene, Maenalus, and the names of classical goddesses to demonstrate their own inferiority to Harefield and its lady.

In *Comus*, even more clearly than in *Arcades*, classical imagery links a contemporary British setting with the mythical milieus of ancient Greece, mixing well-known fables with new mythical inventions and exploiting the pagan marvellous to illustrate or symbolize concepts acceptable to an audience composed of seventeenth-century Christian gentry. Thus employed, myth might function as demonstrative rhetoric — for the praise or blame of contemporary society — or as allegorical and symbolic fiction, shadowing or exemplifying norms of

virtue or vice. Serving the ends of instruction and persuasion as well as
entertainment, performing a semantic function over and above its role
as ornament, it might provide a vocabulary of symbols intelligible not
only to the humanist and scholar but also to many members of the
nobility and gentry: a language of signs all the more powerful for its
frequent ambiguities, its ambivalence, and its potential contradictions.[27]

In celebrating a contemporary event—the Earl's formal
installation—Milton has in a sense transformed it by placing it in a
context of traditional and freshly invented myth. The time is the
present—long after the age of the Greek poets or the reign of the
British king Locrine. The geographical setting is Britain—not Greece
or Italy—and more specifically the Welsh Marches, the countryside
near Ludlow and the river Severn. The final scene indeed presents
Ludlow Town and the President's Castle; the place and time of the
dramatic myth thus narrow to the actual historic place and occasion.
Yet, except for oblique references to the Welsh border country (lines
27–33) and to the "smooth Severn stream" (line 825), the two preceding scenes in the wild wood and at Comus' "stately Palace" are unlo-
calized, and the vagueness that surrounds them enhances their mythical and fairytale character, inviting attention to their symbolic significance. For, as recent critics have observed, both scenes involve images
with complex literary traditions behind them: the forest-labyrinth
(with analogues in Dante's *selva oscura* and Spenser's wandering wood)
and the palace of Circe (with later analogues in the palaces or
pleasure-gardens of Ariosto's Alcina, Tasso's Armida, and Spenser's
Acrasia). This is not ancient Greece or Italy—and repeated allusions to
the ancients serve to emphasize the point—yet Milton nevertheless
takes particular pains to associate the ordeal of the three children with
the mythology of the classical world, inventing a liaison between Bacchus and Circe and conducting their offspring Comus through "the
Celtic and *Iberian* fields" to this ominous wood not far from the banks of
the Severn.

The Elder Brother professes to "call/ Antiquity from the old Schools
of *Greece*/ To testify the arms of Chastity"; and the attendant Spirit
commends the truths underlying the mythical fables "Storied of old"
by wise poets. The action of the masque-fable takes place in the present, long after the time of the ancients; but the mythological conventions of the antique pagan world are, for the most part, carefully maintained, and Christian themes and images are usually shadowed under
pagan symbols. One might expect heathen imagery from Comus himself, the son of Bacchus and Circe; and in fact the tutelary divinity of
banquets and revelry assimilates his orgies to pagan rites, invoking the

sinister goddess Cotytto as "Goddess of Nocturnal Sport." Thyrsis subsequently describes the sorceror and his "monstrous rout" as "Doing abhorred rites to *Hecate*. . . ."

The attendant Spirit is presented as a Neo-Platonic daemon, who dwells before the "threshold of *Jove's* Court" and intervenes to aid Jove's favorites in their passage through the perilous wood. His role is comparable to that of a guardian angel, but Milton avoids making this identification. After death Virtue will crown her true servants "Amongst the enthron'd gods on Sainted seats." Deploring the ill-managed merriment of rustic wassailers at their harvest feasts, the Lady complains that they "praise the bounteous *Pan*" in wanton dance and "thank the gods amiss." Yet elsewhere she can allude to the three theological virtues (lines 213–215), substituting Chastity for Charity; and the song in which the attendant Spirit presents the children formally to their parents combines the Biblical theme of the trial of faith and patience, with the imagery of the dance (lines 970–975). To free the Lady from Comus' enchanted seat, he invokes the aid of the goddess of the river Severn, summoning her in the name of classical water-deities: Oceanus, Tethys, Nereus, Proteus, Triton, Leucothea, and others.

Although the figure of the legendary Sabrina derives from the fabulous history of Geoffrey of Monmouth, the "quick immortal change" whereby the king's daughter is transformed into a river-goddess has been modelled largely on the transformations of mortals into water-divinities in Ovid's *Metamorphoses* and possibly on Spenser's fables of the metamorphoses of various nymphs into fountains and streams. An exception to the predominant classical imagery is the Second Brother's allusion to the books, beads, and maple dish of a Hermit. This essentially Christian motif evokes the indeterminate chronological and geographical context of Spenserian romance: variably medieval, classical, and contemporary. The Lady herself also employs the imagery of medieval Christianity, comparing the "gray-hooded E'vn" to "a sad Votarist in Palmer's weed. . . ."

In contrast to the rustic ducks and nods of the Country-Dancers at Ludlow, the fashionable dancing of the gentry is lauded in mythological terms: "such Court guise/ as *Mercury* did first devise/ With the mincing *Dryades*. . . ." Whatever his ultimate destination — a pagan Elysium or a Christian heaven — the attendant Spirit maintains the decorum of classical myth through his epilogue. He mentions the Hesperides, Venus and Adonis, Cupid and Psyche, the promise of Jove; but he avoids any explicit reference to the Christian Deity.

Both the contemporary British setting and Christian moral or theological concepts are deliberately obscured under the veil of pagan myth. In much the same way, motifs significantly reminiscent of the

morality play (with its Good and Evil Angels and its central personification of Mankind or Everyman) have been accommodated both to the
conventions of Renaissance mythography and to those of the Renaissance masque. For Rosemond Tuve, the Lady was an "endangered
creature in the dark wood of the world," and Milton's "whole invention" moves upon "the great hinge of the Circe-Comus myth. . . ."[28]
C.L. Barber interpreted the masque as "a trial of chastity" in which the
poet "put Revel in the role of villain. . . ."[29] Other critics have interpreted *Comus* as Christian or Neo-Platonic allegory.[30] As Professor
R.M. Adams[31] observed some years ago, it is easy to overread this
masque; the reader should be modest in drawing inferences from the
nature of the imagery or from the philosophical *sententiae* scattered
throughout the dialogue. In advancing one interpretation, however,
we are not necessarily obliged to exclude others. In the Lady's ordeal
we may recognize indeed several complementary motifs. The journey
of the soul through the wilderness of this world and its return to the
heavens through virtue tested and purified by trial. The trial of virtue
by confrontation with its contrary vice. The motif of right rule —
government and discipline in the individual and in the state. Conventional interpretations of Circe and her ectypes in terms of the deceits of
the senses, irrational pleasure, or bestial vice. Etymological associations
of the forest with the realm of matter (*hyle*) and multiplicity (*silva*). A
complex of Platonic images and concepts associated with the education
to be bestowed on children of the state's guardians: images linking
sorcery with pleasure, temperance with harmony, philosophy with
music. The Platonic emphasis on philosophy as a means of purification
and reascent to the heavens.[32]

Significantly the mythological fable of *Comus* — re-enacting if not
parodying the Ulysses myth — reflects and shadows the masque-
situation itself. As participants in the masque, the three children are
indeed exposed to the sorceries of pleasure and nocturnal revelry —
the enchantments of the god of masquing — and in the course of the
action they symbolically enact their own victory over temptation. With
Comus himself expelled — the potentially vicious aspects of the masque
ritually exorcised — the masque-spectacle itself has been purified; the
final dances may justly celebrate the children's triumph over "sensual
Folly, and Intemperance."

In this context, where the fictions of classical myth are represented
as still alive and still valid, the Lady can invoke Echo for aid, comparing
her own lost brothers to "thy *Narcissus*," and on another occasion likening them to Hebe. Comus can remember listening to the songs of Circe
and the Sirens, recalling how they had moved even Scylla and Charyb-
dis. He can hail the lost Lady herself as the tutelary goddess of the
grove, the companion of Pan or Silvan. The Elder Brother interprets

the myths of Diana and Minerva as moral allegory, testimony to the power of Chastity. The attendant Spirit, disguised as the shepherd Thyrsis, defends the myths of the ancient poets as still true, still valid:

> . . . 'tis not vain or fabulous
> (Though so esteem'd by shallow ignorance)
> What the sage Poets taught by th' heav'nly Muse
> Storied of old in high immortal verse
> Of dire *Chimeras* and enchanted Isles,
> And rifted Rocks whose entrance leads to hell,
> For such there be, but unbelief is blind.

This analogy serves to strengthen the literal force of the fabulous tale that follows, and to emphasize the real peril that confronts the Lady; but it also invites the audience indirectly to look beneath the veil of the incredible fable to the moral and spiritual reality concealed beneath the ancient myths.

[IV]

The poetry considered thus far is, for the most part, secular, though it sometimes includes Christian motifs. Let us turn now to Milton's "divine poems" — poetry on Biblical subjects or devoted to Christian religious themes.[33] One of the earliest of these is his ode "On the Morning of Christ's Nativity"; written at the same time as his Sixth Elegy, it presents a striking contrast to the latter in its treatment of classical allusions. With the exception of the verses describing his Nativity Ode (lines 81–87), the Latin poem to Charles Diodati is dominated by references to classical myth (references to Bacchus and Apollo, Liber and Erato, Ceres and Venus, Muses and the Aonian hill); to classical poets (Ovid and Pindar and Horace, Orpheus and Homer); or to classical philosophers and seers (Pythagoras, Tiresias, Linus and Calchas). Even in affirming the sacred office of the poet, Milton retains the decorum of the ancient polytheism: "For truly, the bard is sacred to the gods and is their priest. His hidden heart and his lips alike breathe out Jove."[34]

In contrast, the six Latin verses describing his birthday gift to Christ (the Nativity Ode) avoid mythological allusions. The only reference to the gods of the Gentiles in this passage is their overthrow: "Et subito elisos ad sua fana Deos."[35]

In *Comus* the attendant Spirit alludes to the "heav'nly Muse" who had taught the ancient mythological poets, but there is nothing in the context of this allusion to suggest that she is identical with the heavenly muse of DuBartas' *Uranie* and of Milton's *Paradise Lost*. In the Nativity Ode, however, the "Heav'nly Muse" is closely associated with the

Judaeo-Christian tradition, and in the introductory section Milton invokes her aid in preparing a birthday present to the Infant God:

> Hast thou no verse, no hymn, or solemn strain,
> To welcome him to this his new abode. . .?

The Christmas gift, which the poet hopes to present at the manger before the arrival of the Magi, is the "Hymn" itself — 27 stanzas composed in a verse form adapted from that of the Italian canzone and strongly reminiscent of the Spenserian tradition in its iconographical methods, its treatment of personifications, and its elaboration of conceits.

The genre to which the Hymn belongs is classical as well as Christian. Subsequently, in *The Reason of Church-Government*, Milton would praise Biblical as well as classical models for lyric poetry: "Or if occasion shall lead to imitate those magnific odes and hymns wherein Pindarus and Callimachus are in most things worthy, some others in their frame judicious, in the matter most an[d] end faulty. But those frequent songs throughout the law and prophets beyond all these, not in their divine argument alone, but in the very critical art of composition, may be easily made to appear over all the kinds of lyric poesy to be incomparable."[36] As lyric poetry correlated with a festival of the Church — even though he did not design his poem for choral performance — Milton's "Hymn" belongs to a tradition of Judaeo-Christian hymnology that includes poems as diverse as the Psalms and Canticles, Spenser's hymns of heavenly love and heavenly beauty and the hymns of Richard Crashaw. On the other hand, his poem is a deliberate Christian counterpart of the Homeric and Orphic hymns, and of other lyric poems celebrating the gods of ancient Greece. One of the hymns formerly attributed to Homer had recounted the feats of the infant Hermes, who had managed, even in his cradle to outwit Apollo. The infant Heracles had similarly strangled the serpents that his stepmother Hera had sent against him. In Milton's hymn the first *aristeia* of the divine child is the cessation of the oracles and the rout of the entire pantheon of heathen gods:

> Our Babe, to show his Godhead true,
> Can in his swaddling bands control the damned crew.

If this passage evokes the memory of the exploits of the infant Hermes and the infant Heracles, it does so only to undercut them, banishing them to outer darkness with the whole tribe of Gentile idols.

This is the first assault on the kingdom of Satan, the "old Dragon"; and the heathen gods are introduced only to portray their expulsion. The majority, significantly, as in the catalogue of devils in *Paradise Lost*, do not belong to the classical pantheon; they are the idols of barbarian peoples, indigenous to regions near or adjacent to the Holy Land. As such, they have been traditional rivals of the Judaeo-Christian Deity. Along with classical divinities (Apollo, nymphs, local genii, lars and lemures) appear the idols of the Middle East (the Canaanite Baal, the Philistine Dagon, the Ammonite Moloch, the Egyptian Hammon and Osiris, the Phoenician Ashtaroth and Thammuz) as well as the half-serpentine Typhon and sundry ghosts or fays.

In the earlier sections of this poem classical imagery is either subordinated or assimilated to biblical motifs. In personifying Nature and Peace, Milton is following the example of both Christian and pagan poets. Both of these "machining persons," however, have lost whatever pagan connotations they once possessed, and have been converted to the praise of the Christian Deity. Nature is aware of her true Maker and Master and also of the fact of His Incarnation. Peace is prompt in obeying His command.

In introducing an allusion to the Arcadian shepherds' god Pan in his description of the shepherds of Bethlehem, Milton has consciously evoked the classical pastoral tradition. Yet this inconsistency is not obtrusive, inasmuch as Pan had become virtually a synonym for Christ in Renaissance humanist tradition. The allusions to "the age of gold" and to "*Cynthia*'s seat" (the moon) are likewise too conventional to seem discordant. In this section of the hymn Milton associates the angelic music at Christ's nativity with the Old Testament motif of the angelic song at the creation of the world (Job xxxviii. 6–7), but also with the classical motif of the music of the spheres. Similarly, his prophecy that "Truth and Justice then Will down return to men" combines the Biblical motif of the Four Daughters of God (Psalm lxxxv. 10–11) with the classical myth of Astraea's having forsaken the earth and returned to the heavens.[37] To speculation about a return to the Golden Age (a classical myth frequently assimilated to the motif of the Biblical Garden of Eden) Milton opposes the prophetic certainty of the future day of doom, thereby emphasizing both parallels and contrasts between the First and Second Advents and placing the Incarnation and the Last Judgment in the same perspective.

Begun within the year following the Nativity Ode and left incomplete, "The Passion" was apparently intended as a companion piece. The eight stanzas extant employ the same verse-form and rhyme-scheme as the four introductory stanzas of the Christmas ode. They form an introduction to the poem that Milton felt himself too immature to write; but whether the body of this work would have retained the stanzaic form of the introductory stanzas, whether it would have utilized the same stanzaic form as "The Hymn," or whether it would have substituted an entirely different stanza we cannot know. The elaborate conceits that characterize this poem, and various other English works composed in Milton's youth, are usually ascribed to the influence of Giles Fletcher the younger and other English Spenserians, to the example of DuBartas, and to the diffusion of a vaguely defined "marinism" from Italy into western Europe.

An implicit parallel with the *enfances* of a classical hero or divinity underlies the Nativity hymn; "The Passion," in turn, emphasizes an analogy with the trials and labors of Hercules and other mythical heroes. Just as "The Hymn" has celebrated the victory of the new-born Christ over all the gods of the Gentiles, its sequel asserts His superiority to the Gentile worthies and heroes, establishing His unique position as "Most perfect *Hero*. . . ."

The allusions to classical sources of poetic inspiration ("My muse," "my *Phoebus*") are so conventional that they do not seem inconsistent with a Biblical theme; and both allusions are introduced in the context of Christian sacred poetry. Of "joyous news of heav'nly Infant's birth,/ My muse with Angels did divide to sing." Now Milton's "*Phoebus*" is bound to the "Horizon" of Christ's passion and death. When he invokes night for aid, as "best Patroness of grief," he is elaborating a conventional personification; he is not treating her here as the Gentile goddess whose genealogical claims he had denounced in his First Academic Exercise and whom he would later include among the powers of the abyss in *Paradise Lost*. Such indeterminate images — neither strictly classical nor strictly Biblical — are, moreover, immediately countered and complemented by clearly Scriptural themes. If the allusion to Christ as "perfect Hero" suggests an analogy with Hercules, the difference is immediately made clear by emphasizing Christ's sacerdotal role in His incarnation and sacrifice: "He sovran Priest, stooping his regal head . . . Poor fleshly Tabernacle entered. . . ." Similarly, after the references to Phoebus and to night, Milton introduces the chariot of Ezekiel; like a prophet, the poet is carried in spirit on a visionary journey to Jerusalem:

> See, see the Chariot and those rushing wheels
> That whirl'd the Prophet up at *Chebar* flood;
> My spirit some transporting *Cherub* feels,
> To bear me where the Towers of *Salem* stood. . . .

Like the Nativity Ode and "The Passion," Milton's brief lyric "Upon the Circumcision" is correlated with the sequence of events in the life of Christ and with the liturgical calendar of the Church. Unlike the opening lines of "The Passion," it does not refer explicitly to the Nativity Ode, nor does it employ the same metrical forms. In form (as F.T. Prince observed) it follows the pattern of the Italian canzone.[38] The same rhyme-scheme and (with one minor exception) the same metrical patterns are followed in both halves of the poem; it is composed essentially of two symmetrical stanzas of 14 lines each. The imagery throughout is biblical, without classical intrusions. Milton begins by invoking the angels who had sung at Christ's nativity to mourn the first (and premonitory) shedding of His blood; the poet then takes up, quite briefly, the topic of Christ's humiliation and vicarious atonement. Just as the Nativity hymn moves freely in time from the Nativity itself retrospectively to the creation of the world and proleptically to the Last Judgment, this brief lyric moves retrospectively from the circumcision to the doom pronounced on Adam and proleptically to the crucifixion.

The two other italianate lyrics, with which this canzone is often compared, appear to be almost contemporary with it. Both are madrigals,[39] both are occasional poems (though not in precisely the same sense), both are religious verse. Apparently intended for a clock case, "On Time" is a brief meditation on eternity. "At a Solemn Music" adapts the traditional analogy (inherited from classical musical theory) between cosmic harmony, the harmony of man's body and soul, and instrumental harmony (*musica mundana, humana,* and *instrumentalis*) to the service and worship of God.[40] With its union of voice and verse, the concert serves as an image of the celestial music of the angels before the throne of God; obedience and disobedience to Him are translated into musical metaphors, as concord and discord. The reference to Voice and Verse as *"Sirens"* is an echo from classical mythology, just as the analogy between instrumental music and human and cosmic harmony is a legacy from classical theory. Both of these motifs, however, had become so conventional that Milton could, without manifest inconsistency, exploit them in a Judaeo-Christian context, associating them with the "sapphire-colour'd throne" and celestial music of Old and New Testament apocalypses and with the fall and restoration of mankind.

[V]

The fact that all three of Milton's major poems are "divine" poetry — poems based on Biblical arguments — is of central importance for the character of their imagery and for the relationships between classical and Judaeo-Christian values in all three works. Speaking *in propria persona*, in his own voice, the epic narrator has comparative freedom to draw his images from both classical and Biblical sources and to introduce modern as well as ancient comparisons. The characters in the poem, on the other hand — his epic *personae* — would have far less liberty. Without special revelation Adam and Eve could have no knowledge at all of Greek and Latin civilization, or of Judaeo-Christian history. Any information of this sort must necessarily be revealed to

them by an angel. Allusions to Greek and Latin myth by divine or
angelic persons, on the other hand, might seem to violate decorum.
The burden of classical allusions, mythological comparisons, and the
like must fall predominantly on the epic narrator.

In the case of *Paradise Regained* — where the action occurs over 4000
years after that of *Paradise Lost*, and where the events of Old Testament
history and the empires of Assyria and Persia and Greece belong to the
past — the range of allusions available to the principal *personae* is ap-
preciably greater. Of the two antagonists in this brief epic, one is a
fallen angel, the Prince of this World; he still possesses, however darkened and diminished, the powers of his angelic intelligence. The other
spiritual combattant is the incarnate Logos, the divine Wisdom in
human form — but the question of how much, precisely, He may know
about the wisdom of the Gentiles is a point that the Messiah Himself
does not clarify, and that the poet deliberately leaves indeterminate. In
the drama, where the poet cannot speak at all in his own person,
allusions to other cultural traditions must be accommodated to the
capacities and experience of the speaker. One would not expect Samson or Dalila or any of their companions to have Greek mythology at
their fingertips; and any reference to the Greece of Pericles or to
Roman history would be a glaring anachronism.

On the other hand — leaving aside such limitations on classical imagery and allusions for the moment — all three poems belong to classical
genres and, in varying degrees, conform to the principles of classical
structure, as Milton believed them to be. The example of the three
Athenian tragic poets — Aeschylus, Sophocles, Euripides — was in his
opinion the "best rule to all who endeavour to write Tragedy." He
bestows a Greek title on his tragedy of Samson; and long before, in his
list of dramatic plans, he had given analogous Greek titles to projected
tragedies on other biblical subjects: "Achabaei Cunoboroomeni,"
"Amaziah Doryalotus," "Salomon Gynaecocratumenus," and the like.
He includes the conventional parts of Greek tragedy in his biblical
drama: prologos, parados, epeisodion, stasimon, exodus. In situation,
characterization, and dialogue he recalls analogical, if not prototypical,
scenes in classical tragedy; and in the final chorus of *Samson Agoniste* he
echoes a concluding chorus of Euripedean drama.[41]

In *Samson* the conflict between true and false divinities is focused
primarily on the contest between Jehovah and Dagon and their respective champions, Hebrew and Philistine. Accordingly, the conflicting
loyalties and contrasting modes of heroism are presented largely in
terms of local or regional traditions. The heroic age is that of the
Nephilim, and the Anakim of Canaan, whose descendants survived in
Philistia); and both Samson and Harapha allude to the Anakim as a
standard against which they measure their own heroism.[42] Samson has

given "some proof/ Of acts indeed heroic, far beyond/ The Sons of *Anak*, famous now and blaz'd . . ." (lines 526–528). Harapha claims to belong to a "stock renown'd/ As *Og* or *Anak* and the *Emims* old/ That *Kiriathaim* held . . ." (lines 1079–1081). Dalila compares herself to the Hebrew heroine Jael as the pious deliverer of her country from a fierce destroyer (lines 984–994). Even in his oath Harapha observes the decorum of an idolater, swearing by Baal-zebub and Astaroth. (One recalls the worship of Baal and Ashtaroth by the Ten Tribes in *Paradise Regained*, Book III, line 417.) Samson's friends draw moral exempla from their own national history—from the stories of Gideon and Jephthah (lines 276–289). When they compare the sumptuous Dalila to a vessel under full sail, it is a vessel from a nearby port: a "Ship/ of *Tarsus*, bound for th' Isles of *Javan* or *Gadire* . . ." (lines 714–716).[43]

References to Greek myth are, for the most part, presented obliquely. The Circe allusion (lines 934–935) is implicit rather than overt, and neither the sorceress nor the Sirens are mentioned by name. Other classical myths are branded as Gentile fables. Although the Chorus compares Samson to either Atlas or Hercules, it names neither of these legendary figures directly, and the myth is introduced in terms that undercut its validity: "Like whom the Gentiles feign to bear up Heav'n" (line 150).[44] Samson regards the myths of the Greeks as merely Ethnic fables, but he also exploits them to heighten his own sense of guilt, to aggravate his self-condemnation for revealing a divine secret to a Philistine woman. The allusion serves, in fact, as the basis for an *a minori* argument, an argument "from the lesser to the greater." If (the argument seems to run) such a betrayal of divine secrets has seemed especially heinous even to the Gentiles (who do not know the true God and whose divinities are false gods, vain and empty idols), how much more heinous is this sin in me—in me who know and worship the true God, yet have betrayed His secrets. Those were imaginary sins, committed only in empty fables; my sin is real.

Although Professor Hughes identifies this passage as a reference to the Tantalus myth,[45] Samson phrases his allusion to heathen mythology in terms that Milton has made deliberately vague and oblique (liness 499–501):

> . . .A sin
> That Gentiles in thir Parables condemn
> To thir abyss and horrid pains confin'd.

As "*Chalybean* temper'd steel" (line 133) was a product of Asia Minor, this classical allusion to a Middle Eastern setting is hardly out of place in this dramatic context. Normally in this drama, however, Milton utilizes Oriental place-names unknown to classical poetry. They correspond to the Greek place-names that had adorned the tragic verse of Sophocles and his peers; and Milton treats them in the classical manner, adding characteristic epithets: "in *Ramath-lechi* famous to this day"; "the Hill by *Hebron*, seat of Giants old"; "From *Eshtaol* and *Zora's* fruitful Vale."

Yet, except for the reference to the tabernacle at Shiloh (line 1674), the two Semichoruses which preceded Manoa's final speech would hardly seem out of place in a drama on a classical theme—though in their context they are well adapted to this neoclassical drama on an Old Testament miracle. Although the imagery of "sudden flame" had been applied to Achilles and other classical heroes and though the 'fiery virtue" of this Danite hero recalls the *ignea virtus* of Lucan and other classical writers, these metaphors are not essentially pagan and could therefore be transferred readily to an Old Testament subject without violating decorum. The simile of the "ev'ning Dragon"[46] may recall classical similes likening a powerful warrior to a deadly serpent, but in evoking the classical tradition it embellishes the biblical theme instead of clashing with it. Taken separately, the eagle simile and the imagery of "cloudless thunder" would seem neutral—neither exclusively Biblical nor exclusively classical—but in conjunction they inevitably recall the classical Zeus. This oblique allusion to the pagan imagery of divine justice is, however, implicit rather than explicit, and would not normally strike the reader as out of place. Finally, although the legend of the Phoenix[47] circulated primarily through classical poetry and bestiaries, it had long since been accommodated, allegorically and typologically, to the Christian tradition. Milton's Semichorus of Danites does not refer to it by name; and the reference to "the *Arabian* woods" would seem to preserve the decorum of a Middle Eastern setting. (I shall consider other aspects of the imagery in this passage later, at the end of this section.)

The type of post-sepulchral honors that Dalila anticipates for herself, and that Manoa foresees for Samson, significantly resembles the conventions of the Greek hero-cults and the rites associated with the sepulchral shrine or *heroum* of the dead warrior. Here again the classical parallel is merely implicit, and its pagan associations are not obvious.

In the encounter between Samson and Harapha, Milton is handling a motif—the challenge to single combat, the affair of honor—that possessed notable antecedents in Homeric epic and Biblical narrative and that was still very much alive in Renaissance Europe. Primarily Milton has his eye fixed on Goliath's challenge to Saul's army, but he is also keenly aware of the duels in classical epic, the reliance of classical heroes on "gorgeous arms" (sometimes produced by divine craftsmen and not infrequently charmed), and the formalities of judicial combat in medieval and Renaissance aristocratic society. The anachronisms in this scene—the appellant's triple challenge, the giant's insistence on the "honour" to be lost in such an encounter with "no worthy match" — are an inheritance from medieval chivalric conventions and Renaissance duelling codes.[48] They would appear to be as out of place in Philistia as in the Attic theater — as Milton himself surely realized. Yet in the age of the heroic play — of the extravagantly anachronistic dramas and operas of Davenant and Dryden — these anachronisms might seem very slight indeed.

The dialogue between Samson and Dalila exploits medieval as well as classical motifs, though the speakers themselves belong to pre-Davidic Palestine. Dalila's phraseology ("Mine and Love's prisoner," "Love's law") exploits commonplaces of the Ovidian and medieval erotic tradition still current in seventeenth-century lyric and drama. Other images in this scene belong to both Biblical and classical traditions. When Samson denounces Dalila as a Hyaena[49] (line 747), accusing her of deception, betrayal, and "feign'd remorse" ("these are thy wonted arts,/ And arts of every woman false like thee"), he seems to be exploiting the associations between the Hebrew words for *hyaena*, *hypocrite*, and *painted* or *colored*. The implications of this metaphor become more fully apparent later, when he accuses Dalila more explicitly of "feign'd Religion, smooth hypocrisy. . . ."

In the song of victory that precedes Manoa's last speech and the exodos of his drama Milton introduces a chain of linked similes that underline the essential values and meaning of the action. Three of these comparisons — flame, serpent, eagle — recall heroic similes in Homeric and Virgilian epic; collectively they strengthen the links between Milton's drama and the classical heroic tradition, yet give an additional dimension to the hero's *aristeia* by linking it symbolically with conventional images of rebirth. The spark under the ashes flares up again and destroys a city. The serpent sheds its skin. The eagle renews its eyesight and its plumage. This sequence of images of renewal — further interconnected through the imagery of bird and flame[49a] — reaches its climax in the allusion to the Phoenix, which for centuries had been regard as a symbol of regeneration. In this context the solar associations of eagle and Phoenix seem not irrelevant to the reassertion of the hero's identity; but certain analogies with the hero of the *Odyssey* are also suggestive. The imagery in which Milton alludes to the destruction of the unsuspecting Philistines recalls the omens whereby Homer had foreshadowed Odysseus' revenge.[49b] In different ways both heroes demonstrate fortitude of mind in adversity, and both reassert their heroic identity in lowly and abject conditions. His true identity concealed through a humiliating disguise (the rags and *persona* of a hungry beggar), Odysseus slaughters the lordly suitors in the midst of their feasting; the occasion, moreover, is an athletic contest or *agon*, a demonstration of strength and skill. Through their own insolence and blind folly (as gods and men alike insist throughout the epic) his victims have repeatedly invited their own destruction; and at the critical moment they are smitten with madness by divine agency to hasten their ruin. In accomplishing this act of personal vengeance, moreover, Homer's hero is aided throughout by the sapient goddess Athene. For many of Milton's near-contemporaries she was a symbol of divine Wisdom itself.[49c]

[VI]

As a "brief epic" *Paradise Regained* belongs to the same literary genre as the Book of Job (which Milton once regarded as a potential model) and to a variety of classical and Renaissance epics ranging from the *Argonautica* of Apollonius of Rhodes to Sannazaro's *De Partu Virginis* and DuBartas' *La Judit*. Professor Barbara K. Lewalski has reexamined Milton's poem against a background that includes not only the Book of Job but also the shorter Renaissance epics written in neo-Latin or in the vernacular tongues; and Louis Martz has placed it in the tradition of Virgil's *Georgics*.[50] Like *Paradise Lost*, it presupposes the classical epic, partly as model and partly as foil; and, albeit in condensed form, it utilizes many of the traditional features of Greek and Latin heroic poetry: proposition and invocation, divine (or infernal) councils, epic similes. The similes are comparatively few, however, nor are they elaborated at great length. The celestial council is restricted to one scene in which God the Father addresses Gabriel, foretelling the Son's victory over temptation. Two demonic councils take place, immediately before and after Satan's first encounter with his adversary. On two occasions — before the temptation in the wilderness and after the final victory on the temple tower — an angelic chorus sings a hymn of victory and triumph to the Son of God. As in *Paradise Lost*, Milton invokes the Spirit for inspiration instead of the classical Muses. In contrast to *Paradise Lost*, however, where he had followed Homer in combining the epic proposition with the invocation, he now separates them in the manner of Virgil's *Aeneid*; moreover, in the opening lines he follows the pattern set by the alternative (perhaps spurious) proposition of the *Aeneid* ("Ille ego qui," "I who erewhile," etc.).

The salient features of this brief heroic poem are that it is a monomachia (or duel) and that the contest is dialectical: a verbal, moral, and intellectual struggle rather than a physical encounter. The principal issue at stake is kingship: secular versus spiritual dominion, the four world-monarchies versus the Messianic fifth monarchy, the kingdoms of the Gentiles versus the throne of David, the usurped empire of Satan and his angels versus the kingdom of heaven.

The invocation to the Spirit who had led "this glorious Eremite" into the desert — in place of a conventional invocation to Calliope or Clio — emphasizes the distinction between divine and human poetry and the substitution of a sacred for a secular theme. The promise to sing "of deeds/ Above Heroic" similarly asserts the Messiah's superiority to the worthies traditionally celebrated in heroic poetry, to the heroes of Greece and Rome and indeed to all secular kings and conquerors.

In this context, as in Milton's tragedy on Samson, classical allusions must be introduced with circumspection. Though they are not always treated pejoratively, they frequently form a substantial and significant part of the lures and snares with which the devil attempts to trap his opponent, and they are often deliberately contrasted with Biblical tradition: the literature, history, and institutions of Israel.

The *enfances* of the hero had been prophetic of his future mission. The "heroic acts" of which he had dreamed centered on a future act of deliverance, either national or universal (I, lines 216–220);

> . . .one while
> To rescue *Israel* from the *Roman* yoke,
> Then to subdue and quell o'er all the earth
> Brute violence and proud Tyrannic pow'r,
> Till truth were freed, and equity restor'd: . . .

He has been aware of Gabriel's prophecy that "Thou shouldst be great and sit on *David's* Throne,/ And of thy Kingdom there should be no end" (I, lines 240–241). He now knows, moreover, that the way to his throne lies through "many a hard assay even to the death,/ Ere I the promis'd Kingdom can attain,/ Or work Redemption for mankind, whose sins'/ Full weight must be transferr'd upon my head" (I, lines 263–267). He is thus simultaneously the true king of Israel, the true king and deliverer of all mankind, and the vicegerent of heaven: "heir of both worlds" (IV, line 633), a universal king.

Throughout the epic the majority of allusions utilized for comparisons or as examples are biblical: Christ is "our Morning Star" (I, line 294), and Satan is likened to a falling star in autumn or to lightning (IV, lines 619–620). Hell is Abaddon (IV, line 624) rather than Tartarus. In debate Christ and Satan cite the examples of Moses and Elijah and Job, Ahab and Balaam, Hagar, Antipater, Gideon and Jephthah, David and Judas Maccabaeus (I, lines 351–354, 369–375, 49l; II, 308–319, 423–425, 439–440; III, line 165).

Missing the newly-proclaimed Messiah, the disciples recall parallels in Old Testament history, such as Moses and Elijah (II, lines 13–19). Hungering in the wilderness, Christ dreams of Daniel and Elijah and how their hunger had been satisfied (II, lines 264–278). The typological analogy between Christ and Adam, and the analogy between the temptations of Christ and Eve, also recur frequently throughout the poem. Milton's opening lines emphasize the analogy and contrast between Eden's loss through one man's disobedience and its recovery through one man's obedience (I, lines 1–7); and the final angelic chorus asserts that the Messiah has avenged "Supplanted *Adam*" and founded a "fairer Paradise/ For *Adam* and his chosen Sons . . ." (IV, lines 606–617). God the Father predicts that Christ, the woman's seed, will win "by Conquest what the first man lost/ By fallacy surpris'd" (I, lines 150–155). In undertaking the temptation of Christ, Satan has been encouraged by the memory of his earlier victory over Adam (I, lines 100–105); after his first encounter with his new adversary he is less confident, having found "Far other labour to be undergone/ Than when I dealt with *Adam* first of Men . . ." (II, lines 131–143). In the banquet temptation in the wilderness the poet-narrator himself draws the contrast: "Alas how simple, to these Cates compar'd,/ Was that crude Apple that diverted Eve!" (II, lines 348–349).

Like the allusions to Moses and Elijah, references to Job recur throughout the early books (I, lines 369, 425; II, lines 64–70, 95).

Certain other motifs, though classical in origin, had been so thoroughly assimilated by later writers that they would scarcely seem out of place in an epic on a biblical theme: "this woody maze" (I, line 246), "the top of Virtue's hill" (II, line 217), Occasion's forelock" (III, line 173), "Ambrosial drink" (IV, line 590), the Platonic concept "of good, wise, just, the perfect shape" (III, line 11). In Christ's description of the "false resemblance" of wisdom as an "empty cloud" (IV, lines 319–321) Professor Hughes detects an allusion to the myth of Ixion; but, even if Milton had this analogy in mind, he has phrased it so obliquely that it no longer smacks of paganism.

The first extended reference to the religions of the Gentiles occurs in Christ's rebuttal of Satan's pretense to philanthropy: his claim to have assisted mankind "by presages and signs,/ And answers, oracles, portents and dreams . . ." (I, lines 393–396). In its context this discussion follows logically from the Messiah's earlier reply to the suggestion that he convert the stones of the wilderness into bread: "Man lives not by Bread only, but each Word/ Proceeding from the mouth of God . . ." (I, lines 347–351). It leads logically, in turn, to the topic of the cessation of the oracles and to an assertion of Christ's role as God's "living Oracle" and a further prophecy of the Spirit of Truth as "an inward Oracle. . . ." God has "justly giv'n the Nations up/ To thy Delusions . . . since they fell/ Idolatrous"; but "this thy glory shall be soon retrench'd;/ No more shalt thou by oracling abuse/ The Gentiles; henceforth Oracles are ceast,/ And thou no more with Pomp and Sacrifice/ Shalt be inquir'd at *Delphos* or elsewhere,/ At least in vain, for they shall find thee mute" (I, lines 430–464).

Here, as in *Paradise Lost*, the gods of the Gentiles, including Apollo, are exposed as diabolical; and, as in the Nativity hymn, they are expelled by the incarnate Logos, the Wisdom of God.

In Book II the more sensual aspects of the religion of the Greeks are emphasized. The figments of classical mythology are brought into close association with those of medieval chivalric romance and with diabolical agency: the operations of Belial and his crew or the illusions wrought by Satan himself. As an aspect of the temptation of pleasure, they are emblematic of luxury in its broader aspects: eroticism, prodigality, sloth, gluttony, false magnificence, and the gratification of all five senses.

Belial advises his Prince to seduce the Messiah by "setting women in his eye and in his walk. . . ." He exploits the language and imagery of Renaissance Petrarchism: "more like to Goddesses/ Than Mortal Creatures," able to "draw/ Hearts after them tangl'd in Amorous Nets." Even "wisest *Solomon*" fell victim to their charms and turned idolatrous, "bow[ing] to the Gods of his Wives" (II, lines 153–171). In this passage Milton returns to the theme of a drama he had once considered writing — a tragedy based on Solomon's seduction into idolatry by his heathen wives.

Satan's reply combines an allusion to the biblical "sons of God" and the daughters of men, with classical myths of the love-affairs of gods and nymphs. Belial and his "lusty Crew" have been in the habit of waylaying such rare beauties as "*Calisto, Clymene,/ Daphne,* or *Semele, Antiopa,/* Or *Amymone, Syrinx,* many more," seducing them and subsequently laying the blame on Greek divinities: such "names ador'd" as "*Apollo, Neptune, Jupiter,* or *Pan,/* Satyr, or Faun, or Silvan" (II, lines 178–191). In rebutting Belial's suggestion, moreover, Satan appeals to two classical examples of continence, Alexander the Great and Scipio Africanus; He also refers to the Homeric tale of "the Zone of *Venus*" and its "effect on *Jove*" as merely a myth ("so Fables tell").

In the same book, the "pleasant Grove" where Satan stages his noontide temptation would seem "to a Superstitious eye the haunt/ Of Wood-Gods and Wood-Nymphs . . ." (II, lines 296–197). The "Table richly spread, in regal mode," which he offers to the Messiah, resembles a Roman banquet, to which the coast of Africa, the Black Sea, and the Lucrine Bay have sent their tributes. The servitors are compared to Ganymede and Hylas. Here are nymphs of Diana's train, Naiades, ladies of the Hesperides; and in describing them, Milton brands the pagan myths and medieval romances alike as fabulous. These ladies seem "Fairer than faign'd of old, or fabl'd since/ Of Fairy Damsels met in Forest wide/ By Knights of *Logres*, or of *Lyones* . . ." (II, lines 340–365).

These apparitions are, in fact, devils, although Satan represents them as classical daemons and nature divinities, "Spirits of Air, and

Woods, and Springs," who have come to pay homage to their Lord (II, lines 374–376). A final classical echo concludes the scene on a more sinister note. After Christ has rejected this banquet — citing its biblical counterpart with "flights of Angels ministrant" (II, lines 383–386) — the table abruptly vanishes "With sound of Harpies' wings and Talons heard . . ." (II, line 403(.

In the final speech in this book, however, the ancient Gentiles appear in a more favorable light. In rejecting Satan's temptation of riches, Christ cites the examples of Gideon, Jephthah and David, and then turns to Roman history for further exemplars of virtuous poverty (II, lines 443–446):

> Among the Heathen, (for throughout the World
> To me is not unknown what hath been done
> Worthy of Memorial) canst thou not remember
> *Quintius, Fabricius, Curius, Regulus?*

The third book advances the critique of gentilism still further. After combining the Platonic commonplace of the "perfect shape" of virtue with the imagery of the "oraculous gems/ On *Aaron's* breast," the Urim and Thummim (III, lines 9–15), Satan proposes the bait of glory, adducing the examples of Alexander the Great, Scipio Africanus, Pompey the Great, and Julius Caesar. In countering these arguments, Christ condemns the world's false opinion of glory and the conquerors who claim the title of gods and demand divine honors: "One is the Son of *Jove*, of *Mars* the other. . . ." To these martial conquerors and would-be demigods he opposes the Greek and biblical exemplars of glory achieved through deeds of peace: "patient *Job*" and "Poor *Socrates* (who next more memorable?) . . ." (lines III, lines 81–99).

From the lure of glory Satan proceeds to the lure of kingship, urging the Messiah to reclaim the throne of David *now* and citing the example of Judas Maccabaeus. Then he offers the vision of "The Monarchies of the Earth, thir pomp and state" as an introduction into regal arts and the mysteries of kingship, presenting in succession the Parthian and Roman empires and the wisdom and eloquence of Athens. In these three panoramas geographical, topographical, and historical allusions complement and reinforce each other. After the panoramic view ("wide-angle-lens") of Mesopotamia the focus of the vision narrows to the concentrated might of the Parthian host at Ctesiphon; and at this point a further catalogue of geographical allusions heightens the emphasis on concentrated strength. The "flower and choice/ Of many Provinces from bound to bound" are here, "From *Arachosia*, from *Candaor* East," from Afghanistan to the Caspian Sea and Persian Gulf. Milton concludes this description, however, with a comparison which might undercut as well as enhance this image of embodied force, an allusion to a patently fictitious episode in Boiardo's romance *Orlando Innamorato* (III, lines 337–339):

> Such forces met not, nor so wide a camp,
> When *Agrican* with all his Northern powers
> Besieg'd *Albracca*, as Romances tell. . . .

This equivocal and double-edged comparison serves much the same function as the comparison of Satan's fallen angels to the giants and heroes of Greek myth and to the legendary knights of medieval and Renaissance chivalric romance (*Paradise Lost*, I, lines 576–587). It seems to aggrandise and glorify its subject, while ironically introducing doubts and ambiguities which threaten to subvert it.

The vision of Rome begins with a panoramic view of the city itself, then proceeds to a catalogue of embassies from nations obedient to her and her "great Emperor" (IV, lines 67–81). Just as the temptation of Parthia has offered a vision of concentrated military force, this provides an image of concentrated political power and imperial authority. Yet the moral realities underlying both the *imperium* and its external magnificence are soon apparent; the emperor is a brutish monster, his throne a sty. In this scene, as in the temptation of Athens, the Messiah Himself raises the question as to how much He actually knows about the society of the Gentiles (IV, lines 113–118)

> . . . though thou should'st add to tell
> Thir sumptuous gluttonies, and gorgeous feasts
> On *Citron* tables or *Atlantic* stone,
> (For I have also heard, perhaps have read)
> Their wines of *Setia*, *Cales*, and *Falerne*,
> *Chios* and *Crete*. . . .

This geographical catalogue complements the earlier catalogue of embassies, but the emphasis has shifted significantly from political dominion to *haute cuisine*, from a diplomatist's gazetteer to a vintner's list.

In the temptation of Athens, Biblical and classical learning are finally brought into clear-cut opposition; and, again, the question as to how much of this pagan civilization the Messiah really knows is raised but left unanswered (IV, lines 286–291):

> Think not but that I know these things; or think
> I know them not; not therefore am I short
> Of knowing what I ought: he who receives
> Light from above, from the fountain of light,
> No other doctrine needs, though granted true;
> But these are false, or little else but dreams. . . .

Satan has argued that "all knowledge" is not contained in Scripture, in the Law and the Prophets: "The *Gentiles* also know, and write, and teach/ To admiration, led by Nature's light . . ." (IV, lines 225–228). In reply, the Messiah accuses the Greek philosophers of ignorance or false wisdom. The Greek poets have borrowed their arts from Hebrew sources, and debased them by celebrating their own vices and those of their gods. The orators of Greece and Rome are inferior to the Biblical prophets "As men divinely taught, and better teaching/ The solid rules of Civil Government/ In thir majestic unaffected style . . ." (IV, lines 334–364).

Milton opens the fourth book of *Paradise Regained* with a sequence of similes emphasizing the Tempter's persistence in spite of his ill success; and he concludes the temptation of the tower with two further similes accentuating Satan's defeat. Both of the latter are based on Greek mythology: the fable of Hercules and Antaeus and the myth of Oedipus and the Sphinx. Of the introductory similes, the image of "surging waves against a solid rock" (IV, lines 18–20) had long been a traditional symbol of constancy, widely current in Renaissance poetry and emblem literature.[50a] It is echoed later in the same book, with much the same moral significance, when Satan admits that he has "found thee/ Proof against all temptation as a rock,/ Of Adamant, and as a Centre, firm . . ." (IV, lines 531–534). It acquires additional, and specifically Messianic, significance, however, in the context of the progressively elaborated differentiation of Christ's kingdom from the monarchies of the world. In the same book Christ exploits the imagery of Daniel, likening His future kingdom to "a tree/ Spreading and overshadowing all the Earth," and to "a stone that shall to pieces dash/ All Monarchies besides throughout the world . . ." (IV, lines 146–151). In another Miltonic simile near the beginning of this book — the allusion to "a swarm of flies in vintage time" (IV, lines 15–17) — Professor Hughes finds analogies with Homer's similes, but also calls attention to the symbolic association of flies with demons in Renaissance poetry.[51]

The "Table of Celestial Food" wherewith the angels refresh the victorious protagonist after his ordeal synthesizes several of the dominant motifs and images in this epic. If the "Ambrosial drink" (IV, line 590) recalls the classical Olympus, the "fount of life" from which it is drawn is an inheritance from the Apocalypse (Revelation xxii.1) and the Psalms (Psalm xxxvi. 9), while the fruits from the tree of life are a legacy from the first and last books of Scripture (Genesis ii. 9; iii. 22; Revelation ii. 7; xxii. 2, 14). Counterpointing Satan's illusory "Table richly spread," this motif also recalls the Messiah's insistence on his ability to "Command a Table in this Wilderness,/ And call swift flights of Angels ministrant/ Array'd in Glory on my cup to attend . . ." (II, lines 384–386). The phrase itself (as Professor Hughes points out) recalls Psalm lxxvii.19.[52]

The Ariostean allusion in this book (IV, lines 541–543)

So saying he caught him up, and without wing
Of *Hippogrif* bore through the Air sublime
Over the Wilderness and o'er the Plain; . . .

incongruously utilizes the imagery of Italian romance-epic — itself a fabulous variation on motifs derived from classical mythology — to introduce the climactic episode in this sacred epic. Yet the incongruity may be little more than apparent — superficial if one explores the broader association of this image. It would seem, on the surface, that Milton has introduced this reference in order to heighten the contrast between the fabulous flight undertaken by Ariosto's imaginary heroes on a purely fictitious steed with Christ's real journey through the air to the pinnacle of the temple at Jerusalem through diabolical agency. Yet the context and the character of the image itself suggest further implications. In view of the analogies between the temptation of Eve and that of Christ, recurrent throughout this epic, a further analogy between this real aerial journey and Eve's imaginary flight in *Paradise Lost* might seem implicit here. Both are the result of demonic power, though one takes place in actuality, the other merely in fantasy. Like Eve's imaginary flight above the earth, Astolfo's ascent to the earthly Paradise upon the hippogriff (sometimes interpreted as a symbol for the imagination) was only a fantasy, a figment of Ariosto's own poetic imagination. This fabulous flight serves as a foil for the true, and more marvellous, actions that Milton is describing: for Christ's real recovery of lost Paradise and the true happiness of man.

Finally, the dual and paradoxical nature of the hippogriff, combining the natures of horse and gryphon, ironically hints at the enigma that Satan has been endeavoring vainly and blindly to solve: the riddle of Christ's nature and identity.[53] Having found his adversary "To the utmost of mere man both wise and good,/ Not more," he has resorted to "Another method" to "know what more thou art than man,/ Worth naming Son of God by voice from Heav'n . . ." (IV, lines 535–540). The answer is itself a mystery — the dual nature of Christ "Both God and Man, Son both of God and Man, Anointed universal King" (*Paradise Lost*, III, lines 316–317) — and of course/ Satan cannot solve it. Milton's allusion to Ariosto's hippogriff seems, in this context, especially relevant to the theological mystery that baffles the Tempter and that drives him to this final, desperate method of discovering his opponent's identity. It is, accordingly, particularly appropriate as a transition to the episode of the final test on the pinnacle of the Temple at Jerusalem.

It is also especially appropriate to the motif of "Recover'd Paradise. . . ." As Milton was well aware, the dual nature of the gryphon (both lion and eagle) had made it a conventional symbol of Christ. Dante had introduced this symbol into his Earthly Paradise (*Purgatorio*, Canto xxix, lines 108–114; xxxi, lines 80–81) as "la fera/ ch' è sola una persona in due nature."[54] Behind the seemingly incongruous reference to Ariosto's fabulous creature — both gryphon and horse — there lies (I think) a further allusion, more oblique but also more apposite, to the traditional Christological symbol that Milton had encountered in the paradisal garden of a favorite Italian poet.[55]

If this interpretation is correct, the Hippogriff simile is proleptic, pointing forward to the similes that immediately follow the final temptation. In both of these juxtaposed comparisons Milton treats classical myths not only symbolically but quasi-typologically, as figures that achieve their full meaning and realization in Christ. While exploiting the conventional analogies between Christ and Hercules, as he had done much earlier in the Nativity Hymn, he can adapt the motif of Hercules' victory over Antaeus not only to the triumph of reason over appetite, or the Christian's spiritual warfare against the flesh, but to the conflict between the First and the Second Adam (the Earthly and the Heavenly Man) in the human soul as part of the process of regeneration. Through the same motif he can also stress the correlative antithesis whereby, throughout the epic, he has progressively defined the spiritual nature of Christ's kingdom by contrasting it with secular kingship: the monarchies of the earth.[56] The tension between flesh and spirit thus provides a basis for emphasizing the tension between the world and the church, the Augustinian *civitas terrena* and *civitas Dei*. Through the same allusion Milton accentuates the victory of the King of Heaven over the Prince of this World.

Throughout the temptation, Satan as Prince of this World can see and understand only the earthly; the spiritual escapes him, and it is impossible for him, therefore, to recognize the dual nature of Christ as the Heavenly man—both God and man, and Son of both God and man—or to understand the spiritual and heavenly nature of the Messianic kingdom. This was the mystery that Dante had contemplated, near the end of the *Purgatorio* and again in the final lines of the *Paradiso*: the mystery that Satan cannot solve and that eventually overthrows him.

The Sphinx's riddle had centered on "man." Satan's inquiry is centered on "what *more* thou art than man/ Worth naming Son of God." The heart of the mystery is Christ as *theanthropos* (God-*and*-man) — fully God and fully man, in contradistinction to the heroic demigods of Gentile myth. The mystery itself, moreover, is an object of faith rather than of reason: a miracle beyond the comprehension even of the elect, unfallen angels.

This mythological simile is technically adroit not only for the paradoxical propriety with which it adapts a classical motif to the central doctrine of Christianity, but also for the skill with which Milton exploits the ambiguities and ironic potential inherent in this analogy between the temptation of the tower and the Oedipus myth. It is in some respects a shocking comparison, worthy of the Dean of St. Paul's or even of Góngora; but it is elaborated with tact and sublety. As Milton develops the parallel with no less sensitivity to its connotations than to its overt meaning, he manages to involve his audience to some extent in perplexities that in a degree recapitulate or imitate those of the Arch-fiend. The manner in which he elaborates his primary image raises doubts not so much as to the nature of the divine protagonist Himself (the problem that vexes His Adversary) but as to precisely what the poet means, as to how much Milton's Christ knows previously about His own nature and identity and as to what both protagonist and antagonist learn about themselves or each other during this climactic temptation of the pinnacle.

If the simile is noteworthy for its reversals — not only of Satan's ex-pectations but of the reader's as well — it is also remarkable for the skill with which Milton recreates in the reader something of the surprise and uncertainty which the Adversary experiences in his blundering confrontation with a divine mystery. In some respects the imagery works at cross-purposes, suggesting secondary correspondences and differences that counterpoint or subvert the primary analogy. Though Milton explicitly compares Satan with the Sphinx herself — not with Oedipus, of course — the analogy is valid only to a limited degree; in other ways the contrasts are more significant than the parallels. Though the devil and the Theban monster resemble each other in grief, in spite, and in their sudden fall, in other respects they play contrary roles. The Sphinx proposes the riddle, and already knows its answer before she asks her question. Satan, on the contrary, has not been proposing an enigma; he has been seeking the answer to one.

In Milton's development of the implications of his original comparison — or in the connotations this analogy inevitably suggests — one encounters deliberate ambiguity and asymmetry. The parallel lines are broken by contrary implications. Having begun this episode with what appears to be a singularly capricious allusion to Ariosto's fantasy, Milton has based the turning-point or *Peripeteia* of his epic plot on an ambiguous answer (IV, line 561) to the devil's ultimate challenge; finally he has followed up these equivocal passages with an equally equivocal allusion to classical myth. Taken ensemble, these ref-erences leave uncertain and undetermined the question as to what, if anything, Satan has discovered about the nature and identity of his opponent in this last encounter, and what his opponent has learned about Himself.

Nonetheless it is possible that the miracle on the temple-tower has in fact given Satan at least a partial answer to the enigma of his opponent's identity—that he recognizes in his intended victim the first-begotten Son who had expelled him and his crew from Heaven, and that it is this recognition which smites him with amazement. It is also possible that the Son has made a similar discovery about Himself, learning more about His own divinity as well as the nature of His kingdom.[57] But Milton deliberately leaves these uncertainties unresolved, and his treatment of the Sphinx image enhances the ambiguity.

In this dialectical drama, in which the incarnate Word — the Wisdom of God, and "the true Light, which lighteth every man that cometh into the world" (John i. 9) — confronts the father of lies and prince of darkness, Milton has conflated motifs from the Biblical "epic" of Job (a temptation-drama testing and exercising the hero's faith and patience) and motifs associated with the classical epic of heroic wisdom, the *Odyssey*. Though the latter analogies should not be pressed too far, they have a significant bearing on the motif of the hero's identity as well as on the disguises and shifts of His wily adversary. In Homer's epic the motifs of concealed identity, disguises and false leads and false motives had received elaborate and often subtle development, usually in possibly dangerous situations where the hero is a stranger or even a suppliant or (as in the respective *nostoi* or homecomings of Agamemnon and Odysseus) where he faces mortal peril in his own realm and his own household. (In this respect Odysseus' wary prudence provides as striking a contrast with Agamemnon's credulity as the contrast between their faithful and unfaithful wives.) On several occasions Homer's hero invents false autobiographies. He adapts his behavior, pretended motives, and his arguments to the demands of the changing environments and situations that confront him. On his own island he successively tests the members of his household to determine their reliability. In one scene (Book XIII) he lies to Athene (who is herself disguised), and wins her applause for his craftiness; he is a man after her own heart. He visits Penelope in disguise (Book XIX), and the question as to whether or not she actually guesses his identity and conceals her knowledge from him is still subject to debate. Penelope herself outwits him on a later occasion (Book XXIII), testing him by a secret which only the two of them share. Through a skilful use of this motif of concealed identity the poet can simultaneously raise and maintain suspense, demonstrate the ingenuity and cleverness of his hero, and set the stage for the dramatic moment of recognition. As Aristotle had noted, Homer had made highly effective use of the *anagnorisis* or discovery in constructing his epic plot; and indeed the crucial "turn" or reversal occurs at the point when the apparent beggar reveals his identity and avenges himself on the parasitic suitors who have wasted his goods, courted his wife, sought his son's life, and corrupted his household.[57a]

Though the analogies between Satan and Odysseus are more obvious in *Paradise Lost* than in its sequel, we would miss much of the intellectual drama in this poem, and underestimate its counter-hero, if we should fail to recognize the Odyssean traits in this later Satan. Conversely, the role of Christ in this brief epic seems to acquire additional point and meaning through contrast and analogy with the *Odyssey*. Unlike the wanderer Odysseus, who managed eventually to save himself but not his companions, the hero of Milton's poem will successfully bring back "long wander'd man/ Safe to eternal Paradise of rest" (*PL* XII, lines 312–314). On the other hand, He returns (like the Ithacan) unrecognized, in lowly disguise and as a stranger to His own realm (cf. John i. 9–14), and it does not know Him. As the incarnate Truth however, He fills a very different role from that of the clever Greek, and from that of His adversary. He has no need to test His foe, or to seek to discover His identity. He penetrates Satan's disguise immediately. The problem that remains is to recognize His opponent's lures and sophisms for what they are, and to expose them. The other facets of Odysseus' role Milton assigns to his counter-hero.

Interpretations and representations of Odysseus have (as scholars observe) ranged between the type of the clever villain at one extreme and that of the philosopher and contemplative hero at the other. He had been, for diverse poets or philosophers, an exemplar of wisdom and prudence or an exemplar of hypocrisy and fraud.[57b] Two of the principal terms used to describe him (*polytropos* and *sophos*)[57c] possessed analogous ambiguities; and when applied to Odysseus, they could be interpreted in either a pejorative or a favorable sense. In this "meditative poem" or contemplative epic, where the hero is "to vanquish by wisdom hellish wiles" (*PR*, I, lines 175), Milton exploits the inherent ambiguities in "the Ulysses theme,"[57d] polarizing its diverse and often conflicting meanings and reorganizing them about the contrary images of celestial and infernal knowledge: the antithetical archetypes of Truth and Falsehood.

Many of the conventional interpretations of *polytropos* and *sophos* are appropriate for the Tempter's character and role in both epics. Though one should not overtax the metaphor "of many turns," it is not insignificant that the serpent's coils are represented as symbolic proof of "his fatal guile" long before this subtlest of beasts becomes the devil's instrument (*PL* IV, lines 347–350). Satan is versatile both as tactician and rhetorician, adapting his discourse to his immediate audience; he changes his apparent motives and character when the situation seems to demand it. He has in the course of time become even more widely travelled than the Ithacan voyager to whom Milton has compared him. He knows the mores of many peoples. He is adept at sophistic methods, and he has at least a superficial knowledge of philosophy. He is *polymechanos*, surely, in his invention of artillery in one poem and in his control of optical phenomena in another, where he effectly disposes his "Aery Microscope" (*PR* IV, lines 56–57). There is unconscious irony, of course, in his endeavor to make his divine antagonist likewise a world-traveller—a *polytropos anēr* like himself and like the hero of Homer's epic (*PR* III, lines 236–239):

> The world thou has not seen, much less her glory,
> Empires, and Monarchs, and thir radiant Courts,
> Best school of best experience. . . .

This, to the world's Creator!

On the other hand, Chapman's idealistic conception of the *Odyssey*[57e] as "a demonstration of 'overruling wisdom', of 'the Minds inward, constant and unconquered Empire,'" and of its hero as "'the much-sustaining, patient, heavenly man', "the wise and God-observing man', 'whose genius . . . turns through many and various ways towards the truth'" brings the Homeric exemplar of heroic wisdom close to Milton's image of divine wisdom. Finally, in the context of an Odyssean background the recurrent emphasis on the "private" status of Milton's hero seems to acquire a heightened significance (*PR* II, lines 79–81; III, lines 21–23, 231–235; IV, lines 638–639). One recalls the choice of Odysseus in Plato's *Republic*, where (in contrast to other heroes of the Trojan war) the soul of Odysseus prefers to be reborn in the "body of a 'private, unofficial person'" and to lead "the life of some humble citizen unoccupied with public affairs."[57f]

[VII]

The classical aspects of Milton's Hell impressed many of the earlier readers of *Paradise Lost*. In contrast to the fiends of Dante and Tasso, Milton's devils seemed to resemble Greek or Roman warriors and statesmen;[58] they admired the semblance at least of heroic virtue and freedom, they observed military and social discipline, they showed undeniable courage even in defeat, they applauded merit and aspired to glory and honor. The classical images and motifs interwoven throughout the opening books of this epic were indeed partly responsible for "Satanist" interpretations of the work and for the critical commonplace that, consciously or unconsciously, the poet had elevated the Prince of Darkness into an epic hero and had subsequently felt compelled to degrade him.[59]

Satan's actions, in fact, constitute one of the major links between Milton's poem and the classical epic tradition, on the one hand, and the Biblical "epic" of Job on the other. Up to the moment of his seemingly triumphant return to Pandaemonium, his activities have followed a pattern significantly analogous to the heroic enterprises of the secular epic tradition. A martial context. A vanquished and banished general who refuses to admit defeat and to surrender to his victor. The establishment of a new political order. The inception and execution of the heroic enterprise itself, which is no less than the conquest of an entire world. On the other hand, for all the martial power and ostentation of Hell, the enterprise is accomplished not by force but through guile. The crucial struggle is a moral combat, a temptation-ordeal as in the book of Job.[60] And indeed the *militia-tentatio*, associated with patristic exegesis of Job, underlies all of Milton's major poetry: his "diffuse" epic and his "brief" epic, his unique tragedy and his masque at Ludlow.

Paradise Lost is not the "epic of Satan," however, nor is the devil the true "hero" of the poem;[61] his temporary victory is an integral part of the celestial strategy. Satan has won a battle only to lose the war. Moreover, despite the analogies between his enterprise and those of the martial heroes of antiquity, there are significant moral and spiritual divergences which place his heroic deeds in an entirely different light. As a result his *aristeia*, his "best," becomes, in effect, his "worst."

The limitations of Renaissance genre-theory[62] are painfully apparent today, and their relevance to the actual poetry of the age is variable and often ambiguous. We may be justly skeptical, accordingly, of the obsession of many sixteenth- or seventeenth-century critics with isolating and defining the ideal-form of an heroic poem: a paradigmatic and archetypal epic partially exemplified in the heroic poetry of classical antiquity and partly elucidated by classical literary theorists. We are also, perhaps, more likely than they to emphasize the diversity of the classical epics themselves, and possibly more alert to the dangers of trying to subject them to the tyranny of a generic stereotype or paradigm.

The relation of the gods to the hero and his enterprise is variable both in classical and in Renaissance heroic poetry. In some of the major classical epics the principal action in the poem is willed by Zeus (if not already ordained by a more mysterious Fate) and often strongly assisted by several of the gods, though opposed by others. The gods themselves are often capricious, and the heroes sometimes subject to folly or madness — lust, anger, cruelty, hybris — though the character of both divinities and mortals may be deliberately "tidied up" in the more philosophically-oriented epics. The hero of the *Iliad* is a warrior whom Zeus "hath delighted to honor"; the hero of the *Odyssey* a wanderer whom Zeus intends to return to his home. Both are special protégés and favorites of Athene, just as the hero of Virgil's epic is consistently aided by his mother Venus. Virgil's Aeneas is not merely aided by the gods, however; he is the bearer of Roman destiny and as such the divinely-appointed instrument of Jove. However reluctant he may be at times to accept the full burden of his mission, he is the agent of the Olympians. Favored by certain gods or goddesses, all three heroes eventually cooperate with these divine powers and ultimately emerge victorious. Conversely, the "delaying actions" in all three poems (as Milton's contemporaries would have called them, are engineered by hostile divinities or mortals; and these (as the poet makes clear) are in fact brazenly flouting the decree of Zeus. In Renaissance epic this schema is accommodated, not infrequently, to the Christian marvell-ous. The Deity Himself often ordains the epic enterprise, despatching His angels at crucial moments to assist the hero, while the powers of Hell vainly but vehemently resist. The antagonists of Heaven are, in the majority of such epics, the antagonists of the hero and his enterprise.[63]

Milton's Satan, on the other hand, as the self-styled Antagonist of Heaven, conceives and executes his own heroic enterprise in diametri-cal oppostion to the will of God. The "delaying actions" or counterac-tions designed to frustrate his enterprise — recognition by Uriel, inter-ception by Gabriel's angelic guard, Raphael's warning to Adam and Eve — are initiated by the celestial forces — by God Himself or by His angels; and, as the Deity is fully aware from the beginning, they will be unsuccessful in preventing the immediate success of Satan's enterprise: the seduction and ruin of mankind.

Thus, despite Milton's numerous classical allusions and "imitations," and his frequent exploitation of the conventions of Virgilian and Homeric epic, the plot of *Paradise Lost* varies significantly from both classical and Renaissance norms in giving the victory temporarily to the Antagonist of Heaven, in depicting the defeat of the "epic person" or "principal hero" (Adam), and in presenting the victories of its true heroic archetype (the Son of God as Logos and Messiah) primarily through retrospective and proleptic episodes. This is almost (though not quite) as revolutionary as if Virgil had awarded the victory to Tur-nus, representing Aeneas' future triumph only in a prophetic vignette.

Like other Renaissance poets who had based their epics on Biblical or Christian history, Milton retains the forms and conventions of classi-cal epic, while altering its content by substituting sacred for profane materials.[64] His proposition announces a Biblical theme; and at a later point in the development of the epic fable (Book IX) he reaffirms the superiority of his epic argument to those of classical heroic poetry and medieval romance. Like Homer and Virgil he calls on the Muse for aid, but follows DuBartas and Tasso in substituting the Heavenly Muse for the pagan Muses of Helicon.

Milton explicitly differentiates his Urania from the classical muse of astronomy — as well as from Calliope, the muse of epic poetry and the mother of Orpheus. He asserts his intention to surpass the poets of antiquity, soaring above Mount Helicon. In place of the hills and streams associated with the classical muses he links his own Muse with the sacred mountains and streams of the Old Testament: Sinai and Zion, the brook Siloa. Associating Urania with the Biblical Wisdom, he affirms her existence before the creation of the world. He also calls on the indwelling Spirit who prefers the pure heart before all temples; this divine power may be identical with the Heavenly Muse invoked earlier; but Milton has apparently left their relationship ambiguous.[65]

He retains the divine and infernal councils, the angelic messengers, the device of relating past events over a dinner table and future events through vision and prophecy. He adapts the conventional epic catalogue to the demonic order of battle, representing the fallen angels by the names of Gentile idols who had seduced mankind from the worship of the true God.[66] He retains the conventional epic simile,[67] drawing his comparisons from both Biblical and classical sources, from natural history and travel literature, and from other areas that he had encountered in his wide reading.

Milton's frequent allusions to classical myth serve the dual functions of ornamenting and illustrating the incredible scenes and events he is describing — so remote from the actual experience of his readers, so sketchily or so vaguely mentioned in the Scriptures, and in some respects more familiar and more clearly "realisable" through the imagery of Graeco-Roman antiquity. At the same time these mythological references accentuate the authenticity of Milton's Scriptural argument; for they are, in actuality, fabulous distortions of the truths of sacred history.

His description of Hell and its denizens combines classical and Biblical motifs with the imagery of barbarian migrations and Middle Eastern despotism.[68] The rebel angels are compared to the rebellious Titans and giants of classical myth or to fallen divinities like Hephaestus. Satan lies prone on the fiery flood, "in bulk as huge/ As whom the Fables name of monstrous size,/ *Titanian*, or *Earth-born*, that warr'd on *Jove* . . .," but he is also likened to the biblical Leviathan (I, lines 195–210). In developing this simile Milton introduces the fabulous motif of the whale mistaken for an island. Though this legend appears in Ariosto's *Orlando Furioso*[69] as well as in the bestiaries, Milton prefers to treat it as a seaman's yarn: "Deeming some Island, oft, as Seamen tell. . . ." The architect of Pandaemonium is a demon subsequently known as Hephaestus or Vulcan or Mulciber; but the fables of his fall from heaven "thrown by angry *Jove*" are false, a corruption of sacred history: "thus they relate,/ Erring; for he with this rebellious rout/ Fell long before . . ." (I, lines 739–751). Subsequently (X, lines 578–584) Milton represents the myth of the Titan Ophion and his wife Eurynome as an infernal fable concerning the temptation of Eve:

However some tradition they dispens'd
Among the Heathen of thir purchase got,
And Fabl'd how the Serpent, whom they call'd
Ophion with *Eurynome*, the wide-
Encroaching *Eve* perhaps, had first the rule
Of high *Olympus*, thence by *Saturn* driv'n
And *Ops*, ere yet *Dictaean Jove* was born.

Comparisons with Titans, giants, and fallen gods are reinforced, on the one hand, by allusions to the martial heroes of antiquity and, on the other, by analogies with the classical underworld. The fallen angels march, like ancient Greeks, "In perfect *Phalanx* to the *Dorian* mood," to such music "as rais'd/ To highth of noblest tempers Heroes old/ Arming to Battle . . ." (I, lines 550–555). They stand "in guise/ Of Warriors old with order'd Spear and Shield," awaiting their Leader's command (I, lines 564–567). In sheer might they excell the mythical giants who fought against the Olympian gods, the legendary heroes who warred at Thebes and Troy, and the fabulous heroes of Arthurian and Carolingian romance (I, lines 575–587). The infernal capital bears a Greek name, *Pandaemonium*. Beëlzebub is compared to the mythical Atlas, who had supported the heavens on his shoulders: "shoulders fit to bear/ The weight of mightiest Monarchies . . ." (II, lines 305–307). Satan's journey through chaos is more perilous than the voyages of Ulysses and of Jason's Argonauts (II, lines 1016–1020); and there are implicit analogies with Ulysses in Satan's duplicity and skill at inventing ruses and disguises and in fabricating ingenious lies, in his role as spy, and in his insistence on his "faithful" and responsible leadership. The sports of the fallen angels are likened to the Olympic and Pythian games, or (more equivocally) to the rage of Typhoeus and the fury of the dying Hercules (II, lines 539–546). Later, in the temptation of Eve, Satan affects the stance of "some Orator renown'd/ In *Athens* or free *Rome*, where Eloquence/ Flourish'd . . ." (IX, lines 670–672).[70]

Yet, if Satan and his angels resemble the Titans and giants in stature and in might, and in sacrilegious ambition, they also share the doom of these mythical and archetypical rebels. Hell is a dungeon, a place of punishment—even though the fallen angels (unlike the fallen giants and Titans) endeavor to convert their dungeon into a seat of empire. Though disguised by architectural magnificence and barbaric splendor, its harsh realities—the reality of punishment for evil by further and greater evils—are emphasized by frequent references to the underworld of classical mythology. The nine days' fall through Chaos (Book VI, line 871), along with the nine-day period that the fallen angels lie stunned and confounded in the fiery gulf (I, lines 50–53), has been compared, both thematically and chronologically, with the fall of Hesiod's Titans; and the location of Hell—"As far remov'd from God and light of Heav'n/ As from the Centre thrice to th' utmost Pole" (I, lines 72–74) — has reminded several commentators of the cosmological position of Virgil's Tartarus.[71] Milton's Hell contains Medusa and her "*Gorgonian* terror," and other monsters even "worse/ Than Fables yet have feign'd, or fear conceiv'd, *Gorgons* and *Hydras* and *Chimeras* dire" (II, lines 611, 626–628). The poet alludes also to the myth of Tantalus (II, lines 612–614), and he introduces all of the traditional infernal rivers (Styx, Acheron, Cocytus, Phlegethon, and Lethe) into his underworld. The council chamber in Pandaemonium is "that *Plutonian* Hall" (X, line 444); and the fallen angels and their dungeon are frequently described through such allusions as "*Stygian* flood" (I, line 239), "*Stygian* Council" (II, line 505), "*Stygian* throng" (X, line 453), "*Tartarean* Sulphur" (II, line 69), "this gloom of *Tartarus* profound" (II, line 858).

In comparing the fallen angels, afloat on the "inflamed Sea" to Busiris' "*Memphian* Chivalry," drowned in the Red Sea (I, line 307), Milton exploits the typological associations of Pharaoh's Egypt with Hell and its angels.[72] The next extended simile in this book—the plague of locusts raised up by Moses (I, lines 338–346)—introduces yet another allusion to "the realm of impious *Pharaoh*," while suggesting a further symbolic association with the locust-imagery of the Apocalypse (Revelation ix. 1–11).[73] This simile, in turn, leads to a further simile based on the Germanic migrations and invasions (I, lines 351–355); and this allusion is followed by the catalogue of devils. In classical epic this device had been frequently (though not exclusively) associated with the order of battle; and Milton deliberately evokes and exploits these martial associations, transferring them from physical to spiritual warfare. These infernal peers and princes are the rivals and antagonists of Israel's God — warlords in a universal theomachy — and Milton describes them in terms of the idolatrous cults of the ancient Near and Middle East (I, lines 364–375). In the future history of the world, as in the central plot of *Paradise Lost*, their strategy is one of deception and seduction, directed toward the apostasy of mankind.

The order in which these fallen angels appear is significant. The "chief" among them are demons who belong to the areas in and around Palestine and who will erect "Thir Seats . . . next the Seat of God": Moloch, Chemos, Astoreth, Thammuz, Dagon, Rimmon. These are followed by the gods of Egypt: "*Osiris, Isis, Orus* and their Train." Belial comes last. These are "the prime in order and in might" among the fallen angels; most of them had been explicitly denounced in the Old Testament, and Milton regarded all of them as rivals of the true God or corrupters of the true faith. The gods of Greek mythology follow, but in the poet's opinion they are of merely secondary importance. In describing them (I, lines 508–521), he challenges their divinity ("held/ Gods, yet confest later than Heav'n and Earth/ Thir boasted Parents") and stresses the pattern of displacement and usurpation among the successive rulers of the gods in their struggles for supremacy.

The description of Sin combines motifs drawn from Hesiod's serpent-woman Echidna (and analogous monsters in classical and medieval or Renaissance literature), iconographical conventions associated with the serpent of Genesis, and the myths of Scylla and Cerberus. The account of her miraculous birth parodies the myth of Athene's emergence from the head of Zeus; but Milton fuses this motif with the Biblical metaphor of the genesis of sin and death (James i. 15), and in the interrelationships of Satan, Sin, and Death several scholars have recognized a grotesque infernal parody of the Trinity.[74] Into his account of the stupendous bridge that Sin and Death construct over the abyss,[75] Milton introduces references to the Gorgon myth, to the myths associated with the creation of the floating island Delos and its subsequent fixation by divine power, and to the bridge that Xerxes erected over the Hellespont (X, lines 295–311). The abyss itself, as Milton portrays it, closely resembles the original chaos described by Ovid and Lucretius; and it is peopled by a variety of primeval divinities derived from Greek mythology: Chaos and Night, Orcus and Hades, Demogorgon.[76] In depicting Satan's voyage through chaos, he alludes to the Roman war-goddess Bellona and to Greek legends concerning the hostility between gryphons and Arimaspians (II, lines 921, 943–945, 960–967). In portraying the Limbo of Vanity he takes Ariosto's fabulous romance as the point of departure for his satiric fantasy, but includes imagery drawn from travel literature about Central and East Asia and from Biblical and Greek tradition: the builders of the tower of Babel, and the Greek philosophers Empedocles and Cleombrotus.[77] His cosmology utilizes Biblical motifs like Jacob's ladder—though ironically it is through Satan's eyes that we behold the mysterious stairs before the Gate of Heaven, and they have apparently been deliberately let down to torment him: "whether to dare/ The Fiend by easy ascent, or aggravate/ His sad exclusion from the doors of Bliss" (III, lines 510–525)—but it also includes details adapted from classical myth, such as the "golden Chain" that links this "pendant world" to Heaven (II, line 1051).[75] But the "golden Compasses"[79] (VII, lines 224–231) wherewith the world is circumscribed derive from Biblical tradition.

Raphael's account of the warfare in Heaven begins and ends with the exaltation of the Messiah. The divine proclamation (based on Psalm ii) which declares Him the anointed head over all the host of Heaven provides the occasion or pretext for Satan's revolt; and the narrative concludes with the Messiah's victory over His enemies, "Mightiest in [His] Father's Might" and mounted upon "The Chariot of Paternal

Deity. . . ." These primary Biblical motifs, both Messianic in character and significance, serve as a frame for Raphael's description of the battles of the angels.

The Archangel's narrative corresponds formally to the retrospective narratives of Odysseus and Aeneas at the tables of their royal hosts, though there are significant differences. Unlike the Greek and the Trojan narrators, the angel is no storm-driven voyager and suppliant, nor is he the protagonist of *Paradise Lost*, in the sense that these classical heroes were the epic persons of the *Odyssey* and the *Aeneid*. He was not, moreover, the principal figure in the events that he is narrating, as Aeneas and Odysseus had been. Though he alludes to his own actions in combat (VI, line 363), he places greater emphasis on Abdiel's moral heroism, the sword of Michael, and the *aristeia* of the Messiah. The contrast with both Odysseus and Aeneas as narrators is significant; for "those elect/ Angels contented with thir fame in Heav'n/ Seek not the praise of men . . ." (VI, lines 374–376).

Raphael's "angelomachia" juxtaposes motifs derived from classical and Scriptural sources and from Renaissance warfare. Chariot warfare belonged, of course, to the battlefields of the Old Testament as well as to Homeric epic; but Milton invests this motif with an altogether different significance when he places the Messiah in the chariot of Ezekiel's vision. Dante had similarly combined a Messianic motif with the imagery of Ezekiel (i. 4–14) and the Apocalypse (Revelation iv. 6–9) in depicting the chariot of Beatrice (*Purgatorio* xxix); this is drawn by a gryphon, emblematic of Christ (see the discussion of *Paradise Regained*, *supra*). This enigmatic pageant alludes symbolically to the Church Militant;[80] and, though Dante and Milton develop this in quite different ways, it retains its association with the Church Militant in *Paradise Lost*. Milton heightens the metaphor of spiritual combat by introducing the visionary chariot onto the battlefield itself in the climactic scene of the war in heaven.[81] In this scene Professor Hughes finds echoes of Homer's description of Hector in the *Iliad* (VI, lines 832–838), and other commentators have emphasized the influence of Hebraic traditions associated with the Merkabah.[82]

In this final episode in his angelomachia Milton has transformed and transcended the conventional imagery of chariot warfare in classical epic, but he has also, through this Messianic and apocalyptic chariot, heightened his emphasis on the Messiah's supremacy. The poet has prepared for the Messiah's victory not only by portraying the stalemate that results from the successive battles between the angelic forces, and its ruinous effects, but also by presenting the image of chariot warfare among the angels in a series of different contexts. When, just before the outbreak of battle, we see Satan the Apostate "exalted as a God" and seated "in his Sun-bright Chariot," an "Idol of Majesty Divine" (VI, lines 99–101), we recognize that he is miming the glory of the Father; but the image is also both contrapuntal and proleptic, pointing forward to the Son's advent in the chariot of "Paternal Deity" and to Satan's own expulsion. When Moloch defies Gabriel and threatens "to drag him bound" at "his Chariot wheels" (VI, lines 355–360), the comparison with Achilles and Hector seems inescapable. Allusions to chariot warfare on this first day of battle are almost invariably associated with confusion: "Arms on Armor clashing bray'd/ Horrible discord, and the madding Wheels/ Of brazen Chariots rag'd" (VI, lines 209–211); "all the ground/ With shiver'd armor strown, and on a heap/ Chariot and Charioteer lay overturn'd/ And fiery foaming Steeds . . ." (VI, lines 388–390). Like some classical warrior, the wounded Satan is carried "Back to his Chariot" on the shields of his fellows (VI, lines 337–338). Milton's treatment of the motif of chariot warfare on the third day of battle, on the other hand, is quite different, associated as it is with Messianic victory and triumph. Having ascended the paternal chariot, the Son advances attended by "twenty thousand . . . Chariots of God" (VI, lines 769–770): a detail that derives (as Professor Hughes has observed) from the Psalms (lxviii. 17). At His approach peace returns to Heaven. Bidding his faithful angels to rest "this day from Battle," He proceeds alone against His adversaries, mounted in his "fierce Chariot" and "Grasping ten thousand Thunders. . . ."

In this battle-scene Milton similarly combines Biblical and classical allusions in describing his hero's armor. The Messiah appears "in Celestial Panoply all arm'd/ Of radiant *Urim*, work divinely wrought . . ." (VI, lines 760–761). The epic appositive, reminiscent of Homer and Virgil, heightens the analogy with heroes like Achilles and Aeneas, whose arms and armor had been fashioned by Hephaestus himself. Since the word *ûr* was usually interpreted as light or fire, this symbolic detail in Milton's epic links the oracular stones of Aaron's breastplate with the traditional image of the Son of God as light (John i. 4–9; viii. 12; ix. 5) and the analogous imagery associated with the divine Wisdom of the Old Testament (Wisdom of Solomon vii. 25–26). Milton's imagery thus implies Christ's high-priesthood besides emphasizing His prophetic role as God's living Oracle" (cf. *PR* I, lines 460–461). In the Nativity Hymn, as in *Paradise Regained*, Milton develops the theme of the cessation of the pagan oracles at the advent of the incarnate Logos; and in the latter poem the Tempter significantly alludes to the "Lights and Perfections" in the breastplate of the high-priest (*PR* III, lines 12–16):

> Thy Counsel would be as the Oracle
> *Urim* and *Thummim*, those oraculous gems
> On *Aaron's* breast. . . .

In the Son's radiant panoply the imagery of fire and light associated with the divinely fashioned arms of classical heroes (*Iliad* XIX. 367 ff.; *Aeneid* (Book X) has been transferred to the metaphorical and spiritual armor of the New Testament: "the armor of light" of Romans xiii. 13, and the "armor of righteousness" and "whole armor of God" of 2 Corinthians vi. 7 and Ephesians vi. 13. Primarily, however, this imagery reinforces the qualities shared by Sapientia (Wisdom vii. 25–26) and the Son as Logos (Hebrews i. 2–3): "the brightness of his glory, and the express image of his person, and upholding all things by the word of his power. . . ."

Other motifs in this angelomachia are either a Scriptural or a classical legacy. The insults and defiances exchanged by the combattants, and the sardonic jests and taunts that the rebels hurl against their opponents, were conventional in epic combat; they occur frequently in the *Iliad* and to a limited extent in the *Aeneid*. The combat between Satan and Michael is ultimately based on the Apocalypse (Revelation xii. 8), and the Archangel's two-handed sword may possibly involve allusions to the Biblical "sword of the Spirit, which is the word of God" (Ephesians vi. 17) and the correlative simile in Hebrews (iv. 12) comparing "the word of God" to a "two-edged sword."[83] On the other hand, Raphael's account of how Satan, wounded by Michael, first experiences pain — and how "A stream of Nectareous humour issuing flow'd/ Sanguine, such as Celestial Spirits may bleed . . ." (VI, lines 325–334) — is to some degree reminiscent of combat-scenes in the *Iliad* and of the wounds suffered, and ichor shed, by Aphrodite and Ares.

One battle-scene in Raphael's "angelomachia" opens with artillery fire, in Renaissance fashion, but concludes with tactics reminiscent of the classical giants and Titans, as "Hills amid the Air encountered Hills/ Hurl'd to and fro with jaculation dire . . ." (VI, lines 662–665). In his summaries of individual combats Milton imitates the manner of Homer and Virgil, while substituting Canaanite names (or names derived from related Middle Eastern tongues) for the onomastics of classical epic. Such names as Ariel and Arioch, Adramelech and Ramiel and Asmodai are a legacy from Biblical or Apocryphal tradition, but Milton manages to accommodate them to the formulaic style of Homeric epic (VI, lines 354–372):[84]

> On each wing
> *Uriel* and *Raphael* his vaunting foe,
> Though huge, and in a Rock of Diamond Arm'd,
> Vanquish'd *Adramelech*, and *Asmodai*,
> Two potent Thrones, that to be less than Gods
> Disdain'd, but meaner thoughts learn'd in thir flight. . . .

Adam describes the speaker as a "Divine Historian," rather than as a divine poet. Yet the Archangel's narrative has seemed to some observers very much like a brief epic on a sacred theme; it centers, in fact, on a subject very similar to that of Valvasone's brief epic *L'Angeleida*. Its manner and style have raised questions that are still controversial. It has been variously interpreted as a critique of heroic warfare, an epic farce, a serious imitation of classical epic and a serious adaptation of classical mythology to a sacred theme.[85] The introduction of artillery into Heaven might seem as dubious and as equivocal as the imitation of the titanomachia. Valvasone had anticipated Milton on this point, linking this diabolical invention with the war of the angels; but, as both poets were aware, Ariosto had already associated the invention of firearms with infernal agency and had introduced it anachronistically into the context of Carolingian romance. All three poets were consciously "myth-making," centering their fables on the conceit that so murderous a weapon could only have been invented by the devil himself and exploiting the *topos* of the "infernal machine." Professor Hughes calls attention to the infernal origins of Spenser's "divelish yron engin" (*FQ*. I, vii. 13) and to the analogy with Ariosto's "abominoso ordigno,/ che fabricato nel tartareo fondo/ fosti per man di Belzebú maligno/ che ruinar per te disegnò il mondo . . ."[86] (*OF*. IX. 91). Milton alludes to this commonplace in describing the Foe's "devilish Enginry" (VI, line 553), varying the metaphor with a pun in an earlier passage (VI, lines 501–506):

> Some one intent on mischief, or inspir'd
> With dev'lish machination might devise
> Like instrument to plague the Sons of men. . . .

In the Tenth Book of Milton's epic Satan and his angels are publicly humiliated by divine agency, transformed into hissing serpents at the moment in which he announces the success of his mission and awaits the applause of his peers. The scene begins with similes based on travel literature and centered on the motif of strategic retreat and withdrawal, but the allusions are Oriental rather than classical: references to the Tartar retiring from his Russian foe, and to the retreat of the Bactrian Sophi from the Turk (X, lines 431–436). In withdrawing from the outer regions of Hell to the Metropolis, Satan's angels are obeying their Leader's parting command, as Milton informs us; but in fact the poet is setting the stage for his transformation-scene. The devils are concentrated in and about Pandaemonium, so that none of them can escape the "horrid sympathy" that will associate them in the same punishment, sharing in common the doom pronounced on Satan and his serpentine instrument in the Garden of Eden. The nature of their metamorphosis is correlated with the nature of Satan's vehicle in the temptation of Eve and with Biblical allusions to him as dragon and serpent;[87] there is also a remote possibility that Milton may have had in mind a current etymological interpretation of "Leviathan" as signifying "society of serpents": an allusion that might have bearing on the kind of political order delineated in his Hell.[88]

This transformation-scene has been frequently compared with Ovid's description of the transformation of Cadmus and his wife into serpents or with the metamorphosis of Buoso degli Abati and his fellows in Dante's *Inferno* (canto xxv).[89] Milton had previously alluded to the metamorphosis of Hermione and Cadmus in emphasizing the beauty of the serpent of Eden (IX, lines 505–506); here, on the contrary, his emphasis falls on the hideousness of this "crowd/ Of ugly Serpents. . . ." Besides references to the myth of Python and to the legendary origin of Libya's serpents from the Gorgon's blood, Milton draws on classical geography and pseudo-natural-history for an allusion to the isle Ophiusa and for a catalogue of fabulous serpents (X, lines 524–531): "*Amphisbaena* dire,/ *Cerastes* horn'd, *Hydrus*, and *Ellops* drear,/ And *Dipsas*. . . ." Punished in the shape in which Satan had sinned, they find their penance aggravated by a delusive grove of trees "laden with fair Fruit, like that/ Which grew in Paradise, the bait of *Eve*/ Us'd by the Tempter . . ." (X, lines 515–516, 547–555). This too is a magnified and multiplied reflection of a Satanic instrument in the temptation and fall of man. Having taken the point of departure for this image from a Biblical motif, Milton has elaborated it with the ingenuity of a baroque composer elaborating a musical theme, introducing meanwhile comparisons based either on classical myth ("the snaky locks/ That curl'd *Megaera*") or on late classical reports concerning the region of the Dead Sea (the apples of Sodom). The invention of such images, drawn from such diverse sources and traditions, is ingenious; and they are brilliantly accommodated to the dramatic situation and to its moral and spiritual content.

The major figures among Milton's faithful angels are generally represented through combined Biblical and classical motifs and imagery, though the names themselves have a diversified background. Some are the names of biblical or Apocryphal angels; some appear in pseudepigraphal literature or occultist tradition. Some have been adapted from the names of human beings mentioned in the Scriptures; and some apparently are Milton's own coinages. Raphael's role as the sociable Archangel is based on his actions in the Book of Tobit; but it is significant that, unlike Milton's angel, the angelic companion of Tobias eats no food (Tobit xii. 19). One might also note that the angel's associations with ophthalmology (for he has been sent by God to restore Tobit's eyesight as well as to assist Sarah, daughter of Raguel — iii. 17) are transferred, metaphorically at least, to Milton's divine seer, the Archangel Michael. Raphael's descent from heaven is depicted through imagery based on Aegean navigation and on the recently-invented telescope;[90] and the angel himself is likened both to a Phoenix and to the

winged Hermes, a god of wisdom as well as the mythical messenger of
the gods (IV, lines 261–286). The fact that the Renaissance associated
this divinity (as Hermes Trismegistus) with mystical theology and
physicotheology would lend additional point to Milton's simile. Homer
presents him in an amiable light, and he intervenes on the hero's behalf
at a crucial moment in Virgil's epic. Disguised as a courteous youth, he
leads the aged Priam through the Greek camp to Achilles' quarters and
escorts him safely back through the enemy lines. In the *Odyssey* he bears
Zeus's command to Calypso, instructing her to release Odysseus and
speed him on his way back to Ithaca. But he is tactful about delivering
this unwelcome message to the nymph. He waits until they have dined
together and, prefacing the divine command with an apology, dis-
claims personal responsibility. In the *Aeneid* he is somewhat less graci-
ous and more abrupt, for the message he bears contains a rebuke.
Nevertheless the fate of the future Roman empire is at stake, and the
god delivers Jove's command to Aeneas with despatch, bidding him
quit Carthage and pursue his glorious destiny in Italy.

The Archangel Michael's "military Vest of purple" is compared to
the purple of Tyre and of the Thessalian town Meliboea; the rainbow-
goddess Iris (herself a messenger of the goddess Hera) "had dipt the
woof ..." (XI, lines 240-244). The cherubim who descend with
Michael to expel Adam from Eden are described through details based
on Ezekiel's vision (for each of them has four faces) and through similes
drawn from classical myth: allusions to the double-visaged god Janus
and to the hundred-eyed Argus, the custodian of the Garden of the
Hesperides, whom Hermes had lulled asleep. (XI, lines 126–133). Subsequently, however, the same "heav'nly Bands" are compared to the
angels whom Jacob encountered in Mahanaim and to the angelic hosts
who protected the Prophet Elisha from the Syrian army at Dothan (XI,
lines 213–218).

The angel Uriel had been associated with rabbinical tradition; but in
identifying him with the angel whom St. John the Divine beheld in
the sun (Revelation xix. 17), Milton is apparently developing metaphorically and figuratively the associations of the Hebrew word *ûr* with light
and fire.[91] The same verbal and etymological associations seem to
underlie the mixture of Biblical and alchemical imagery in terms of
which he describes the sun. The allusion to the twelve stones in Aaron's
breastplate seem to link (albeit obliquely) the Urim and Thummim
("lights" and "perfections") of the high-priest both with the angel of the
sun (through the etymological association with fire or light) and with
the Stone of Perfection (or elixir) of the alchemists. Here, as elsewhere
in the poem, Milton applies the imagery of the telescope to his Archfiend (though he also exploits it in relation to Raphael); and he
deliberately contrasts the real powers of transmutation possessed by

"Th' Arch-chemic Sun" with the vain imaginations and fruitless experiments of contemporary alchemists. In this context, his use of technical terms based on classical mythology ("Volatile *Hermes*," "old Proteus"; III, lines 603–604) heightens the rhetoric of depreciation.[92]

In an early draft for a tragedy on the fall of man ("Adam Unparadised") Milton had introduced the Biblical angel Gabriel (cf. Daniel viii. 16; ix. 21; Luke i, 19, 26) into the Garden of Eden, glossing his name as signifying "a Prince of Power." The "watch" (a Chorus of angels) enter separately; and there is no indication that Milton regards Gabriel as captain of the angelic guard. Nor is there any suggestion that Gabriel is present in the following scene when "Lucifer appears," the "Chorus prepares resistance," and there is some "discourse of enmity on either side. . . ."[93] In the epic, however, he is now "Chief of th' Angelic Guards"; the latter are presented in heroic terms; at the end of the book he confronts Satan directly, and a battle that might have wrecked the universe is averted only by divine intervention (IV, lines 990–1015):

> Th' Eternal to prevent such horrid fray
> Hung forth in Heav'n his golden Scales, yet seen
> Betwixt *Astrea* and the *Scorpion* sign,
> Wherein all things created first he weigh'd. . . .

As Professor Hughes points out, this passage combines a motif common to Homeric and Virgilian epic with the scales imagery of Daniel and Isaiah as well as with an astronomical sign.[94] Again, Milton is "myth-making"; and by validating his fable with a reference to the zodiacal sign Libra he has converted it indeed into an aetiological myth. There is, however, a significant divergence from the Homeric and Virgilian treatment of this image. In classical epic, where Zeus weighs the fates of individual contestants or of entire armies against each other, the descending scale identifies the doomed or defeated warriors. In *Paradise Lost*, on the other hand, when the Deity weighs "the sequel each of parting and of fight,/ The latter quick up flew, and kickt the beam"—thereby demonstrating "how light, how weak" the devil will prove if he should resist.

Though the golden scales, golden chain, and golden compasses derive from different traditions—the compasses from Scripture and from iconographical tradition, the golden chain from Homeric epic, the scales from both Homeric and Biblical imagery—Milton treats them in much the same manner: as essentially figurative or mythical elements which symbolize profounder truths. The compasses and scales, taken together, emphasize the providential order operative in the creation of the world, when God made all things (Wisdom xi. 21) "In Number, Weight, and Measure. . . ."[94a] In developing the metaphors implicit in this biblical motif, Milton has associated them with other Scriptural figures of weight and measure (Job xxviii. 25, Isaiah xxvi. 7) referring to the creation of the world or with similar figures associated with the providential government of the created universe and evaluation of the just or unjust (Job xxxi. 6, Isaiah xxvi. 7, Daniel v. 27); but he has also altered these motifs by introducing them into the framework of neoclassical epic and accommodating them, in varying degrees, to classical conventions.

The compasses-motif had appeared originally in the context of Wisdom's account of dwelling with God before and during the creation of the world, "when he set a compass upon the face of the depth" (Proverbs viii. 22–31) — the passage Milton recalls in the invocation to Book VII preceding Raphael's account of "how and wherefore this world was first created. . . ." Though the substitution of the metaphorical compasses for the more abstract motion of circumscribing may have resulted from a mistranslation, it had exerted a decisive influence on iconography. The epithet "golden" — a non-Biblical addition — tends to assimilate the compasses to the Homeric motifs of golden scales and chain, thereby blurring the distinction between Scriptural and classical imagery. Milton had interpreted the golden chain earlier (in his Second Prolusion) as a symbol of universal harmony and concord; but the notion of earth's symbolic dependence on divine Providence is implicit in his adaptation of this motif in *Paradise Lost*.

The complex nexus of gold-symbolism in the epic involves deliberate contrasts or correspondences between diverse planes of being — celestial, infernal, terrestrial — and between the states of innocence and corruption. Milton exploits it to stress the majesty of Heaven, the alchemical powers of the sun, the natural beauty of Eden (whether "sands of Gold" or fruits of "Golden Rind"), or Mammon's sordid avarice and the counterfeit magnificence of Hell. In elaborating this imagery, Milton has his eye on Biblical associations with the testing and purification of the just and with the Holy City of Revelation, but he also has in mind the precious vessels of classical epic, the state feasts of Renaissance monarchs, Renaissance alchemical theory, and the gold-mines of the New World.[94b]

Although much of the gold-imagery in Milton's descriptions of Heaven was ultimately based on the Old and New Testaments, in developing it he introduced either his own inventions or variations on classical motifs. In the Apocalypse "that great city, the holy Jerusalem," is "pure gold, like clear glass; and the street of the city was pure gold, as it were, transparent glass" (Revelation xxi. 10, 18, 21). In describing the Messiah's triumphal re-entry into Heaven after creating the world, Milton combines this Biblical image with a motif from Ovid's *Metamorphoses* (I, 163ff.), where the Olympian gods, summoned to council, proceed along the Milky Way to the palace of Jove. Milton adapts this motif to the royal-road of Heaven, adding gold-dust to complete the analogy. In this scene the Messiah leads the way to God's Eternal house" along a stellar thoroughfare that closely resembles the Galaxy (VII, lines 574–581):

> A broad and ample road, whose dust is Gold
> And pavement Stars, as Stars to thee appear,
> Seen in the Galaxy. . . .

This is not the Galaxy itself, and the passage exemplifies Raphael's narrative technique of likening things in heaven to those on earth, to the things that Adam himself has seen and experienced. For the first man has already beheld "that Milky way/ Which nightly as a circling Zone thou seest/ Powder'd with Stars." Raphael's method of teaching the *invisibilia Dei* by analogy with visible, created things hinges on essentially the same doctrine as that set forth in the Psalms (xix. 1–4) and the Pauline epistles (Romans i. 10–20) concerning the knowledge of God through His creatures — though in this instance the relationship between visible and invisible, or earthly and heavenly, is (in a sense) presented in reverse: from the viewpoint of the celestial being who is endeavoring to find earthly and visible analogies for the invisible realities he already knows.

Earlier in the epic Milton had utilized the same Biblical motif to illustrate Mammon's avarice. Characteristically the personification of Riches had preferred the sight of wealth ("The riches of Heav'n's pavement, trodd'n Gold") to the Beatific Vision (I, lines 680–684). The gates of Heaven move on "golden Hinges" (VII, lines 205–207), in contrast to the hinges of Hell-gate; and the stairway to Heaven (adapted from Jacob's vision at Bethel; Genesis xxxviii. 12–17) "scal'd by steps of Gold to Heav'n Gate . . ." (III, lines 549–541). In contrast to the "rod of iron" (Psalm ii. 9) with which the Messiah punishes the rebels, He rules the faithful angels with a "Golden Sceptre . . ." (V, lines 886–887; cf. II, lines 325–328). The elect angels quaff "rubied Nectar" from vessels of pearl or diamond or "massy Gold . . ." (V, lines 633–635). Although this imagery, reminiscent of an Olympian feast, heightens the decorum of divine majesty, it may also involve an oblique allusion to the imagery of election in the Pauline epistles: the "vessels of gold and of silver" elected to honor (2 Timothy ii. 20) and "the vessels of mercy" on whom the Deity has chosen to bestow "the riches of his glory . . ." (Romans ix. 23). The golden crowns and the harps of the blessed (III, lines 349–365) are also Biblical in origin (Revelation iv. 4, 8; xiv. 2), although Milton has altered both of these details, weaving amarant into the golden crowns and gilding the harps of the harpers.

The "Golden Censer" in which the Son as Intercessor presents the first prayers and sighs of the penitent Adam and Eve before His Father's throne, and the "Golden Altar at which he presents them (XI, lines 16–25), derive directly from the Apocalypse (Revelation viii. 3; cf. also iv. 4; v. 8; ix. 13): "And another angel came and stood at the altar, having a golden censer; and there was given unto him much incense, that he should offer it with the prayers of all saints upon the golden altar which was before the throne." Both of these details — golden censer and golden incense-altar — had belonged to the Holy of Holies in the tabernacle at Mount Sinai (Exodus xxxix. 38; xl. 5; Leviticus xxxvii); and this according to the author of Hebrews (chapters viii and ix), had been a type and figure of a more perfect tabernacle "not made with hands," in which Christ Himself fulfilled the office of high priest.[94c] But this is a subject that I shall take up later.

To describe the earthly Paradise and the state of innocence, Milton again interweaves imagery drawn from classical and Biblical traditions or from his wide reading in world history and geography.[95] The fruits of Eden, "burnisht with Golden Rind," are *"Hesperian* Fables true,/ If true, here only . . ." (IV, lines 249–251). "Universal *Pan*" joins the Graces and the Hours in dance (IV, lines 266–268). The poet compares this Assyrian garden with Enna in Sicily, the gardens of Daphne in Syria, the island Nysa in the river Triton in North Africa, and Mount Amara in Ethiopia, obliquely introducing allusions to the rape of Proserpina and to the myth of the child Bacchus and his mother Amalthea (IV, lines 268–283). In *Du Bartas His Second Weeke* he had encountered earlier a similar contrast between pagan myths of Elysium and the historical reality of the Biblical Garden of Eden:[96]

> Ye Pagan Poets that audaciously
> Have sought to dark the ever-Memory
> Of God's great Works; from henceforth still be dum
> Your fabled prayses of *Elysium*;
> Which by this goodly Module you have rought,
> Through deaf tradition that your Fathers taught:
> For, the Almighty made his blissful bowrs
> Better indeed then you have fainèd yours.

The works of God surpass the inventions of the poets; and, as Sylvester's gloss on this passage comments, "The *Elysian* Fields of the Heathen Poets are but dreams."

Milton likens Adam and Eve themselves to Olympian gods; in youthful dalliance with his bride, Adam "Smil'd with superior Love, as *Jupiter*/ On *Juno* smiles, when he impregns the Clouds/ That shed *May* Flowers . . ." (IV, lines 497–501). At their bridal, "heav'nly Quires the Hymenaean sung . . ." (IV, line 711), and their nuptial bower surpasses the haunts of mythical wood-gods (IV, lines 705–708):

> In shadier Bower
> More sacred and sequester'd, though but feign'd,
> *Pan* or *Silvanus* never slept, nor Nymph,
> Nor *Faunus* haunted.

Eve herself is likened to Pandora, both in beauty and in fate: (IV, lines 712–719):

> ... when to the unwiser Son
> Of *Japhet* brought by *Hermes*, she ensnar'd
> Mankind with her fair looks, to be aveng'd
> On him who had stole *Jove's* authentic fire.

On one occasion she is Narcissus (IV, lines 456–469); but she is also a type of Mary "second *Eve* . . ." (X, line 183).

Upon awakening, Adam whispers "with voice/ Mild, as when *Zephyrus* on *Flora* breathes . . ." (V, lines 15–16). The paradisal fruits with which Eve welcomes their angelic visitant include species found in the mythical garden of Homer's Alcinoüs as well as plants of the East and West Indies, the Black Sea coast, and the Carthaginian shore (V, lines 338–341). Her own "Silvan Lodge" is likened to *"Pomona's* Arbour"; and she herself is fairer "Than Wood-Nymph, or the fairest Goddess feign'd/ Of three that in Mount *Ida* naked strove . . ." (V, lines 377–382). The Judgment of Paris, evidently, would have been in her favor; but this comparison is in some respects equivocal. It preserves the decorum of a sylvan setting; but it also suggests an analogy between Paris's decision and that of Adam. Choosing the goddess of love and beauty instead of the divinities of wisdom and dominion (or, in other terms, the voluptuous life before the lives of contemplation or action), Paris had won the most beautiful woman of her time, but his decision had resulted in the ruin of Troy. Confronted with a decision between obedience to God and his companionship with Eve, Adam chooses Eve; and his decision results in the ruin of mankind.

Similar imagery recurs ironically in the idyllic description of Eve in her flower garden immediately before her temptation and fall. As she unwisely eschews Adam's protection, to expose herself needlessly to moral peril in solitude, she withdraws her hand from her husband's "and, like a Wood-Nymph light,/ *Oread* or *Dryad*, or of *Delia's* Train,/ Betook her to the Groves, but *Delia's* self/ In gait surpass'd and Goddess-like deport. . . ." Again, the mythical allusions are sylvan— but with the additional connotation of unviolated purity. The comparison with Diana, moreover, suggests analogies with other epic heroines whose beauty had been extolled through variants of the same simile: Homer's Nausicaa (*Odyssey* VI), Virgil's Dido (*Aeneid* I), Spenser's Belphoebe (*FQ*. II. iii. 31). With her gardening tools, Eve bears a further resemblance to the classical goddesses of agriculture (IX, lines 385–396):

> To *Pales*, or *Pomona*, thus adorn'd,
> Likest she seem'd, *Pomona* when she fled
> *Vertumnus*, or to *Ceres* in her Prime,
> Yet Virgin of *Proserpina* from *Jove*.

Similarly, her rose-garden surpasses the fabulous gardens of Greek myth as well as the historic garden of Solomon's Song of Songs (IX, lines 439–443) — though in the context of her own imminent ruin and her seduction of Adam both allusions seem ominous:

> Spot more delicious than those Gardens feign'd
> Or of reviv'd *Adonis*, or renown'd
> *Alcinoüs*, host of old *Laertes*' Son,
> Or that, not Mystic, where the Sapient King
> Held dalliance with his fair *Egyptian* Spouse.

Eve is also compared to Homer's enchantress, though the more sinister overtones of this allusion are suppressed. The beasts of the field (the poet informs us) are "more duteous at her call,/ Than at *Circean* call the Herd disguis'd" (IX, lines 519–520).

In delineating the effects of the Fall on Adam and Eve, Milton bases his imagery both on Scriptural history and on recent travel literature. As *"Herculean Samson"* had risen from Dalilah's lap shorn of his strength, the ruined couple awake after their intoxicated sleep "destitute and bare/ Of all thir virtue . . ." (IX, lines 1059–1063). Concealing their nakedness with the leaves of the banyan tree, they resemble the feather-girded Americans discovered by Christopher Columbus. As they address their prayers penitently to Heaven, they resemble the mythical Deucalion and his wife, the sole survivors of the flood according to Hellenic legend. For it is through their agency that mankind is to be perpetuated (XI, lines 8–14):

> . . .yet thir port
> Not of mean suitors, nor important less
> Seem'd thir Petition, than when th' ancient Pair
> In Fables old, less ancient yet than these,
> *Deucalion* and chaste *Pyrrha* to restore
> The Race of Mankind drown'd, before the Shrine
> Of *Themis* stood devout.

In unfallen Eden even the serpent is beautiful, and Milton emphasizes its loveliness after it has already become the victim of demonic possession and perverted into the instrument of Satan. In an age which still admired the S-curve, the *figura serpentinata*, as a formula for beauty in the visual arts[97] this emphasis on the serpent's original loveliness prior to its own perversion and the fall of Eve might have seemed more convincing than to a later age. Milton consciously accentuates its beauty through a series of comparisons based on classical myth and legend: allusions to the metamorphosis of Cadmus and Hermione, to the god Aesculapius, and to the serpent-forms in which Zeus had appeared to mortal women and begotten such historical heroes as Alexander the Great and Scipio Africanus (IX, lines 503–510).

References to the classical divinities Aurora and Leucothea (V, line 6; XI, line 135) in Milton's chronographias are conventional, as are the Homeric and Virgilian echoes in allusions to the "rosy steps" or "rosy hand" of Morn (V, line 1; VI, line 5). The cave within the Mount of God, "Where light and darkness in perpetual round/ Lodge and dislodge by turns" (VI, lines 4–8), has been traced by Professor Hughes to Hesiod's *Theogony*.[98] Besides introducing "grateful vicissitude" into Heaven, it also introduces the element of time and thereby differentiates the Deity's eternity and timeless Being from the durational existence of His creatures; the angels themselves have been created in time. The frequently-repeated word "ambrosial" (V, lines 427, 642, and elsewhere) is likewise too conventional to seem distinctively pagan; nevertheless its mythical associations with the Olympians as the food and drink of the gods are not out of place in Milton's earthly paradise or in his celestial paradise. When applied to the forbidden fruit which Eve extends to Adam (IX, line 852) the classical associations acquire ironic overtones; for, instead of conferring immortality and divinity, this seeming food of the gods will bring mortality and death. Ironically, the same epithet is applied both to the fruit of the deadly tree of knowledge and to that of the tree of life: "Ambrosial Fruit/ Of vegetable Gold . . ." (IV, lines 219–220; cf. *PR* IV, lines 588–590).

Metaphorically the sin of devouring the forbidden fruit is debased to a particularly repulsive mode of cannibalism. Milton likens it to the feast at which Thyestes had unwittingly devoured his own children. This allusion to the myth of Atreus appears in the context of Milton's account of the climatic changes that followed the fall of man; and this account is itself largely a poetic fiction, a mythical invention. God has commanded His angels to change the courses of the planets, to teach the fixed stars malign influences, to "turn askance/ The Poles of Earth twice ten degrees and more/ From the Sun's Axle" or to alter the course of the sun itself (X, lines 650–691):

> At that tasted Fruit
> The Sun, as from *Thyéstean* Banquet, turn'd
> His course intended. . . .

The efficacy of this allusion lies less in the overt reference to astronomy and climatology than to its unstated implications. In devouring the

forbidden fruit, Adam and Eve have metaphorically devoured their
own sons, bringing death to their future posterity.

The tradition behind the "*Amarantin* Shade" of Milton's Heaven (XI,
line 78) is a complex one. The Greek adjective meant "unfading" or
"unwithering," and in antiquity there apparently existed a real plant
(or plants) which bore this name. It reappears in Renaissance herbals,
but in Renaissance poetry it is sometimes a purely imaginary flower.[99]
Through a false etymology based on analogy with the Greek word for
flower (*anthos*) the original word was corrupted to *amaranthus*, and it
appears in this form both in the Garden of Adonis in Spenser's *Faerie
Queene* (III. vi. 45):

> And all about grew every sort of flowre,
> To which sad lovers were transformd of yore;
> Fresh *Hyacinthus*, *Phoebus* paramoure, . . .
> Foolish *Narcisse*, that likes the watry shore,
> Sad *Amaranthus*, made a flowre but late,
> Sad *Amaranthus*, in whose purple gore
> Me Seemes I see *Amintas* wretched fate,
> To whom sweet Poets verse hath given endlesse date [;]

and in the flower catalogue of Milton's *Lycidas* (lines 149–150):

> Bid *Amaranthus* all his beauty shed
> And Daffadillies fill their cups with tears. . . .

In *Paradise Lost* (III, lines 350–364) it has become a plant symbolic of
eternal life or everlasting bliss, indigenous to heaven and no longer
found on earth:

> Immortal Amarant, a Flow'r which once
> In Paradise, fast by the Tree of Life
> Began to bloom, but soon for man's offence
> To Heav'n remov'd where first it grew, there grows,
> And flow'rs aloft shading the Fount of Life. . . .

References to an amarantine (unfading) crown occur in both classical
and Christian writers (cf. Philostratus' *Heroicus* and 1 Peter v. 4, "a
crown of glory that fadeth not away"), but Milton has significantly
interwoven this motif, literally and metaphorically, with the Apocalyptic motif of the golden crowns which the twenty-four elders cast down
before the throne and the sea of glass (Revelation iv. 4–11):

> . . .down they cast
> Thir Crowns inwove with Amarant and Gold. . . .

Milton renders the literal meaning in his description of the Elysian
flowers "that never fade," with which the elect spirits bind their locks.
The phrase "Impurpl'd with Celestial Roses" recalls an additional
meaning common to both Latin and English: *amarant* as the color red

or purple. The introduction of this flower-symbolism at this point in the narrative, immediately after the Father has predicted man's fall into misery and death, but has also promised him immortality and eternal bliss in Heaven, reinforces a central motif in the epic: the contrast between the earthly paradise lost and the heavenly paradise to be gained. If it recalls Satan's earlier allusion to man's "faded bliss,/ Faded so soon" (II, lines 375–376), it also anticipates the imagery of the scene in which Adam first learns of Eve's ruin (IX, lines 892–893): the garland of flowers dropped, "the faded Roses shed. . . ."

Like Homer and Virgil before him, Milton introduces omens — signs that nature has "imprest/ On Bird, Beast, Air" — as cryptic prophecies of future changes (XI, lines 181–190). Though Adam does not understand "these mute signs in Nature," he realizes that they point to "some furder change . . ."; and indeed the eclipse, and the double pursuit — by eagle and by lion — toward the eastern gate point to their imminent expulsion. If the comparison to birds of paradise is appropriate for Adam and Eve, the reference to the "Bird of *Jove*" has been selected with no less propriety to emphasize the Archangel's role both as divine messenger and as agent of divine justice. The choice of the king of birds and king of beasts as pursuers emphasizes the offense against divine majesty (*lèse majesté*).

Finally, in the actual scene of their expulsion, as Adam and Eve look back and behold "that flaming Brand" waved over Paradise and "the Gate,/ With dreadful Faces throng'd and fiery Arms" (XII, lines 641–644), there may be an oblique but significant allusion to the fall of Troy. Just before Aeneas, guided by divinity, quits the doomed city to commence his own wanderings through the world, he beholds a vision of the wrathful gods fiercely engaged in destroying Troy:

> apparent dirae facies inimicaque Troiae
> numina magna deum.

In the "celestial cycle" — and in both of Milton's epics — the loss of Eden is the precondition for regaining an interior paradise happier far, and the fall of man a preparation for his ultimate exaltation to an even higher state. In the Trojan cycle the fall of Ilium and the exile of the Trojan remnant were (as later generations reinterpreted the story) preconditions for the foundation of the Roman empire and for the establishment of a New Troy on the Thames. As Adam and Eve forsake Eden to begin their wanderings (like Aeneas) with "Providence thir guide," the analogy with the Trojan myth seems fitting; and at least one classical scholar has emphasized the parallel by rendering Virgil's Latin (*Aeneid* II, 622–623) in Milton's English:[100]

The dreadful faces throng, and, hating Troy,
Great presences of gods.

[VIII]

Whether classical or biblical in origin, or derived from other
sources, Milton's images are usually closely correlated with his theme
and subject matter and with the conventions of literary genre. In his
First Prolusion the terms of the debate virtually dictated the kind of
imagery he would employ, compelling him to ransack the mythographers for references to the genealogy of Night and Day. Again, in his
Second Prolusion the subject led him, almost inevitably, to explore the
symbolic and mythical associations of the doctrine of celestial harmony.
Allusions to the Hercules myth in both of his epics, in *Samson Agonistes*,
in the Nativity Hymn, and in the introductory verses on "The Passion"
emphasized the superiority of Judaeo-Christian heroic ideals to those
of pagan antiquity. In varying degrees each of these poems managed to
evoke the decorum of some classical literary genre devoted to the deeds
of gods or heroes, only to distinguish it from the higher decorum of the
"divine poem." In much the same way, direct or oblique allusions to
Odysseus or Jason, Caesar or Aeneas, or the heroes of Renaissance
romance-epic could emphasize the links between Milton's heroic poem
and the secular heroic tradition, while affirming its superior merits as a
Biblical epic based on truth rather than myth and celebrating a loftier,
more spiritual conception of heroic virtue and heroic action or passion.

By centering much of his heroic poetry on spiritual rather than
physical combat — on the moral warfare of temptation, on verbal or
meditative debate, or on the victory of the Incarnate Logos over his
own spiritual foes within or without the human soul — Milton suc-
ceeded in spiritualizing and internalizing not only the concept of
heroic virtue, but also the central action in the heroic poem itself. As a
result of this internalization of the epic tradition, much of the external
description and narration in his poem acquires figurative value as a
system of metaphorical analogies for otherwise indescribable spiritual
events. The topographias and chronographias, the representations of
persons and actions, become in a significant degree moral symbols; and
their symbolic nature becomes increasingly apparent as the characters
in the poem (and the reader with them) move from an external to an
internal Hell, or from an exterior Paradise to the promise of a Paradise
within. Similarly, in his prose and poetry alike, Milton exploits the
imagery of physical light and darkness, freedom or confinement, as a
point of departure for exploring their internal and spiritual correla-

tives: the darkness of the mind, the bondage of the will, inner illumination and inner freedom; the hell or heaven within the human soul.

In both epics, geographical and topographical allusions, sometimes based on recent explorations but frequently derived from biblical or classical literature, reinforce the central theme. In *Paradise Regained* they heighten the contrasts between secular and spiritual kingship, world-conquest and self-conquest: world-dominion and the paradisal freedom that man had enjoyed before his fall as an essential aspect of the divine image in which he had been created. The vast prospects and expansive vistas serve, by comparison and contrast, to suggest the greatness of the soul: the magnitude and nobility of the spiritual kingdom that the hero of this "interior epic" is to regain. In *Paradise Lost*, similarly, images based on geography or natural history or the history of mankind — together with the panoramic surveys of the world and its history in the final books — emphasize the universal significance of Adam's decision. His choice affects not only his own descendants but the beasts of land and air and sea; and it results in radical alterations in geography and uranography, in heaven and earth and the relationships between them. The cosmic scope of this epic serves — again by comparison and contrast — to dramatize the superior nobility of the soul, and to heighten the poet's dual emphasis on man's original dignity and on the dignity of his own epic action. Created a little lower than the angels, Adam shares with his Creator (VIII, lines 440–441) an inner freedom which differentiates him not only from the brute but from the rest of created nature. He holds the key to his own fate, for it has been divinely entrusted to him; and in this lies his essential and intrinsic nobility. Yet it is also the key to his own ruin and that of the created universe with him. For the destinies of the macrocosm are inseparably interinvolved with those of the microcosm. As part of the same universal order, the same universal harmony, they have joined originally in the same universal hymn of praise, and they will subsequently share the same universal ruin. Adam's ruin, and that of the world created for his delight and profit, hinges upon his own free will, his original endowment from Heaven. The freedom that constitutes the essential dignity of man is also (paradoxically) the source of his misery.

The bond that thus links the destinies of microcosm and macrocosm so intimately in Milton's epic belongs to that system of universal analogy — correspondences and "sympathies" among diverse levels and kinds of beings — in which many of Milton's contemporaries still believed and which (for some of them) provided a philosophical basis for metaphor and allegory. "O Earth, how like to Heav'n . . .!" Satan exclaims, immediately prior to entering the serpent in Eden (IX, line 99). In endeavoring to "relate/ To human sense th' invisible exploits/ Of warring Spirits," Raphael follows the poet's method of "lik'ning

spiritual to corporal forms,/ As may express them best. . . ." Yet (like
the fallen Archangel) he is also conscious of the symbolic analogies
between the terrestrial and the celestial (V, lines 564–576):

> . . . though what if Earth
> Be but the shadow of Heav'n, and things therein
> Each to other like, more than on earth is thought?

In Mazzeo's view, the "principle of universal analogy" underlay the
poetry of the English metaphysicals as well as seventeenth-century
Continental theories of the conceit. Through the influence of Graciàn,
Tesauro, and other literary theorists, Giordano Bruno's "conception of
the poet as one who discovers and expresses the universal analogies
binding the universe together" was "made the basis for a poetic of
'concettismo' or . . . 'a poetic of correspondences.'"[101] Other critics
have associated this principle with allegory. "The basis of allegorical
reading," Roche suggested, "is this analogical nature of the universe.
In an hierarchical universe where each thing has a fixed place the
relationship of any two things in the same world or sphere may adum-
brate the relationship of two other things in another world or sphere."
According to Pico della Mirandola, the three worlds — sublunary, celestial, supercelestial — were "analogically correspondent."

Roche has applied this approach to Spenser's *Faerie Queene*, and (as
he points out) Simon Fornari had cited Pico's views in his exposition of
the *Orlando Furioso*.[102] In the course of a lunar journey to recover
Orlando's lost wits, the English knight Astolfo learns from his guide
(Canto xxxv. 18) that "'there cannot wag a straw/ Below on earth but
that the sign is here,/ And each small act doth correspondence draw/
Although in other show it doth appear . . .'":

> Ogni effetto convien che corrisponda
> In terra, e in ciel, ma con diversa faccia.

Though Ariosto treats the theory of correspondences facetiously, his
commentator Fornari seems to have taken the doctrine in high seri-
ousness, basing his own theory of allegory on correspondences between the human microcosm and the three worlds (sublunary, celestial,
supercelestial) of Pico's *Heptaplus*.[103]

Milton was undoubtedly familiar with the theory of universal analogy. Moreover, as he was well aware, correspondences between heaven
and earth would have significantly greater relevance for the still-
unfallen world that he was portraying than for the world after the fall,
when the original harmony existing among all orders and levels of
created beings had been broken. As a basis for his similes he would
(almost inevitably) be compelled to search for analogies with earthly
things to illustrate the celestial things he was describing; but in seeking

and elaborating such correspondences he was not obliged to regard them as metaphysically true. In fact he encountered similar problems, sought the same kind of similes and analogies, in endeavoring to give sensuous reality to his image of Hell. Raphael's remarks on analogies between earth and heaven are consistent with Renaissance Neoplatonic or neo-Hermetic doctrines, but they are quite intelligible in the context of classical Platonism and New Testament typology. Both of the latter profoundly influenced Milton's analogical thought and imagery, despite the highly significant differences between them.

Though the imagery of shadow and substance and an emphasis on the analogical relationship between the earthly and the heavenly are common to both, for Plato the analogy is essentially metaphysical and almost exclusively vertical. It has little or no historical relevance, no horizontal dimension. In the New Testament epistles, on the other hand, the analogy between the earthly and the heavenly is operative in human history; it exists on a horizontal level as well as in a vertical dimension. Plato had described earthly things as shadows and reflections of heavenly archetypes, copies and *eidola* of the true. St. Paul had declared that "the invisible things" of God could be clearly seen and understood by the things that He had made (Romans i. 19–20); but when he (or the author of Hebrews) speaks of the earthly as shadows and copies of the heavenly, or as figures of the true (Colossians ii. 17; Hebrews viii. 5; ix. 23–24; x. 1), the context is essentially typological and Christological. He is comparing and contrasting the imperfect types of the Old Testament with their fulfilment and perfect realization in the antitypes of the New.

These analogical relationships between the earthly and the heavenly, as St. Paul develops them, comprehend the parallels or antitheses between Adam and Christ, the Earthy and the Heavenly Man (Romans v. 18–21; 1 Corinthians xv. 21–22, 45–49); between the law and the gospel and the old and new covenants; between Mount Sinai and Mount Zion and between the earthly and the heavenly Jerusalems. They also include further correspondences — between the mediatorial office of the old high-priesthood, ministering on earth in a sanctuary built with hands, and the heavenly high-priesthood of the risen Christ, interceding in the very presence of God; between the blood-offerings of the old dispensation and the perfect sacrifice of the new; and between citizenship on earth and in heaven (cf. Colossians iii. 1–4, 9–10; Galatians iv. 24–26; Philippians iii. 20–21; Ephesians i. 10, ii. 6; Hebrews iv. 14; viii. 10, 16; ix. 8–15, 23–25; xi. 10, 13, 16, 27; xii. 9, 18–23). The earthly things are not only copies or shadows of the true and perfect patterns laid up in heaven; they are also types and shadows of the "good things," the heavenly and spiritual things, that are to come. As presented in the Pauline epistles and in Hebrews, this typological symbolism is inseparably linked with either the first or the second advent of Christ, and with His role as mediator, with the divine promises first obscurely and later more clearly announced, and with faith itself as the means of knowing the *invisibilia Dei*, as "the substance of things hoped for, the evidence of things not seen" (Hebrew xi. 1).[104]

In Michael's survey of human history in the last two books of Milton's epic, the Archangel's method and imagery are essentially typological, but there are nevertheless significant differences in his presentational modes. These coincide with Milton's division of what was originally a single, prophetic book into two books: the first concluding with destruction of the first world by water and with the Noachic covenant; the second recounting the course of the second world until its destruction and purgation by fire, and ending with Adam's expulsion from Paradise. As a result of this division the mythological allusion at the beginning of Book XI, likening Adam and Eve to Deucalion and Pyrrha, acquires additional significance through its relevance to the Biblical episode that now concludes this book. On the other hand, . Milton's image of Christ as heavenly intercessor and high-priest at the beginning of this book — a motif which had received elaborate typological development in Hebrews — is thematically more relevant to the concluding events in Michael's prophecies in Book XII; this relationship is partially obscured by the structural revisions which separate the beginning of the original book from its end. In this passage Milton effectively applies imagery based on the Old Testament type (the Aaronic high-priesthood) and on its reinterpretation by the authors of Hebrews and the Apocalypse, to his own image of Christ as antitype: as the heavenly high-priest who intercedes in the immediate presence of the Father.

Milton's structural division coincides with the destruction of the antediluvian world and the beginning of another: like his angelic narrator, the poet himself has paused "Betwixt the world destroy'd and world restor'd . . ." (XII, line 3); and he emphasizes this discontinuity in world-history both by breaking the continuity of the original book and by the discontinuity in the Archangel's prophetic mode, a shift from primarily visual to exclusively verbal presentation. In Book XI Michael reveals the future effects of Adam's sin through a series of visionary tableaux, which he complements by verbal explication: the murder of Abel, the diseases of the Lazar-house, the seduction of the sober "sons of God" by the worldly "daughters of men," the translation of Enoch, Noah's ark. In Book XII, on the other hand, he relies on verbal prophecy alone.[105] Adam learns by hearing rather than by prophetic vision, depending not on the evidence of his eyes but on a verbal revelation which is essentially a précis of the Scriptures. It is through verbal discourse rather than visual images that he first finds "Mine eyes true op'ning" (XII, lines 273–274), and through faith as "evidence of things unseen" that he can contemplate the distant and still invisible objects of the divine promises, "the substance of things hoped for. . . ."

Both Michael and Raphael are relating "heavenly things" to the "earthy Man" (Adam), accommodating them to his limited human understanding. Yet there are significance differences between these narratives both in presentational modes and in the relationships they imply between the "earthly" images or types and their celestial parallels or paradigms. Raphael is portraying discord in Heaven, and the final restoration of peace, while in the created universe the original harmony among all things and the original concord between earth and Heaven still remain unbroken. He is addressing unfallen man; and he presents his brief epic of the war in Heaven as an exemplary warning against the analogous revolt and disobedience through which Adam himself will (all too shortly) fall, incurring an analogous expulsion from Paradise. The archangel's narrative is relative primarily to the original covenant between God and Adam (Genesis ii. 16–17). The events that he recounts occur in Heaven rather than on earth. They are invisible exploits by warring spirits; and these battles are essentially (though not exclusively) spiritual. These actions (it would appear) have already taken place; they belong apparently to the past rather than to the future. Finally, the archangel's "method of tradition" (as Bacon might have called it) is rather poetic than historiographical: an imaginative reconstruction of the angelomachia based on scattered and cryptic allusions in the Scriptures. (This aspect of Raphael's "brief epic," however, is probably less representative of what Milton thought the narrative mode of a "Divine Historian" ought to be than of Milton's own conception of epic poetry as a fictional image of a true historical action. The brevity and ambiguity of his Scriptural sources gave him ample freedom to invent and reconstruct his own imaginary version of the angelomachia.)

Michael, on the other hand, is instructing a fallen creature in the future history of a fallen world. The events that he relates are, for the most part, confined to the earth; their actors are men and women, rather than angels. Whereas Raphael's representation of the creation of the world on six consecutive days is a concession to the limitations of his human audience, as God's acts are immediate, Michael's survey of world-history does not require this sort of accommodation since the events themselves will occur in process of time. There are very few fictional embellishments in his austere chronicle-history of the world after the flood. The implications of the veiled predictions concerning the woman's seed unfold progressively in time, becoming increasingly clearer as the series of shadowy types culminates in the prophecy of the Messiah's advent, and in Adam's confession of faith in the Christ-to-come. Interweaving the motifs of punitive justice and the grace vouchsafed to fallen man, Michael proceeds through a series of covenants to the covenant of faith.

The fact that Michael's narrative is prophetic and proleptic, in contrast to Raphael's retrospective epos, has a significant (though not decisive) bearing on their exploitation of typological symbolism. In the Pauline epistles and in Hebrews the relation between earthly type and celestial antitype is usually conceived and represented in chronological terms, in terms of human history. The earthly shadows are on the whole "foreshadowings": veiled symbols of the "good things to come." Thus the Aaronic high-priesthood under the Law was a type or shadow of the heavenly high-priesthood of Christ under the New Dispensation, the Gospel. Similarly Moses, Joshua, David are types of Christ. Typological symbolism would seem, accordingly, less appropriate for Raphael's account of past events in Heaven than for Michael's visionary and verbal prophecies of the future history of mankind and, more particularly of the Holy Community from the age of the patriarchs to the Second Coming.

Nevertheless we must regard the sociable Archangel's "angelomachia" as considerably more than divine history. This epic of warring spirits would seem to be normative also, and exemplary, for the pattern of man's spiritual warfare in the fallen world. Though represented as past history, it is also to some extent symbolic and prophetic of the Second Advent. The invention of the cannon by the devil anticipates the weapons and tactics of Renaissance warfare; and the poet's treatment of Messianic symbolism in the angelic war recalls the imagery and Messianic expectations of his earlier prose treatises: *Of Reformation . . . in England, The Reason of Church Government,* or indeed *Areopagitica.* Raphael is delineating the heavenly paradigm of the future battles of the Church Militant [105a] (which will reach their climax in an analogous Messianic advent and triumph), just as Michael will subsequently trace the future course of the Church Militant, in his survey of world-history. This narrative also will conclude similarly with a Messianic advent, "in glory and power" with contrary rewards for the faithful and the unfaithful.

Though Adam hails Raphael as an historian and Michael as a seer, it is the latter who in certain respects foreshadows the methods of the historiographer, and the former who anticipates those of the poet and the seer, singing of invisible things and presenting them through visual imagery. Raphael's images and presentational modes are, not surprisingly, fairly characteristic of Milton's images of "heavenly things" elsewhere in his epic, when the poet is narrating or describing actions and scenes in his own voice instead of the voice of one of his epic *personae.* In portraying these invisible paradigms of things on earth —

archetypal "patterns laid up in heaven" — the poet complements Scriptural images and motifs with other details drawn from the resources of his own imagination, his classical education, his wide reading in world history, geography, and science. With imagery derived from the visionary and apocalyptic literature of both testaments, or from the Psalms or Proverbs or the New Testament epistles, he may combine details reminiscent of Homer and Hesiod and Ovid; or he may describe the revealed antitypes of the New Covenant partly in terms of their earthly types and shadows.[105b]

Analogies between heaven and earth[106] in Milton's epic are further enhanced by the presence of time in Heaven. Because of the alternation of light and darkness, he can include the conventional epic chronographies in Raphael's account of the battle in Heaven, as well as in the poet-narrator's description of events on earth. In this context the image of the cave within the mount of God is also suggestive; through the influence of Platonic tradition, it had long been a conventional symbol of the world.

Besides correspondences and analogies on diverse planes of reality and different levels in the hierarchy of being, the *personae* in Milton's epic frequently imitate or parody one another. The devils deliberately imitate God's light or mime his thunder. Satan's throne and chariot are imitations of those belonging to the true God; and as idol of divine majesty he affects divine honors. Though the degree to which Sin can be regarded as a parodic imitation either of the Son as Logos or of the Biblical Sapientia (cf. Proverbs viii. 30; Wisdom of Solomon vii. 26; Hebrews i. 3) is debatable, the Sapientia-allusion would seem to have a significant bearing on the central episode in *Paradise Lost*. As a parody of divine knowledge, and as an infernal, diabolical wisdom whose offspring are death and remorse, Sin herself as an allegorical *persona* is representative not only of "sin" in general, but also of Satan's particular offenses against both God and man — as well as the particular sin of Adam and Eve. This was not only a transgression of a divine command, but also a perverted mode of knowledge: the immediate and personal experience of evil. The genealogical relationships between Satan, Sin, Death, and Sin's brood of hellhounds both foreshadow and symbolize the progressive stages of man's fall.

A hierarchical metaphysics (as Professor Roche observed)[107] lends itself readily to a system of universal correspondences. In Milton's poetic universe the hierarchies are not rigidly defined, and the ascent from matter to spirit is gradual; the angels themselves are in part material beings, and God Himself is not only the beginning and end of all things — their formal, final, and efficient cause — but also their material cause. In *Paradise Lost* body and soul are less sharply differentiated than in earlier works like *Comus*, and, in contrast to the imagery of the afterlife in Milton's Latin epicedia or in his sonnet on Mrs. Catharine Thomason, the epic apparently reflects the mortalist view expressed in his theological treatise, *The Christian Doctrine*. But Death is an alien intruder in Milton's cosmos — an invading monster from outer space — and prior to the fall of man, the possible levels and gradations of being in Milton's universe would seem to be virtually infinite. Its hierarchical structure is not rigid and static but in constant motion. It allows a continuous movement upwards from matter toward spirit. Yet, on the other hand, the highest and most spiritual of created beings can forfeit their station and, sinking to lower levels, become increasingly grosser and darker in essence. It is a dynamic universe, not unlike that of the alchemists, in which all things are either in process of becoming more spiritualized or more material, or are maintaining their respective states of being through continuous motion. (Even seemingly pointless activities, like Raphael's excursion to Hell-gate, are motions that confirm the loyal angels in their original state of being; they move, like the spheres, in love of an Unmoved Mover.)

In this universe of perpetual movement the principal images that link the various levels of the unfallen world are, as in Dante's *Paradiso*, images of light and music. As in the prolusion on the music of the spheres and in several of Milton's earlier poems — the Nativity Hymn, *Arcades* and *Comus*, *At a Solemn Music* — the original harmony of the prelapsarian universe is expressed in terms of song and dance. For Pico (as Roche observed) the different levels of being were united through God's love. In Milton's poetic universe they are united through worship: through praise of the Creator and love of "Him whom to love is to obey . . ." (VIII, line 634; cf. V, lines 535–540). In the unfallen world all things both reflect and minister to their Creator; and, through imagery derived from both Biblical and classical sources, Milton represents this original state of universal harmony through the symbolism of a universal *molpe*: choral song and choral dance. There are significant correspondences between the movements of the planets and fixed stars and the mystic dances of the angels about the divine throne. The earthly Paradise resounds with the music of nature — fountains and birdsong, rustling leaves, the unpremeditated songs of unfallen man — as Heaven with the sound of the harp and the hymns of the angels. All things, except the apostate angels, are united in a universal hymn of praise: a cosmic symphony in which the poet-narrator himself also bears a part.

He is also intimately involved in the symbolic motions — circular or linear, intricate or plain, vertical or horizontal, spatial and temporal — that recur throughout his poem. Taught by his heavenly muse, he ascends or descends to the contemplation of Heaven or Hell or the earthly Paradise. With the revolving year, "Seasons return"; but for the blind man there can be no grateful vicissitudes of morning or evening twilight, no return of day. Yet it is paradoxically in the outer darkness that seems to surround him that he can behold, by the inner, celestial light things invisible to mortal sight.[108]

The poet himself thus shares not only in the symbolic movements within the poem — in its ascents and descents, the alternation of the seasons — and in the song of the angels, but also in the complex imagery of light and darkness that pervades his poetic cosmos and provides a basis for its moral and epistemological symbolism. Light and darkness (typologically associated with the elect and the apostate angels in exegetical tradition) acquire architectonic value as an essential part of the elaborate system of analogies and contraries underlying the temporal and spatial structure of Milton's universe and the structural organization of his narrative. Besides functioning as the basis for a kind of spiritual counterpoint or *contrapposto*, they enhance the dramatic immediacy of a scene: the sudden blaze of light in Hell as the millions of fallen angels brandish their swords; or conversely the darkness in heaven symbolic of divine wrath (VI, lines 56–59, 824–834). The artificial glory of Pandaemonium (which mimics God's light, just as the infernal cannon parody His thunder) stands in striking contrast not only to the prevailing "darkness visible" of Hell but also to the divine glory of Heaven and the natural glory of the newly created sun and stars. Conversely the dazzling obscurity of the Godhead, "Dark with excessive bright," introduces a paradoxical (though traditional) variation on the motif of celestial light. The waning lustre of the Archangel's glory after his fall is ironically counterpointed by the artificial lustre of his barbaric throne; but even this diminished or artificial glory is subsequently undercut by Satan's tactical resort to the cover of darkness. Both in Eden itself and during his nocturnal flight about the world he deliberately shuns the light: a voluntary, and highly symbolic, transition from Lucifer to lucifuge.

Milton's variations on the motif of inner illumination and inner or outer darkness belong to the same complex system of symbolic chiaroscuro; but they are also closely correlated with the imagery of the temptation (Genesis iii. 5–7): ". . . then your eyes shall be opened, and ye shall be as gods, knowing good and evil. . . . And the eyes of them both were opened, and they knew that they were naked. . . ."

Milton's Heaven and Hell are described, on the whole, in general terms. It is their light and darkness respectively (along with their spatial opposition, at contrary poles of Milton's imaginary universe) which gives "sensuous immediacy" (in Professor Grose's phrase)[108a] to these spiritual realities: bestowing a "local habitation" on spiritual states and making the *invisibilia Dei* and the *invisibilia diaboli* visible and apprehensible to us.

It is inspired song, then, that links the hierarchies of being in Milton's epic, and that involves the poet himself in the symbolic structures of his own poem. Through song he joins in the concert of angelic praise. Through song he takes part in the ascending and descending movements, and the spiralling structures of his own poetic universe.

Similarly it is through the divine light itself that he can see and tell of the *invisibilia Dei* invisible to mortal sight. The "invisible things" of God are perceived, however dimly, both through the poet's imitation of the visible things that the Creator has made, and through the visual and aural imagery of the poet's own creation; the poetic "heterocosm" and minature world that he himself has fashioned through the inspiration and illumination of the same divine Spirit who had created the cosmos itself, the larger world.

Both the genre of *Paradise Lost* and its argument held significant implications for Milton's imagery. As he was well aware (and as modern critics have also recognized) he must depict the state of paradisal innocence to readers who belonged to a fallen world.[109] In an early draft for a tragedy on this theme, the prologue (delivered in the persona of Moses as author of Genesis) had informed the spectators of the drama that "they cannot se Adam in the state of innocence by reason of thire sin."[110] The technical reason for this statement may have been Milton's concern to rationalize his failure to portray the actual temptation-scene, which would have entailed inevitable difficulties in costuming if and when the tragedy should be staged; but the fact that he choses this particular explanation is significant. In the epic there are no staging difficulties, no problems in costuming; and he can portray at length not only the crucial temptation-scene but the state of paradisal bliss that Adam has forfeited. Yet in describing this life in Eden, in his rendering of its topographical and geographical setting as well as in his treatment of prospective or retrospective episodes involving events that take place elsewhere, the poet deliberately "brackets" both Paradise itself and the actions that occur within it from the outside world. Morally and spiritually, temporally as well as spatially, this prototype of all subsequent pleasure-gardens is literally a *hortus conclusus*.[111] Unique and set apart not only from the world but from the common experience of mankind, it enjoys the status of a Platonic (if not a Jungian) archetype, but with this significant difference: that the Idea in all its uniqueness exists on earth.

Only through the poet's own proleptic allusions, or through the prophetic speeches of Michael, do we encounter the world familiar to us: the world of classical or Renaissance geography and of Biblical or classical history. The earthly paradise has not survived the flood; it exists only as a barren island in the Persian Gulf.

Yet if the poet must face the problem of making the state of unfallen man comprehensible and "sensible" to his fallen readers, the angelic narrators face similar difficulties with regard to Adam. Raphael must not only make heavenly things apprehensible to human sense and reason, but must describe the origin of evil to a creature who mercifully does not yet possess the knowledge of good and evil. Michael in turn must recount the future course of mankind to a man who has encountered no other human being except his own wife and who has not yet set foot outside of Paradise into the world without.

These problems were, on the whole, the results of Milton's choice of theme. Other difficulties, arising from his choice of genre, he shared with other Renaissance poets who had endeavored to accommodate the Christian marvellous to the conventions of classical epic: the representation of Hell and Heaven, of good and evil angels, and of other things invisible to mortal sight. Having selected an argument that he believed to be more heroic than those of classical epic — and having chosen to portray the magnalia of spiritual beings more numerous, more powerful, more intelligent than mankind — Milton repeatedly calls attention to the technical difficulties he must encounter, to the problem of achieving plausible and "sensible" representation. He adapts to his own subject matter the Virgilian formula of comparing great things with small — [112]contrary to the normal rhetorical methods of amplification. (By orthodox procedures an orator or poet would consciously magnify his subject by comparing it with greater things; to liken it with lesser things, conversely, was a conventional technique of extenuation and depreciation.) Milton similarly alludes, either in his own person or in that of Raphael, to his deliberately-elected technique of representing the heavenly through comparison with the earthly or the invisible through analogy with the visual.[113] He must portray the instantaneous and immediate acts of God in terms of temporal process. He makes frequent, and often elaborate, use of the inexpressibility-*topos*; for he must describe the invisible, relate the unutterable.

He introduces comparisons not only with the supposed facts of human and natural history but with the figments of fable and romance. The truths he is endeavoring to describe (he suggests) transcend not only the concrete realities of the world as we know it, but even the wildest fantasies and inventions of the poetic imagination. In drawing his comparisons, he exploits not only images based on "likes" and "unlikes" (*similia* and *dissimilia*) and on "equals" (*pares*), but also "unequals" (*impares*): things greater or less in quality or quantity than the objects or events that he is depicting. On occasion he invites attention not only to problems of description but to those of nomenclature. The figure of Death, of instance, cannot justly be called "shape" or "substance" or "shadow."

[APPENDIX]

Milton's Prose

Finally, let us turn, however briefly, to the attitudes Milton expresses towards antiquity in some of his prose works.[1] Most of these are serious compositions, though their tone and mood may vary radically as Milton alters his argument or his stance: now grave and now jocose, now sardonic and now inspired. In personal diatribe he often hurls whatever sort of metaphorical ammunition comes most readily to hand; ridicule based on classical myth is among them. Salmasius' name may suggest fish, but it also evokes the myth of Salmacis and Hermaphroditus. The name More prompts a series of botanical images centering upon the word *morus* (mulberry) and inevitably recalling the myth of Pyramus and Thisbe. In the same work — and in his own defense as well as that of his nation — Milton can exploit mythical allusions to the gods and prophets of the Gentiles to illustrate his own peculiar relationship to divine Providence and the singular protection he receives from Heaven as a blind man and as a propagator of truth. "Shall I mention," he asks, "those wise and ancient bards whose misfortunes the gods are said to have compensated by superior endowments, and whom men so much revered that they chose rather to impute their want of sight to the injustice of heaven than to their own want of innocence or virtue?" This noble digression on the motif of blindness leads — through allusions to the myths of Tiresias and Phineus, the "two destinies, which the oracle of Delphi" announced to Achilles, and other classical or modern references — to his reassertion of the Christian paradoxes of strength through weakness and inner illumination in blindness; see John Milton, *Complete Poetry and Major Prose*, ed. Merritt Y. Hughes (New York, 1957), pp. 824–827). In the same personal apology Milton compares himself to Euripides' tragic heroes and suggests (albeit obliquely) a further analogy with Socrates.

In Sidney's opinion, "a fayned example hath as much force to teach as a true example . . ."; *An Apologie for Poetrie*, in *English Literary Criticism: The Renaissance*, ed. O.B. Hardison, Jr. (New York, 1963), p. 114. As for its power "to moove, it is cleere, sith the fayned may bee tuned to the highest key of passion. . . ." Yet whatever its efficacy in instruction and persuasion or in arousing delight, whatever its utility in rhetoric as well as in poetry, a fictional example might seem ill-adapted to serve as logical proof, as valid evidence in serious causes. Milton often employs it, however, as evidence as well as ornament, in pleading the gravest of causes and in reassessing the fundamental doctrines and concepts of political and ethical theory or of theology.

In *Areopagitica* and the preface to *Samson Agonistes* Milton cites both apostolic and patristic examples, to defend the study of Hellenic learning in one instance and the nobility of tragedy in the other. Moses, Daniel, and Paul were "skilful in all the learning of the Egyptians, Chaldeans, and Greeks," he tells us; and indeed Paul had "thought it no defilement to insert into holy scripture the sentences of three Greek poets, and one of them a tragedian. . . ." After Julian the Apostate had denied Christians the right to study heathen learning, the two Apollinarii managed "to coin all the seven liberal sciences out of the Bible, reducing it into divers forms of orations, poems, dialogues, even to the calculating of a new Christian grammar"; see John Milton, *Complete Poems and Major Prose*, ed. Merritt Y. Hughes (New York, N.Y., 1957), p. 726. Subsequently, in defending the dignity and utility of tragedy — and, more narrowly, tragedy modelled on ancient Attic exemplars— Milton adduces Christian and pagan testimonies and examples: Aristotle and Cicero, Plutarch and Seneca, Augustus Caesar and Dionysius the elder; but also St. Paul the Apostle, Gregory Nazianzen, and David Paraeus.

In both instances the context of these allusions to pagan literature and learning is polemical. In the former instance, Milton is attacking government censorship of the press, maintaining that the "reading of books, whatever sort they be," is more beneficial than harmful; see *Major Prose*, p. 725. In the second case he is justifying his own literary practice — in composing a tragedy at all (in the first place), and in fashioning his drama according to the model of Greek tragedy. In neither instance is he concerned with classical mythology *per se*, with its function as a stylistic ornament or symbolic mode, or with its use and abuse.

In other prose treatises he frequently exploits classical allusions along with Biblical references to make his point. He begins *The Reason of Church-Government* with a reference to Plato and subsequently alludes to the examples of Cyrus and Scipio. Correlating Scriptural with classical traditions, he asserts that "all the ancient lawgivers were either truly inspired, as Moses, or were such men as with authority enough might give it out to be so, as Minos, Lycurgus, Numa . . ."; see *Major Prose*, p. 643. In *The Doctrine and Discipline of Divorce* he compares Eve to Pandora, and Adam to Epimetheus. He exploits Plato's myth of Eros and Anteros to demonstrate that without mutual love wedlock can be only the empty husk of matrimony. Even more significantly, he praises several of the ancient poets and philosophers Homer and Manilius, Plato and Chrysippus on theological grounds. They have exonerated heaven of responsibility for the crimes of men and have insisted "that man's

own will self-corrupted is the adequate and sufficient cause of his disobedience besides fate. . . ." These men were "not ignorant in their
heathen lore that it is most godlike to punish those who of his creatures
became his enemies with the greatest punishment. . . . Thus were the
common sort of Gentiles wont to think, without any wry thoughts cast
upon divine governance"; see *Major Prose*, pp. 714–715.

In *The Tenure of Kings and Magistrates* Milton counters Royalist arguments based on Scripture (Psalm li. 4) with references to Greek and
Latin tragedy. After citing arguments in favor of tyrannicide in the
dramas of Euripides and Seneca, and the view of "the prime authors"
of Greece and Rome on this subject, he leaves these Ethnic examples
"lest it be objected they were heathen" and turns instead to Old Testament history, drawing his evidence from "another sort of men that had
the knowledge of true religion . . ."; see *Major Prose*, pp. 760–761.
Again, in his theological treatise, *The Christian Doctrine*, he concludes
his discussion of predestination with quotations concerning "the justice
of God" taken from "the heathen Homer" (*Odyssey* I, lines 7, 32–34);
see *Major Prose*, pp. 931–932.

Of particular interest is the fact that Milton credits the "heathen"
poets and philosophers with opinions very like his own concerning the
operations of divine justice and the hardening of the heart. His state-
ments on this subject in *The Doctrine and Discipline of Divorce* anticipate
the manner in which he would depict Satan's punishment in *Paradise
Lost*. Cicero and Homer and other Gentile poets and philosophers
believed (he declares) that there could be no greater punishment than
when "God himself throws a man furthest from him; which then they
held he did when he blinded, hardened and stirred up his offenders to
finish and pile up their desperate work since they had undertaken it."
"To banish for ever into a local hell" — whether in the air or at the
earth's center, or in "that uttermost and bottomless gulf of chaos,
deeper from holy bliss than the world's diameter multiplied" — this
"they thought had not a punishing so proper and proportionate for
God to inflict as to punish sin with sin"; see *Major Prose*, p. 715.

In these passages mythological allusions constitute only one of several kinds of evidence and proofs that Milton draws from classical
antiquity; but it is significant that he does not hesitate to utilize poetic
myth as logical proof — not merely as extrinsic ornament — in serious
controversial subjects which he regarded as vitally important for the
individual and for church and state. In some of his earliest surviving
prose, the Latin academic exercises, the case is different. Designed for
oral delivery, either in college or in the Public Schools of the University,
these are exhibition-pieces as well as apprentice-work, both testing and
exercising the student and giving him a chance to display his rhetorical
and logical skill on issues that were in the literal sense merely

"academic" — far different from those that would engage his pen during the 1640's and 1650's. In these exercises, where the speaker must demonstrate both erudition and ingenuity, Milton adorns his discourse with frequent allusions to classical literature — echoes of Horace and Persius and Martial, of Homer and Hesiod and Pindar, of Virgil and Ovid, Plato and Pythagoras, Aristotle, Plutarch, Athenaeus, the Orphic Hymns. When his subject seems to require it, he bases his arguments as well as his ornaments on the mythographers. In the First Prolusion his subject compels him to consult the latter, but (finding the majority of these authorities against them, he dismisses "these inventions of the poets" as unreliable: "gay fables" unable to endure the test of reason. The testimony and "assertions of the mythologists" to the contrary, "I dare assert that Day is older than Night. . . ."; see *Major Prose*, pp. 596–599. In the Second Prolusion, "On the Music of the Spheres," he argues initially that Pythagoras had not intended this doctrine to be taken literally. It was merely a poetic symbol referring to the same universal harmony and concord of all things that Plato subsequently taught through his myth of the celestial Sirens and that Homer had signified through his "figure of the golden chain which Jove suspended from heaven." In this use of symbol Pythagoras seemed "to have followed the example of the poets—or, what is almost the same thing, of the divine oracles—by which no sacred and arcane mystery is ever revealed to vulgar ears without being somehow wrapped up and veiled"; *Major Prose*, p. 603.

CHAPTER TWO

Milton's Urania and the Renaissance Tradition: An Overview

> O heavenly muse, that not with fading bays
>   Deckest thy brow by th' Heliconian spring,
> But sittest, crown'd with stars' immortal rays,
>   In heaven, where legions of bright angels sing,
> Inspire life in my wit, my thoughts upraise,
>   My verse ennoble, and forgive the thing,
> If fictions light I mix with truth divine,
> And fill these lines with others' praise than thine.

LIKE MILTON, Torquato Tasso has chosen a sacred (though not a Biblical) subject for his epic, invoking a celestial muse for aid and specifically contrasting this truly heavenly source of poetic inspiration with the Aonian mountain Helicon, haunt of the pagan muses.[1]

Nevertheless, while emphasizing her celestial character and explicitly distinguishing her from the Muses of Helicon, Tasso does not call her the "heavenly muse" (the phrase is Fairfax's addition), nor does the poet or his translater address her as Urania. The stellar imagery in the opening lines of the *Gerusalemme Liberata* could befit the classical muse of astronomy; but *that* Urania had been one of the nine sisters who haunted Mount Helicon, and Tasso's opening lines patently contrast his heavenly (i.e. Christian) muse from those of ancient Greece:[2]

> O Musa, tu che di caduchi allori
> non circondi la fronte in Elicona,
> ma su nel cielo in fra i beati cori
> hai de stelle immortali aurea corona. . . .

Although other identifications have been proposed, Italian scholars have identified the muse whom Tasso invoked as Urania, "pero modificata alquanto dal concetto pagano e considerata piuttosto come celeste intelligenza protettrice dei poeti."[3]

The use of this name by Christian poets of the Renaissance to emphasize their conscious selection of a sacred rather than a secular argument is, on the whole, a reflection of the "Christian humanism" that (despite recent reassessments) was a prominent, if not distinctive, feature, of both the "northern" and the "southern" Renaissance. If poets retained the conventional invocation to an obsolete divinity like the Muse or Apollo, it was to assert their self-conscious relationship to the classical tradition. If they distinguished their own Urania from her mythological counterpart (and from Clio or Calliope as well), it was to underline their conscious preference for a sacred, if not a biblical, subject and (in some instances) for the Christian rather than the pagan marvellous. The muse is "heavenly" not because she teaches the movements and influences of the stars, but because she symbolizes the inspiration and/or revelation of the true God, in contrast to the divinities of ancient paganism. She is associated with the "heavenly" wisdom and eloquence of the biblical tradition, in contrast to the "worldly" and "earthly" wisdom of heathen antiquity.

The antecedents of Milton's muse have been investigated with the zeal of some genealogist endeavoring to establish some recent title to a throne.[4] Some have traced her to the Aphrodite Urania of Plato's *Symposium*, or to the heavenly ("uranian") muse whom Plato contrasts with Polyhymnia and associates with heavenly love. Others associate her with the heavenly Wisdom or Sapience of Spenser's *Fowre Hymnes*, who in turn reflects the influence of the Old Testament wisdom literature.[5] Dante had called on Urania for aid in the *Purgatorio*, but without explicitly differentiating her from the muses of Helicon, whom he also invoked. (In commenting on this invocation, Benvenuto da Imola had stressed her heavenly character because of the literal meaning of her name: "quia latine sonat coelestis").[6] An ambiguous reference to the nine muses in Dante's *Paradiso*, moreover, had sometimes been glossed as a reference to "new" — i.e. "Christian" — muses. In this passage (Dante had declared) he is coursing waters never traversed before; hence he invokes the aid of Minerva, Apollo, and "nove Muse." Bernardino Daniello (whose commentary on Dante's *Commedia* was familiar to Milton) and other critics interpreted this phrase as signifying "Muse nuove," the *new* Christian muses as distinguished from the ancient muses invoked by pagan poets of Graeco-Roman antiquity.[7]

William Alabaster had used the phrase "heavenlie muse" in a sonnet on Christ's passion, but he had neither invoked nor even personified the muse:[8]

> Then since my holie vowes have undertooke
> to take the portract of Christs death in mee
> then lett my love with sonnetts fill this booke
> with hymnes to give the onsett as did hee
> That thoughts enflamed, with such heavenlie muse
> The Coldest Ice of feare, may not refuse.

In this context "heavenlie muse" might refer to sacred thoughts and holy meditations, as well as to a celestial *inspiratrix* of divine poetry.

For Lily B. Campbell the Urania of DuBartas' poem *L'Uranie* in *La Muse Chrestiene* (1574), together with the Urania of Spenser's *The Teares of the Muses* and the Sapience of his *Fowre Hymnes* were among the primary influences in shaping the tradition behind Milton's own heavenly muse. Calling attention to Spenser's reference to DuBartas' "heavenly Muse" in the "L'Envoy" to *The Ruines of Rome*, she found it "impossible to dissociate the Urania speaking in *The Teares of the Muses* and the Urania of DuBartas. . . . Certainly she is the Christian Muse as she recounts the fruits of knowledge. . . ."[9]

The Urania of Spenser's *Teares* belongs to the traditional "sacred Sisters nine,/ The golden brood of great *Apolloes* wit . . ."; but Spenser converts her into something more than the classical muse of astronomy. He identifies her with "th' heavenlie light of knowledge" — the "onelie comfort" and "loadstarre" in "this wide world in which they wretches stray. . . ." Describing her in terms reminiscent of the Wisdom of the Old Testament, he associates her with knowledge of the world's creation, with self-knowledge and awareness of one's duties to both God and man, and finally with knowledge of the celestial spheres, of the "Angels waighting on th' Almighties chayre," and of the majesty of their Creator. Urania's "heavenlie discipline" belongs to "the schoole of arts divine" (the usual term for sacred theology, the "divine science"), and she possesses the skill "To make men heavenly wise, through humbled will."[10]

The Urania of the *Teares* is virtually a personification of theology. The principal influence in converting the classical muse of astronomy into the patroness of divine poetry and the inspirer of the Biblical revelation seems, however, to have been DuBartas' poem *L'Uranie*.[11] Adapting the motif of Hercules' Choice to the poet's vocation, DuBartas hesitates, like a pilgrim at a crossroads, still undecided as to which way he should choose among the many flowery paths that lead to Apollo's hill. While he is still "unresolved of my Course," he beholds a "sacred Apparition," who identifies herself as Urania. It is she herself (she informs him) "Who humane-kinde above the *Poles* transport,/ Teaching their hands to touch, and eyes to see/ All th' enter-course of the *Celestiall Court*." Her dress and discourse recall her traditional association with astronomy, however; for her seven-fold diadem symbolizes the planets, her mantle is adorned with constellations, and her nine-fold voice imitates "Th' harmonious Musick of Heav'n's nimble Dance." Exhorting DuBartas to allow her to guide his pen and lead him up to heaven, she bids him sing the praise of the Almighty and "tuning now the *Jessean* Harp again,/ Gaine thee the *Garland* of eternall *Bayes*."

Poetry (Urania continues) is a "meer *Heav'nly gift*," a "*Divine-Fury*" and "sacred *Phrenzie*" which causes a man to transcend himself and which lifts him above the heavens. Originally invented to "handle onely sacred Mysteries/ With more respect," poetry has been debased by vicious and profane writers. Insisting that a base argument inevitably debases a poet's style and that (conversely) "of it selfe a lofty *subject* raises/ Grave stately words," Urania urges DuBartas to consecrate his eloquence to "those Heavenly *Oracles*," to choose Christ as his Parnassus ("your *double* Mount/ Whereon to Muse"), and (instead of "the winged hoove/ Of *Pegasus*, to dig th' Immortall Fount") to "Take th' Holy-Ghost, typt in a *Silver-Dove*."

Milton alludes to a "heavenly muse" in a variety of contexts, and it is by no means certain that she bears the same meaning in all of these instances. In *Comus*, for example, she appears in association with pagan myth. In the Nativity Ode she is invoked to assist the poet in preparing a birthday gift for the new-born Christ. In *Paradise Lost* she is a source of inspiration superior to the muses of Mount Helicon; only in this epic does Milton actually call her Urania, and it is not altogether clear whether she should be regarded as identical with the Spirit invoked by the poet, or not. In *Paradise Regained* he again invokes the spirit for aid, but does not explicitly name Urania or use the phrase "heavenly muse."

The literary affinities of Milton's Urania and her theological significance have been complicated by our awareness of his wide erudition and of his ability to evoke and simultaneously transcend a literary tradition by bringing elements drawn from diverse and seemingly incompatible sources into new and signficant relationships and thus achieving an original creation, a new synthesis. In invoking Urania Milton was certainly aware of the Platonic associations of her name as well as of the various idealized versions of the classical muse Urania by Spenser and Dante and the more radical transformations by DuBartas and his imitators. Milton was no less aware, however, that in displacing the classical muses by a "Christian muse" the divine poets of the Renaissance had adapted rather than rejected the classical imagery and the literary formulas associated with it: that the invocation to a "muse"—even to a muse native to the Christian Heaven and resident among the hills and fountains of the Holy Land—remained essentially a poetic symbol, a "Christianized myth" rather than an object for adoration and faith.

He was also fully aware that the "heavenly muse" herself, as a Christian variant on a classical literary convention, had also become well established as an alternative convention and that it had acquired a wide variety of alternative senses on which the *poeta Christianus* might draw at will. The same symbol might be figuratively applied to the poet's own holy meditations or "musing" on sacred themes or to other poets who had chosen Biblical subjects or celebrated heavenly love or beauty instead of their earthly counterparts. It could also serve as a metaphor for the Christian revelation itself; for theology as a divine science, for the Scriptures, for the Sapientia of the Old Testament Wisdom books, or for the Christian God as the object of faith and worship and the source of divine knowledge and inspired utterance.

The metaphor of a "Christian muse" was, if not an oxymoron, a paradoxical compromise between truth and myth, sacred and profane traditions — imitating a classical motif while altering its original referent — and in his later epic *Paradise Regained* Milton discards this metaphor, avoiding any overt reference to a muse, and instead invokes the Spirit directly.

On this point he follows the precedent set by other Renaissance poets who had deliberately emphasized their choice of a sacred argument by addressing the Christian God (or alternatively a saint or an angel) in lieu of classical divinities such as the Muses of Olympus and Helicon or Apollo Musagetes. Thus in *La Judit* Saluste duBartas had invoked the "true God" — as a gloss in Sylvester's translation points out[12] — and in the latter's translation of *La Sepmaine* similar comments direct the reader's attention to the poet's invocation of the true Deity:

> The Poet imploreth the gracious assistance of the true God
> of Heaven, Earth, Aire, and Sea. . . .
>
> The Translater knowing and acknowledging his own insufficiency for so excellent a labour, craveth also the aid of the All-sufficient God.
>
> Again he cals upon God, for Assistance in the description of the second daie's Work.
>
> He calleth upon the true God to be assisted in the description of these two Elements and the things therein.
>
> . . . calling upon the God of Heaven, our Poet prayeth to be lift up in the Heavens that he may discourse (as he ought) of the stars, fixed and wandring.
>
> . . . to discourse in this day of the creation of Fishes and of Fowles . . . he calleth on the true God.

Again, in the Sixth Day of the First Weeke, DuBartas had prayed the "Almighty Father" to guide him and to "pour upon my faint influent tongue/ The Sweetest hony of th' *Hyanthian* Fount,/ Which freshly purleth from the Muses Mount. . . ."[13]

In "An Hymne of Heavenly Beautie" Spenser had likewise invoked the true God to aid him in describing the beauty and glory of heavenly things to mortal men (lines 8–14):[14]

> Vouchsafe then, O thou most almightie Spright,
> From whom all guifts of wit and knowledge flow,
> To shed into my breast some sparkling light
> Of thine eternall Truth, that I may show
> Some litle beames to mortall eyes below,
> Of that immortall beautie, there with thee,
> Which in my weake distraughted mynd I see.

In the opening lines of *Il Mondo Creato* Tasso had significantly addressed his invocation to all three persons of the Trinity ("Padre del Cielo, e tu del Padre eterno/ Eterno Figlio, e non creata prole . . .;/ E tu, che d'ambo spiri, e d'ambo splendi,/ O di gemina luce acceso Spirto"),[15] beseeching the gift of the Holy Spirit ("Divino Amore") to dwell within his own heart and inspire his song of the creation of the world:

> Tu dal Padre, e dal Figlio in me discendi,
> E nel mio core alberga, e quinci e quindi
> Porta le grazie, e inspira i sensi e i carmi,
> Perch'io canti quel primo alto lavoro,
> Ch'e da voi fatto, e fuor di voi risplende
> Maraviglioso, e'l magistero adorno
> Di questo allor da voi creato mondo,
> In sei giorni distinto.

Praying God as "celeste Fabro" to reveal the causes that moved Him to create the world and the divine "Idea" that He had taken as His model ("Tu che 'l sai, tu 'l rivela"), Tasso had likened himself to a musical instrument ("cetra" or "roca tromba") on which the Lord must play this new song.[16]

The accommodation of classical conventions to Biblical materials (and vice versa) may result in ambiguities in the works of poets more orthodox than Milton. Though DuBartas alludes frequently to his "Muse," in *La Sepmaine* it is by no means clear that he means to identify her with the Godhead or (more specifically) with any of the persons of the Trinity. The tone of the concluding verses of The Seventh Day of the First Weeke would seem incompatible with such an interpretation:[17]

> But, soft my Muse: what? wilt thou re-repeat
> The Little-World's admired modulet?
> If twice or thrice one and the same we bring,
> 'Tis tedious; how-ever sweet we sing.
> Therefore a-shore: Mates, let our Anchor fall:
> Here blowes no Winde: here are we welcom all.
> Besides, consider and conceive (Pray)
> W' have row'd sufficient for a *Sabbath-day*.

Similarly in invoking the Deity for inspiration in the Third Part of the First Day of the II. Week Sylvester alludes to his Muse, but gives no indication that she should be identified with the Holy Spirit:[18]

> All quickning Spirit, great God, that (justly-strange,
> Judge-turned-Father) wrought'st this wondrous-change;
> Change and new-mould me, let thy hand assist,
> That in my Muse appear no earthly mist:
> Make me thine organ, give my voyce dexterity
> Sadly to sing this sad Change to Prosperity.

In Milton's case, the problems of interpretation are further complicated by the inevitable differences between the methods of the poet
and those of the logician, the historian, or the theologian. The boundaries between poetic fiction and personal belief are not always clearly
defined; and his analysis elsewhere of the various senses of the phrase
"the Spirit of God, or the Holy Spirit" in the Scriptures and the views
he expressed concerning the invocation of the Holy Ghost have raised
further difficulties in regard to the Muse of *Paradise Lost* and the spirit
invoked in *Paradise Regained*. In contrast to the method of his theological treatise, in his poems he avoids differentiating the various senses of
"Spirit"; there remains, however, considerable disagreement among
scholars as to the theological identity of the power (or powers) invoked
in both of his epics. Milton's widow apparently identified his Muse with
the Holy Spirit. This would be consistent with traditional interpretations of references to the Spirit in Genesis i. 2 ("And the Spirit of God
moved upon the face of the waters") and in Matthew iii. 16 ("and he saw
the Spirit of God descending like a dove, and lighting upon him") and
consonant with the practice of a number of other Renaissance poets.[19]
Moreover, according to the Nicene creed, this was the power "Who
spake by the Prophets. . . ."

Yet, as Maurice Kelley pointed out, Milton's discussion of the Holy
Spirit in his theological treatise *De Doctrina Christiana* tended to undercut this interpretation since, in Milton's opinion, the Holy Ghost could
not be "an object of invocation."[20] When the phrase "the Spirit of God,
or the Holy Spirit" occurs in the Old Testament, Milton believed, it
should be "variously interpreted; sometimes it signifies God the Father
himself . . .; sometimes the power and virtue of the Father, and particularly that divine breath or influence by which every thing is created and
nourished." Sometimes it means Christ, sometimes an angel, sometimes "that impulse or voice of God by which the prophets were inspired." It also signifies "that light of truth . . . wherewith God enlightens and leads his people"; and more particularly "it implies that
light which was shed on Christ himself." In the New Testament the
same phrase possessed a comparable range of meanings: the Father
himself; "the virtue and power of the Father"; "a divine impulse, or
light, or voice, or word, transmitted from above"; "the person itself of
the Holy Spirit, or its symbol." Kelley associated the Spirit invoked in
both epics with the power and virtue of the Father and the "divine
impulse, or light, or voice, or word . . . from above." William B. Hunter,
Jr. identifies Milton's muse (and also the light invoked in Book III) with
the Son of God.[21]

In his allusion to the spirit's preference for "the' upright heart and
pure" before "all Temples," Milton is, of course, echoing the imagery
of the Pauline epistles: "Know ye not that ye are the temple of God, and

that the Spirit of God dwelleth in you?" (1 Corinthians iii. 16).[22] Nevertheless, following as it does the references to Mount Sinai and Mount Zion (associated respectively with tabernacle and temple, and with sites of "the Oracle of God"), this passage may also involve an oblique allusion to the contrasts developed in the Epistle to the Hebrews between the old covenant and the new, and between the earthly and the heavenly tabernacle: "For this is the covenant that I will make . . .: I will put my laws into their mind, and write them in their hearts."[23] The reference to "the Oracle of God" near "*Siloa's* Brook" in Zion, as contrasted with the upright and pure heart as the favored abode of the Spirit, suggests a further affinity with Milton's later reference to the indwelling Spirit in *Paradise Regained* (I, lines 460–464):

> God hath now sent his living Oracle
> Into the World, to teach his final will,
> And sends his Spirit of Truth henceforth to dwell
> In pious Hearts, an inward Oracle
> To all truth requisite for men to know.

The two oracles in this passage are, respectively, Christ Himself in His office as Prophet, and the Holy Ghost ("the Spirit of truth" who will "abide with you for ever . . ." cf. John xiv. 16–17).[24] Similar imagery in association with the Holy Spirit recurs in the final book of *Paradise Lost* (Book XII, lines 485–502, 519–526):

> . . . but from Heav'n
> Hee to his own a Comforter will send,
> The promise of the Father, who shall dwell
> His Spirit within them, and the Law of Faith
> Working through love, upon thir hearts shall write,
> To guide them in all truth, and also arme
> With spiritual Armour. . . .

The ambiguities that his readers have found in Milton's Muse are analogous to those that he himself, in a different context, detected in both Old and New Testament references to Spirit. We cannot exclude the possibility that, as with "that two-handed engine" of *Lycidas*, he was consciously exploiting the aesthetic and allusive values of obscurity and ambiguity. He was uncertain about the meaning and reference of "the Spirit of God" in Genesis i. 2, and he has left his readers uncertain about the meaning and identity of the Spirit he invokes in the first books of both epics. As he must have realized, for the majority of his contemporary audience the dove was the conventional symbol or emblem of the Holy Ghost. The image of the Spirit brooding "Dove-like" on the abyss would suggest analogies with the descent of the Spirit at Christ's baptism in the waters of Jordan, and (conceivably) with the dove of Noah's ark flying over the waters that covered the earth.

Though he himself hesitated between alternative identificátions of the Biblical text underlying his image — between a reference to the Son and an allusion to the Father's "divine power" — his readers would, in all likelihood, regard this passage as an invocation to the Third Person of the Trinity.[25]

This probability could be enhanced by their familarity with the practice of other Renaissance poets who had either invoked the Holy Ghost directly for inspiration or implored God the Father for the gift of the Spirit. As Professor Campbell observed, DuBartas invoked God to fill his heart with "sacred furie" and "with thy *Holy* sprite, my sprite enspire."[26] Though Tasso invoked all three persons of the Trinity, his line ("Tu dal Padre, e dal Figlio in me discendi") indicates that he was specifically seeking the inspiration of the Holy Spirit. (The subsequent shift from *tu* to *voi* emphasizes the cooperation of all three persons of the Trinity in creating the world.)

By invoking the divine power who had been present at the creation of the world and had inspired the prophet and seer traditionally regarded as the author of Genesis, Milton emphasizes the superior authority of his own poetic argument, based as it is on the Biblical revelation, and the superior source of his own poetic inspiration, in contrast to the subject matter and inspiration of classical epics. His own epic argument, derived from the book of Genesis, is founded on truths divinely revealed to Moses; and he underlines this point by echoing the first word in Genesis ("In the Beginning": *Bereshith*). But Milton is also (it would seem) stressing the internal, spiritual guidance and illumination essential for understanding and interpreting the written word, the operation of the Holy Spirit. The truth (as he declares later in his poem) has been "Left onely in those written Records pure,/ Though not but by the Spirit understood" (*PL* xii, lines 511–514). The Christian doctrine (as he asserts elsewhere), "that DIVINE REVELATION disclosed to all ages by CHRIST," is to be obtained "from the Holy Scriptures alone, under the guidance of the Holy Spirit."[27]

This allusion to Moses and the power that inspired him is also relevant, however, to the poet's plea for divine instruction and inspired utterance. For Moses had deplored his own lack of eloquence, being "slow of speech, and of a slow tongue" (Exodus iv. 10–12): "And the Lord said unto him, Who hath made man's mouth? Or who maketh the dumb, or deaf, or the seeing, or the blind? Have not I, the Lord?/ Now therefore go, and I will be with thy mouth and teach thee what thou shalt say."

There would, however, be an additional reason for alluding to Mosaic inspiration at this point, followed by the allusion to Mount Sion, so closely associated with the Psalms of David. For, according to traditions associated with Josephus and Origen and Saint Jerome and cited

by later writers, the art of poetry had originated earlier among the
Hebrews than among the Greeks. In portions of the Pentateuch Moses
employed the heroic meter long before Pherecydes and Homer. The
prophet David had composed and sung hymns in God's praise prior to
the poets of Greece. Milton could have encountered these views in the
Etymologies of Isidore of Seville, in the works of Rabanus Maurus, and
(in modified form) in Boccaccio's *Genealogy of the Gods of the Gentiles*.[28]
Sir Philip Sidney, moreover, had adduced the example of David to
"shew the reasonablenes of this worde *Vates*" (i.e. "a Diviner, Fore-seer,
or Prophet") when applied to the poet. Are not the Psalms themselves
"a divine Poem?" The book of Psalms had been "fully written in meter,
as all learned Hebricians agree, although the rules be not yet fully
found." David's manner of "handeling his prophecy . . . is merely poetical," a "heavenlie poesie. . . ."[28a]

The first invocation, then, with its implicit contrast between the external sites associated with God's presence and inspiration and His
indwelling within the temple of the heart, also suggests an analogous
distinction (underlined by the two separate invocations, to Heav'nly
Muse and Spirit) between the Scriptural records which provide the
source of Milton's epic argument and the "guidance of the Holy Spirit"
by which they must be understood. In the 1667 edition of *Paradise Lost*
each of the two "sub-invocations" constitutes a separate and distinct
period, as the original punctuation indicates (lines 1–16, and lines 17–
26), thus accentuating the difference between them. The first part, by
invoking the power who inspired Moses, also acknowledges the Biblical
source and hence the divine authority for Milton's "great Argument.
. . ." The reference to the Shepherd Moses on Mount Sinai, followed
soon after by the allusion to the "*Aonian* Mount" Helicon, suggests a
veiled comparison with the Boeotian "shepherd" Hesiod, who had
been taught by the Muses of Helicon. As Hesiod's muses informed him,
they knew how to sing both true things and false things. Milton is
singing the truth, guided by the Scriptural revelation and illuminated
by the Spirit of truth. This is a true account of the origins and beginnings of things (based on the book of beginnings) in contrast to
Hesiod's *Theogony* and the works of other Greek theological poets.[28b]

The second part of the invocation, addressed to the Spirit, is in effect
a prayer for inner illumination and elevation. It involves, surely, a
petition for cleansing and purifying the heart so that the Spirit may
dwell within, and for guidance in understanding the Biblical revelation.

In the close association between the heavenly muse Urania and eternal Wisdom in the presence of God the Father (*PL* VII, lines 1–12)
Milton has portrayed a sort of heavenly paradigm of divine poetry: a
harmony of celestial wisdom and celestial song that corresponds in

certain respects to the union of wisdom and eloquence, or truth and discourse, sought by Saint Augustine and by various Renaissance humanists and to the union of inspired knowledge and inspired utterance that Milton and his contemporaries recognized in the Scriptures.[29] This is an ideal not unrelated to his conception of the poet as *vates* — as prophet and seer — and it raises a further problem, not unrelated to that of his Muse's identity: the visionary and prophetic stance which he shared with other poets of his age.

In recent years critics have placed increasing emphasis on the *persona* of the *vates* in Renaissance poetry and on the prophetic and visionary elements in the writings of Milton and Spenser or their near-contemporaries.[30] The extent to which any of these Renaissance poets seriously regarded themselves (or one another) as divinely inspired seers and prophets, and (conversely) the degree to which they adopted the *persona* of the inspired bard and the formulas of celestial inspiration as little more than literary conventions, are still controversial. Some would share Romantic views of Milton as a bardic seer. Some would emphasize his respect for logic and right reason, recalling the admonition of his angel Raphael: "Heav'n is for thee too high/ To know what passes there; be lowlie wise. . . ." Others would stress Milton's relationships with the English sectaries of his period, and the importance that some of them attributed to prophetic and visionary experiences.

But there is a significance difference between the "enthusiasm" of the Puritan left wing and the "enthusiasm" conventionally associated with the poet.[31]

No less significant, however, are the different (sometimes radically different) values that various poetic conventions — such as the invocation to the Muse to inspire the poet and recite hidden or forgotten truths inaccessible to him, the convention that the Muse alone knows the causes and details of the action and can report the order of battle, the stance of the inspired bard or seer — may acquire once the fiction of the pagan Muses has been dropped and the Christian Deity substituted as the object of the poet's invocation and the source of his inspiration. As a result of the substitution of Christian for pagan content and intent, while retaining the external structure of the original formulas relatively intact, the conventions themselves may acquire different and at times startling connotations. Can the poet call on the Deity to recite the usual epic catalogue? If he beseeches the Muse to recite the circumstances and causes of the actions he has selected as his subject matter, can he pretend to verbal inspiration as well as inner illumination? In the context of the Renaissance "divine poem," with its Biblical subject matter and its invocations addressed to the "true God," how does the poet expect his reader (the *Christianus lector*) to interpret his claim to a divinely inspired "enthusiasm" or his stance as vatic bard, as

Christian prophet and seer?[32] These problems arise primarily as a result of the adaptation of classical poetic conventions (which had long since lost their original religious associations with Graeco-Roman paganism) to Judaeo-Christian beliefs. Some of these problems perplexed sixteenth- and seventeenth-century critics. They worried Samuel Johnson. But to some extent they still persist, though in different form, in twentieth-century criticism; and they have a significant bearing on the question of Milton's elusive relationship to what has been called "the visionary company."

By linking his Muse with the divine Wisdom of the Old Testament, who had been "brought forth" before the fountains and the hills (Proverbs viii. 22–31), Milton accentuated her superiority to the Olympian muses both in antiquity and in nobility of origin. Like Wisdom her sister, Urania had been born long before the classical "Muses nine" or the mountains and springs with which they had been traditionally associated. Moreover, she was of higher birth, a native of Heaven itself. Such arguments, based on the commonplaces of *dignitas* and *antiquitas* were conventional in the rhetoric and poetics of encomium. Milton had utilized them years earlier in his First Prolusion on the superiority of Day to Night and in his account of the contrasting genealogies of Mirth and Melancholy in the twin poems *L'Allegro* and *Il Penseroso*. The same *topoi* or *loci communes* had frequently been exploited by poets and orators in extolling the ancestry of some scion of an ancient family, in glorifying a university or a city or a nation, or in arguing the dignity and nobility of a particular art or science. The art of sculpture, for instance, might be traced back to the creation of Adam and Eve, and music or architecture to the creation of the world. In *Paradise Lost* both of the latter are in fact older than the universe itself, arts indigenous to Heaven.

Abraham Cowley was not alone in calling poetry a "divine science,"[33] and the Renaissance apologists made much of its celestial origins as well as its antiquity and its early associations with religious ceremonies and with primitive philosophy or theology. ". . . In all ages, and even amongst the most barbarous," asserts the Argument to Spenser's October Eclogue, poetry has been "always of singular accounpt and honor, and being indede so worthy and commendable an arte: or rather no arte, but a divine gift and heavenly instinct not to bee gotten by laboure and learning, but adorned with both: and poured into the witte by a certaine *enthousiasmos*, and celestiall inspiration. . . ."[34] In *An Apologie for Poetrie*, Sidney similarly referred to Plato's *Ion*, albeit with more caution: "he [Plato] attributeth unto Poesie more then my selfe doe, namely, to be a very inspiring of a divine force, farre above mans wit. . . ."[35] According to Puttenham, "this science in his perfection can not grow but by some divine instinct — the Platonicks call it *furor*; or by excellencie of nature and complexion; or by great subtiltie of the spirits & wit; or by much experience and observation of the world, and course of kinde. . . ." "The profession and use of Poesie is most ancient from the beginning, and not, as manie erroniously suppose, after, but before, any civil society was among men." Poets were the "first priests, the first prophets, the first legislators and politicians in the world," in addition to being the world's first philosophers, the first astronomers and historiographers and oratours and musitiens. . . ."[36] For Ben Jonson, Poetry was "the Queene of Arts, which had her Originall from heaven, received thence from the '*Ebrewes*, and had in prime estimation with the *Greeks*, transmitted to the *Latines* and all Nations that profess'd Civility."[37]

In Milton's own opinion, the abilities of the poet were "the inspired gift of God rarely bestowed. . . ." The major poetry that he hoped some day to write could (he knew) be accomplished only through divine inspiration and his own painstaking labor:[38]

> . . . nor to be obtained by the invocation of Dame Memory and her Siren daughters, but by devout prayer to that eternal Spirit who can enrich with all utterance and knowledge, and sends out his seraphim with the hallowed fire of his altar, to touch and purify the lips of whom he pleases. To this must be added industrious and select reading, steady observation, insight into all seemly and generous arts and affairs. . . .

To Milton's nephew, writing more than thirty years after his uncle's treatise *The Reason of Church-Government*, poetry was "a science certainly of all others the most noble and exalted, and not unworthily termed divine, since the height of poetical rapture hath ever been accounted little less than Divine Inspiration. . . ."[39]

In Boccaccio's *Genealogia Deorum Gentilium* Milton would have encountered opinions concerning the antiquity and heavenly origins of poetry not unlike those that he himself would express in both of this epics. Boccaccio had associated poetry with heavenly Wisdom; like his personification of Philosophy, poetry dwelt *in gremio Dei*, in the very bosom of God. In discussing the priority of poetry among various nations, moreover, Boccaccio had (like Milton in *Paradise Regained*) assigned priority to the Hebrew tradition. Moses (he believed) had been one of the very earliest poets to compose heroic verse — a point not irrelevant to Milton's allusion to Moses' special relation to the heavenly muse, in the invocation in the first book of *Paradise Lost*.

Poetry "dwells in heaven," Boccaccio had asserted, "and mingles with the divine counsels. . . ." She "moves the minds of a few men from on high to a yearning for the eternal, lifting them by her loveliness to high revery. . . ." She is "ethereal and eternal," and has no dealings with things that perish. . . ." It is "absolutely certain," Boccaccio continued, ". . . that poetry, like other studies, is derived from God, Author of all wisdom. . . ." She "proceeds from the bosom of God; and few . . . are the souls in whom this gift is born. . . ."[40]

Arguing that poetry had originated among the Hebrews, Boccaccio maintained that "Moses was a master of poetry before either Babylonians or Greeks." He could not "believe that the sublime effects of this great art were first bestowed upon Musaeus, or Linus, or Orpheus. . . . Rather was it instilled into most sacred prophets, dedicated to God. For we read that Moses, impelled by what I take to be this poetic longing, at dictation of the Holy Ghost, wrote the largest part of the Pentateuch not in prose but in heroic verse. In like manner others have set forth the great works of God in the metrical garment of letters, which we call poetic. And I think the poets of the Gentiles in their poetry — not perhaps without understanding — followed in the steps of these prophets; but whereas the holy men were filled with the Holy Ghost, and wrote under His impulse, the others were prompted by mere energy of mind, whence such a one is called 'seer.' Under fervor of this impulse they composed their poems."[41]

Led by his muse, Milton descends into Hell, journeys through Chaos, soars into the Heavens (rapt above the Pole, like Urania's earlier devotee DuBartas), and returns safely to earth again.[42] The visionary flights that he makes reflect the tradition of the contemplative journey into the underworld or the celestial realm associated with classical heroes such as Aeneas and Scipio or with Renaissance voyagers like Ariosto's Astolfo.[43] Yet they are also related to the visionary journeys of Biblical and medieval prophets and saints and, more particularly to the convention of the poet's imaginary ascent or descent under the guidance of his muse or the aid of some other natural or supernatural power (Philosophy or Theology, Reason or Imagination) and the like. Milton would have encountered this tradition in the works of such favorite poets as Dante and Chaucer and Spenser, as well as in DuBartas' imaginary journeys with his Muse into the Heavens, over the earth, and into the depths of the ocean in accordance with the nature of his changing subject matter and its correlative changes in scene.[44] With these traditions are interwoven the imagery of poetic and religious rapture, the metaphors of wingéd words and wingéd song, and the correlative *topoi* of the poet's flights of fantasy and the visionary journeys of the prophet or seer.[45] In this context also, Milton's comparison of his own situation with that of Orpheus — the *priscus theologus* associated with mystical hymns to the gods, with a descent into the underworld and reascent and a mythical demonstration of the affective power of song, and with the cult of the afterlife — would seem significant. In much the same way he compares himself with blind bards and prophets associated with classical legends — Homer and Thamyris, Phineus and Tiresias (*PL* III, lines 26–36), while simultaneously expressing his preference for Biblical over classical literature and extolling "*Sion* and the flow'ry Brooks beneath" above "the Muses" of classical literature. Soaring "above th' *Olympian* Hill" (as also above and beyond the Aonian mount Helicon) and "Above the flight of *Pegasean* wing" (VII, lines 3–4), he has outflown the pagan poets, inspired as they were by false divinities, just as he has outflown Bellerophon (VII, lines 15–20).

Milton's Muse, and the manner in which he invokes her and represents her, are in large part traditional — but they also constitute a major innovation on tradition. We can understand them better if we view them in the wider context of the Homeric and Virgilian and Hesiodic Muses, of the invocations by Tasso and DuBartas and other Renaissance poets, and of the parallels and differences between classical and Scriptural notions of divine inspiration. But the context itself will not, I think, fully explain them; and in some respects their meaning and function is peculiar to Milton's verse.

CHAPTER THREE

Urania: "Meaning" and "Name."

Descend from Heav'n Urania, by that name
If rightly thou art called, whose Voice divine
Following, above th' Olympian Hill I soare,
Above the flight of Pegasean wing.
The meaning, not the Name I call: for thou
Nor of the Muses nine, nor on the top
Of old Olympus dwell'st, but Heav'nlie borne,
Before the Hills appeerd, or Fountain flow'd,
Thou with Eternal wisdom didst converse,
Wisdom thy Sister, and with her didst play
In presence of th' Almightie Father, pleas'd
With thy Celestial Song.*

(PL, VII, lines 1-12)

T HOUGH the transformation of the classical muse of astronomy into
the Renaissance muse of "divine poetry" has been well explored by
Professor Campbell,[1] insufficient emphasis has, I believe, been placed
on the multiple significance and consequent ambiguity of such key
words as "Urania", "Muse", and "divine poem". As part of the difficulty
of interpreting Milton's references to his own Urania stems from this
semantic uncertainty, it is useful to distinguish those senses which apparently apply to *Paradise Lost* from other current meanings of these
terms.

In the Renaissance the label "divine poetry" could cover several
meanings. The epithet "divine" could refer not only to the subject of a
poem but also to its author and source of inspiration. A work might be
called "divine" because its author was God, because its human author
had been divinely inspired, because its argument had been taken from
the Scriptures, or because it treated the central doctrines or mysteries
of the Christian faith. The Song of Songs was a "divine pastoral
Drama"[2] because it had been dictated by God and because it was believed to figure the love between Christ and the Church. Dante's *Commedia* was "divine" because its subject-matter was Christian eschatology,
the "state of souls after death." *Paradise Lost* has been called "divine"[3]
because its argument was based on Genesis. Besides these essentially

---

*The Poetical Works of John Milton, ed. H. C. Beeching (New York, 1935).

Christian interpretations, which involved a contrast with profane or secular poetry, the term "divine" could also refer to the classical conception of the poet as a man inspired by the gods, a bard rapt by a sacred fury, or to the poet's role as "maker" or creator.[4]

Obviously, it is absurd to apply *all* of these meanings to Milton's divine poetry. If *Paradise Lost, Paradise Regain'd,* and *Samson Agonistes* are "divine", the reason is not that the Spirit of God supposedly wrote them (neither Milton nor Addison was so naive), but that all three contain "divine arguments", subjects taken from Scripture. As Milton himself would have recognized, *Paradise Lost* and *Paradise Regain'd* are not divine epics in the same sense as the Book of Job,[5] nor does the term "divine tragedy" have precisely the same meaning when applied to *Samson Agonistes* as when attached to the Apocalypse.[6] The Nativity Ode is not a divine lyric in the same sense as the Psalms. The Renaissance was fully aware of the distinction between the poetry of the Bible and poetry *based* on the Bible. The former was divine because dictated by God, because it was God's Word. The latter was divine only because derived from God's Word. In the first instance subject, author, and diction were divine. In the second case, only the subject was divine, and even this possessed only a mediate divinity, based as it was not on a direct revelation but on the previous revelation recorded in the Scriptures.

Milton might well believe that he had been divinely aided to understand the Biblical revelation and to record his understanding in answerable style. But he would be quite aware of the distinction between the divine aid vouchsafed him in interpreting a prior revelation and the original revelation recorded in the Bible itself. Whatever functions he believed his Heavenly Muse to fulfill, he did not expect her to add "historic details to the Scriptures" or to reveal to him "special truth".[7] Though he believed himself inspired by the same power which had inspired Moses and David, he would not have claimed that *Paradise Lost* constituted a direct revelation like Genesis or that it was divine poetry in precisely the same sense as the Psalms and Job.

[I]

"From Hesiod to Natalis Comes", Professor Campbell has observed, "Urania had received her meed of praise as the muse of astronomy, as the muse the of heavens". With DuBartas' *Uranie,* however, she became "the muse of Christian poetry" and the "center of a whole doctrine and defense of Christian poetry which had been gradually growing up in Christian Europe and in England".[8] These are, however, only two of several Renaissance conceptions of the "Heav'nly Muse". Professors Starnes and Talbert have called attention to the fact that in the Renaissance dictionaries of Stephanus and Calepine, "as in *Paradise Lost,* Urania is the heavenly Muse who lifts learned men to the sky".[9] Linocier, Ripa, and others advanced additional interpretations of the Heavenly Muse. As Urania derived her name from Uranos (Heaven) and literally signified "heavenly", she could appropriately symbolize not only astronomy and the elevation of the learned, but also such concepts as the heavenly origin of poetry, the act of proairesis or choice, the contemplation of the sublime, the universality of erudite men, and celestial music or heavenly song.

1. For Macrobius, Urania was associated specifically with the sphere of the fixed stars:[10]

> In the *Theogony,* Hesiod calls the eighth Muse Urania because the eighth sphere, the star-bearer situated above the seven errant spheres, is correctly referred to as the sky . . .

John the Scot likewise placed the Heavenly Muse in the sphere of highest pitch:[11]

> *Ourania* celestis ab ouranoi, id est celo, denominata quae propter vocis acumen acutissimo spere sono coniungitur. . . . *Uraniem* id est celestem Musam.

The title-page of Gafori's *Practica Musicae* located her in the "celum stellatum", and the *Theorica Musicae* similarly assigned her to the eighth sphere:[12]

> . . . hoc orbe reliquorum infra se orbium melodia comprehenditur omnem penitus harmoniam exuperans. ideoque ubi uranem musam poctarum quidam posuerunt: eam quidem que ex musis novem quas Iovis & memoriae filias finxerunt omnem dicendi dulcedinem complectitur & superat.

Linocier identified her with astrology and declared, with Plutarch, that she dwelt in heaven and presided over celestial things:[13]

> *eodem pacto nos unam Musarum in coelo & circa res coelestes collocamus, quae est Urania: nam coelestia varia gubernatione non videntur indigere, unam cum habeant causam universalem, naturam: ubi vero multi sunt errores, excussus, & transgressiones, ibi octo reliquiae debent transmitti, et una hoc vitium, altera illud corrigat.* Urania igitur coelestibus praeficitur secundum Plutarchum: quae quanto his inferioribus praestant, tanto etiam difficilia.
> . . . contenti itaque erimus ostendere, illam Uraniam nihil aliud esse quam coelestem Astrologiam, dictam *apo tou ouranou,* à coelo. Nam ut scribit Pharnutus [*sic* for Phornutus] "holon ton kosmon oi palaioi, ekaloun ouranon" [Greek transliterated], id est integrum mundum antiqui coelum vocabant. Et sic Urania universi scientiam perfectissime callebat.

2. She could also symbolize heavenly speculation or the contemplation of supernal things. According to Plato's *Cratylus,*[14] "the upward

gaze is rightly called by the name urania *(ourania)*, looking at the things above *(horō ta anō)*, and the astronomers say . . . that from this looking people acquire a pure mind, and Uranus is correctly named". This etymology was echoed by both Charles Stephanus ("quasi *ta ano horosan* hoc est, sublimia speculantem")[15] and Henry Stephanus:[16]

> Latini quoque Uraniam appellant. de qua Plato in Cratylo, "hē d' au es to anō opsis, kalōs echei touto to onoma kaleisthai ourania, horōsa ta anō."

Linocier found a similar interpretation in Plato's *Republic* and in Fulgentius:[17]

> . . . vel [dicitur Urania] denique quod gloria & sapientia animos elevat ad coelestium contemplationem, ut ait Fulgentius.
> Est igitur Platonis 7. de repub, sententia verissima, qua Uraniam existimat animi nostri oculos ad superiora dirigere, & hinc illud ipsum perducere.

Robert Stephanus derived the name Uranus from the same verb *(horao)*, but suggested that this etymology referred to the transparency of the heavens, "looking through" rather than "looking upwards":[18]

> Uranos vero dicitur quasi *oranos* (ut ait Ambrosius libro Hexaemeron) ab *horao* quod sit visui pervium & minime densum, ut est aqua et terra.

3. Boccaccio reiterated Fulgentius' interpretation of Urania as choice, a power belonging to a heavenly mind and a stage in the acquisition of knowledge and doctrine.[19]

> Urania octava est, id est celestis. Post enim diiudicationem eligis quid dicas, quid despuas; eligere enim utile, et caducum despuere celeste ingenium est.
> L'ottava si chiama Urania, cioè 'celestiale'; perchioche, dopo l'aver giudicato, elegge l'uomo quello che egli debba rifiutare; percioché lo eleggere quello che sia utile e rifiutare quello che sia caduco e disutile, è atto di celestiale ingegno.

Similarly, according to Linocier, "Caeterum caelestis illa contemplatio, quam Astrologiam vel Uraniam appellarunt, nihil aliud significat, quam post diiudicationem eligere quod dicas, vel despuas. eligere autem utile caducumque aspernari, coelestis est animi, & sapientiae fama perillustris".

4. Linocier and Ripa explained that Urania elevates learned men to the skies:

> . . . vel dicitur Urania: quod viros doctos sui studiosos ad coelum usque evehat:[20]
> La presente Musa e detto da Latini celeste, significando *ouranos,* che e l'istesso, che il Cielo. Vogliono alcuni che ella sia cosi detta, perche inalza al Cielo gl' uomini dotti.[21]

Linocier also pointed out that learned men are born everywhere—under all parts of the sky:

> A coelo itaque dicta est, quoniam docti ubique gentium nascuntur . . .

5. For John the Scot, Urania was the guardian of celestial music, in contrast to Calliope, who presides over artificial music:[22]

> Praesul est Urania caelestis musicae, Calliopea artificialis musice praesul.

A Dutch translator of Ripa's *Iconologia* explained her name as meaning "Hemel-Sangh",[23] and Calepine suggested such interpretations as "song of heavenly things" or "the divinity of song".[24]

6. Henry Stephanus suggested several alternative meanings of Urania—the celestial Venus, the gods, showers, and a game of ball:[25]

> Est & Venus quadam *ourania,* siut *erōs ouranios* apud Plutarchum in Erot
> . . . Rursum *ourania* ludi genus quo pilam in altum iactabant & exilientes,
> antequam in terram deferrentur, manibus eam excipiebant. Hesych. &
> Pollux lib. 9. pag. 292, necnon Eustath . . . Unde *ouraniazein,* id est *tēn
> ouranian* ludere, Ludere ludum illum qui *ourania* vocatur. Hesych.)
> Interdum absolutè ponitur, ut quum dicuntur Dij pro *hoi ouranioi theoi,*
> seu *epouranioi.* Hesychio *ouranioi* sunt *hoi ton ouranon katakootes,* caelicolae.
> Ovid. Mater caelestum. Cicero, Voluntas caelestium: qui etiam dicit Col-
> ere caelestes. A poetis vocantur *ouraniōnes* quoque, & *ouranidai.* Itidem
> *Ourania* dicuntur Imbres, pro *ourania hydāta.*

7. Whereas most Renaissance commentators explained Urania's name in terms of her subject matter or her effects, Ripa regarded it as an allusion to her origin, an indication of the heavenly source of poetry. Like his representation of Urania,[26] two of his personifications of "Poesia" wore clothing emblematic of the heavens, and he explained that poetry had its origin in heaven. Urania was the muse who bestowed the spirit of poetry:[27]

> Donna vestita del color del cielo . . . Si veste del color del ciclo, perche il
> cielo in greco si dice *Uranos,* & la Musa, che da spirito di Poesia, e Urania,
> & per testimonio di tutti i poeti non puo un'huomo esser valente in queste
> arti, se non e di particolar talento del cielo dorato: & pero si dicono i Poeti
> haver origine dal cielo . . .
> Giovane bella, vestita d'azzurro celeste, sopra il qual vestimento vi
> saranno molte stelle . . . Poeta, secondo Platone, non e altro ch'espres-
> sione di cose divine eccitate nella mente da furore, & gratia celeste . . . La
> veste con le stelle, significa la divinita, per conformita di quello, che
> dissero i Poeti haver origine dal Cielo.

Milton's general indebtedness to this tradition is, perhaps, more apparent than any debt to particular sources. When he invokes the "meaning" rather than the "name" of Urania, he is not necessarily invoking the Spirit as the "reality behind the name",[28] but merely following the etymological approach fashionable among his predecessors and contemporaries and interpreting the name of his muse literally as "Heavenly". As this had long been the standard etymology of Urania, it indicates the poet's conformity with a tradition rather than a specific indebtedness to a single source.

Other current explanations find only limited parallels in Milton's epic. Though Starnes and Talbert suggest that "descriptions of Urania, in the dictionaries, as one of the nine Muses would be a basis for Milton's elaboration",[29] there are actually few close resemblances. His reference to Urania's "Celestial Song" (VII, 12) may echo Calepine's interpretation of her name as "coelestium rerum cantu" or Pers' explanation, "Hemel-Sangh". In raising learned men to the skies, she plays a role similar to that of Milton's Muse, who leads the poet "Into the Heav'n of Heav'ns" (VIII, 13) and lifts him "above the Pole". As a symbol of the poet's heavenly inspiration, dictating to him nightly and inspiring his unpremeditated verse, she is comparable to Ripa's Urania, who bestows the spirit of poetry—a divine gift which originates in heaven. As a "Goddess", an inhabitant of heaven, and the sister of God's Wisdom, she possesses a significance similar to that Henry Stephanus had found in Urania—"Dij" and "caelicolae". Finally, there is a very remote parallel between the "playing" in which Milton's Urania engages and the definition of *ourania* as "ludi genus". Though the analogy is obviously far-fetched, the notion of sport or play is common both to Stephanus' definition of *ourania* and to Wisdom's *ludus* in Proverbs viii. 30–31.[30]

[II]

Like the particular muse Urania, the more general concept—Muse—had been subjected to a variety of interpretations. In a limited sense the Muses could denote certain types of songs. In a broader sense they might symbolize music and poetry. Or they might refer to remoter concepts—the tones of the diapason, the celestial spheres, the organs of speech, the liberal arts, and inquiry, doctrine, or discipline. If one is to re-investigate the "meaning" of Milton's "Heavenly Muse", one must consider not only the implications of the word "Heavenly" (i.e. Urania), but also the ambiguity and multiple significance of the name Muse.

1. In the simplest sense, the Muses were songs or guardians of songs. From Macrobius to Linocier, mythographers emphasized the derivation of the word *Camenae* from *canere* (to sing):

> the Etruscans also recognize that the Muses are the song of the universe, for their name for them is *Camenae,* a form of *Canenae,* derived from the verb *canere.*[31]

John the Scot observed that "omnis Musa bene canens Camena dicitur".[32] Boccaccio declared, on Macrobius' authority, that the Muses are the "song" of the world and derive their name from the verb *to sing*:[33]

> . . . aggiugnendo poi le muse essere il canto del mondo, e questo, non che dall' altre genti, ma eziandio dagli uomini di villa sapersi, perchiochè da loro sono le muse chiamate 'camene', quasi 'canene', dal 'cantare' cosi nominate.
> . . . Musas esse mundi cantum a rusticis etiam sciri, qui eas Camenas, quasi canenas, a canendo dixerunt.

Henry Stephanus defined Muse both as goddess of song and as song itself:[34]

> *Mousa* . . . Musa: dea cantus . . . *Mousa* aliquando accipitur pro ipso cantu, ut & Eust, testatur:

According to Calepine, "Musa latine significat cantum . . . Musam pro cantu posuit Vergil. cum inquit . . . Pastorum musam Damonis & Alphesiboei". Elyot defined "Musa" as "a sweete songe"; Holyoke, as "a song"; and Morel and Thomas, as "a sweet song".[35] Linocier explained the Muses as "celestial songs":

> Musarum enim nomine coelestes cantus intelligunt: quo argumento Camenas dici aliquando existimant, ex Melanchthonis sententia, qui in scoliis & illustrationibus versus illius Virgilij:
>
> > Alternis dictis; amant alterna Camenae,
>
> per Camenas Musas intelligit, vultque illas a canendo dictas: hasce vero a Iove proficisci, quoniam (uti est apud Plotinum) mundi totius animum frequenter Iovis appellatione nuncupat Platonis schola.

2. Macrobius identified the Muses with Plato's celestial Sirens and thus associated them with the music of the spheres:[36]

> In a discussion in the *Republic* about the whirling motion of the heavenly spheres, Plato says that a Siren sits upon each of the spheres, thus indicating that by the motions of the spheres divinities were provided with song; for a singing Siren is equivalent to a god in the Greek acceptance of the word. Moreover, cosmogonists have chosen to consider the nine Muses as the tuneful song of the eight spheres and the one predominant harmony that comes from all of them.

According to John the Scot,[37]

> Novem Musae sunt iuxta numerum mundane constitutionis quae similiter VIIII ambitus habere perhibetur, VII videlicet planetarum circuli et duo extremi terre profecto atque ultime spere, quapropter enneaptongon chelin, hoc est novem sonorum liram Iovis, id est mundus, dicitur habere.

Boccaccio followed Macrobius in linking the nine Muses with the eight celestial spheres, "equiparando quelle a' canti delle otto spere del cielo, vogliendo poi la nona essere il concento che nasce della modulazione di tutti e otto i cieli".[38] Gafori associated the Muses with the spheres in the text of his *Theorica Musicae* and on the title-page of his *Practica Musicae.* Conti echoed the traditional explanation of the Muses in terms of the tones of the eight spheres and the "bonum concentum" of all.[39] Cartari observed that "the heavens (according to the opinion of the Platonickes) have every one their severall Muse, called by them often-times Syrens, as most harmoniously and sweetly singing, alluded unto the celestiall orbes, which in number are likewise nine . . ."[40] Linocier ascribed to each of the spheres a different Muse as well as a different form of Bacchus:

> Singulis porro Musis unum praefecit Bacchum, quoniam is symbolicōs divinae cognitionis nectare prudentioribus monstrat. Licet autem singulis sphaeris coelestibus unam praefecerim Musarum cum Baccho, non inferendum est tamen coelos esse animatos, anima informante, sicut per animas animalium carnes informantur.

In Scaliger's opinion, the ancients had erred in deriving the number of the Muses from that of the heavens, but the belief lent additional propriety to the mythical status of the Muses as daughters of Heaven.[41]

> Antiqui item errarunt, qui a caelorum numero eum numerum ductum voluerint. Nam octo tantum quum agnoscerent eo tempore, totidem faciebant Musas: nonam autem matrem potius, aut nutricem arbitrabantur: . . . quare Mimermnus non male Caeli filias cecinerit in Elegiis.

3. Both Boccaccio and Linocier cited Fulgentius' suggestion that "per queste nove muse doversi intendere la formazione perfetta della nostra voce", for the voice is produced by nine organs of speech — four front teeth, two lips, the tongue, the palate, and the windpipe.[42]

4. Domitius Calderinus and Badius Ascensius identified the Muses with poetic inspiration: "Nec pierides subeunt .i. furor poeticus": "Pierides .i. poetici furores".[43]

5. John the Scot and Boccaccio derived the word *muse* from *moys,* or water:

> Fontigenae enim dicuntur Musae eo quod in undis prius musica artificialis inverta est, nam *mousa* dicitur aqua.[44]
> Nondimeno pare ad alcuno che le muse si debbano dinominare da *"moys"*, che in latino viene a dire "acqua". E questo vogliono, perciochè il comporre, e ancora il meditare alcuna invenzione e la composta esaminare, si sogliono con meno difficultà fare su per la riva di un bel fiume o d'alcun chiaro fonte che in altra parte, quasi il riguardar dell' acqua abbia alle predette cose e muovere e incitar gl'ingegni.
> Nec non arbitror Musas a moys, quod est aqua, dictas, causa in sequentibus ostendetur.[45]

6. For Charles Stephanus, the Muses primarily signified poetry and music: "Praecipue tamen Musarum voce Poesis, & Musica designantur."[46] Elyot regarded them as "givers of eloquence" or as "poetrie or study of humanitie". Holyoke defined them as "goddesses of learning, also learning and poetrie itself". Thomas explained them as "goddesses of learning, poesie, and musicke. also poetrie, studie of good letters, learning". According to Conti, "Musae . . . poetarum praesides, omniumque cantilenarum authores fuisse putabuntur, . . . & carminum & musicae inventrices fuerunt, & totius sapientiae moderatrices . . ."[47]

7. A wide variety of etymological interpretations were advanced to explain the Muses in terms of intellectual disciplines, such as knowledge, inquiry, doctrine, or the liberal arts. Plato's suggestion that "the Muses and music in general are named, apparently, from $m\bar{o}sthai$, searching, and philosophy"[48] was frequently quoted during the Renaissance and appears to have influenced both classical and medieval conceptions of the Muses. Cornutus' *De Natura Deorum* derived *Mousa* from $m\bar{o}sis$ (searching),[49] and Isidore of Seville explained that "Musae autem appellatae *apo tou mysthai*, id est a quaerendo, quod per eas, sicut antiqui voluerunt, vis carminum et vocis modulatio quaereretur"[50]. Isidore's etymology, in turn, influenced Boccaccio's conception of the Muses as symbols of knowledge, the offspring of God and Memory:[51]

> . . . e possiam dire, queste muse, cioè scienza, in noi gia abituata per lo intelletto e per la memoria, potersi dire figliuole di Giove, cioè di Dio Padre e della Memoria. E dico Giove doversi intendere qui Iddio Padre, percioche alcuno altro nome non so più conveniente a Dio Padre che questo . . . Cosí adunque . . . meritamente di Giove e della Memoria possiam dire le muse essere state figliuole, in quanto egli è vero dimostratore della ragione di qualunque cosa; le quali sue dimostrazioni, servate nella memoria, fanno scienza ne' mortali, per la quale qui, largamente prendendo, s'intendono le muse . . . Le quali dice . . . Isidoro . . . esser nominate "*a quaerendo*", cioè da "cercare"; perchiochè per esse, si come gli antichi vogliono, si cerca la ragione de' versi e la modulazione della voce . . .
>
> Placet Ysidoro . . . has Musas appellatas a querendo, eo quod per eas, sicut antiqui voluerunt, ius carminum et vocis modulatio quereretur, et ob id per derivationem ab eis musica, que est moderationis peritia, denominata est.

According to Cassiodorus, "the Muses themselves received their name from the word *maso,* that is, 'to seek', since through their agency, according to the ancients, the power of song and the harmony of the voice were sought".[52]

This conception was shared by Calepine[53] ("Dicitur enim Musa Herodiano teste inquisitio. Quaerendo enim disciplinas adipiscimur") and Sabinus[54] ("Musae, ab inquirendo dictae sunt"), while Plato's etymology was widely quoted during the Renaissance:

[Scaliger:] hi autem Poetae, quare soli sibi Musarum tutelam vindicant atque patrocinium, quarum spiritu, quae alios lateant, ab ipsis inveniantur. Nam Musae *para to maiōsthai* a Platone deductae sunt: quibus scilicet inventio attribuatur.[55]

[Linocier:] Nam & . . . Plato Musas dictas vult indagatrices, utpote quae per sensus, & exteriora, quae superna & coelestia sunt, excogitent . . . Ab indagine enim dicitur Musa, secundum Platonem in Cratylo; vel inquisitione *apo tou mōeisthai;* cui Pharnutus [*sic*] libro de natura Deorum subscribit, cum ait: *kalountai de mousai apo tēs mōseōs, ho esti zēteseōs, Musae* (inquit) dicuntur ab *inquisitione.* idem sentit Suidas, proptereaque ait eas ab inquirendo dictas, quoniam ipsae sint omnis disciplinae causa.

[R. Stephanus:] Musas Plato in Cratylo dictas affirmat *apo tau mōstai,* quod est inquirere, quasi indagatrices: cui Pharnutus in libro de Nat. deor, subscribit, Ita enim ait, *kalountai de mousai apo tou moseos, ho esti zeteseos.* Musae, inquit, dicuntur ab inquisitione. Idem sentit Suidas, idem & Palaephatus. Unde & aliquando Mosas eas antiqui vocavere.
Unde & aliquando Mosas eas antiqui vocavere.

[C. Stephanus:] *Musa, Latine vestigatio,* seu *inquisitio* dicitur. Sic enim Phornutus in lib, de Nat. Deorum. *kalountai de Mousai apo tou mōsthai ho esti zētein* . . . Scal. Poet. 1. 2. *apo tou maiōsthai,* quod iis inventio tribuatur, Platonem secutus deducit.

[H. Stephanus:] Ab Eust. traditus *mousas* allegoricè dici *kata noun gnōsin:* Suidae autem *mousa* simpliciter est *gnōsis* qui a *mō* derivat, signif. *zēto,* quoniam est *hapasēs paideias aitia.* De etymo dixi paulo ante ex Suida, quod & Eust. sequitur: *Mousas* videlicet dictas esse à *maō.* Similiter & Plato in Crat. *Tas mousas te kai holēn tēn moisikēn* à verbo *mōsthai* dictas videri scribit: cognominatas nimirum *apo tēs zēteseos te kai philosophias:* accipiens illud *mōsthai* pro *zētein,* sicut & *maiesthai* suprà.

An alternative derivation from *myein* (to teach or instruct) also strengthened the interpretation of the Muses as symbols of instruction. According to Eusebius' *De Praeparatione Evangelica,*[56] the Muses were so called because they taught men *ta kala* (beautiful things): *apo tou myein tous anthropous, touto de esti didaskein ta kala.*

This etymology was likewise well known during the Renaissance. According to Calepine, "Musae Iovis coeli et terrae filiae dictae [sunt], quoniam *myein* graece honesta bonaque doctrina instituere significat". Scaliger explained that "alii *apo tou myesthai* unde Mystae & Mysteria: quo verbo iudicium designetur. Arcana enim selecta sunt: electio autem ab iudicio. Nempe omnia quae in opere posita sunt, ab intellectione, aut ab inventione, aut ab iudicio proficiscuntur".[57] Robert Stephanus observed that "Eusebius tamen in Evangelica praeparatione, Musas tradit sic appellatas, quia *myeo* apud Graecos honesta bonaque doctrina instituo significat. quamobrem eas Orpheus & Proclus hominibus religionem monstrasse in hymnis suis cecinerunt". Charles Stephanus noted that "Euseb[ius] de Praep. Evang. a *myēo Musae* deducit, id significat *instituo, instruo".* Henry Stephanus cited the same etymology: "Euseb[ius] vero *para to myein,* significante *didaskein & paideuein.*" Ripa declared that "Eusebio nel lib. della preparatione Evangelica dice esser chiamate le Muse della voce Greca *myēo,* che significa instruire di honesta & buona disciplina; onde Orfeo nelli suoi hinni canta come le Muse han dimostrata la Religione, & il ben viver' a gli huomini".[58]

A further etymology—the derivation from *homoiousas or homousas*— suggested the interdependence of the liberal arts, or the interconnection of the virtues, sciences, and disciplines. According to Cassiodorus, "Musae vero Eoa lingua quasi *homousai* dicuntur, quod invicem sicut virtutes necessariae sibi esse videantur".[59] Echoing this opinion, Linocier observed that "Alij, ut Cassiodorus, propter scientiarum & disciplinarum inter se convenientiam, Musas vocarunt quasi *homousas,* vel certe quod invicem sicut virtutes sibi esse videantur". Robert and Henry Stephanus noted that "alij vero propter disciplinarum inter se convenientiam, quasi *homoiousas,* quod uno nexu disciplinae omnes teneantur, atque ita fiat encyclopaedia", and Charles Stephanus declared that "sunt qui a convenientia, seu nexu disciplinarum, & encyclopaedia Musas quasi *homoiousas* dictas putent". The conventional conception of the Muses as sisters and inseparable companions was also interpreted in terms of this etymology. According to Calepine,

> ... alij musas denominatas perinde atque *homousas* omusas, praesunt enim orationi. Una enim utentes convenientia quam *harmonian* vocant & simul canunt & simul tripudijs exercentur, nec unquam invicem separantur. Nam tametsi earum quaeque suam vim habeat, et alia in astronomia, alia in geometria, & alia in alijs disciplinis, in unaquaque tamen earum musas omnis invenias. In astronomia enim atque geometria facile reperias & carminum & historiae pulchritudinem atque dignitatem. Et eodem modo in caeteris scientijs.

Robert Stephanus observed that "Musas simul versari & in chorum numerumque ludos agere, dixerunt antiqui, propter scientiarum copulam & nexum, quo inter se disciplinae quodam quasi nodo copulantur & coniunguntur. Eadem de causa sorores existimata putant". Cartari found the same conception in the classical iconography of the Muses:[60]

> The auncients when they intended to set down how the liberall arts, and all other sciences, depended one upon the other, and were as it were knit and coheared together, depictured the Muses, holding one another by the hand, and heedfully dauncing (as it were in a round) lead and guided by Apollo: which meaneth that superiour light and understanding, which illuminateth and enknowledgeth the intellectual parts of men.

Other, less familiar etymologies also interpreted the Muses in terms of knowledge or discipline. Charles Stephanus cited Heinsius' suggestion that the Muses derived their name from the Hebrew word for discipline *mosar* (Hebrew transliterated):[61]" Dan. Heinsius in Aristarcho sacro ab Ebraeo *Musar* quo disciplinam significat, derivat. Musas autem Poetae *Jovis*. i.e. intellectus, & *Memoriae* filias fecerunt". In Linocier's opinion, Homer addressed his Muse as "goddess' (*thea*) because of the clarity of knowledge:

> [Eustathius] Musam interpretatur animae cognitionem, quae non minus sit divinum quiddam quam anima ipsa. Eius sententiae videtur esse Homerus, quam *thean* dixit *apo tou theein*, id est a cognitionis claritate. . . . Vel denique (ut Diodorus scriptum reliquit) Musae vocantur, quod modulandi artem caeterasque disciplinas probe teneant.

The Muses symbolized mental concepts (Linocier explained), the offspring of God's knowledge and memory:

> Alij vero ita interpretantur: Iupiter, aiunt, rerum omnium parens e Mnemosyne (id est, memoria & cognitione sui) Musas genuisse dicitur; quae mentis conceptus significant, acternarum rerum contemplatores, quae quidem res intellect u tantum percipi possunt.

Conti cited Tzetzes' conception of the Muses as knowledge and intelligence: "Nam scriptum reliquit Zez. hist. 90. chil. 6. nihil aliud esse Musas quam cognitionem & animi vim illam quae intelligit . . ."[62]

Though not all of these interpretations of the Muses are applicable to Milton's Urania, several would seem to be appropriate when qualified by the adjective *heavenly*. If Muses are songs or guardians of songs, a "Heav'nly" Muse could simply denote a "heavenly song" or its patroness—a meaning consistent with Milton's reference to Urania's "Celestial Song". If one accepts the more general conception of the Muses as music and poetry, a Heavenly Muse might well symbolize "heavenly poetry" in general, divine or sacred utterance. This reading would seem to be compatible with the Renaissance conception of Urania as the "Christian Muse", the Muse of "divine poetry". If the Muses denote knowledge and instruction, a Heavenly Muse might well represent sacred wisdom, heavenly instruction, or the Divine Science, theology. This interpretation would, however, have only a limited applicability to *Paradise Lost*. Since Milton's Urania is the sister of celestial Wisdom, she can hardly be identical with God's sapience or with theology. She could, however, represent the *expression* or *utterance* of wisdom, even though she does not symbolize wisdom itself; and indeed the fact that she has inspired Moses suggests that she may personify in part—not divine truth—but the verbal revelation of divine truth through the Scriptures.

Milton's Heavenly Muse bears, in fact, a relationship to Celestial Wisdom which is not dissimilar to Renaissance conceptions of the Muses. If the sisterhood of the Muses traditionally denoted the interdependence of the arts and sciences, the reference to Urania and Wisdom as "sisters" might well point to the interconnection between divine poetry and theology. As sacred poetry merited the epithet "divine" largely through the nature of its content and could hardly be separated from divine wisdom, Urania and Sophia would be appropriately represented as sisters. Milton would attempt to achieve in *Paradise Lost* a fusion of poetry and theology similar to that in the Psalms—to mix "the powre of divine doctrin, with delectable melodie of song, that whiles the eare is allured with swete harmonie of musicke, the hart is indued with heavenlie knowledge pleasant to the mind, and profitable to the soule".[63]

The ties between Wisdom and Urania are also analogous to those between the two Muses *Meleta* and *Aoide* (Meditation and Song) in Renaissance theory and between religious meditation and "unpremeditated verse" in the Third Book of *Paradise Lost*. Robert Stephanus followed Pausanias in declaring that there were three Muses— meditation, memory, and song:

> Alias vero idem Pausanias tres Musas connumerat, . . . sic nominatas: primam *meletēn*, hoc est, meditationem: secundam *mnēmēn*, hoc est, memoriam: tertiam *aoidēn*, hoc est, cantilenam.

According to Scaliger, on the other hand, theologians had originally recognized only *two* Muses, concerned respectively with meditation and poetic—the invention of an argument and the disposition of a poem.[64]

> Iccirco duae tantum Musae per initia creditae a priscis theologis, qui sese earum discipulos cecinere: quarum alter dicta sit *meleta*, quae quidem meditando inveniret: altera *poēta*, quae inventa certo disponeret iudicio. Propterea vero quod eruerent ex ipsis exordiis rerum ignota vulgo monumenta: tertiam quidam adiecere, quam a memoria *mnēmēn* nominarent.

Significantly, Milton's account of the circumstances of his composition (III, 26ff.) seems to attribute the origin of his "unpremeditated verse" primarily to his meditation on the Holy Scriptures. In Verity's opinion, lines 26–29 refer to his "love of . . . classical poetry, . . . those ancient poets inspired by the Muses", whereas the following lines declare that "his love of the classics is exceeded by his love of Scripture . . . [T]he Psalms of David and the works of the singers of Israel . . . are dearest to him".[65] Then, Milton continues, he "feed[s] on thoughts, that voluntary move Harmonious numbers". The passage suggests that Biblical poetry leads to meditation ("thoughts") and that this in turn prompts his "unpremeditated verse".

If Urania's association with Wisdom is analogous to the interrelationship of the Muses, it is also similar to the latter's relationship with such mythical personifications of wisdom as Pallas and Apollo. According to

John the Scot, it was Pallas who inspired the Muses; ipsa enim inspirat omnem musicam".[66] In Cartari's opinion, the Muses were "lead and guided by Apollo: which meaneth that superiour light and understanding, which illuminateth and enknowledgeth the intellectuall parts of men".[67] In both instances the Muses are directed by a higher type of wisdom.

The closest parallel to the Muses' divine genealogy is to be found in the Father's close association with Urania and Wisdom before the creation of the world — a detail which illustrates two traditional conceptions of poetic origins. The notion that poetry originated in Heaven and is a divine gift had been a commonplace perpetuated once for all in Plato's *Ion*. The further belief—that sacred poetry is far older than profane or secular verse—had been traditional since the Greek and Latin fathers and was held by both Protestants and Catholics. According to the Douai Bible, the "holie Psalmodie was before anie profane poetrie now extant", and other Hebrew poetry antedated Amphion, Orpheus, and Musaeus.[68] And, as Milton was subsequently to declare,

> With Hymns, our Psalms with artful terms inscrib'd,
> Our Hebrew Songs and Harps in *Babylon,*
> That pleas'd so well our Victor's ear, declare
> That rather *Greece* from us these Arts deriv'd . . .

In declaring that Urania played in God's presence "Before the Hills appeer'd or Fountain flow'd," Milton is affirming the heavenly character and origin of poetry and the priority of "divine poetry" ("Celestial Song") to all secular or worldly poetry, and indeed to the world itself.

CHAPTER FOUR

Urania: Wisdom and Spiritual Exegesis

> The Lord possessed me in the beginning of his way, before his works of old. I was set up from everlasting, from the beginning, or ever the earth was. When there were no depths, I was brought forth; when there were no fountains abounding with water. Before the mountains were settled, before the hills was I brought forth: While as yet he had not made the earth, nor the fields, nor the highest part of the dust of the world. When he prepared the heavens, I was there: when he set a compass upon the face of the depth: When he established the clouds above: when he strengthened the fountains of the deep: When he gave to the sea his decree, that the waters should not pass his commandment: when he appointed the foundations of the earth: Then I was by him, as one brought up with him: and I was daily his delight, rejoicing always before him; Rejoicing in the habitable part of his earth; and my delights were with the sons of men.*

In the opening lines of Book VII, Milton has invested his Muse with some of the attributes of her "Sister" the "Eternal Wisdom". Wisdom had been "brought forth . . . before the hills," when "there were no fountains abounding with water." Similarly Urania was "Heav'nlie borne, Before the Hills appeerd, or Fountain flow'd." Both had contributed to the "recreations" of the Father "before the world was built." The "eternal wisdome" was *dayly his delight, playing always before him.*"[1] Similarly, the Heavenly Muse "with her [did] play In presence of th' Almightie Father, pleas'd With [her] Celestial Song." This "Song", in fact, is the only attribute which the Muse of lines 7–12 does *not* share with the Wisdom of Proverbs VIII. 23–30. It is based on a current etymology of Urania[2] and has no parallel in the Biblical text.

Although scholars have long recognized Milton's exploitation of Proverbs in this passage[3], they have not yet reached agreement as to the precise significance of the close relationship between Urania and Wisdom or the extent to which this relationship finds Biblical authorization. In the following pages I shall re-examine these problems against the background of Scriptural exegesis and Renaissance lexicography.

*Proverbs viii. 22-31. AV.

[I]

In Professor Fletcher's opinion, "there is nothing in the Biblical passage which in any way suggests the presence of *two* Spirits at Creation with the Son of God, or, in the Old Testament, God himself . . . Certainly throughout the chapter, and especially again in these verses, she [Wisdom] makes no reference whatever to a companion or sister Spirit having been present with her during the accomplishment of the events described . . . The text of Scripture, therefore, could not have suggested to Milton the strange idea of having two, apparently equal Spirits with the Son on his mission of Creation." As the notion of *two* spirits present with God at the creation — Understanding and Wisdom — can be found in the writings of Ben Gerson, Professor Fletcher suggests that Milton's Muse is "a poetic conception of Ben Gerson's Understanding."[4]

Milton's apparent innovation could, however, find limited justification in an earlier reference to Wisdom as plural. In Proverbs I. 20 ("Wisdom crieth without; she lifteth up her voice in the streets") the Hebrew text employs the plural form *hokhmoth*. (Hebrew transliterated.) Pagninus retains the plural number in his Latin translation of this passage ("Sapientiae in platea praedicabit: in plateis dabit vocem suam")[6], and later translators and commentators likewise call attention to this detail, though they differ in their interpretations of its significance. For Tremellius and Junius[7], it is essentially a rhetorical device to honor Christ, the wisdom of God and the source of true wisdom in man:

> Est autem Christus summa haec sapientia, de qua
> hic & capite 8. agitur, ipsissima Dei sapientia,
> in qua re conditi sunt omnes thesauri sapientiae
> & intelligentiae, & per quam sapientiae rivi in
> homines diffunduntur verbo. Quamobrem honoris
> causa plurali numero dicitur sapientiae, quasi
> dicas tota sapientia, & omnis sapientiae auctor.

Commenting on the same text ("Summa sapientia foris recantat"), Piscator[8] explains the plural number as a reference to the manifold wisdom of the Son of God: "Heb. Sapientiae. Numero plurali. Id est, Filius Dei: qui describitur infra cap. 8. qui praeditus est multiplici sapientia." Peter Muffet[9] regards the plural as a superlative, but also interprets it as an allusion to the multiple means and instruments whereby divine wisdom inspires and enlightens man:

> Because he [Solomon] speaketh of perfect wisedome,
> which excelleth in the highest degree, therfore in
> the originall text, he calleth hir wisdomes in the
> plurall number, according to the Hebrew phrase.

> Indeed there is but one wisdome in regard of the
> authour and fountaine of all knowledge, who is Iesus
> Christ the personal wisdom of his father, but in
> regard of the meanes and instruments, which this
> eternal wisdom useth to lighten men by, wisdom is
> manifold, . . . for what corner or countrey is there,
> wherein the light of trueth shineth not, or is not
> revealed, either by Gods messengers, creatures,
> operations, or inspirations?

Unlike these and other commentators, Milton did not identify the Wisdom of Proverbs viii with "the Son of God," but regarded her as essentially "a poetical personification of wisdom."[10] This divergence does not, however, diminish the significance of the plural number of the Biblical Wisdom as a possible justification for Milton's allusion to *two* spirits who "play" before the Father and are prior to the creation of the world. Other factors may have been 1) Muffet's allusion to the *sapientiae* of Proverbs i. 20 as "muses", 2) the interpretation of the verb "cries" in the same text in terms of song, 3) the conception of the muses as the inventers and guardians of all wisdom, 4) the application of the term "divine science" to music and poetry[11] as well as theology, 5) the association of "wisdom and instruction" in Proverbs i.2 and the explanation of "Musa" as a derivation from the Hebrew *Musar* (instruction), and 6) the musical connotations of the verb "play" in Hebrew, Latin, and English.

[II]

For Muffet, the *sapientiae* of Proverbs i.20 are "muses full of heavenlie wisdom," who "lift up their voices" and "sing" to "publish the will of God":[12]

> But wheres it skilleth much after what manner speeches
> are delivered, it is worthie the observing that these
> wisdomes well seen in musicall harmonie, or muses so
> full of heavenlie wisdom, are said to crie, and to lift
> up their voices. For do they publish the will of God
> unto us after the maner of criers, who make proclamation?
> do they lift up their voices as trumpets, to tell us of
> our transgressions? do they utter their wordes after the
> maner of Orators, to perswade us unto the practize of all
> sorts of vertues? finallie, do they sing as the Levites
> of Israell, to affect us with the feeling of matters spirituall? and do we like
> deafe adders stop our eares
> at the voice of the charmers, charme they never so wiselie?

The same passage had also been interpreted as a song *about* Wisdom rather than as a song *by* her:

Tertullian according to the Septuagint, reading the
verse thus, *Sophia in exitibus canitur hymnis, in*
plateis constantiam agit, wisdome in the goings out
is sung with hymnes, and in the streets she exerciseth
constancy, he applieth it unto Martyrs, whose spirituall
wisedome doeth make them to sing to God, even when
they are going by torments out of this life; and the
praise of whose wise dying is sung in hymnes by the
Church of God.

Moreover, Wisdom and the Muses had been subjected to very similar
interpretations. Wisdom *hokhmah* (Hebrew transliterated) could mean
"quaelibet Ars,"[14] and the Muses themselves had been explained as
personifications of the arts and sciences. For Conti, they are the guardians of all wisdom, and music is a "divina scientia":[15]

Eaedem [Musae] & carminum & musicae inventrices fuerunt,
& totius sapientiae moderatrices sicuti testatur idem
Orpheus: . . . Temonem sacrae Sophiae haec audite tentes . . .
Inde accidit ut musicam divinam scientiam crediderit
Pythagoras, ut ait Strabo, libro primo Geographiae.
Cum crederent igitur antiqui omnes res humanas a mente
divina, & a corporibus coelestibus aliquo pacto gubernari,
omnem cujusque peritiae praestantiam deorsum mitti
tradiderunt a Sole, & a caeteris planetis: cum re ipsa
sine ope divina vis humana debilis & imbecilla sit ad
omne opus perficiendum: quare Musae saepius ad ferendum
opem vocantur a poetis.

For Carolus Stephanus, the name "Muse" meant inquiry or instruction,
and for Heinsius the word was derived from the Hebrew *Musar,* signifying discipline or instruction:[16]

Musa, Latine *vestigatio, seu inquisitio* dicitur. Sic enim Phornutus in lib. de
Nat. Deorum. "Kalountai de Mousai apo tou mosthai ho esti zetein . . .
(Greek transliterated) Eusebius de Praeparatione Evangelica a myeo
(Greek transliterated) *Musae* nomen deducit, id significat *instituo, instruo.*
Scal. Poet. 1. 2. *apo tou* maiosthai (Greek transliterated) quod iis inventio
tribuatur, Platonem secutus deducit. Dan. Heinsius in Aristarcho sacro
ab Ebraeo *Musar* quo disciplinam significat, derivat.

As "wisdom and instruction" *musar* (Hebrew transliterated) are closely
associated in Proverbs i.2 and elsewhere in the same book,[17] Heinsius'
etymology would provide some justification for linking the Heavenly
Muse and Eternal Wisdom.

[III]

Milton's allusion to Urania's "Celestial Song" suggests, that, unlike
most lexicographers and commentators, he was exploiting the word

"play" (Proverbs viii. 30–31) in a musical sense. The Hebrew verb *sahaq* (Hebrew transliterated) the Latin *ludere,* and their English equivalent "play" were sufficiently ambiguous to warrant this interpretation. Though *sahaq* (Hebrew transliterated) could mean "make sport" or "jest," it could also denote "play" in the more limited sense of "instrumental music, singing, and dancing."[18] *Ludere* could likewise be interpreted not only in the sense of sport, but also in terms of music and verse. According to Calepine and Robertus Stephanus, it signifies "canere, pulsare," and "versibus scribere," while "ludere in numerum" means "Saltare ad modum rhythmi & cantilenae, ut ait Servius. Virgil. 6 eclog. 6."[19] For Elyot *ludo* means "to plaie as one doeth on instruments, to write verses," while "ludere in numerum" signifies "to daunce measure."[20] Similar interpretations appear in the dictionaries of Cooper, Thomas, Morel, and Holyoke.[21]

There is, however, little reason to conclude that Milton's use of the word "play" in the invocation of Book VII or the quotation from Proverbs viii. 30 in *Tetrachordon* represents "an independent translation from the Hebrew"[22] or that it indicates his "use of . . . rabbinical material."[23] This reading was far more common in the Biblical translations of the Renaissance than has generally been recognized. Though Milton could have encountered it in the Hebrew text, where *mesaheqeth* (Hebrew transliterated) is "a *piel* participle with feminine ending of the verb *sahaq* (Hebrew transliterated) and clearly means *playing* or *sporting*,"[21] and in the Vulgate ("Cum eo eram cuncta componens: & delectabar per singulos dies, ludens coram eo omni tempore: ludens in orbe terrarum: & deliciae meae, esse cum filijs hominum"), he could also have met it in the translations by Pagninus and Piscator and the commentaries of Jermin and Cleaver. In Pagninus' translation, the passage reads "& eram deliciae, die die: ludens coram eo in omni tempore. Ludens in orbe terrae eius; & delectationes meae cum filiis hominum." Arias Montanus' notes[25] substitute "ludebam" for "ludens". Munster[26] renders it as "fui quoque (ei) oblectamento per singulos dies, ludens coram eo omni tempore. Ludo praeterea in orbe terrae eius, & delitiae meae sunt, ut sim cum filijs hominum." Though Tremellius and Junius prefer "laetificans," Piscator[27] amends their version to "ludens": "sumque deliciae ejus quotidie, ludens coram eo omni tempore: Ludens in orbe habitabili terrae ejus . . ." According to Jermin,[28] "the originall word here translated *rejoycing*, is *sahaq* (Hebrew transliterated) and doeth most properly signifie *ludere*, to play and to sport, according as the Vulgar Latin and *Arias Montanus* doe read it. And what shall we understand this sporting to be, but that praeludium as it were of Gods eternall pleasure, wherein all things are from everlasting disposed and ordered by Gods eternall decree. And therefore *Rupertus* sayeth, *O ludum sapientiae deliciosum, praescire atque praedestinare certum aliquem numerum angelorum & hominum, & in libro vitae nomina conscribere singulorum!* O the delicious sporting of wisdome, to foreknow and predestinate a certain number of Angels and men, and to write the names of every one in the booke of life!"

In these translations and commentaries Milton could have found ample justification for his interpretation of Proverbs viii. 30 in the sense of "play", but very little precedent for the musical sense of the word. Most explain "ludere" as sport, and Lyranus[29] goes so far as to interpret Wisdom's play as a cosmic ball-game:

> Ludens coram eo omni tempore. & quid sit iste ludus
> subditur: Ludens in orbe terrarum. i. ludem faciens
> de orbe terrarum: qui similis est ludo pilae: quae
> de uno transfertur in alium secundum quamdam revolu-
> tionem: quia regna terrae transfert atque constituit
> de gente in gente.

Piscator[30] finds an allusion to child's play:

> *Sum deliciae ejus*] Sicut pueruli ludentes in conspectu
> eorum a quibus educantur, sunt deliciae ipsorum . . . .
> *Ludens*] Sicut scil. pueruli ludere solent. Synodoche
> generis.

Similarly, in Cleaver's[31] opinion, "hee compareth himselfe to a nursling, smiling and laughing with his nurse; and to a little child, sporting & playing before his father. The latter is set downe, first, in one of the same borrowed speeches, *laughing,* and *sporting in the habituall parts of the earth,* that is, taking pleasure in the creatures, beholding therein the fruit of the most absolute wisdome, power, and goodnesse of the whole Trinitie."

Though none of these commentators or translators interpret the *ludens* of Proverbs viii. 30–31 in a musical sense, this reading could be justified by other passages in the Old Testament (I Samuel xviii. 7; 2 Samuel vi. 5, 21; I Chronicles xiii. 8, xv. 29), where this word is applied to vocal or instrumental music.[32] In the Pagninus—Montanus version[33] the passage "Et respondebant mulieres ludentes" is glossed as "cantabant" (I Samuel xviii. 7). Piscator[34] finds in 2 Samuel vi. 5 an allusion to "playing" on musical instruments: "*Gestiebant* prae laetitia] Heb. ludebant . . . Sed vertendum *ludebant:* quia continenter commemorantur instrumenta musica quibus luserunt . . . *Cum:* sic postulante Lat. praeposito] hic notat instrumentum. Sic apud Virgilium, Ludere calamo. Eclog. I."

In representing his "Heav'nlie Muse" as the sister of Heavenly Wisdom and as the power of "Celestial Song," Milton was exploiting a conventional interpretation of the name Urania, the affinity between the *sapientiae* of Proverbs i. 20 and the Muses, and the musical and

poetic connotations of the verb *ludere*. In its context, moreover, the
sister-image is not inappropriate. It recalls the imagery of Proverbs vii.
4 ("Say unto Wisedome, Thou art my sister")[35]. It emphasizes the contrast between the classical Urania, who is sister to the "Siren daughters"
of "Dame Memory,"[36] and Milton's Urania, who is sister to God's "Eternal Wisdom." Finally, it permits the poet to give additional emphasis
to this contrast by delegating to Urania some of the salient characteristics of the Biblical Wisdom — her existence before the creation of hills
and fountains and, accordingly, her priority to the mythical Muses and
their haunts — Parnassus, Helicon, Olympus, and the Castalian spring.

[IV]

Unlike the "harmonious Sisters, Voice and Vers,"[37] Wisdom and
Urania are not "Sphear-born," but have existed prior to the creation of
the celestial orbs. In this respect they also differ from the classical
Muses, whom Platonic tradition had associated with the spheres.
Urania's "Celestial Song" antedates the creation of the world and is
therefore distinctly different from the "celestial songs" of the heavenly
bodies and their indwelling sirens, Muses, or angels.

In what sense, however, does she "play" in the presence of God and
before the creation? In other contexts her "Celestial Song" might denote the "heavenly harmony" ("illo coelesti concentu")[38] of the spheres,
but in the invocation to Book VII this interpretation is not applicable.
The hills and fountains were created a whole day prior to the celestial
orbs (*PL*, VII, 276–386). In the context of Milton's invocation, the only
feasible interpretations are that Urania's song symbolizes an attribute
of the Father or an idea pre-existing in the divine mind or else that it
represents the song of the angels before the creation of the world.

Urania's kinship with Wisdom suggests that, like her sister, she may
be "a poetical personification of an attribute of the Father." If so, then
the most likely probability is that she represents the original harmony
existing in the divine mind, reflected in the divine decrees, and subsequently realized in the "pulcherrimo ordine"[39] of the visible and
invisible worlds.

First, if one regards her as prior to the invisible, as well as the visible,
creation, she clearly pertains to God's "internal effiency," which is "independent of all extraneous agency," as are "his decrees."[40] Secondly,
the close association between Urania and Wisdom is analogous to that
between the Father's decrees and his foreknowledge. According to the
De Doctrina, the two are inseparable, and divine foreknowledge is identical with divine wisdom:

. . . . it is absurd to separate the decrees or will of
the Deity from his eternal counsel and foreknowledge,
or to give them priority of order. For the foreknowledge
of God is nothing but the wisdom of God, under another
name, or that idea of every thing, which he had in
his mind . . . before he decreed anything.[41]

Thirdly, both Rupertus and Jermin had explained Wisdom's "play" as
an allusion to divine foreknowledge and predestination. Fourthly, Milton's prolusion *On the Harmony of the Spheres* had allegorized the concept
of heavenly harmony ("coelestis concentus") as "universal concord and
sweet union of all things" and conformity with "the laws of destiny."[42]
Fifthly, according to *The Wisdom of Solomon* xi. 20, God had "ordered all
things, in measure, and number, and weight."[43] The idea of proportion and musical harmony must, therefore, have existed prior to creation in the mind of the Father. For John Peter, "the *Reason* of *Numbers*"
served the Creator as a rule for the framing of the world and an instrument for its preservation:[44]

As the *Reason* of *Numbers* (if we dare credit *Solomon,*
Wisd. II.20) was *One* of the chiefest *Rules,* according to which *God* fram'd
the *World;* so is it also none
of the meanest *Instruments,* by which he still upholds
its *Fabrick:* so that to *set light* by the *power* of
Numbers, is to undervalue the *Wisdom* of the *Almighty,*
who thereby at first modulated the *whole Creation;*
and *still* makes use of an *Harmonical Concert* and
Physical Proportion to keep all in *Tune. By which*
means also is the *Reciprocal Harmony* maintained
betwixt the *Macrocosme,* and the *Microcosme* . . . .

Urania may appropriately signify harmony as a divine attribute, as a
characteristic of the divine decrees, or as a divine idea antecedent to the
world, but subsequently embodied in the "musica mundana" of the
spheres, the "musica humana" of soul and body, the "musica instrumentalis"[45] of human voice and artificial instruments, and the "celestial consort' of blessed spirits. The Father's delight in her "Celestial
Song" would, accordingly, appear to be the pleasure he derives from
contemplating his own decrees, in observing in his own Idea the musical proportions and preordained harmony of all things.

The alternative view—that Urania's playing refers to the song of the
angels—is, however, consistent with the angelology[46] of *Paradise Lost*
and the *De Doctrina,* and with the *Nativity Ode.* The latter refers to the
"Musick . . . made . . . when of old the sons of morning sung, While the
Creator Great His constellations set." In *At a Solemn Musick* God's "celestial consort" is an "undisturbed Song of pure content" sung by angels
and spirits of the just. The theological treatise advances the arguments

that the angels existed prior to the world's creation and that one of their primary functions is "praising God"; both theses find support in Job xxxviii. 7 ("When the morning stars sang together, and all the sons of God shouted for joy")[47]. In *Paradise Lost* the chief example of celestial music is the song of the angels. The council in Book III terminates in angelic "symphony" and "sacred Song" (III, 365–417). In Book V the angels devote the day to "song and dance about the sacred Hill." Like Urania herself, "harmony Divine" is personified as feminine ("*her* charming tones"); and just as the "Almighty Father" is "pleas'd" with Urania's "Celestial Song," so in this instance "God's own ear Listens delighted" (V, 618 ff.). Upon the Son's victorious return from battle, "each order bright, Sung Triumph, and him sung Victorious King" (VI, 885–886), and angelic song celebrates the creation of the world (VII, 180 ff., 253 ff., 274–275, 565 ff., 594 ff.). In most of these instances of "Celestial Song," the angelic symphony occurs *prior* to the creation of the world—"Before the Hills appeerd, or Fountain flow'd."

The close association of the angels and the Muses as tutelary spirits of song and the common application of stellar symbolism to Urania and the angels lend additional weight to the possibility that the "Celestial Song" of Milton's muse refers to the music of the angels. Gafori represents both angels and Muses as heavenly spirits responsible for the music of the spheres. The title page of his *Practica Musicae*[48] assigns each of the Muses to a separate sphere, with the exception of Thalia, who is relegated to the earth. Urania is appropriately associated with the sphere of the fixed stars ("celum stellatum"). The *Theorica Musicae*[49] echoes Plato's account of the celestial spirits (sirens, or "singing deities") and stresses the analogy with angels:

> At celestium ipsorum spirituum quos Socrates in republica
> Platonis syrenes nominavit non unus idemque modus est
> quem ipsi foelices & celi omnes quibus insident decantare
> dicuntur sed pro illorum diversitate tam diversus quam
> consonus . . . . Supersedunt autem hi spiritus secundum suos
> ordines & eorum congruentiam ad spheras quatenus omnis
> harmonie vis reddundet quod Georgius anselmus in primo
> sue musices persuadet. Interpretatur enim syren deus
> canens sed proprius incessantes a cantu spiritus sicut
> spheras a motu significari voluit. Nostri vero theologi
> melius hos spiritus angelos nominant & in ordinem novem
> distinguunt unicuique officium atque ordinem suum tribuentes . . . .

Moreover, though Milton himself regards the creation of the angels as considerably prior to that of the spheres, and accordingly represents the "sacred song" of the angelic hierarchies as distinct from the movements of the stars, he nevertheless draws on the latter convention for his description of the angelic "song and dance about the sacred Hill":

Mystical dance, which yonder starrie Spheare
Of Planets and of fixt in all her Wheeles
Resembles nearest, mazes intricate,
Eccentric, intervolv'd, yet regular
Then most, when most irregular they seem:
And in thir motions harmonie Divine
So smooths her charming tones, that Gods own ear
Listens delighted.

Like the heavenly "song and dance" of Milton's angels, Urania's "Celestial Song" may represent an extension of the concept of "musica
mundana"—the music of the spheres—to a period prior to the creation
of the celestial orbs. By this adaptation of a Pythagorean and Platonic
motif, he could emphasize the superiority of the Christian Heaven to
that of classical mythology and of the Christian Muse to her pagan
predecessors. Whereas the classical muses inhabited the visible
heavens, Milton's Urania dwells in the Empyrean. Whereas they were
an "empty dreame," she is a reality. Whereas they were no older than
the spheres they were alleged to inhabit, she has existed before the
spheres were formed and dwells in the "Heav'n of Heav'ns" with God
himself.

The significance of this difference appears all the more striking
through the contrast with Gafori's representation of Urania. In the
Theorica Musicae she occupies a position comparable to that of Calliope
in other authors[50]; she dwells in the highest sphere, which embraces
the tones of all the lower orbs. None of the Muses, however, inhabit the
Empyrean, which belongs to God alone:[51]

> hoc orbe reliquorum infra se orbium melodia comprehenditur
> omnem penitus harmoniam exuperans. ideoque ibi uranem
> musam poetarum quidam posuerunt: eam quidem que ex musis
> novem quas Iovis & memoriae filias finxerunt omnem dicendi
> dulcedinem complectitur & superat. Si quidem Teologi decimum
> asserentes coelum dei altissimi novam sedem nemini habitatam
> dixerunt ut inquit Georgius ipse anselmus. Nulla enim
> infra deum maiestati aut meretur aut potest prior fieri:
> neque omnino tantum valet vigorem tamque exuperantem
> pati aut cognitione concipere. sunt quippe omnia ad
> illam sicuti oculi nicticoracis ad lucem.

Milton's Urania is unique in dwelling above the spheres in "Empyreal
Aire."

Finally, Urania and the angels are linked by stellar symbolism. In
Ripa's *Iconologia,* she is characterized by an azure robe, a garland of
stars, and a celestial globe as signs of her traditional role as the Muse of
Astronomy and her ability to "inalza[re] al Cielo gl' huomini dotti."[52]
Similar details recur in Ripa's delineations of "Poesia": "Si veste del
color del cielo, perché il cielo in greco si dice *Uranos,* & la Musa, che da

spirito di Poesia, è Urania . . ."[53] The stellar symbolism of Job xxxviii.7 had been interpreted in terms of the angels and their song at the creation of the world. The Tremellius—Junius Bible explains "filii Dei" as "angeli."[54] Munster observes that the Hebrews interpret *stellae matutinae* as a reference to heavenly bodies, but that Christians explain it as an allusion to the angels:

> Stellae matutinae.] Hebraei per stellas intelligunt
> corpora coelestia, quae hic referuntur pro modulo
> suo laudasse deum, cum poneret fundamentum terrae.
> Sed cum coelum & terra simul sint fundata, ut patet
> ex principio Gen. nostri per stellas intelligunt
> angelos[55].

In Beza's opinion the first part of the text referts to the "daunce" of the stars and latter half to angelic praise:

> Where wert thou] *when the starres of the morning merily sung together, and all the sonnes of God reioyced?* . . .
> where wert thou then, when those heavenly torches first
> beganne to shine, and ioyfully to daunce, as it were in
> number and measure, one after another, and when for
> this worke these blessed spirits with one acorde sang
> praises unto me?

Piscator[56] interprets the entire text as a reference to the angels' hymn of praise at the creation:

> *Quum canerent simul stellae matutinae*] Per stellas
> matutinas intelligo angelos, partim ex collatione
> membri sequentis, ubi hae stellae per epexegesin
> nominantur filii Dei: partim ex veritate historiae.
> quia quum terra crearetur, videl. die primo, tum
> stellae nondum erant; quippe quae die demum quarto
> creatae sunt. Vocantur autem angeli stellae matutinae
> per metaphoram, propter pulchritudinem qualis cerni-
> tur in stella matutina, quae dicitur lucifer seu
> phosphorus . . . *Quum canerent*] Quum laeto cantu
> celebrarent Deum propter terram creatam, tanquam
> materiam e qua creaturus es et reliqua mundi partes . . . .
> *Filii Dei*] Id est, angeli.

[V]

In identifying his Heavenly Muse[57] as the sister of Heavenly Wisdom, Milton was building on the foundation set by expositors of Proverbs and by Renaissance lexicographers. The former had not only stressed the plural form of the word *hokhmôth* in several texts, but also identified the Wisdom (or wisdoms) of Proverbs with the Muses. The latter provided ample authority for conceiving Wisdom's "play" in a musical sense. The chief remaining ambiguity in these lines is the question of whether Urania's "playing" should be regarded as prior to the invisible creation or to the visible universe alone. Both alternatives are feasible, and it is possible that Milton did not intend his readers to choose between them.

CHAPTER FIVE

Urania: "Spirit" and "Muse."

And chiefly Thou, O Spirit, that dost prefer
Before all Temples th' upright heart and pure,
Instruct me, for Thou knowst; Thou from the first
Wast present, and with mighty wings outspread
Dove-like satst brooding on the vast Abyss
And mad'st it pregnant: What in me is dark
Illumine, what is low raise and support;
That to the highth of this great Argument
I may assert Eternal Providence,
And justifie the wayes of God to men.

(*PL* I, lines 17–26)

Thou Spirit who ledst this glorious Eremite
Into the Desert, his Victorious Field
Against the Spiritual Foe, and broughtst him thence
By proof the undoubted Son of God, inspire,
As thou art wont, my prompted Song else mute,
And bear through highth or depth of natures bounds
With prosperous wing full summ'd to tell of deeds
Above Heroic, though in secret done . . . .*

(*PR*, I, lines 8–15)

Though the identity of Milton's 'Heav'nly Muse' has long been a matter for controversy, little attempt has been made to resolve one of the crucial ambiguities in the exordium of *Paradise Lost*. Do the opening lines contain two separate and distinct invocations to different powers, or a single, extended appeal to one divinity? Is the 'Muse' of line 6 identical with the 'Spirit' of line 17 or an altogether different entity? Does the critical word 'chiefly' refer to the verb 'instruct,' to its immediate neighbor 'Thou,' or to 'prefer'?[1] These questions are of major importance for the interpretation not only of the initial invocation, but also of Milton's subsequent references to his celestial patroness (III, 18; VII, 1: 39; IX, 21–47).

Though the problem has not hitherto been couched in precisely these terms, scholars are nevertheless divided on the issue. Some have preferred to read the entire passage (lines 6–26) as a single, continuous invocation to Urania. According to Professor Hanford, 'The Heavenly

The Poetical Works of John Milton, ed. H. G. Beeching (New York, 1935).

Muse . . . is in reality that divine inspiration which revealed the truths of religion to Moses. It is also the spirit of God which dwells in the heart of every believer. Milton's invocations are, therefore, really Christian prayers'.[2] Professors Whiting and Gossman maintain that 'the essential idea, the soul of Milton's Muse', is to be found in 'the words of the first invocation,

> *And chiefly thou O Spirit, that dost prefer*
> *Before all Temples, th' upright heart and pure,*
> *Instruct me, for Thou know'st*[3].

Professor Campbell regards the two as identical in meaning, though different in quality. The Muse is symbol, the Spirit reality. The 'first invocation makes the usual association with the Heavenly Muse as the inspirer of the biblical writers and then identifies the Muse with the Holy Ghost . . . .' In 'invoking the Heavenly Muse,' Milton 'makes it clear that he is using a literary symbol when he names *Urania* . . . Finally, he addresses his supplication to the reality behind the name, and here he describes the Third Person of the Trinity. A few lines later, Milton turns again to Urania . . .'[4]

On the other hand, both Masson and Verity have distinguished two separate invocations, to the Muse and the Spirit respectively. According to the former, 'It is expressly the HEBREW Muse that [Milton] invokes . . . In the end, however, this form of an invocation even of what might be called, by a bold adaptation of classical terms, the true, primeval, or Heavenly Muse . . . , passes into a direct prayer to the Divine Spirit'[5]. Verity likewise distinguishes the 'invocation of the Muse' in lines 6–16 from the 'invocation of the Holy Spirit' in lines 17–26, 'a higher power than the Muse addressed above'[6].

That Milton's Muse is identical with the 'heav'nly Muse' of Book III (line 19), the Urania of Book VII (lines 1–39), and the 'Celestial Patroness' of Book IX (line 21) is obvious enough. But that she is to be equated specifically with the 'Spirit' invoked in the exordium of Book I is far from proven. The question requires further examination in the light of the similarities and differences between Milton's initial address to the Spirit and his various references to the Heavenly Muse throughout the poem.

The most significant difference would appear to be the type of aid the poet asks or claims to have received. The guidance he seeks and obtains from his Muse is essentially verbal. He bids her 'sing' of man's first disobedience and implores her aid in an 'advent'rous Song' that intends to pursue 'Things unattempted yet in Prose or Rhyme'. He requests her to state the causes of the Fall ('Say first . . . what cause'), to recite the catalogue of devils ('Say, Muse, thir Names'), to relate the events subsequent to Raphael's account of the angelic war ('Say, Goddess, what ensu'd'). He asks an 'answerable style' appropriate to the 'highth' of his 'great Argument'. He follows her 'Voice divine' and requests her to 'govern' his 'Song'. She 'dictates' to him 'slumb'ring, or inspires . . . unpremeditated Verse'. She brings his poetry 'nightly to my Ear'. Even the references to her ascent and descent involve the problem of appropriate utterance—the adaptation of style to the level of the subject-matter. In declaring that he has

> . . . sung of Chaos and Eternal Night,
> Taught by the heav'nly Muse to venture down
> The dark descent, and up to reascend,

he is emphasizing a shift in the level of his subject, a transition from Hell to Heaven. In bidding Urania to 'descend from Heav'n' or in asserting that he has been 'up led by thee Into the Heav'n of Heav'ns' or in asking her to 'Return me to my Native Element', he is stressing the lowered pitch of his narrative, the modulation from the war in Heaven to the creation of the world. As in *Lycidas,* he utilizes his references to the Muse as a literary device, to underline a change in subject-matter or style.

From the Spirit, on the other hand, he seeks the internal illumination and moral elevation requisite for his unprecedented 'task'. He does not bid the Spirit to 'say', but to 'instruct', to 'illumine', to 'raise and support'. In its request for illumination his invocation to the Spirit shows greater affinity with the subsequent appeal to 'celestial Light' than with the initial address to the Heavenly Muse, and the instruction he asks from the Spirit belongs properly to the province of Eternal Wisdom rather than to that of her sister Urania. In function and office, the "Spirit" of line 7 bears a closer resemblance to divine wisdom and the inner light than to the Muse. From the one he implores 'knowledge'; from the other, appropriate 'utterance'.

Though the appeal to the Spirit may be justly regarded as a 'Christian prayer', it is questionable whether this label is consistently applicable to Milton's invocations to his Muse. When he asks her aid in stating the causes of the Fall, the catalogue of fallen angels, and the creation of the world, is he actually praying to the Christian God? The terse injunctions to 'say . . . what cause', to 'say . . . thir Names', to 'say . . . what ensu'd' hardly display either the form or the spirit of Christian prayers. When he declares that his 'Celestial Patroness . . . dictates to me slumb'ring', does he mean that his verse, like Holy Scripture, has been set down at the Spirit's own dictation? Milton surely knew a hawk from a handsaw and could distinguish the verbal inspiration of his own poem from the verbal revelation of the prophets. Though he may have 'believed himself to be, in some real sense, an inspired man'[7], he certainly did not believe that 'he was adding historic details to the Scriptures' or 'beholding and revealing special truth'[8]. It is, therefore, more than doubtful that Milton's references to the Heavenly Muse invariably refer to the Spirit of God or that his invocations to Urania are in reality Christian prayers.

From his Muse Milton asks appropriate utterance; from the Spirit he asks knowledge and inner purification. This distinction between the 'answerable style' he requires of the one and the instruction he desires from the other are patently reminiscent of the duality of 'utterance and knowledge' in *The Reason of Church Government*. There is, however, a significant difference between the two works in their treatment of this distinction. According to the treatise, knowledge and utterance are to be achieved by invoking the same divinity, the 'eternal Spirit':

> . . . a work not to be obtained by the invocation of dame memory and her siren daughters, but by devout prayer to that eternal Spirit, who can enrich with all utterance and knowledge, and sends out his seraphim, with the hallowed fire of his altar, to touch and purify the lips of whom he pleases[9].

In the epic, however, Milton seeks these divine gifts separately, imploring knowledge from the Spirit and suitable utterance from the Muse.

The chief motivation underlying this difference seems to have been literary rather than doctrinal. Milton did not alter his belief; he merely adapted it to epic convention. If he asks the gift of appropriate style from the Muse rather than from the Spirit, the reason is to be found largely in the principle of decorum. Demands which might be properly addressed to a Muse could seem irreverent if directed to a God. A poet could legitimately emphasize the gravity of his argument, the technical difficulty of a particular passage, or a shift in subject-matter by invoking his Muse; to invoke God in such instances as these might well seem inpious. In such cases the invocation was usually a literary convention rather than a prayer. Though the poet might observe the pretense of imploring divine aid from his Muse, his real motives were to follow classical precedent, to imitate the invocations of Homer, Virgil, and their epic successors, and to emphasize the more important elements in his own poem.

Like other poets, Milton invokes his Muse at the more difficult points in his narrative. He imitates Homer, of course, in combining his proposition with his initial invocation and in re-invoking his Muse in his epic catalogue. He agrees with Tasso, Vida, and classical precedent in invoking her at intervals during the course of his fable. But he invokes the Spirit explicitly only once—at the beginning of his poem. By thus separating his appeals to the Muse and Spirit for utterance and knowledge and observing a stricter economy in his invocation to the latter, Milton achieves a close conformity to epic precedent in one instance and a note of intense religious sincerity in the other. If his appeal to the Spirit of Book I shows the tone and spirit of a Christian prayer, this effect is largely due to the fact that the more conventional aspects of the epic invocation are consistently delegated to the Muse. Hence the 'devout prayer' to the 'eternal Spirit' for 'knowledge' is not marred by further demands on the same power to recite an epic catalogue, announce a theme, or relate the causes of the Fall. The invocations to the Muse are obviously a conventional literary device; the invocation to the Spirit is a prayer.

Thus there is no essential inconsistency between Milton's views on invocation in *The Reason of Church Government* and in *Paradise Lost*. Indeed many of the major concepts enunciated in the prose work find close parallels in the epic. Intending to soar above 'th' *Aonian* Mount', Milton invokes neither Mnemosyne nor her daughters, 'the Muses nine', but a celestial power associated with the Father and his Wisdom before the creation of the world. The motif of internal purity, inherent in the earlier allusion to the Spirit's power to 'purify the lips of whom he pleases', recurs in the subsequent reference to 'th' upright heart and pure'. The duality of utterance and knowledge reappears in the very structure of the exordium, with its dual request for appropriate speech ('Sing, Heav'nly Muse') and instruction ('Instruct me, for thou knowst').

As a personification of 'Celestial Song'[10] or the power of divine utterance, Milton's Urania is not identical with the Spirit of God. Instead, she is rather the *gift* of God. In stressing her heavenly genealogy and habitation, Milton is exploiting the classical notion of poetry's divine origin as well as the Christian concept of the heavenly source of 'every good gift' and his own belief that poetic 'abilities . . . are the inspired gift of God'. Though, unlike the invocation to the Spirit, the appeals to Urania never address the Father directly, they may involve at times an *indirect* application for his aid. First, as Urania is herself a divine gift dependent on the Father's will, to invoke her assistance is to invoke indirectly the assistance of Heaven. Secondly, Conti's *Mythologia* had linked the celestial origin of the Muses with James i. 17:

> Musas alij Mnemosynes & Iovis, alij Antiopae & Iovis, alij Memnonis & Thespiae filias fuisse putarunt: quoniam Musae scientia, & optimus affectus animi ad illam imbibendam creditus est, qui non nisi divinitus in nos influit, cum omne bonum datum sit de coelo descendens a patre luminum[11].

It is possible, therefore, that the invocation in Book VII ('Descend from Heav'n *Urania*') may involve, beside its direct appeal to the Muse herself, an indirect request to 'the Father of lights' for the 'good gift' of celestial song—that the phraseology is intended to characterize Urania as a 'bonum datum . . . de coelo descendens a patre luminum'.

Though Professor Campbell regards Urania as a 'literary symbol' for the Spirit, there is inadequate internal evidence to establish this identification. As her inspiration is consistently represented as purely *verbal*, her meaning seems to be very much narrower than that of the Spirit. Though she is indeed a 'symbol' and the Spirit a 'reality', one need not infer that it is the reality of the Spirit that she personifies. On the whole she seems to symbolize a *gift* of the Spirit—the power of sacred utterance—rather than the Spirit itself.

Nor does the external evidence of *Paradise Regain'd* establish her identity with the Spirit. Both epics invoke the same Spirit, but not the same Muse. While the invocation in *Paradise Regain'd* describes the Spirit as the customary inspiration of Milton's poetry—

> *Thou Spirit who ledst this glorious eremite*
> *Into the Desert . . . inspire*
> *As thou art wont, my prompted Song else mute—*

it never explicitly mentions the 'Heav'nly Muse'. Though both Urania and the Spirit can 'inspire' divine poetry (*PL* I, 7; *PR*, II, 11), this similarity in function does not prove that they are identical.

Though Urania's absence from *Paradise Regain'd* stands in striking contrast to Milton's frequent allusions to her in his earlier epic, this difference is hardly surprising. The 'brief epic' does not require so elaborate an exordium as does the extended epic, nor is there the same need to interrupt the narrative for additional invocations. Moreover, as *Paradise Regain'd* is less classical in tone than its predecessor, there would be less warrant for invoking a figment of Gentile mythology. Even though Renaissance poets had converted Urania from Hellenism to Hebraism and rededicated her to service as a 'Christian Muse', the pagan origin of the names 'Muse' and 'Urania' remained painfully apparent, and a Christian poet could invoke them only in a figurative sense—metaphorically, allegorically, but never literally.

Furthermore, the type of exordium differs significantly in the two epics. In the earlier work, proposition and invocation are combined[12], as in Homer's *Iliad* and *Odyssey*. In the later poem, however, they are separate and distinct, as in Virgil's *Aeneid*. In *Paradise Regain'd,* therefore, Milton could address the Spirit directly, without seeming to demand that God himself recite the story of Christ's temptation. In *Paradise Lost*, on the other hand, where the proposition is fused with the invocation, Milton asks the Muse to recite the narrative of the Fall, and seeks God's aid in a separate invocation. In neither epic does he directly ask the Spirit to 'say' or 'sing', but rather to 'inspire' or 'instruct'.

There is, then, considerable justification for regarding the first 26 lines of *Paradise Lost* as two distinct invocations to two different powers—the first, a personification of the gift of sacred utterance or

'Celestial Song'; the second, God himself. The first invocation is little more than a conventional literary device; the second is a Christian prayer. The poet's primary consideration in observing this distinction seems, on the whole, to have been a compromise between the conflicting claims of humanism and piety—an endeavor to retain the form of classical invocations to the Muse without imposing impertinent or unseemly demands on the Christian God. Though the 'utterance' sought from Urania is ultimately a gift of the Spirit, Milton prefers, for the sake of decorum, to treat the Muse and the Spirit as separate, though related, concepts and to invoke them for diverse ends.

CHAPTER SIX

"Darkness Visible": The Quality of Hellfire

> At once as far as Angels kenn he views
> The dismal Situation waste and wilde,
> A Dungeon horrible, on all sides round
> As one great Furnace flam'd, yet from those flames
> No light, but rather darkness visible
> Serv'd only to discover sights of woe,
> Regions of sorrow, doleful shades, where peace
> And rest can never dwell, hope never comes
> That comes to all; but torture without end
> Still urges and a fiery Deluge, fed
> With ever-burning Sulphur unconsum'd:
> Such place Eternal Justice had prepar d
> For those rebellious, here their Prison ordain'd
> In utter darkness, and their portion set
> As far remov'd from God and light of Heav'n
> As from the Center thrice to th' utmost Pole.*

(PL, I, lines 59–74)

T hat Hell-fire sheds no light was a theological commonplace, well-known to Milton's contemporaries; and various other English writers of his century allude to it. Herrick mentions it in his *Noble Numbers:*[1]

> The fire of Hell this strange condition hath,
> To burn, not shine (as learned Basil saith.)

John Collop refers to it in *Catholicon Medici,*[2] and John Donne in his *Ecclogue.*[3] The same *topos* also occurs (as Masson noted) in Walker's *History of Independency.*[4] Herrick's acknowledged source was St. Basil, and an analogue has been noted in the latter's *Homily on the Twenty-Eighth Psalm.*[5] This concept had also appeared, however, in other writings by St. Basil, and in the works of other Greek or Latin fathers. Any careful reader of the *Hexaemera* of St. Basil and St. Ambrose, of the *Moralia* of St. Gregory the Great, or even of Chaucer's *Parson's Tale* would have known it. Its usefulness for Milton — and its verisimilitude and credibility for Milton's audience — was enhanced by its traditional nature.

*The Poetical Works of John Milton, ed. H. C. Beeching (New York, 1935).

[I]

In Basil's opinion, fire possessed two distinct properties—light and heat. Though to separate them exceeded man's ability, God could divide the caustic power of flame from its illuminative power, as in the miracles of the burning bush and the "three children" in Nebuchadnezzar's fiery furnace. In the separation of the two qualities resided the antithetical rewards of the blessed and the damned. The just enjoyed light without heat. Hell-fire, on the other hand, burned, but did not illuminate.

A fairly full statement of Basil's conception of Hell-fire appeared in Symeon Metaphrastes' sermon *De Futuro Judicio*—one of twenty-four sermons on morals compiled from Basil's various writings. Symeon combined details of the homilies on Psalms 28 and 33 and other works into a lurid portrait of the terrors of Hell. To the man who has sinned during his former life there appear frightful and menacing angels with fiery eyes and fiery breath, beings perverse in mind and depraved in judgment, faces that resemble night because of the inveterate hatred they bear to men. Then appear the profound abyss, the impenetrable darkness, and the fire that consumes in darkness: the fire that has the power of burning but lacks the property of shining. There too are venomous and carnivorous worms, which gnaw him incessantly and insatiably. Finally, there is the heaviest punishment of all: perpetual shame and infamy:

> Dienceps qui refertam variis sceleribus vitam traduxit, ei formidabiles quidam truculentique repraesentantur angeli, candentibus igneisque oculis horridum intuentes, nilque nisi igneum spirantes: adeo perversi animo iudicioque depravati sunt: nocti facie persimiles, prae truculentia atque in homines odio. Profundum postea barathrum ostenditur, atque *impermeabiles tenebrae, ignisque in obscuritate lumine carens, urendi quidem vi praeditus, lucendi vero facultate destitutus:* vermium etiam venenatorum & carnivororum genus quoddam perpetuo comedens, neque edendi satietate se explens, intolerabiles rodendo dolores inurens. Postremo, quae omnium gravissima est poena, opprobrium illud, neque quamlibet longo temporis cursu eluenda infamia . . .[6]

Think, then (Symeon continues) of the terrible penalties that are to be inflicted upon them by God. The fire prepared for the punishment of the devil and his angels is divided by the voice of the Lord. Divine justice has separated the two natural qualities of fire—the properties of burning and of shining—thus aggravating the punishments of wicked men by heat without light and enhancing the rewards of the just by light that does not sear:

> Cogita igitur, quaeso, terribiles in eos qui puniuntur, à deo impendentes poenas . . . *Tum praeparatus ad punitionem diabolo atque angelis eius, ignis, domini voce discinditur, ut quoniam duae in eo sunt facultates, urendi una,*

lucendi altera, quod asperum quidem ultionique in eo idoneum est, penes eos qui ut torreantur, meruerunt, permaneat: eius verò lucem atque splendorem alacris laetantium hilaritas sortiatur: adeò ut qui in punitionem adhibetur ignis, sine lumine sit: qui verò in oblectamentum, absque urendi vi remaneat. Neque ea in re tibi addubitandum esse cogita. In ipsa enim factorum nostrorum remuneratione, ignis dividetur natura: cuius quidem lumen, iustorum oblectamento: urendi verò molestia, puniendorum tribuetur ultioni. Formidabilior autem ipsis tenebris aeternoque igne, infamia illa est, cui perpetuò peccatores sunt ... Dei enim à nobis alienatio atque aversio, illi qui eam patitur, intolerabilior graviorque est quàm caetera gehennae expectata supplicia: ut oculo privatio luminis, licet alius non adsit dolor[7].

In his *Paraenesis sive Adhortatio ad Theodorum Lapsum,* St. John Chrysostom declared that Hell-fire differed from other flames inasmuch as it was inextinguishable and also burned without light:

Etenim cum ignem audis, cave putes esse huic igni similem: hic enim quidquid corripit, devorat et absumit; ille vero quos semel apprehendit, perpetuo comburit, nec unquam desistit; ideoque inexstinguibilis dicitur ... Quis enarraverit terrores a tenebris illis injectos animis nostris? *Quemadmodum enim ignis ille non consumit, ita neque lucet:* alioquin non essent tenebrae. Perturbationem nobis immissam, tremorem, resolutionem, stuporem, illud solum tempus declarare potest[8].

The idea was accessible to the Latin-reading world through Eustathius'[9] *Metaphrasis* of Basil's *Hexaemeron* and through Ambrose's *Hexaemeron,* Gregory's *Moralia,* and other works.

Commenting on the text *Fiant luminaria* (Genesis 1:13)[10], Ambrose cited the miracle of the burning bush and the contrasting rewards of the righteous and unrighteous as examples of the divine ability to divide the nature of flame:

Ignis autem et illuminat et exurit. Unde Dominus volens Moysi ostendere suae operationis miraculum, quo Moysen ad obediendi studium provocaret, atque ad fidem inflammaret ejus affectum, in igne visus est in rubo, et rubus non exurebatur, sed tantum splendere ignis specie videbatur. Alterum igitur munus vacabat, alterum operabatur. *Vacabat exustionis vis, operabatur illuminationis.* Ideo stupebat Moyses, quia contra naturam suam ignis non exurebat rubum, qui etiam vehementiorem materiem consuevit exurere. *Sed Domini ignis illuminare solet, exurere non solet.* At forte dicas: Quomodo scriptum est: *Ego sum ignis consumens* (Deut. iv, 24)? Bene admonuisti. Non solet consumere, nisi sola peccata. *In retributionis quoque meritorum colligimus dividi ignis naturam: ut alios illuminet, alios exurat, illuminet justos, exurat impios. Non eosdem quos illuminat, exurit; et quos exurit, illuminat: sed illuminatio ejus inextinguibilis est ad perfunctionem bonorum, exustio vehemens ad supplicium peccatorum*[11].

In his commentary on Job 10:22, Gregory explained the punishment of the damned as burning without and blindness within:

Sicut mors exterior ab anima dividit carnem, ita mors interior a Deo separat animam. Umbra ergo mortis est obscuritas divisionis, quia dam-

natus quisque cum aeterno igne succenditur, ab interno lumine teneb-
ratur. *Natura vero ignis est, ut ex se ipso et lucem exhibeat, et concremationem: sed
transactorum ille ultrix flamma vitiorum concremationem habet, et lumen non
habet.* Hinc est enim quod reprobis Veritas dicit: *Discedite a me, maledicti, in
ignem aeternum, qui paratus est diabolo et angelis ejus* (Matth. xxv, 41).
Quorum rursus omnium corpus in unius persona significans, dicit: *Ligate
ei manus et pedes, et mittite eum in tenebras exteriores* (Matth. xxii, 13). Si itaque
ignis qui reprobos cruciat lumen habere potuisset, is qui repellitur
nequaquam mitti in tenebras diceretur. Hinc etiam Psalmista ait: *Super
eos cecidit ignis et non viderunt solem* (Psal. lvii, 9). Ignis enim super impios
cadit, sed sol igne cadente non cernitur, quia quo illos gehennae flamma
devorat, a visione veri luminis caecat; ut et foris eos dolor combustionis
cruciet, et intus poena caecitatis obscuret ... *Hic flamma quae succendit
iluminat; illic ... ignis qui cruciat obscurat ... Horrendo igitur modo erit tunc
reprobis dolor cum formidine, flamma cum obscuritate*[12].

Hell-fire, Gregory, declared, denies light for consolation, but provides
it for greater suffering:

> *Quamvis illic ignis et ad consolationem non lucet, et tamen ut magis torqueat ad
> aliquid lucet ... Ignis itaque qui in obscuritate cruciat credendum est quia lumen
> ad tormentum servat*[13].

Like Basil, Gregory regarded the miracle of the "three children" as
evidence of the divine ability to separate the qualities of flame for
rewarding the just and punishing the unjust:

> Tres quippe Hebraeae gentis pueri, per Chaldaei regis imperium suc-
> censis camini ignibus ... quos tamen ... rex ... illaesis vestibus deam-
> bulantes vidit. *Ubi aperte colligitur quia mira dispensatione conditoris ignis
> qualitas, in diversa virtute temperata, et vestimenta non attigit, et vincula incen-
> dit, sanctisque viris et ad inferendum tormentum flamma friguit, et ad solutionis
> ministerium exarsit. Sicut ergo electis ignis ardere novit ad solatium, et tamen
> ardere ad supplicium nescit: ita e diverso gehennae flamma reprobis et nequaquam
> lucet ad consolationis gratiam, et tamen lucet ad poenam; ut damnatorum oculis
> ignis supplicii et nulla claritate candeat, et, ad doloris cumulum, dilecti qualiter
> crucientur ostendat. Quid autem mirum si gehennae ignem credimus habere
> supplicium simul obscuritatis et luminis,* quando experimento novimus quia
> et taedarum flamma lucet obscura[14]?

The *Glossa Ordinaria* on Job 10:22 also noted the peculiar property of
Hell-fire:

> "Umbra mortis." Mors est separatio a Deo; umbra obscuritas ejus; *quia
> ignis poenalis cremationem habet, et non lucem,* ut in utroque puniantur, qui
> in utroque peccaverunt[15].

Haymo, bishop of Halberstadt, quoted extensively from both Gregory
the Great[16] and John Chrysostom[17], in his discussion of Hell in *De
Varietate librorum, sive de Amore coelestis patriae:*

> Nulli enim occurrent oculis nostris, nisi soli poenarum ministri, et facies
> ubique dira tortorum, et, quod est omnium tetrius, *nec aerii quidem ipsius*

erit ullum solamen aut lucis. Circumdabunt enim nos poenarum loca, tenebrae exteriores. Sed ignis ille, sicut naturam *non habet consumendi, ita nec illuminandi, sed ignis obscurus et flamma tenebrosa*[18].

The same idea reappeaed in Rupert's *Commentaries on Job:*

... nec flamma lucet ibi sicut hic ...,

and in the writings of the schoolmen. In his *Expositio* of Job, St. Thomas Aquinas commented on 10:22 as follows:

Nullus ordo esse: vel propter confusionem mentium, quam patiuntur damnati: vel propter hoc, quòd ille ordo non ibi servatur, qui hic. *hic enim ignis ardet & lucet, quod ibi non est*[20].

In the *Summa Theologica* he devoted an entire article to the problem of "Whether the damned are in material darkness?"[21] Here, as elsewhere,[22] he cited the opinions of Basil and Gregory:

For commenting on Job. x. 22, *But everlasting horror dwelleth,* Gregory says (*Moral.* ix): *Although that fire will give no light for comfort, yet, that it may torment the more it does give light for a purpose, for by the light of its flame the wicked will see their followers whom they have drawn hither from the world*[23].
Commenting on these words ("*exterior darkness,*" Matth. xxii. 13) Gregory says (*Moral.* ix.): If this fire gave any light, *he would by no means be described as cast into exterior darkness.*
Further, Basil says (*Hom.* i. *in Ps.* xxviii. 7, *The voice of the Lord divideth the flame of fire*) that by God's might the brightness of the fire will be separated from its power of burning, so that its brightness will conduce to the joy of the blessed, and the heat of the flame to the torment of the damned. Therefore the damned will be in material darkness[24].
I answer that, The disposition of hell will be such as to be adapted to the utmost unhappiness of the damned. Wherefore accordingly both light and darkness are there, in so far as they are most conducive to the unhappiness of the damned ... Consequently in hell the place must be so disposed for seeing as regards light and darkness, that nothing be seen clearly, and that only such things be dimly seen as are able to bring anguish to the heart. Wherefore, simply speaking, there is a certain amount of light, as much as suffices for seeing those things which are capable of tormenting the soul[25].

St. Bonaventura, in his commentary on the *Sentences,* also discussed the darkness of Hell-fire:

... ignis infernalis caret luce, secundum quod dicitur Iob decimo octavo: *Nonne lux impii exstingetur*[26]? et sicut melius patebit infra, cum dicantur impii proicii *in tenebras exteriores*[27].
Item, similiter Basilius dicit in Hexaëmeron, exponens illud Psalmi: *Vox Domini intercidentis flammam ignis,* quod "ignis materialis sedet ad punitionem damnatorum, quantum ad id quod habet ardoris[28]."

For both theologians, the peculiar quality of Hellfire involved the problem of its nature and species. Thus Bonaventura found it advisable to discuss the question "Utrum ignis inferni sit verus ignis,"[29] and Aquinas debated "Whether the fire of Hell is of the same species as ours?"[30]

The Pricke of Conscience declared that Hell-fire gave no light, but that the torment of the damned was increased by the sights of woe revealed by sparks of fire:

> *Palpabunt tenebras in meridie*
> *sicut in media nocte.*
> "In helle es never day bot ever nyght;
> þat brynnes ay fire, bot it gyf[es] na light."
> Bot yhit þe synful sal ay se
> Alle þe sorowe þat þar sal be,
> And ilka payne and ilka tourment,
> Thurgh sparkes of fire þat obout sal sprent.
> Bot þat sight sal be til þam þare,
> Na comfort, bot sorowe and kare.
> þus to eke þair paynes, þai sal haf sight,
> With-outen any comfort þar of light;
> And for-þi þat helle es ay lightles,
> It is cald þe land of myrkenes . . .[31]
> For Saynt Austyn says on þis manere:
> *Demones igne scintillante*
> *videbunt, et miserabilem*
> *clamorem flencium et la-*
> *mentancium audient.*
> þai sal se þar devels with eghe,
> Thurgh sparkes þat of þe fire sal fleghe . . .[32]
> And alle-þogh þai in helle want light,
> Yhit sal þai of alle payns haf sight,
> Thurgh þe sparkes of fyr þar, als says Saynt Austyn
> Noght til þair comfort bot til þair pyne . . .[33]

Chaucer's *Persones Tale* expressed a similar conception of the infernal flames:

> The thridde cause that oghte moeve a man to Contricion, is drede of the day of dome, and of the horrible peynes of helle . . . The cause why that Job clepeth helle "the lond of deknesse"; understondeth that he clepeth it "londe" or erthe, for it is stable, and nevere shal faille; "derk", for he that is in helle hath defaute of light material. For certes *the derke light, that shal come out of the fyr* that evere shal brenne, shal turne him al to peyne that is in helle; for it sheweth him to the horrible devels that him tormenten[34].
> For as seith seint Basilie: "the brenninge of the fyr of this world shal god yeven in helle to hem that been dampned; but the light and the cleernesse shal be yeven in hevene to his children . . .[35]

[II]

Various texts were cited in support of this conception of Hell-fire. Basil believed that Psalm 28:7, *Vox Domini intercidentis flammam ignis*[36], authorized this opinion. God's separation of day and night on the fourth day (Genesis 1:14) was comparable to his division of the dual properties of flame[37]. The singular quality of Hell-fire, moreover, added to its horror; by contemplating this and other torments of Hell, the Christian should acquire the fear of God (Psalm 33:12)[38]. Furthermore, the same distinction between the caustic and illuminative powers of fire explained how God could illumine Israel and also purify her by burning away her sins (Isaiah 10:17)[39].

Later theologians sometimes cited one or more of these texts in discussing the nature of Hell-fire, but many of them followed Gregory the Great in applying the idea to Job 10:22. Protestant theologians generally explained this text as a reference to the grave rather than to Hell[40]. A few Catholic commentators, however, continued even after the Counter-Reformation to interpret it as a reference to the darkness of the infernal flames.[41]

[III]

In declaring that

> . . . from those flames
> No light, but rather darkness visible
> Serv'd only to discover sights of woe . . .

Milton followed a tradition developed by the Greek and Latin fathers, analyzed by the schoolmen, exploited by Chaucer and Rolle, and still familiar to seventeenth-century Englishmen.

Certain aspects of this description deserve further comment. In the first place, it involves the Christian marvellous; indeed it appears to be the first clear-cut example of the marvellous in *Paradise Lost*. It was, moreover, particularly appropriate to the heroic poem. In the opinion of many Renaissance critics the essential end of this genre was to arouse admiration or wonder. Tasso had recommended the Christian supernatural as the only source of the marvellous consistent with verisimilitude and probability.[42]

Milton's flames without light represented the same sort of divine miracles as the burning bush and the "three children" in the fiery furnace. The separation of the dual properties of light and heat was analogous, but the effect was diametrically opposite. Basil and Gregory had stressed the miraculous character of the two latter incidents. For Gregory, the three Hebrews had been saved through a "mira dispensatione"[43], and for Basil their salvation was more wonderful than the crossing of the Red Sea:

> Longè est admirabilius ignis naturam intercidi,
> quàm mare rubrum in partes dividi[44].

In the burning bush, Basil argued, God had performed a similar wonder:

> . . . Deus autem volens famulum suum reddere sibi attentiorem illo admirabili spectaculo, in rubum ignem splendore solùm agentem . . .[45]

Ambrose held the same view:

> Unde Dominus volens Moysi ostendere suae operationis miraculum, quo Moysen ad obediendi studium provocaret . . . Ideo stupebat Moyses, quia contra naturam suam ignis non exurebat rubum . . .[46]

Like the two analogous miracles, the darkness of Hell-fire constituted a distinct breach of the natural order. It resulted directly from the action of divine justice and represented the same sort of punitive intervention as the subsequent metamorphosis of the evil angels in Book X.

Moreover, though obviously contrary to nature, this detail acquired verisimilitude and probability from patristic and medieval explanations of the singular quality of Hellfire and the miracles of the "three children" and the burning bush. Milton's "darkness visible", moreover, had behind it the authority of Job 10:22, "A land of darkness . . . where the light is as darkness"[47].

Similarly, it emphasized the penal character of Hell. For the fathers as well as the schoolmen, the darkness of Hell-fire represented a deliberate act of divine justice for the purpose of intensifying the torments of the damned by depriving them of the possible consolation of light. In Basil's opinion, moreover, God had specifically performed this miracle in preparation for the devil and his angels[48]. Similarly, as Gregory and others observed, the faint light cast by the infernal flames was intended to enhance the torture of its victims. In declaring that

> . . . darkness visible
> Serv'd only to discover sights of woe,

Milton expressed essentially the same conception of Hellfire as Gregory, Aquinas, Rolle, and Chaucer before him.

[IV]

Visible darkness is an essential element in establishing the decorum of Milton's underworld. ". . . God spared not the angels that sinned, but cast them down to hell, and delivered them into chains of darkness, to be reserved unto judgement . . . " (2 Peter ii. 4). ". . . the place from which I shall not return, even to the land of darkness and the shadow of death; A land of darkness, as darkness itself; and of the shadow of death, without any order, and where the light is as darkness" (Job x.

21-22).[49] Perhaps the primary significance of this motif, however, consists in its psychological and cognitive associations: its implications for the epistemology of Hell.

It is our first introduction to the pervasive imagery of light and darkness, the "spiritual chiaroscuro," that underlies the symbolic structure of *Paradise Lost* as well as the Ludlow masque and *Samson Agonistes*. Though Milton's allusions to his own blindness lend a peculiar poignancy to this motif, the imagery itself is a legacy from diverse cultural traditions: Platonic and Hermetic, Iranian and Orphic, Hebraic and Hesiodic, Homeric and Christian. Behind Milton's exploitation of this motif lie the classical image of the blind poet and seer, the poetic elaboration of light-and-darkness imagery by Spenser and other Renaissance poets, and perhaps recent experimentation with chiaroscuro in the visual arts. The theory of vision was, indeed, so closely interwoven with the theory of knowledge, that their concepts and vocabulary were virtually interchangeable. The terminology of physical vision ("idea," "insight," "vision," "blindness," and the like) provided a metaphorical basis for describing psychological and epistemological process.

Besides its relationship to the larger pattern of light-and-darkness symbolism in the poem, this imagery is also associated closely with the pattern of discovery[50], which constitutes one of the *Leitmotifs* of Milton's epic. The "darkness visible" is both a mode of consciousness—a correlative of the Archangel's own fallen intelligence—and an instrument of discovery. But the consciousness (as the fallen angel and the fallen reader gradually perceive) is essentially the experiential knowledge of evil, and the "discovery" is the progressive realization of good lost forever and the prospect of eternal evil, eternal pain. The visionary mode (so to speak) of the evil eye.

As a correlative to the experience of evil, this motif reinforces the paradoxes of knowledge and vision implicit in the temptation of Adam and Eve (Genesis iii. 5): ". . . in the day ye shall eat thereof, then your eyes shall be opened, and ye shall be as gods, knowing good and evil." After the intoxicating "force of that fallacious Fruit" has worn off, Adam and Eve uprose (IX, lines 1046-1057)

> As from unrest, and each the other viewing
> Soon found thir Eyes how op'nd, and thir minds
> How dark'nd; innocence, that as a veile
> Had shadow'd them from knowing ill, was gon,
> Just confidence, and native righteousness,
> And honour from about them . . . .

Since tasting the "defended Fruit," man has come to "know both Good and Evil," (XI, lines 84-89):

> . . . but let him boast
> His knowledge of Good lost, and Evil got,
> Happier, had it suffic'd him to have known
> Good by it self, and Evil not at all.

Satan's first dramatic action in Milton's epic is an act of vision. Still immobile on the flaming sea, he looks about him, and what he beholds is a torture-chamber. Earlier (though we ourselves as readers discover this subsequently) he had first experienced pain, as a direct consequence of his sin. Now his present torment is intensified and heightened by reference to past and future: by the memory of forfeited happiness (his own "Paradise Lost") and by the prospect of enduring and unremittent pain. Since he is still (according to Milton's angelology) a being primarily and essentially spiritual, though coarsened and made gross by sin, his pain is both spiritual and physical; and, as the poet develops these motifs, there are significant correspondences between them. The physical and sensible torments have their moral and intellectual correlatives in a spiritual dimension. The unquenchable fire and the perpetual darkness have their spiritual counterparts in the progressive darkening of the angelic intellect and in the enslavement of the will to its own fierce and insatiable appetites, its spiritual "chains of fire" and "chains of darkness."

Satan's penalty is (in a significant degree) epistemological; a fallen mode of knowledge. Like Adam and Eve after their fall, he has tasted the "Bad Fruit of Knowledge": "Good lost, and Evil got" (IX, 1072–1073). Revolting through an insatiable appetite for divine glory, as they through hunger for divine knowledge, he is punished by the knowledge of evil itself: by the immediate experience of sin and its consequences, by a continuous and renewed dedication to evil, and by a progressive recognition of its true deformity and of his own spiritual deformation. This is the contrary of the Beatific Vision that he and his peers had known in Heaven. Now that evil must be his good, the highest values are reversed and perverted into their logical contraries. Instead of the Summum Bonum, the fallen angels now adore the author of evil!—a fallen intelligence alienated from the Highest Good and supreme only in misery. They will rejoice in the sight of their matchless chief, just as the faithful angels have received beatitude past utterance from the Vision of God.[51] Satan himself, who had earlier fallen in love with his own perfect image—his newly conceived Sin, a diabolical caricature of heavenly Wisdom—is shortly to encounter her once again, at Hell-gate, and behold in this perfect image of himself the true moral deformity of the evil that has now become his good.

The act of vision that begins Milton's epic fable will unfold in a continuous process of discovery, as Satan and his angels progressively recognize the nature of their dungeon and the limitations of their own fallen nature, as they attempt to disguise the realities of their situation from themselves and from one another, and as they proceed (in a Hogarthian progress) from the knowledge of a local Hell without to the realization of a spiritual Hell within. As they gradually learn, they can never truly escape their dungeon, for they are in a sense "incorporate" with Hell itself; and when they conquer the new world and become powers of the air, they will carry Hell with them. And indeed the very celebration of their apparent victory over God and man will be a reenacting of the Sin in which they and their Leader Satan, and fallen Mankind are all sharers. Their infernal feast on the illusory fruit simultaneously counterpoints the celestial repasts of the elect angels, and recapitulates the physical and spiritual gluttony of Adam and Eve.

As spiritual states, Sin and Death involve modes of knowledge; and in the progressive knowledge and re-enactment of evil lies one of the primary torments of Milton's Hell.

It is through the chiaroscuro of the penal fire that surrounds him from without, and consumes him within, through this paradoxical light in darkness, that Satan successively discovers the grim topography of his place of exile, his fallen companions "o'rewhelm'd/ With Floods and Whirlwinds of tempestuous fire," and his boon-companion Beëlzebub "weltring by his side . . . ." By this light he glimpses the shore of the fiery sea:

> . . . yon dreary Plain, forlorn and wilde,
> The seat of desolation, voyd of light,
> Save what the glimmering of these livid flames
> Casts pale and dreadful[.]

The motifs of vision and discovery receive further development— though from the poet's rather than the Archangel's point of view— through the optical imagery whereby Milton describes Satan's shield. In this instance Milton may be exploiting a conventional association between optical illusions (including meteorological phenomena) and demonic agency. The poet's reference to Galileo's "Optic Glass" (I, line 288) suggests the deliberate production of an *eidolon*, the artificial enhancement of natural vision and enlargement of visual phenomena. This is an instrument of discovery, but it also suggests techniques of magnification and deception not dissimilar to the skills of the sophist and the rhetorician in the verbal arts. The analogous references to Satan's "Aerie Microscope" and to his "strange Parallax or Optic skill/ Of vision multiplyed through air, or glass/ Of Telescope" (*PR*, IV, lines 40–60) are more directly related to his status as prince of the powers of the air as well as to his skills at juggling tricks and deception.

At Hell-gate he encounters the visible personifications of Sin and Death and is compelled to recognize the essential ugliness of evil in general and of his own sin in particular. In Sin he beholds the image of himself without recognizing it, and finds the sight detestable. He escapes the confines of his dungeon only to discover that he can never escape them, that he brings his dungeon with him:

> . . . for within him Hell
> He brings, and round about him, nor from Hell
> One step no more then from himself can fly
> By change of place . . .

He beholds "undelighted all delight . . . ," finds his former lustre visibly impaired, and discovers his own weaknesses.

Meanwhile the exploratory parties of fallen angels, the expeditions sent out "On bold adventure to discover wide/ That dismal World, if any Clime perhaps/ Might yeild them easier habitation," acquire only a wider and sadder knowledge of their dungeon and their miserable fate:

> Thus roving on
> In confus'd march forlorn, th' adventrous Bands
> With shuddring horror pale, and eyes agast
> View'd first thir lamentable lot, and found
> No rest . . . .

They have gained experience, but this is merely the empirical knowledge of mortality and evil, the realities of spiritual death:

> A Universe of death, which God by curse
> Created evil, for evil only good,
> Where all life dies, death lives, and nature breeds,
> Perverse, all monstrous, all prodigious things . . . .

This expedition of discovery, which concludes in terror and horror, is the climax to the account of the pastimes that have engaged the other fallen angels, "somwhat rais'd/By false presumptuous hope," during the absence of their Chief. It leaves no more room for hope. But the leisure pursuits themselves are scarcely encouraging, though they entertain the participants and audience. The athletic games are suggestively reminiscent of the celestial battles in which the rebels had been painfully and ignominiously defeated. The heroic songs lament their overthrows. The theological discourses concerning Providence and Fate find "no end, in wandring mazes lost," and the topic of "free will' is now ironically irrelevant; the last rebels have fallen through abusing their own freedom of choice, and they can never regain their moral freedom. The ventures into moral philosophy—

> Of good and evil much they argu'd then,
> Of happiness and final misery,
> Passion and Apathie, and glory and shame,
> Vain wisdom all, and false Philosophie:—

can have no satisfactory resolution, since good and glory and happiness are now unattainable; and the philosophy seminars can only "charm" them for a time into forgetting or disguising the realities of eternal evil and misery and shame.

The final scenes in this drama of forbidden knowledge are devoted to man's repentance and instruction in the faith; he leaves Paradise content with "my fill/ Of knowledge, what this vessel can containe," and enheartened by faith and hope in a future Deliverer. This is a different kind of wisdom from the knowledge he had sought earlier; and he finds his eyes truly opened at last; open at last to the truth. His pursuit of knowledge has ended in the "evidence" of faith. The wisdom of Hell, conversely, has ended in delusion: in the re-enaction of Adam's sin, and Satan's, and in the reiterated experience of the fruit of forbidden knowledge:

> ... imagining
> For one forbidden Tree a multitude
> Now ris'n, to work them furder woe or shame;
> Yet parcht with scalding thurst and hunger fierce,
> Though to delude them sent, could not abstain, ...
> ... so oft they fell
> Into the same illusion, not as Man
> Whom they triumph'd once lapst.

Their punishment is perpetual hunger and thirst after unrighteousness and a false and illusory good: perpetual concupiscence, perpetual re-enactment of the same sin, and perpetually the taste of the same bitter ashes of remorse. Their understanding darkened by "vain" imaginations, they are punished by their very alienation from the truth and (inalienably) the "strong delusion, that they should believe a lie ...."[53]

Visual illusions occur frequently in *Paradise Lost,* sometimes in association with optical effects and images of light and darkness, sometimes in relation to deliberate imitations and disguises. When Satan makes his first assault on Eve, attempting to "Breach/ The Organs of her Fancie/ and with them forge/ Illusions as he list,/ Phantasms and Dreams" (*PL,* IV, lines 800–803), he appears to her as angel, and the delusions with which he inspires her are associated with the enticements of sight as well as scent. All things seem more beautiful by moonlight than by daylight, just as (in Milton's earlier description of Satan's shield) the moon itself seems much larger when viewed through a telescope than when seen with the naked eye (V, lines 41–53):[54]

> ... now reignes
> Full Orb'd the Moon, and with more pleasing light
> Shadowie sets off the face of things; ...

> . . . I pass'd through ways
> That brought me on a sudden to the Tree
> Of interdicted Knowledge: fair it seem'd,
> Much fairer to my Fancie then by day: . . .

In the second temptation-scene the Tempter resembles a "delusive Light . . . ." As he guides Eve to "the Tree/ Of prohibition, root of all our woe," Milton likens him to an *ignis fatuus,* the "wandring Fire" whereby some evil spirit misleads the night-wanderer (IX, lines 633– 640). In this scene (as in Genesis) the metaphorical associations of vision and taste as modes of knowledge are not only interwoven but specifically concentrated in the central image of the forbidden tree ("good for food, . . . pleasant to the eyes, and . . . to be desired to make one wise") with its fruit "of Divine effect/ To open Eyes, and make them Gods who taste . . . ." What Eve now experiences is a new mode of knowledge—the darkened and distorted vision of the fallen creature, which she mistakes for the wisdom of the gods—and Milton describes her experience through the imagery of intoxication: "height'nd as with Wine, jocond and boon"; and (later) "the force of that fallacious Fruit/ That with exhilerating vapour bland/ About thir spirits had plaid,/ and inmost powers/ Made erre . . . ." Ironically her ambition to "be as gods" in wisdom results in forfeiting potential immortality for mortality; and these ironies are further accentuated by the "ambrosial" odors as- sociated with the forbidden fruit (and with the Tempter himself in Eve's dream) and by her own superstitious faith in the tree's "sciential sap, deriv'd/ From Nectar, drink of Gods."

Greedily ingorging without restraint, Eve "knew not eating Death . . . ." Metaphorically she is already "tasting death"; and in the penance inflicted on Satan and his angels for the seduction of man, Milton elaborates the figurative meaning of this phrase (cf. Matthew xvi. 28; Hebrew ii. 9) into a myth centered on the empirical knowledge of evil. Although the apparition involves sensuous appeals similar to those that had attracted Eve ("The Frutage" is "fair to sight"), it is not "good for food," and (like Tantalus) the fallen angels are "plagu'd/ And worn with Famin," tormented with perpetual hunger and thirst.

In presenting the moral realities of sin and death Milton has moved progressively from the vision of evil—the discovery and exploration of a universe of death, and the recognition of Sin and Death themselves at Hell-gate—to their realization in human terms in Adam and Eve, and finally to a magnified and enhanced image of man's experience of sin and death in the delusions that afflict Hell's angels.

Hell is thus a mode of knowledge; and sin a kind of degenerative disease affecting both sight and appetite. In the course of Milton's epic action, the progressive depravity of the apostate angels—from the godlike to the bestial; from a colony of martial expatriates, entrepreneurs and explorers, architects and philosophers and poets to a society of serpents—is signalized not only by their fading glory but also by the darkening of the mind. Internally and externally they become assimilated to their surroundings, becoming like their "sin and place of doom" increasingly "obscure and foul" (PL IV, lines 835–840). They bear within them the "darkness visible" of Tartarus and the tangible darkness of the abyss: that "palpable obscure" which links the original Chaos with the "palpable darkness" of Pharaoh's kingdom.

With these changes there is a correlative and simultaneous shift from higher modes of perception and cognition to the lower: from the visual experience of evil to the gustatory. In the final transformation-scene, the fallen angels like fallen man are literally as well as metaphorically "tasting death." With these illusions of sight and taste, deceptions of the intellect and the senses, Milton has associated the perversion of the appetite and will. In their uncontrollable craving for the fruit of forbidden knowledge, their insatiable hunger and thirst for unrighteousness, the poet has delineated the same kind of spiritual gluttony that he had portrayed earlier in Eve. Moreover, he portrays it through essentially the same moral and intellectual symbols, the same kind of images, infinitely magnified. The depravity of appetite and will he depicts as morbid and unnatural hunger for delusive and merely apparent goods, a rabid and "hydroptic" craving for evil instead of the love of the Supreme Good.[55] The corruption of the understanding he delineates through its credulous acceptance of evil as good. The early visions and discoveries of Hell's spiritual topography—the early recognitions of evil as evil, and the realities of Sin and Death—have concluded finally in this symbolic metamorphosis into the typical, emblematic shape of evil and the recapitulation of original sin. These epistemological motifs, closely associated as they are with the modes of knowledge left to the fallen angels, reach their climax in the delusive apparition which deceives both sight and taste.[56] At the beginning of the poem, Satan could still recognize evil as evil, could still distinguish between good and evil, and consciously substitute evil for good. At the end of the epic action the devil and his angels have become habituated to this inverse perspective. They are the victims of the same kind of delusion to which they had voluntarily committed themselves earlier, and by which they had voluntarily deceived others. Formerly they had deliberately chosen evil instead of good; now the results of this choice are apparent in its effects on their vision and understanding. They are no longer able to see evil as evil; and evil itself, inevitably, actually looks like the good.

CHAPTER SEVEN

Eyelids of the Morn

> Together both, ere the high Lawns appear'd
> Under the opening eye-lids of the morn,
> We drove a field, and both together heard
> What time the Gray-fly winds her sultry horn. . . .*
>
> *(Lycidas, lines 25–28)*

Commentators on Lycidas have usually traced the origin of Milton's line, "Under the opening eyelids of the Morn," to a marginal reading in the Authorized Version of Job. As several scholars have observed, "the alternative reading for "dawning of the day' [Job iii. 9], offered in the margin as more true to the Hebrew, is 'the eyelids of the morning,'"[1] and in Job xli. 18 [Heb. 41:10 ᷟ] this image occurs in the text itself—"By his neesings a light doth shine, and his eyes are like the eyelids of the morning."[2]

Despite these similarities, however, there is no conclusive proof that the Authorized Version was the source of Milton's phrase. He could have encountered it elsewhere—in the Hebrew text, in numerous Latin and vernacular translations, and in several secular poets. On this point, as in certain other problems involving Milton's reading, the basic issue is not his specific indebtedness to a particular source, but his relationship to a distinct but comprehensive tradition. A brief examination of this tradition from the Vulgate to Lycidas should throw further light both on its Scriptural origin and on its meaning.

Literally the Hebrew phrase *'aphapei shahar* (Hebrew transliterated) means the "eyelids" or "eyelashes" of "morning,"[3] and appears to be related to the verb *uph* ("flicker" or "flutter").[4] As a result of this etymology, the two passages in Job were conventionally interpreted as allusions to the sun's rays, with the double implications of light and swiftness. Schindler's Lexicon Pentaglotton[5] defines the noun *aphapayim* (Hebrew transliterated) as "palpebrae," explains it as a metaphor for the rays of dawn ("Per metaphoram, radij diluculi"), and associates it with the verb *uph* ('*ûp*), signifying "volitare" (to fly or flutter). Castell's Lexicon Heptaglotton[6] similarly derives the Hebrew noun for eyelids from the verb signifying flutter or vibrate and explains this etymology as a reference to their swift movement: "Palpe-

---

The Poetical Works of John Milton, ed. H. C. Beeching (New York, 1935).

brae, à vibratione, & celeri motu, Job. 3.9.c.41–9. *Palpebrae aurorae, ob crispationem radiorum.* . . ."

The literal sense of the Hebrew was sometimes sacrificed in translations. The Septuagint translates both passages in Job as references to the morning star: "kai mē idoi heōsphoron anatellonta" (Greek transliterated.) (Job iii. 9, "& non videat luciferum orientem"), "hoi de ophthalmoi autou eidos Heōsphorou" (Greek transliterated.) (Job xli. 18, "at oculi eius species luciferi").[7] The Vulgate renders the former passage as "surgentis aurorae," but retains the literal meaning in the latter text ("& oculi eius ut palpebrae diluculi"), where the phrase "palpebrae diluculi" is sometimes glossed as signifying "splendores aurorae."[8]

Pagninus' Latin translation[9] preserves the Hebrew sense in *both* passages from Job ("palpebras aurorae") and explains the metaphor in a marginal note as signifying "splendores." In Leo Juda's translation,[10] Job iii is rendered as "nec intueatur palpebras aurorae," and Job xli translated as "eiusque oculi referunt palpebras aurorae." Castalio,[11] on the other hand, sacrifices the metaphor in both passages for the reading "aurorae lumina." Though Sebastian Münster[12] translates Job iii as "primordia aurorae," he points out that the Hebrew word means eyelids and that the "Chaldean," i.e., Aramaic, renders it as rays:

> Hebraica habent,palpebras aurorae: pro quo Chald. interpres vertit, radios aurorae.

He retains the eyelid-image in Job xli ("& oculi eius sunt veluti palpebrae aurorae") and explains this figure as rays of light:

> Sic oculi eius rubent, ut similes esse videantur primis radijs aurorae.

The Junius-Tremellius version[13] retains the Hebrew sense in both instances and calls attention to its figurative nature — as hyperbole in Job xli and as a metaphor for the first rays of the rising sun in Job iii:

> . . . neque vidisset palpebras aurorae . . . i. primum splendorem radiorum ab exorituro sole utrinque in palpebrarum speciem assurgentium: metaphora ab eo qui experigiscitur & palpebras attollit, quocum aurora poëtice comparatur.
> . . . & quidem oculorum ejus, velut palpebrae aurorae . . . hyperbole quae etiam frequens est versibus sequentibus. . . .

Piscator preserves the same literal meaning[14] and explains the phrase not only in terms of the solar rays and the splendor of dawn, but also as an allusion to their swiftness:[15]

> *Palpebras aurorae*] Radios quos spargit sol oriens. Elegans metaphora, propter celeritatem motus.

> Sunt *ut palpebrae aurorae*] Id est,splendent ut aurora.

Abraham Aurelius'[16] poetic "metaphrasis" of Job interprets both passages in terms of the rays of dawn, but does not retain the original eyelid-metaphor:

> . . . nec cernat clara rubentis
> Aurorae eoo quae mittit spicula tractu.

> ·. . . atque oculi lato circum orbe micantes
> Aurorae radios, & solis clara lacessunt
> Spicula.

The dawn-eyelid-metaphor had, moreover, appeared in English translations of the Book of Job long before the Authorized Version. The Wycliffite[17] Bible translates Job xli as "hise iyen *ben* as iyelidis of the morewtid," and a marginal gloss explains this phrase as "briytnesse." In the Geneva Bible[18] a marginal note on Job iii.9 ("the dawning of the daye") cites the Hebrew meaning ("Ebr. the eyeliddes of the morning"), and the original sense is retained in Job xli ("his eyes [are] like the eyelids of the morning"). The Bishops' Bible[19] similarly notes the Hebrew meaning in the marginal comments:

> . . . neither let it see the dawning of the day. . . . The Hebrew speach is, the eye liddes of the morning.
> . . . and his eyes like the morning shine. . . . Or, eieliddes of the morning.

Golding's translation[20] of Calvin's sermons on Job renders iii.9 as "eye liddes of the morning twilight." In the English version of Beza's Job Expounded,[21] the Hebrew phrase is translated as "eyelids of the morning" and explained as a reference to the sun (Job iii.9) — "the day starre, the messenger of light" — or as an allusion (Job xli) to "the golden beames of the morning." Sylvester's Job Triumphant[22] preserves the Hebrew meaning in both references:

> May the Evening Stars be dark: No light returning:
> May it no more see th' Eye-lids of the Morning.

> His Neesings cause a Light, as brightly burning;
> His Eyes are like the Eye-lids of the Morning. . . .

On the other hand, the eyelid-metaphor does not appear in many English Bibles of the early sixteenth century[23] nor in the Douai version of 1609.[24]

Other vernacular translations also preserve the literal meaning of the Hebrew phrase. A marginal note on "l'aube du jour" (Job iii.9) explains that the eyelids of morning are the sun's rays ("Hebr. les paupieres du matin, c'est, les rayons du soleil").[25] Another version renders the same text as "les rayons de l'aube du iour," but translates Job xli.9 as "les paupieres de l'aube du iour."[26] A Spanish Bible[27] published at Basle prefers the eyelid-image in both passages ("los parpados de la mañana," "los parpados del alva") and interprets the latter phrase as "Como el sol." In Luther's version[28] the Hebrew phrase appears as "die augenbrün der Morgenröte" and "die augenliede der Morgenröte." A Dutch translation[29] renders it as "den opganck des dagheraets" and "die oochscheelen der dageraet." Diodati translates it both times as "palpebre dell' alba."[30]

Though Milton probably encountered the eyelid-daybreak-metaphor in Sophocles' Antigone,[31] as well as in the writings of several English poets,[32] the popularity of this image during the English Renaissance was probably due, in large part, to the tradition we have examined. Though it had long been familiar to Latin Christendom through the Vulgate Version of Job xli ("palpebrae diluculi"), it acquired additional emphasis and currency during the Reformation period through the Hebrew text and through Latin and vernacular translations from the Hebrew. Many of these retained the eyelid-image not only in Job xli, but also in Chapter iii.

Moreover, both Milton and his immediate predecessors may have been influenced by the standard interpretation of this image in the Biblical glosses of the Renaissance. Usually it was explained as a reference to the rays of the rising sun, with the additional implications of speed and splendor. This interpretation was not only current at the time of Lycidas, but still standard in Bibles published by Elzevier in 1663 and 1669:

> . . . de oogenleden des dageraets. . . . Soo worden genaemt de stralen der sonne, die in den morgenstont haeruytbreyden, ende openen, eer de sonne opgestaen is; gelijck de oogenleden haer opdoen, eer dat de ooge siet.

> . . . de oogenleden des dageraets. . . . D. als de stralen des dageraets; waer by de oogen van den Leviathan vergeleken worden, om hare grootheyt, roodigheyt, ende klaerheyt.[33]

> . . *les paupieres:* C'est ainsi que se nomment les premiers rayons que le Soleil commence de verser & qui s'épandent çà & là sur les cimes des montagnes avant qu'il se leve; car c'est là comme la premiere ouverture de l'oeil du monde, ainsi que les auteurs profanes appellent le Soleil, & on sçait que les paupieres se doivent ouvrir & hausser avant que l'oeil voye.

> . . . les paupieres de l'aube du jour. . . . C. que ses yeux brillent tellement, qu'ils semblent imiter les premiers rayons du soleil, a cause de leur grandeur, de leur rougeur & de leur clarté. . . . C. sont comme les rayons de l'aurore, ou du soleil, que commençent de paroître immediatement avant son lever.[34]

Against the background of this tradition, Milton's description of "the high lawns" appearing "Under the opening eyelids of the Morn" almost surely refers to the first rays of the sun "qui s'épandent çà & là sur les cimes des montagnes avant qu'il se leve." The imagery depends on the conventional conception of the sun as the "eye" of the day, on the analogy between the solar rays and eyelashes, and on the representation of dusk and dawn as closing[35] or opening eyelids.

In altering his original version ("the *glimmering* eyelids of the Morn") to "*opening*" eyelids,[36] Milton substituted an epithet largely suggestive of motion for one primarily suggestive of light. This emendation serves to stress both the traditional meaning and conventional character of his image. The concept of motion had been inherent in the etymological derivation of the Hebrew *'ap'ap* and Latin *palpebra* from a verb meaning flutter or palpitate. The Elzevier Bibles of 1663 and 1669 were subsequently to explain the imagery of Job in terms of opening eyelids—"la premiere *ouverture* de l'oeil du monde," "de stralen der sonne, die . . . *openen* . . . gelijck de oogenleden haer *opdoen,* eer de ooge siet." Though the epithet "glimmering" has no parallel in known analogues of Milton's eyelid-metaphor, his revised reading bears a close resemblance to images already familiar[37] in the works of Marlowe ("Now, Phoebus, *ope* the eye-lids of the day") and Middleton ("the *opening* Eye-lids of the Morne").

Though Milton's emendation is more *obviously* appropriate to the eyelid-image, the original epithet was, perhaps, more subtle in its use of *double-entendre.* In one sense ("to shine faintly") the word merely refers to the early glow of dawn, but in another sense ("to look or glance with half-closed eyes")[38] it serves to elaborate and accentuate the eyelid-figure.

Like other elements in Lycidas, Milton's eyelid-metaphor is rooted in a dual tradition; it recalls classical as well as Biblical prototypes. Reminiscent of both Greek and Hebrew poetry—of the imagery of Sophocles' Antigone as well as that of the Book of Job—it serves, like Phoebus' digression on fame and St. Peter's diatribe against the "corrupted Clergie," to fuse the sacred and the profane. In its context it preserves the mood and spirit of the pastoral elegy, without sacrificing its Biblical and classical overtones.

CHAPTER EIGHT

Haemony: Etymology and Allegory

> Amongst the rest a small unsightly root,
> But of divine effect, he cull'd me out;
> The leaf was darkish, and had prickles on it,
> But in another Countrey, as he said,
> Bore a bright golden flowre, but not in this soyl:
> Unknown, and like esteem'd, and the dull swayn
> Treads on it daily with his clouted shoon,
> And yet more med'cinal is it then that *Moly*
> That *Hermes* once to wise *Ulysses* gave;
> He call'd it *Haemony*, and gave it me,
> And bad me keep it as of sov'ran use
> 'Gainst all inchantments, mildew blast, or damp
> Or gastly furies apparition. . . .*

> (*A Mask*, lines 629–641)

Recent interpretations of Thyrsis' magic herb have usually employed one or more of several angles of approach: (1) the implications of its name, (2) its similarities with, or differences from, the herb moly, and (3) its function in a larger context—its relation to the theme, dramatic structure, and ethical allegory of Milton's masque. Though all three approaches are necessary for a valid solution of this crux, each has encountered certain inherent difficulties. The third has been especially vulnerable to subjective bias; reading into haemony whatever meaning has best fitted his own conception of the poem's overall structure and sense, the individual critic has been prone to find in the herb the particular concept he had wanted to find. The second has been complicated not only by the variety of meanings commentators have ascribed to moly, but also by critical disagreement as to how far the two plants represent similar or dissimilar ideas. The first approach has hitherto failed to establish a solid basis for the allegory. The only etymology on which scholars are agreed—Keightley's suggestion that haemony was named after "Haemonia or Thessaly, the land of magic"[1]—tells one very little about its allegorical significance. Possible clues to the allegory have been discovered in several alternative etymologies, but these have not yet won general acceptance.

As none of these approaches has been eminently successful in iden-

---

The Poetical Works of John Milton, ed. H. C. Beeching (New York, 1935).

tifying the allegorical referent of Milton's herb, it is hardly surprising
that recent scholarship has challenged not only the abuse of the allegorical method, but the method itself. Thus Adams correctly observes that
"an important reason for Milton's introduction of haemony is not allegorical at all; it has to do with the demands of his story."[2] Arthos
prefers a magical to an allegorical interpretation: "It seems that the
generally universal failure to demonstrate that the *Mask* is an allegory
depends on the inability to establish the significance of an herb, or a
potion, or a wand. But if the central conflict is regarded as a magical
one, the instruments of magic would by definition be without significance. . . . What seems to be true is that all of these things—magic dust,
an enchanted seat, a wand, haemony, and the rest—are meant to be
mysterious, not for whatever purposes concealment may have in allegory, but for the purpose of emphasizing the strangeness by which the
spirit controls nature. Magic has no laws, and the power of these things
depends on magic."[2]

In actuality, however, the element of magic and romance in *Comus*
does not provide a valid argument against an allegorical interpretation.
In "Il Penseroso" Milton recognizes an allegorical element in the
romantic tales "Of Forests, and inchantments drear, / Where more is
meant than meets the ear." How widespread this opinion was during
the Renaissance is evident from its major epics and romances—the
Orlando Innamorato, the *Orlando Furioso*, the *Italia Liberata*, the
Gerusalemme Liberata — not to mention *The Faerie Queene*. In all of these
works the magical elements are rationalized through the moral allegory. Berni urges his readers to look for the doctrine concealed under
the enchantments and monsters of the poem:

> Questi Draghi fatati, questi incanti,
> Questi Giardini, e libri, e corni, e cani,
> Ed huomini salvatichi, e Giganti,
> E fiere, e monstri, ch'hanno visi umani,
> Son fatti per dar pasto agli ignoranti,
> Ma voi, ch'avete gl'intelletti sani
> Mirate la dottrina, che s'asconde
> Sotto queste coperte alte, e profonde.

The enchanted water ("acqua incantata") of the "river of oblivion," he
explains, really symbolizes the psychological quality variously known as
passion, opinion, affection ("affetto"), or impression. The garden represents the world, and the woman who gives Orlando a book so that he
can pass through it safely signifies prudence. The ass, the bull, the
dragon, and the giant he encounters there symbolize "I varj vizj, e le
fatiche, e' guai" which are within the world. The chain under the tables
represents the punishment of the people given to gluttony ("ch'al ven-
tre si son date"). The two female monsters—"quella Fauna, e quell'altra

Serena"—stand for innumerable vain pleasures ("Mille altri van piacer"), which show a fair face but terminate in poison and filth. Underneath these "fantastiche chimere" there is a hidden ("nascosto") allegory.[4]

Ariosto likewise reminds his readers that the strange things he is describing are not lies, and explicitly identifies Angelica's magic ring as reason. It possesses the power to render all enchantments vain, for it can detect the ugly reality behind the beautiful appearance and expose dissimulation and fraud:

> Chi l'anello d'Angelica, o più tosto
> Che havesse quel de la ragion, potria
> Veder'à tutti il viso, che nascosto
> Da fintione, e d'arte non saria.
> Tal ci par bello, e buono, che deposto
> Il liscio, brutto e rio forse parria.[5]

This ethical approach to the magical elements in Ariosto's romance was carried still further by allegorical commentaries on the text. Thus in Valgrisi's edition, the celestial virtue which enables Angelica's ring to "far vano ogni incanto" is interpreted as the divine aid which enables reason to conquer the senses and truth to overcome appearance and falsehood ("quanto benignamente esse virtù celesti aiutino che vuol valersene, à far che la ragion vinca i sensi, & il vero, l'apparente, e'l falso"). Similarly, Alcina's palace, where the sorceress' lovers are transformed into plants and beasts, indicates "quanto le lascivie habbian forza di privar d'ogni forma di persona umana, non che de la ragione, & dell' intelletto, che si da loro in preda."[6]

The allegorical character of the magical elements in Trissino's poem is evident not only from the name of his sorceress (Acratia), but from those of her brother (Faulo, i.e., *phaulos*, "mean" or "bad"), her giants (Dolone and Crisonio), and other characters involved in the Acratia-episode (Areta, Sinesia, Palladio, Metanea, and Ligridonia).[7] Spenser's magicians—Archimago, Duessa, Acrasia, Busyrane—symbolize hypocrisy, falsehood, incontinence, and tyrannic love. Tasso's "two magicians, Ismen and Armida," are allegorized as "two devilish temptations which do lay snares for two Powers of the Soul"—that which "seeketh to deceive with false belief the virtue . . . opinative" and that which "layeth siege to the power of our desires"—and the "enchantments" of the haunted forest signify "deceiving allurements" and "deceitful enticements" which dissuade from virtue and persuade to vice. Whereas Ismeno's enchantments represent "the Errors of Opinion," Armida's spells signify the errors "of the Appetite." Accordingly, when Rinaldo serves Armida, he denotes "anger not governed by reason," but when "he disenchanteth the wood," he symbolizes "anger directed by reason."[8]

In the Renaissance poetic tradition, then, "the instruments of magic" are far from being "without significance." On the contrary, both text and commentary emphasize their allegorical import. In most instances the enchantments themselves represent the illusions of the senses, the passions, or false opinion, and the particular agent or talisman which dispels them is generally interpreted as reason or prudence, aided as a rule by divine power. The fact that "all of these things — magic dust, an enchanted seat, a wand, haemony, and the rest — are meant to be mysterious" does not, as Arthos has argued, preclude an allegorical interpretation. When Thyrsis declares that the tales of "dire *Chimeras* and enchanted Isles" are "not vain or fabulous," as the ignorant suppose, he seems to be echoing the warnings of Berni and Ariosto; there is a true moral signfiicance hidden beneath these myths. It seems probable, therefore, that the magical elements of *Comus,* like those of the Italian epics and romances, mean more "than meets the ear" — that haemony, like Angelica's ring, has an allegorical content.

If there is considerable justification for seeking an allegorical significance in Milton's magic herb, there is an equal need to curb the excesses of the allegorical approach. As part of the responsibility for these excesses lies with the failure of the etymological method to provide a definitive key to the allegory, it seems appropriate to reexamine the various derivations already proposed and to ascertain their relative value for interpreting Milton's symbolism. Despite the obvious difficulties presented by the etymological approach, it is not out of place in a Renaissance allegory. From Plato to Conti, it had been frequently employed for the allegorical interpretation of myth, and it is significant that the name *moly* had been etymologized in terms of *mōlos* (struggle or contest).[9]

Three types of derivation have been proposed for Thyrsis' herb: (1) from a geographical placename, (2) from some form of the Greek word for *blood (haima),* and (3) from a psychological quality (the Greek adjective *haimōn, skillful).* To these one should add a further, but less plausible possibility — a derivation from *haimos (thorn).*[10] Though the first provides the most probable explanation of the name, the third offers, I think, the most satisfactory clue to its symbolism.

1. To the first category belong the derivation from "*Haemonia,* an old name of Thessaly, the land of magic in classical writers,"[11] and the parallel with the "grassie bancks of Haemony" in Spenser's *Astrophel.* In Miss Watson's opinion, Spenser uses the word *Haemony* "as a synonym for Thessalia or Arcadia,"[12] but even this is by no means certain. Haemonia is not a usual synonym for Arcadia, and it seems not improbable that Spenser, unlike Milton, may be referring not to Thessaly, but to the river Haemon."[13] A third geographical derivation — the sugges-

tion that the name haemony contains an allusion to Thrace and thus recalls the charm of the Thracian physician in Plato's *Charmides*[14]—has little evidence to support it. As the name Haemonia was usually applied only to Thessaly or to Ephesus,[15] the closest verbal link between Thrace and haemony appears to be the name of a Thracian mountain—Mount Haemus.[16] A fourth possibility—that haemony may refer to Ephesus, noted for its temple to Diana, and thus symbolizes chastity—is less probable than the accepted view that the name simply means "the Thessalian plant."[17] Though this interpretation throws little light on its symbolic meaning, a rather tenuous basis for an ethical or religious allegory can be found in Milton's earlier allusion to the "Haemonio . . . succo" whereby Medea had rejuvenated the aged Aeson.[18] Haemony could, therefore, with some justification be regarded as a symbol for the *cause* of regeneration or sanctification, and its "divine effect," accordingly, could conceivably be identified with regeneration itself— "that change operated by the Word and the Spirit, whereby *the old man being destroyed,* the inward man is regenerated by God after his own image, in all the faculties of his mind." As the cause of this spiritual effect, haemony could possess several possible meanings: (1) the Word or the Spirit, whereby this change is "operated," (2) "the death and resurrection of Christ," which constitutes the "external cause of regeneration or sanctification," or (3) faith, which is "an instrumental and assisting cause in its gradual progress."[19]

The association of Haemonian herbs with Aeson's rejuvenation could, however, suggest a purely ethical, as well as a religious, interpretation of haemony. In Horologgi's opinion, Medea signifies persuasion, and Aeson's rejuvenation symbolizes his renewed virtue; "Esone ringiovanito per opra di Medea significa l'huomo che si spoglia de i vitij, ne' quali era già invecchiato, e ringiovanisce nella virtù dando orecchie alla persuasione."[20] Conti equates Medea with counsel ("est enim ipsa Medea *mēdos*, consilium"), and Aeson with prudence. She is the daughter of the sun ("consideratio sive prudentia") and Idyia ("cognitio"), and the fables concerning her were designed to exhort us "ad animi moderationem, & ad rectam institutionem vitae." Prudence is the medicine of the mind, and for this reason Jason ("cùm medicum sive medicinam significare possit, *apo tou lasthai* à medendo dictus") takes Medea with him:

> quid hoc significat? *quòd qui medicinam animo suo sit adhibiturus, quae prudentia est,* ut vir bonus, & sanae mentis, & prudens efficiatur, omnia reliqua parvifaciet vel carissima. Qui enim voluptatum desiderium, è quo natus est, non neglexerit, qui parum honestam & effraenatam appetantiam non discerpserit, ille nihil admirabile, nihilque gloriosum potest committere: quare dicta est Medea filios & fratrem discerpsisse, & patriam reliquisse, ut Iasonem sequeretur.

As Medea signifies counsel, prudence, moderation of mind—the true medicine of the soul and "antidotum ... adversus voluptates impuras"[21]—the name haemony, so closely associated with Medea's herbs ("Aemoniâ radices valle resectas") could appropriately symbolize prudence or temperance. Like Medea's art, as conceived by Conti and Horologgi, Milton's herb is "med'cinal" for the mind, rather than the body.

The chief advantages of this interpretation are: (1) that its etymological basis is the soundest and most widely-accepted of the various derivations of haemony—the derivation from Thessaly, (2) that it is consistent with Milton's use of the adjective "Haemonios" in the Second Elegy, (3) that it lends additional support to the recent conception of the masque in terms of the "regeneration of the soul" through temperance and philosophical instruction, and (4) that it accords with the conventional explanations of moly as temperance or prudence. At the same time it presents several difficulties. In the first place, it is by no means certain that Milton had the rejuvenation of Aeson by Haemonian herbs specifically in mind. Secondly, the Medea-myth was subject to a pejorative interpretation; according to Conti, "Haec dicta est senes nonnullos iuventuti restituisse per herbas & ignem, quia in sui desiderium vel senes attraxerit artificiosé, feceritque ut tanquam iuvenes imprudentes & impudentes essent."[22] Thirdly, an allusion to the Aeson-myth seems out of context, in view of the brothers' extreme youth.

The derivation of haemony from Haemonia provides, therefore, only a tenuous clue to the allegory.

2. Nor does the derivation from *haima (blood)* prove a reliable index to the allegory. The evocative but elusive symbolism of blood—so rich in a variety of religious and literary associations—is altogether too ambiguous to provide a clear solution to this crux. As LeComte has remarked apropos of an alternative derivation, it "explains an obscurity by an obscurity."[23]

In Coleridge's opinion, haemony is a compound of *haima* and *oinos*; the name refers to "the blood-wine of the sacrament," and the plant accordingly symbolizes "redemption by the Cross."[24] In this instance the name has been mangled to fit the Procrustean demands of the allegory. The apparent inference concerning the plant's symbolic meaning would have been justified if Coleridge had based it on a probable etymology. In actuality, however, not only is the derivation itself improbable, but it seems to have been invented for the express purpose of providing evidence for Coleridge's religious interpretation. It is essentially manufactured evidence, and the inference he appears to draw from it is only apparent. This ingenious coinage, minted in the

Romantic imagination, does not provide a sound basis for the interpretation of Milton's allegory.

The *N.E.D.* suggested a possible derivation from *haimōnios (blood-red)*, but, in LeComte's opinion, this does not have "the slightest appropriateness."[25] This etymology could, however, provide limited support for the interpretation of haemony as a symbol of charity, which had been traditionally signified by this color. Cesare Ripa's *Iconologia* invests the image of "Carità" with a red garment because this is the color of blood: "Il vestimento rosso, per la simiglianza che hà co'l colore del sangue, mostra che sino all' effusione d'esso si stende la vera carità, secondo il testimonio di S. Paolo . . . : però la Sposa nella Cantica amava questo colore nel suo diletto."[26] This is, of course, very conventional color symbolism, and the fact that haemony bears a "golden flower" in another country does not entirely invalidate this interpretation. Milton was perfectly aware that gold may be "ruddy" and that Shakespeare had described Duncan's blood as "golden." Moreover, the color yellow was also associated with charity; Spenser's Charissa (*FQ,* i.x.30) is arrayed "in yellow robes."

It is significant, moreover, that the name *Haemonia* had been applied to another plant specifically because of its blood-red color. Though the plant is very different from Milton's and throws no light on its allegorical significance, this parallel provides the only unmistakable precedent for Milton's use of the word haemony as the generic name of a specific plant. He could have encountered this use of the name *Haemonia* in Athenaeus' *Deipnosophists,* in Eustathius' commentary on the *Odyssey,* or in Henry Estienne's *Thesaurus Graecae Linguae.* Athenaeus had described a species of fig growing on the island of Paros and called "blood red" *haimōnia* because of its ruddy color.[27] According to Eustathius, "hōs de polla edē sykōn, dēlousin hoi palaioi en hois kai haimōnia ta en tēi nēsōi Parōi, klēthenta houtō dia to erythrōdes."[28] Estienne cites the same etymology: "*Haimōnia syka,* Ficium genus in Paro insula, ita dictorum ob ruborem, inquit Athenaeus lib. 3, & post eum Eustathius: qui quum tradunt ita dicta *dia to erythrōdes,* id est ob ruborem, ab *haima* derivari innuunt, quasi dicerent *dia to haimatoeides chrōma,* id est ob sanguineum colorem. Eadem & Lydia vocata scribit ibidem Athenaeus."[29]

Thus the name *Haemonia* really possessed *two* botanical associations. It had been applied to Medea's magical herbs and to the Parian (or Lydian) fig. In the first instance its significance is purely geographical, and it does not denote a specific plant. In the second case it distinguishes a particular botanical species and derives its meaning from the color of blood. If Milton's haemony resembles the former in its magical character, it also resembles the latter as the generic name of a particular plant. Though it is possible that, like Athenaeus' *Haemonia syka*, Thyrsis' herb may signify the color of blood and accordingly symbolize charity or modesty,[30] Milton's description of the plant contains no clear suggestion of blood or of the quality of redness. This etymology, therefore, is also inadequate as a basis for the analysis of its symbolism.

Le Comte's suggestion that Milton recalled "the bloody origin of haemony's prototype"—the herb moly—from the blood of the giant Pikoloos and accordingly gave his plant a name suggestive of the Greek adjective *haimōn*, "derived . . . from *haima*,"[31] has much to recommend it. It is appropriate in the context of Milton's explicit comparison between the two herbs and their obvious similarities in appearance and function. Nevertheless in itself this derivation provides scant foundation for a definitive interpretation of the allegory. Between the root-meaning (bloody) and its allegorical correlative (divine grace) there is an intervening chain of inferences which is not altogether convincing. The conclusion that haemony represents "the grace given those who are virtuous" rests largely on the assumption that the herb symbolizes "the Saviour's blood."[32] But the chief evidence for this "connection between haemony and Christ's blood" is the questionable hypothesis that Milton's plant is Christ's thorn, a species of rhamnus or paliuros believed to be the thorn-bush used for the crown of thorns.[33] In actuality, it seems more likely that Milton is not describing a real plant at all and that haemony—like Fame in *Lycidas*, "Immortal Amarant" in *Paradise Lost*, and probably Homer's moly—has a purely allegorical significance. The very passage LeComte cites from Eustathius has been taken as evidence that moly is not "eine wirkliche Pflanze," but "rein allegorisch zu verstehen sei."[34]

3. Though the *N.E.D.* suggested a derivation from *haimōn (skillful)*, this has been rejected as both inappropriate and obscure, "for no one is certain just what this *haimōn* (which makes a single appearance in the *Iliad*) means."[25] This uncertainty, however, does not appear in many of the older Greek lexicons available to Milton, which usually define this adjective in terms of knowledge. To apply their conception of this term to Milton's haemony may, therefore, serve rather to illuminate an ambiguity than to explain "an obscurity by an obscurity."

According to the *Iliad*, skillful (*haimōn*) Scamandrios had learned the art of hunting from Artemis. In his commentary on this passage, Eustathius defines this adjective as *epistemōn (wise, prudent, skilled)* and equates it with *daimōn* or *daēmōn (knowing, experienced, skilled)* and *memathekos (learned):*

> Skamandrion tina legei hypo Menelaou pesein thērēs haimona, ēgoun epistēmona, esthlon thērētēra, ekēbolias kekasmenon, hou edidaxen Artemis . . . esti de haimōn hoionei daimōn ētoi daēmōn, toutesti memathēkōs. hou adaēmōn, hoion: machēs adaēmoni phōti.[36]

Hesychius similarly defines *haimona* as *epistēmona* and *empeiron*.[37] In the *Etymologicon Magnum*, *Haimōn* is explained as *ho empeiros (experienced, skilled)*, and the *Iliad (Haimona thērēs)* is cited as an example. The word *haimōn* is regarded as a variant of *daimōn* and defined in terms of knowing and learning:

> Esti daiō, to gignōskō ē manthanō, ex hou [daskalos, kai didaskalos: kai daialos: kai pleonasmōi tou D, diadalos, ho epistēmōn: kai] daimōn, ho autodidaktos: kai kata apobolēn tou D, haimōn.[38]

Milton could have encountered the same definition in the Renaissance lexicons of Budé and Estienne. According to the former's *Lexicon Graeco-Latinum*, "Est autem *haimōn* idem quod *epistēmōn, empeiros,* id est, peritus: fit autem à *daimon* literae detractatione."[39] Estienne's *Thesaurus* declares that "*Haimōn*, aphaeresi *tou d* putatur factum ex *daimon*, idem significante quod *daimon*, Gnarus, Peritus. ut Hesych. quoque *haimon* exp. *epistemona, empeiron,* respiciens ad *haimona thērēs* apud Homer. Iliad (Book V) v. 49."[40]

Haemony, then, carries the sense of *daēmon* and *epistēmon;* the person who possesses it is *gnarus* and *peritus.* As *haimon* had been consistently defined by synonyms meaning wise, prudent, knowing, and instructed, the name of the herb apparently signifies wisdom, prudence, knowledge, or instruction. The chief merit of this derivation is that, unlike the alternative etymologies which have been proposed, it reveals the allegorical significance in the literal meaning of the name. In the case of most alternative derivations there is a marked gap between the suggested meaning of the name and the allegorical significance of the plant—a gap which the critic can bridge only by a perilous stretch of the imagination. The proposed derivations of haemony from words meaning *Thessalian, bloody,* or *blood-red* are legitimate conjectures as to what the name itself literally signifies, but they do not in themselves explain what the herb symbolizes on the allegorical level. Accordingly, the critic has been forced back upon his own resources, compelled to base his allegorical interpretation on one of the many tenuous and ambiguous associations of Thessaly and blood. As the foundation for his allegory, he has had to rely on the *connotations* of his proposed etymology, rather than on its denotation. This gap between etymon and symbol— between the literal meaning of the name and the allegorical significance of the plant—disappears, however, if one accepts the *N.E.D.*'s suggestion that haemony is derived from *haimōn*.

[II]

Though it has been argued that this etymology has not "the slightest appropriateness,"[41] there are several factors which make this interpretation of haemony seen highly appropriate in its context. In the first place, the Attendant Spirit describes haemony's effects specifically in terms of knowledge:

> . . . by this means
> I knew the foul enchanter though disguis'd.

On the other hand, the Lady, who does not have the protection of this herb, is deceived "with blear illusion" and "false presentments" through "the virtue of [Comus'] Magic dust." This derivation lends additional support to recent interpretations of haemony in terms of ethical or theological doctrine—as 'lofty moral wisdom," the "Christian and Platonic doctrine of virtue," "Christian philosophical knowledge," and "divine philosophy."[42] The allegorical significance of haemony, according to this interpretation, is very similar to that of other magical talismans and antidotes against enchantment—Angelica's ring (reason), Orlando's book (prudence), and the herb moly (reason, prudence, erudition, Hellenic philosophy, divine philosophy, and education).[43]

As *haimōn* and *daimōn* were believed to have stemmed from the same word for *knowing*,[44] it is especially fitting that the spirit who bestows the herb of knowledge—haemony—should have been described in the Cambridge MS. as a *daemon*. There is thus a verbal connection between the name of the plant and the quality of the ethereal being who imparts it to the brothers. According to Plato's *Cratylus*, these spirits were called *daimones* "because they were wise and knowing (*daēmones*)."[45] Hierocles' commentary on the *Golden Versus of Pythagoras* explains that certain intermediate spirits are sometimes called "good daemons" because they are blessed and versed in the divine laws ("periti delle leggi divine") and sometimes known as angels because they declare and announce the norm for the blessed life. They are endowed with "perpetua dottrina, & scienza."[46] This etymology recurs in Renaissance lexicons. Budé defines *Daimon* as "deus, genius, larva, ingenium, sapiens: quasi *daemon, i. sciens*,"[47] and Estienne likewise derives *Daimon* from *daemon*, which he defines as "Doctus, id est Gnarus, Peritus."[48]

The context of the word *haimona* in the *Iliad* invests it with certain supernatural associations which are consonant with those of haemony. Scamandrios (who is called *skilled —haimona*) has been divinely taught; his instructress was none other than Artemis, the goddess of the chase. Eustathius lays considerable stress on the divine origin of his knowledge and terms him *theosophon* ("divinâ sapientia praeditum").[49] Haemony itself—a herb bestowed by a celestial spirit and bestowing a "divine effect"—could appropriately symbolize "the wisdom of God" (*theou sophia*).[50] The divine associations of Homer's *haimōn* seem to reinforce the recent interpretation of Milton's plant in terms of re-vealed truth—*divine* philosophy.

Sixthly, this etymology seems all the more appropriate in view of the fact that Lawes himself played the part of the Attendant Spirit. If (as Hanford believes) this musician had "certainly" been "employed in [the] instruction" of the Egerton children,[51] it is especially fitting that they should receive at his hands the herb denoting knowledge or skill.

[III]

Though this derivation seems to provide the most satisfactory clue to both the literal meaning and the allegorical significance of Milton's herb, it does not in itself constitute a complete answer. It informs us that haemony signifies knowledge, but precisely what kind of knowl-edge this is one must gather from its description and context. The fact that it flowers "in another Countrey" makes a religious interpretation seem virtually inescapable, and Professor Jayne is surely correct in inferring that it represents Christian wisdom. The contrast between the dark and prickly leaf it bears on "this soil" and the golden bloom it displays in another land may, indeed, be emblematic of St. Paul's an-tithesis between the partial and obscure knowledge attainable on earth and its perfection in Heaven ("For now we see through a glass *darkly*; but then face to face: now I know in part; but then shall I know even as also I am known"). As John Smith, the Cambridge Platonist, observes on this passage, "S. *Paul* distinguisheth *the knowledge* of *this life . . .* and of *the life to come:* that *now we see di' esoptrou in a glass,* which is continually sullied and darkened, while we look into it, by the breathing of our Animal fansies, passions, and imaginations upon it; and *en ainigmati darkly: but* we shall see *then prosōpon pros prosōpon face to face. . . .* And in the like manner does a Greek Philosopher compare these two sorts of Knowledge which the Soul hath of God in this life and in that to come, "Tous epistēmonikous logous mythous hēgēsetai synousa tōi patri kai synestiōmenē tēn alētheian tou ontos, kai en augēi katharai," *The Soul will reckon all this knowledge of God which we have here by way of Science but like a fable or parable, when once it is in conjunction with the Father, feasting upon Truth it self, and beholding God in the pure raies of his own Divinity.*"[52] Haemony's "darkish" leaf is thus an appropriate symbol of the obscur-ity of our knowledge on "this soil" in comparison with the "bright golden flow'r" of the Beatific Vision. Its "prickles" emphasize the diffi-culty and "labour" involved in the pursuit of "Heav'nly Truth," for the path to Heaven is proverbially "steep and thorny."[53] The fact that it is "Unknown, and like esteem'd" by the "dull swain" is also appropriate,

for the multitude prefer "the broad way and the green," and to pursue
Divina Scientia — Theology — one must forsake the "volgare schiera."[54]
A Christian interpretation of haemony is consistent with its characteristics as Thyrsis describes them.[55]

The derivation from *haimōn* does not preclude other etymological
interpretations, and it is possible that Milton may have intended to
suggest other meanings in addition to the root-meaning, *knowledge*. If
haemony signifies *Christian* knowledge (as recent scholarship has proposed), the ideas of regeneration, charity, and "the Saviour's blood,"
suggested by alternative etymologies, would tend to reinforce this religious interpretation. Nevertheless, these inferences are extremely
dubious and introduce an unnecessary complication into a relatively
simple symbol. We can say with reasonable certitude that haemony
means knowledge; to superimpose additional meanings is to court
obscurity again.

[APPENDIX]

Haemony and Christian Moly.

The mysterious herb, "more med'cinal . . . than that *Moly* That *Hermes*
once to wise *Ulysses* gave,"[1] has not infrequently been interpreted in
terms of Christian symbolism.[2] In a recent article LeComte suggested
that the name "haemony" referred to Christ's blood and that Milton
had in mind a species of Rhamnus or Paliuros known as "Christ's
Thorn." "It is a fascinating assumption . . . ," he concluded, "that the
Homeric plant was subtly exalted in Milton's mind or (rather) fused
with the conception of another and more glorious plant. The very
word 'haemony' can be viewed as ingeniously exemplifying this blend
of two worlds, classical and Christian."[3]

If one accepts this essentially Christian conception of "haemony,"
Milton would appear to have deliberately contrasted the Christian
antidote to sensual vice with its pagan predecessor, symbolizing this
ethical antithesis through two sorts of magic herb. He had, however,
been anticipated by Guillaume Budé. In *De Transitu Hellenismi ad Christianismum*, Budé had drawn a similar distinction between "moly
Homericum" (representing Greek philosophical doctrine) and "moly
nostrum" its Christian equivalent (the supernatural wisdom which
proposed the Gospel as a rule and Christ's cross as an ethical norm).

In the opinion of learned men (Budé declared) Homer intended the herb moly as a symbol for the doctrine of philosophy. For it possesses the power to reform the brutish and degenerate morals of human beings and restore them to their human nature. If so much can be said of Greek philosophy (which was the invention of mortal men), how much more appropriately may we refer this symbol to the divine discipline of our religion? For "our moly" springs from the wells of heavenly wisdom, whereas Homer's moly sprang only from the earth:[4]

> Sub nomine autem molyos herbae Homerus philosophiae doctrinam significasse symbolicè creditur à doctissimis. Cuius vim eam esse, ut volunt arbitratus est ille vir mortalium ingeniosissimus, eamque facultatem,mores ut hominum degeneres & efferatos aut veterinarios factos, atque pecuarios, sibi tandem illa, naturaeque humanae restitueret. Id quod si de Hellenica philosophia dictum est, quae mortalium revera inventum fuit, quanto nos congruentius id tribuere divinae disciplinae potuimus? Inter moly enim nostrum & moly Homericum, cùm plurimum tum hoc referet, quòd illud è puteis sapientiae coelestis: hoc è terra effoditur, humanisque inventis. Quare plus est oxymoriae in vita & moribus Hellenismi philosophiae, quàm verae solidaeque sapientiae. Ad hominem verò philosophum perficiendum, qui ad regulam evangelicam, ad normam (ut sic dicam) atque perpendiculum crucis dominicae eiusdemque savatoriae [*sic*] respondeat. . . .

Regardless of whether Milton got his "cue" from Budé, the fact that both writers apparently exploited the antithesis between Homeric and Christian moly is itself significant. Living in an uneasy tension between two worlds, classical and Christian, the Renaissance humanist found himself enforced to evaluate and, when possible, to reconcile them. Usually he preferred to adapt the idiom and aesthetic values of antiquity, to the moral values and spiritual content of Christianity. Budé expressed the contrast between Hellenism and Christianity through a symbol derived from the *Odyssey.* Milton adopted the same symbol to express essentially the same antithesis.

Dalila, Ulysses, and Renaissance Allegorical Tradition

> ... I know thy trains
> Though dearly to my cost, thy ginns, and toyls;
> Thy fair enchanted cup, and warbling charms
> No more on me have power, their force is null'd,
> So much of Adders wisdom I have learn't
> To fence my ear against thy sorceries.*
>
> (SA, lines 932–937)

In rejecting Dalila's blandishments, Samson asserts his immunity in terms reminiscent of classical mythology:

> Thy fair enchanted cup, and warbling charms
> No more on me have power, their force is null'd,
> So much of Adder's wisdom I have learn't
> To fence my ear against thy sorceries.

Though the 'enchanted cup' has been generally recognized as an allusion to the Circe myth, there has been less certainty in the interpretation of the 'warbling charms'. The phrase was often regarded as a reference to the Sirens, but, in Verity's opinion, it may allude merely to the 'spells spoken over [Circe's] cup at its brewing'.[1] The context of Milton's line, however, would appear to support the former interpretation. Samson has learned to turn a deaf ear to Dalila's persuasions, to 'fence' his 'ear' against her 'sorceries'. The idea of safety in deafness belongs properly to the story of the Sirens rather than to the legend of Circe. Whereas the herb moly sufficed to protect Odysseus against the latter, he was compelled to 'fence' the ears of his crew with wax[2] in order to shield them from the 'warbling charms' of the Sirens. Dalila's 'warbling charms' and Samson's metaphorical deafness are an apparent allusion to the myth of Odysseus and the Sirens.

Milton's 'fair enchanted cup, and warbling charms' is strongly reminiscent of Horace's *Sirenum voces et Circae pocula* (*Epist.* I, ii, 23) though in the interest of decorum Milton has suppressed these direct allusions to classical fable. As in the Chorus's earlier reference to the

*The Poetical Works of John Milton, ed. H. C. Beeching (New York, 1935).

Atlas myth (150), he prefers to introduce his allusions to Gentile legend with deliberate caution, through indirect suggestion rather than explicit statement.

Critics have frequently overlooked the close relationship between Renaissance allegorizations of the Ulysses myth and Milton's characterization of Dalila. The latter's proficiency in the arts of the *meretrix*, her appeal to the delights of the senses, her flattery and deceit, link her with the mythical temptresses of Odysseus as Renaissance mythographers had conceived them. For the full significance of Milton's Horatian echo and its bearing on the role of Dalila and Samson's 'bondage' to her, one may examine the Renaissance interpretation of Circe and the Sirens, as exemplified by Conti and Alciati.

The importance of this parallel lies not only in the apparent imitation of a single line, but also in the close analogy between the immediate contexts of the two verses. Both involve the theme of moral slavery to a loose woman. After mentioning 'the Sirens' songs and Circe's cups', Horace points a moral equally applicable to Milton's hero:

> quae si cum sociis stultus cupidusque bibisset,
> sub domina meretrice fuisset turpis et excors,
> vixisset canis immundus vel amica luto sus.

Just as Odysseus refuses to 'become the shapeless and witless vassal of a harlot mistress', so Samson likewise declines to 'live uxorious to thy will In perfet thraldom' (945).[3] The *meretrix*-label, which Horace applies to Circe, is conventional among Renaissance mythographers. Alciati's emblem of the sorceress (no. 76) bears the motto *Cavendum à meretricibus,* and the accompanying verses refer to the 'harlot named Circe' (*illustri meretricem nomine Circe*). Claude Mignault's commentary explains that by this *figmento effingitur meretricis & libidinis foedae typus* and quotes the pertinent lines from Horace's *Epistle.*[4] The same interpretation had also been applied to the Sirens. The explanatory verses to Alciati's Emblem no. 115 observe that *est doctis cum meretrice nihil;* and Mignault adds:

> Revera meretrices fuere, ut tradunt Servius & Palaephatus. . . . Ad hanc fabulam alludens D. Hieronymus, ait in Epistola quadam: Et nos ad patriam festinantes, mortiferos Sirenum cantus surda debemus aure transire.[5]

The *meretrix*-epithet is equally applicable to Samson's 'deceitful Concubine'—'unclean, unchaste' (527, 321). Milton refers elsewhere to her 'Harlot-lap' (*Paradise Lost*, IX, 1060) and 'strumpet flatteries' (*Reason of Church Government,* conclusion).

There is, moreover, an additional parallel between Dalila's appeal to the 'delights' of the 'senses' (916) and allegorical interpretations of the allurements of Circe and the Sirens. All three cases involve the depraving effects of the *vita voluptuosa*. Samson indicts Dalila for her 'lust' (837) and lasciviousness (536) and condemns the 'venereal trains' of 'pleasure and voluptuous life' whereby she had ensnared him (532). Mignault quotes Erasmus's explanation of the Circe myth in terms of *turpibus affectibus* and Plutarch's opinion that *mulieres, quae amoris poculis & veneficiis viros captant, voluptateque in suam potestatem redigunt, stupidos eos, amentes & depravatos vitae socios deinceps habent.*[6] Explaining Horace's line (*Sirenum voces et Circae pocula*) as a reference to *voluptate turpi*, he also cites Synesius's conception of the Sirens as *voluptates sensum oblectantes, quae eos perdant qui ipsarum cantui & blanditijs aurem praebuerunt.*[7] Conti likewise interprets Circe as *libido* and *voluptates* and explains the Sirens as *voluptates, & earum titillationes*, to whose enticements the wise man must stop up his ears:

> Si quis igitur calamitates complures, & aerumnas multas devitare voluerit, is ad voluptates illegitimas, & ad turpia humanae vitae lenocinia ad Ulyssis exemplum aures obturet opus est. . . .

Dalila's appeal to 'leisure and domestic ease' (917) has a classical analogue in the Horatian conception of the Siren as Idleness (*improba Siren desidia; Sat.* II, iii, 14) — an interpretation echoed by both Conti and Mignault.[9] Similarly, her 'flattering prayers and sighs' (392) are paralleled by Conti's explanation of the Sirens as *adulatorum voces*,[10] and Mignault's statement *quod blanditiis illiciat*. If Dalila is 'false' and 'fallacious' (320, 749), she shares these qualities with her classical analogues. Milton characterizes Circe as *malefida* (Elegy I, 87), and Mignault refers to the *fallaci & captioso Sirenum cantu.*[11]

Like Dalila, the Sirens are a 'specious Monster' (230) and an accomplished 'snare' (230, 532, 931-2). Because of their hybrid nature, the 'monster' label was conventional. According to the verses on Alciati's emblem,

> Illicium est mulier quae in piscem desinit atrum,
> Plurima quod secum monstra libido vehit.

Mignault quotes similar lines:

> Sic blandas vocisque notas, & carmina vicit;
> Sic tandem exitio monstra canora dedit[12]

and Conti includes the same concept in his definition:

> Sirenes & ipsae periculosa hominibus monstra propter cantus suavitatem, dictae sunt ita cantilenis navigantes homines demulcere, ut in profundissimum somnum inducerent; quos postea ita sopitos in mare deiiciebant ac necabant: excogitabant enim ex omnibus cantilenis, quas pro cuiusque ingenio iucundiores fore putabant.[13]

The 'snare' label is likewise traditional. Mignault observes that

> Quamplurimas certè calamitates ex libidine proficisci nemo nescit: tamen eius tres sunt praecipuae illecebrae. siquidem aut visu, aut cantu, aut commercio capiuntur, & in turpis amoris pedicas illaqueantur humani animi. . . .[4]

In Conti's opinion, *dictae sunt . . . Sirenes, quasi cathenae, quia allectos vincirent in amore.*[15]

Like the Sirens, Dalila plies the 'wonted arts' of the *meretrix* (the 'arts of every woman false like thee', 748–9), lulls her victim to sleep, brings to him to 'shipwreck' (192–200, 1044–1045), and despoils him of his most precious possessions in his sleep. Conti had described how the Sirens brought *navigantes homines . . . in profundissimum somnum* and afterwards *sopitos in mare deiiciebant.* Horologgi's 'Annotationi' on Anguillara's version of *Le Metamorfosi di Ovidio* similarly explained how these *meretrici,* the Sirens:

> hanno voci e canti soavissimi, che adormentano i miseri che passano per là e adormentati gli affogano, privando di tutti i beni quelli che danno nelle loro mani . . . solo Ulisse fugge da le loro insidie; perche la sola prudenza sa spregiare de dannose arti delle meretrici, chiudendo l'orecchie à i canti loro.[16]

Samson similarly suffers spoliation and metaphorical shipwreck in his sleep. Dalila 'made him sleep upon her knees' (Judges xvi. 18) and then, says Milton's Samson, she

> shore me
> Like a tame Wether, all my precious fleece,
> Then turn'd me out ridiculous, despoil'd,
> Shav'n, and disarm'd among my enemies.

Unlike Odysseus, Samson had been 'a foolish Pilot' and had failed to take precautions against the Sirens' songs. Hence he had 'shipwrack't My Vessel trusted to me from above' (198–9). Despoiled and shipwrecked, he suffered the conventional fate of the victim of the Sirens.

Dalila's 'enchanting voice' and 'bait of honied words' (1065–6) are characteristic not only of the Sirens, but also of the Renaissance Circe. A marginal gloss on Alciati's emblem of the Sirens explains that *Verba inflammant ad amorem;* and, in commenting on the verse *Aspectu, verbis, animi candore trahuntur,* Mignault observes that *verba certè non minorem vim habent ad pelliciendos animos quàm oculi: imò verò maiorem plerumque* and that *eloquentia compta ornataque, qua vel pertinacissimi, vel etiam maximè refractarij molliri, & in aliam penè formam mutari queunt.*[17] In the *Odyssey* Ulysses's companions hear Circe singing at her loom, but her 'beautiful voice' is not, strictly speaking, the cause why they have sought out her dwelling. In Renaissance adaptations of the myth, however, her voice becomes an important instrument of seduction. The *Orlando Innamorato* describes how

> Cantando ad ir da lei la gente alletta,
> E chi vi della sua forma priva.

And later in the same poem Alcina, a sorceress of the Circe type, is represented as fishing with the bait of words alone:

> sopra la marina,
> Facea venir con arte, e con incanti,
> I pesci fuor dell'acqua tutti quanti.

> Or com'io dissi, la Fata pescava,
> Nè rete non avea, nè altro ingegno,
> Sol le parole, che all'acqua parlava
> Facean tutti qua' pesci stare a segno.[18]

A similar concept occurs in Plutarch's comparison of Circe's victims to fishes caught *dia tōn pharmakōn* (Greek transliterated) (*Ut pisces quibusdam medicamentis celeriter capiuntur, sed esui tamen fiunt inutiles: ita mulieres,* etc.)[19]

Indirect though they are, Milton's allusions to the myths of Circe and the Sirens serve to emphasize several of the basic ethical values underlying Samson's relationship with Dalila. Many of the latter's salient characteristics—her meretricious and libidinous nature, her skill in the arts and snares of the harlot, her flattery and deceit, her appeal to the *vita voluptuosa,* her eloquence—are qualities she shares with her classical analogues, as Renaissance mythography had allegorized them. If her 'enchanting cup' recalls that of Homer's sorceress, her 'warbling charms' are equally reminiscent of other 'specious monsters' of Homeric fable, the Sirens.

These references to classical myth not only reinforce the characterization of Dalila, but also contribute to that of Samson. The 'Adder's wisdom' he has learned, which enables him to 'fence' his ear against her 'sorceries', serves to link him with Odysseus. Recent scholarship has stressed 'heroic knowledge' as the key to Milton's drama,[20] and in the light of this argument the analogy between Odysseus and Samson assumes additional significance. The antithesis between wisdom, on the one hand, and 'sensual folly and intemperance' (*Comus,* 975), on the other, is of major importance in *Samson Agonistes* (52-7, 201-9, 377-80, 496, etc.); but it is also inherent in Renaissance interpretations of Odysseus's encounters with Circe and the Sirens. According to Conti, *Ulyssis prudentia fuissent aures omnibus obturatae adversus Sirenum cantus;* and, when Circe had bewitched his companions *ipse invictus ob sapientiam, quae verè est Dei munus, perstiterit. Ego Ulyssem rationis participem animae nostrae partem esse crediderim.*[21] Similarly, Mignault explains Ulysses as *mentem animae ducem,* whereas the fate of his companions under Circe's spells indicates the irrational folly of the lover (*Et rationem animi perdere, quisquis amat*):

> Ideo mythologici Venerem *aphroditēn* quasi *aphrosynēn* (Greek transliterated), id est stultitiam & mentis privationem interpretantur.[22]

In Samson's final interview with Dalila the former disproportion between his 'immeasurable strength' and 'wisdom nothing more than mean' has been significantly reduced. If his earlier lapse into sensual folly recalls the victims of Circe and the Sirens, his final ability to counter Dalila's blandishments with 'Adder's wisdom' proves that he has acquired something at least of the *sapientia* of Odysseus.[23]

CHAPTER TEN

Eve's Dream and the Conventions of Witchcraft

> Taste this, and be henceforth among the Gods
> Thy self a Goddess, not to Earth confind,
> But somtimes in the Air, as wee, somtimes
> Ascend to Heav'n, by merit thine, and see
> What life the Gods live there, and such live thou.
>
>   Forthwith up to the Clouds
> With him I flew, and underneath beheld
> The Earth outstretcht immense, a prospect wide
> And various: wondring at my flight and change
> To this high exaltation. . . .*
>
>   (PL, V, Lines 77–81, 86–90)

In Satan's initial temptation of Eve, he exercises "his Devilish art" to beguile "her Fancie" and thus "forge Illusions . . . , Phantasms and Dreams." In the spiritual war between heaven and hell for the *anima humana,* this appeal to the irrational faculties of man is the diabolical counterpart of the celestial appeal to higher faculties, through Raphael the divine historian and Michael the heavenly seer. Eve's dream is thus Satan's opening foray in the psychic battle between falsehood and truth.

In an earlier examination of this scene, Professor Hunter has argued convincingly that Milton "conceived of this dream in terms of contemporary dream and demon lore" and that the poet was exploiting current beliefs in "the powers of devils over dreams" and their "operation upon the imagination or fantasy."[1] But this is hardly the whole story, and the scene also draws extensively on other aspects of contemporary demonology. In several respects Eve's dream of aerial "flight" bears a marked resemblance to current interpretations of the witches' Sabbath. In the long-standing controversy over the existence and efficacy of witchcraft, the popular belief in the nocturnal flight of *lamiae, maleficae,* or *strigae* was often accepted as fact,[2] but sometimes rejected as a diabolical illusion. Only the latter, however, has a direct bearing on *Paradise Lost.*

The Poetical Works of John Milton, ed. H. C. Beeching (New York, 1935).

As witchcraft itself was commonly regarded as a "Devilish art,"[3] the terms in which Milton describes Satan's psychological assaults on Eve strongly suggest the idea of sorcery. Satan's disguise as a toad recalls one of the most conventional forms which familiar devils assumed in their association with the sorceress.[4] Conventional too is Satan's attempt to taint the "animal Spirits." As Weyer and other writers on witchcraft had observed, the "melancholici" are, of all human beings, the most vulnerable to "daemonum illusionibus artibusque."[5]

In directing his attack on Eve as the weaker of the human pair, Satan foreshadows the rôle he will subsequently play among mankind. In his chapter "On the Credulity and Frailty of the Female Sex," Weyer observes that women are by nature more susceptible than men to the devil's illusions, and that it was for this very reason that Satan had chosen Eve as his initial victim rather than Adam:

> Chiefly that sly trickster [the devil] seduces the female sex, which is temperamentally unstable, credulous, malicious, weak-minded, and melancholy, as it can control its emotions only with difficulty. In particular, he misleads weak, stupid and vacillating old women. Hence in the beginning, when there were only two human beings in existence, he attacked Eve as a more suitable instrument for his persuasion than Adam. And he conquered her by a trifling argument.[6]

Thus the same reasons—frailty and credulity—underlay woman's vulnerability to the delusions of witchcraft and Eve's vulnerability to Satan's temptation. Her dream is, on the whole, the archetype of Satan's subsequent attacks on woman's phantasy; it contains most of the essential elements of witchcraft, as many Renaissance demonologists conceived it.

The principal analogy between this scene and contemporary witch-lore is the illusion of flight. Eve's tempter promises her a life "among the Gods,"

> . . . not to Earth confind,
> But somtimes in the Air, as wee, somtimes
> Ascend to Heav'n, by merit thine, and see
> What life the Gods live there, and such live thou.

In her dream, the taste of the forbidden fruit confers the power of flying:

> Forthwith up to the Clouds
> With him I flew, and underneath beheld
> The Earth outstretcht immense, a prospect wide
> And various: wond'ring at my flight and change
> To this high exaltation; suddenly
> My Guide was gone, and I, me thought, sunk down,
> And fell asleep; . . .

In this passage Milton has skillfully combined elements derived from the Biblical account of the temptation with details reminiscent of traditional witch-lore and the fall of Lucifer. In urging Eve to "be a Goddess" and enjoy the life of gods, Satan is employing the argument of Genesis iii.5, "ye shall be as gods." In exhorting her to "ascend to Heav'n" by her own merits, he is echoing the idiom of his own crime, as expressed in Isaiah xiv.13–14, "I will ascend into heaven . . . : I will ascend above the heights of the clouds; I will be like the most High."[7] In producing the illusion of nocturnal flight, he is employing the same tactics he will subsequently practice on mistresses of the "devilish Art" of witchcraft to induce an erroneous sense of power and thus draw them into destruction.

Unlike the deluded sorceresses among her posterity, Eve is still unfallen and is therefore able to recognize her aerial journey as a mere "dream." The traditional witch was less fortunate. In the opinion of some writers, her ability to fly was real; for the more skeptical, it was an illusion fostered by the devil, and the woman's inability to recognize it as a delusion was the direct result of insanity or demonic agency. Thus, in his chapter, "How the Devil Corrupts Men's Phantasy and Seems to Prophesy, According to Augustine's Opinion," Weyer draws on the mediaeval *Canon Episcopi* and on Pseudo-Augustine's *Liber de Spiritu et Anima,* as evidence that the nocturnal flight was no more than an illusion. Both of these documents had long served as standard authorities for the more skeptical attitude towards witchcraft in general and the myth of demonic transportation[8] in particular:

> Whence certain women devoted to Satan and seduced by demonic illusions and phantasms, believe and declare that they ride at night with the pagan goddess Diana or with Herodias or Minerva or a countless multitude of women, or obey their orders. Wherefore God's priests ought to preach to the people, so that it may know that these opinions are utterly false and that such phantasms are imposed on the minds of the faithful not by a divine but by an evil spirit. For Satan himself, who transforms himself into an angel of light, when he overcomes the mind of any woman and subjugates her to himself through infidelity, immediately transforms himself into an angel of light, in appearances and likenesses of various forms. And he leads the captive mind astray, deluding it with dreams.[9]

Again, in his chapter "How and Why Witches are Maddened by the Devil So That They Believe and Declare That They Have Done What They Could Not Possibly Do," Weyer rejects the belief in the demonic transportation of witches as a diabolical illusion and "idol of the phantasy":[10]

> When evil women resolve to put these wicked fictions into practice, they consecrate themselves with spells and ointments to the devil, who exploits

them for his own work and rules their phantasy, leading it to places where they desire to be. Nevertheless their bodies remain without sensation, and the devil covers them with shadow so that they are invisible. And when he observes that their desires have been fulfilled in their imaginations, he restores them to their own movements and removes the shadow. Nevertheless they have not moved from the spot; but an idol, which the devil had fashioned, has appeared to the phantasy.

In support of this interpretation, Weyer cited Ponzinibio's *Tractatus de Lamiis* and the *Canon Episcopi*.[11] Witches have been misled by the devil ("mentis errore à diabolo affectae") and suffer from a corrupted imagination ("vitiatam phantasiam").[12]

Since the *Canon Episcopi* and Pseudo-Augustine's book represented a distinct challenge to the very notion of witchcraft, both were often quoted in mediaeval and Renaissance demonology. Writers who dismissed sorcery as demonic illusion invoked them as authorities for a skeptical attitude towards demonic transportation. On the other hand, Sprenger and other witch-hunters sought to limit their relevance to demonology by contending that they pertained to a witch-cult altogether different from "new witches" of contemporary popular belief.[13] As both works were widely cited, the ideas expressed there should have been familiar to Milton's audience. Against this background, which explicitly associates the illusion of flight with Satan's ability to transform himself into "an angel of light" (2 Corinthians xi.14), Satan's appearance in Eve's dream is all the more appropriate; he seems an angel from Heaven, "One shap'd and wing'd like one of those from Heav'n by us oft seen; . . ."

Weyer's skeptical attitude towards the witch's flight was shared by a variety of Renaissance and late-medieval authors. The *Corrector Burchardi* refers to women deceived by the devil into believing that they ride at night with demons and ascend (like Milton's Eve) "up to the Clouds":

> Have you believed that there is any woman who would possibly do what some (deceived by the devil) affirm that they ought, of necessity and by command, to do—that is, to ride on certain nights with a throng of devils transformed into the likeness of women (which they superstitiously call *holda*) and be numbered in their company? . . . Have you believed what certain women are accustomed to believe—that with other members of the devil, in the silence of the night, you are lifted up into the air, through closed doors, as far as the clouds . . . ?[14]

Similarly, the *Roman de la Rose* dismisses as deceptive "visions" the belief of many women in their nocturnal ride with Dame Habonde:

> Et les cinq sens ainssi decoivent
> Par les fantosmes qu'ils recoivent,
> Dont maintes gens par leur folies

Quident estre par nuit estries,
Errans avecque Dame Habonde.[15]

In the XVth century, as Huizinga has observed, "the opinion that the rides through the air and the orgies of the witches' sabbath were but delusions which the devil suggested to the poor, foolish women, was already rather widely spread." In Martin Lefranc's *Champion des Dames,* the "Champion" refuses to believe

Que femme corporellement
Voit par l'air comme merle ou grive . . . .
Quant la pourelle est en sa couche,
Pour y dormir et reposer,
L'ennemi qui point ne se couche
Se vient encoste allé poser.
Lors illusions composer
Lui scet sy très soubtillement
Qu'elle croit faire ou proposer
Ce qu'elle songe seulement.[16]

Cardinal Juan de Torquemada, in discussing the *Canon Episcopi,* argues "that all which these women assert is impossible; it is all an illusion produced by the demon and those who believe it lose the faith."[17] The *Somma Pacifica* likewise treats belief in night-flying as a diabolical illusion:[18]

It is stubbornly believed . . . that [certain women] go with Herodias or Zobiana, or are carried into distant places with many other persons to their sport on Thursday nights upon an anointed stick or on certain beasts . . . and other similar things. All this the devils accomplish, to whom they have given themselves in bond, and the devils make them behold [these figments] through the illusion of dreams.

This skeptical attitude recurs in the XVIth and XVIIth centuries, even at the height of the witch-persecutions. According to George Giffard, "The devils make the witches in some place beleeve . . . that sometimes they flie or ride in the ayre, which thinges indeed are nothing so, but they strongly delude the fantasies of the witches."[19] Similarly, William Perkins rejects the nocturnal flight as an infernal delusion:[20]

. . . our Witches [confesse of themselves things false and impossible] when they be examined or consulted with, as that they . . . are carried through the aire in a moment, from place to place . . . ; lastly, that they are brought into farre countries, to meete with Herodias, Diana, and the Devill, and such like; all which are mere fables and things impossible . . . Becoming [Satan's] vassalls, they are deluded, and so intoxicated by him, that they will run into thousands of fantasticall imaginations, holding themselves . . . to be transported in the ayre into other countries, yea to do many strange things, which in truth they doe not.

Montaigne also casts doubt on this superstition: "How much more naturall, that our understanding may by the volubility of our loose-capring minde be transported from his place? then that one of us should by a strange spirit, in flesh and bone, be carried upon a broome through the tunnel of a chimney?"[21] According to Bacon, "witches themselves are imaginative and believe ofttimes they do what they do not. . . . It is worthy the observing, that . . . the greatest wonders which they tell of, carrying in the air, . . . etc. are still reported to be wrought, not by incantations or ceremonies, but by ointments and anointing themselves all over. This may justly move man to think that these fables are the effect of imagination."[22] In the opinion of the Duke of Newcastle, "they imagine their dreams are real exterior actions; for example, if they dream that they flye in the Air, . . . they believe no otherwise, but that it is really so: And this wicked Opinion makes them industrious to perform such Ceremonies to the Devil that they may worship him as their God, and chuse to live and dye for him."[23]

In *Paradise Lost* Milton's use of traditional witch-lore is not obtrusive. There is none of the grotesque paraphernalia of noisome ointments or such ludicrous vehicles as goats and brooms. Such details would obviously have violated epic decorum and been especially unsuitable to Eve in her unfallen state. Nevertheless the essential elements of witchcraft are present. The demonic attempt to corrupt the phantasy, the choice of woman as the weaker and more vulnerable instrument, the apparition as an angel of light, the diabolical illusion, and the nocturnal flight "up to the Clouds" are all conventional features of witchcraft as Weyer and other demonologists had presented them.[24]

How far they reflect Milton's considered views on witchcraft is another matter altogether. In treating the nocturnal flight as a Satanic illusion, he appears—superficially at least—to side with the more skeptical writers on the subject. In *Paradise Regain'd*, on the other hand, he represents demonic transportation as a reality; Satan carries Christ to the temple's highest pinnacle and to the mountain-top not in phantasy but in fact. This discrepancy, however, is more apparent than real, and Renaissance witchcraft-literature offers numerous parallels. Not infrequently the very author who dismisses the nocturnal flight as a mere delusion will nevertheless affirm the possibility of demonic transportation. Conversely, a writer who believes implicitly in the actuality of the witches' sabbath will often admit it is sometimes only an illusion.[25] There is no fundamental inconsistency between Milton's treatment of demonic transportation in the two epics.

The line between poetic imagination and doctrinal belief is sometimes difficult to trace, and in Milton's case it is particularly likely to become blurred. All too frequently the commentator accepts passing allusions to the conventions of sorcery as valid evidence of positive belief. Thus Trevor Davies asserts that the "question" of Milton's "views about witchcraft . . . is a fairly easy one to answer. A number of his writings show that he accepted the current beliefs of the witch-hunters of his day." The poet "was not behind his Puritan contemporaries in his convictions about witchcraft" and, indeed, can be numbered among "witch-hunters of no small credulity."

Yet none of the passages the author cites in support of this startling verdict really proves the point. Some are very weak indeed: an allusion to the "Sorceresse Medea," a comparison between the Church of Rome and a witch, accounts of witchcraft in Russian and Scottish history, a passing jest in a college oration. At most they indicate a rhetorical and poetic exploitation of isolated conventions associated with witch-lore, but not a positive belief in them. It is not Milton whom one suspects of credulity when one reads that "*Comus* lines 513 sqq. were written when men's minds were filled with resentment at the liberation of the Lancashire witches in 1634" and that they were possibly "written with a didactic aim for those who were sceptical about the reality of witchcraft."[26]

Later scholars are more cautious in evaluating Milton's allusions. In the lines on the skill of "*Lapland* Witches" to cause lunar eclipses, Professor Svendsen finds the poet stating "the power of witches here as if it were fact, despite the 'exiling of Satan,' . . . by emergent Renaissance rationalism." In actuality, however, there seems little reason to place greater stress on this allusion than on the mythological reference to Scylla, which immediately precedes it. Svendsen leaves open the question as to "whether this passage . . . puts Milton himself outside the main direction of contemporary thought as to Satan's powers. . . ."[27] Yet if one is to rely on this allusion alone as evidence, one can hardly avoid answering in the negative.

As Professor Schultz has pointed out, the *De Doctrina's* reference to "omnis daemonum invocatio, quaeque eo spectant" suggests that Milton "believed [a supernatural diabolical art] to be, or to have been, theoretically possible." Nevertheless it is by no means certain that Milton regarded the *praestigiatrix, pytho,* and *hariolus* of the proof-texts as comparable to the *striga, lamia,* or *malefica* of mediaeval and Renaissance superstition. Even though it is possible that he may have accepted the existence of witches on Biblical evidence, there is no clear indication that he also accepted the popular conception of witches or the more erudite superstitions entertained by men like Sprenger, James I, Henry More, and Glanvil. On the contrary, his treatment of the convention of demonic transportation in *Paradise Lost* seems to link him with the more skeptical views advanced by Weyer. On the whole, one must agree with Schultz that Milton's views on the subject "must remain largely a topic of conjecture," but that "we may guess with some confidence that he doubted the prevalence and just possibly the existence of sorcery in his own age."[28]

CHAPTER ELEVEN

Paradise Lost and the Apotheosis Tradition

> Ite procul lacrymae, purum colit aethera Damon,
> AEthera purus habet, pluvium pede reppulit arcum;
> Heroúmque animas inter, divósque perennes,
> AEthereos haurit latices & gaudia potat
> Ore Sacro. Quin tu coeli post jura recepta
> Dexter ades, placidusque fave quicunque vocaris . . . .
>
> *(Epitaphium Damonis*, lines 203–208)

> Thy Works and Alms and all thy good Endeavour
> Staid not behind, nor in the grave were trod;
> But as Faith pointed with her golden rod,
> Follow'd thee up to joy and bliss for ever.*
>
> (Sonnet XIV, lines 5–8)

In its treatment of the commonplaces of the apotheosis tradition, *Paradise Lost* differs significantly from Milton's minor poems. In his epicedia and his Neoplatonic masque he usually follows tradition; he presents these conventions, when he finds occasion to employ them at all, in a conventional manner. In his heroic poem, on the other hand, he frequently subverts or inverts them. Some of them may have seemed too closely associated with pagan conceptions of the hero to fit conveniently into a Biblical epic centered on Christian heroism. Their exaltation of human merits might appear out of place in a poem on original sin. Their exhortation to transcend the human condition, to despise the earth, and to ascend to the heavens (albeit through virtue and knowledge) might, in the context of *this* epic argument at least, seem an ironic recapitulation of the original crimes of Eve and Lucifer. And indeed Milton does, on the whole, tend to treat them ironically.

The apotheosis tradition itself is too complex for examination in a single study, and the mutations of the astral flight motif are even more varied.[1] As a point of departure I shall consider only one facet on this tradition—the conventions associated with Lucan's account of Pompey's ascent to the "convex of the Thunderer", where "with blacke ayre the starry poles doe meet." Here dwell the shades of half-deified soules

---

The Poetical World of John Milton, ed. H. C. Beeching (New York, 1935).

(*semidei manes*) whom fiery worth (*ignea virtus*) has taught to endure the lower part of heaven and brought to the eternal spheres. Filled with true light, Pompey's soul admires the wandering planets and fixed stars, perceives how dark are our "brightest dayes" in comparison with this celestial light, and laughs at the fate of his body. Subsequently adapted by Dante and Boccaccio and Chaucer, this passage was frequently interpreted in the light of Stoic and Neoplatonic pneumatology and sometimes correlated with analogous commonplaces in Boethius' *Consolation of Philosophy* and Macrobius' commentary on Cicero's *Somnium Scipionis.*

The salient feature of this tradition was the flight of the separated soul, released from the fetters of the body, to its native and natural element. Composed of the lighter elements (fire or air, or both), the spirit or *pneuma* ascends to the proper *locus* of these elements, rising (like a balloon) in accordance with the principle of levity. The purer the soul, the more rapid and the loftier its flight. In the course of its ascent, it may be progressively purified of earthly grossness and contagion. According to several commentators, the lunar concave itself may serve as a sort of aerial purgatory, preparing the spirit for its consort star. According to other expositors, the soul itself will be ultimately dissolved, dispersed into its original and component elements.[2]

Ascending to luminous regions of pure air or ether beyond the darkness of earth and the turbid lower atmosphere, the souls of the virtuous dwell in the lunar concave (sometimes identified with Elysium), in the sphere of the fixed stars (the *aplanes*), or beyond. From this celestial vantage-point they judge and re-evaluate the comparative merits of earth and heaven. Admiring the planets and fixed stars, marvelling at the magnitude and harmony of the heavens, they despise the minute earth and its transient and deceptive glories.

In the hands of poets and philosophers alike, the apotheosis may serve as the basis for a critique of secular values, for arguing the vanity of the world and the flesh and the insignificance of earthly beauty or wisdom or fame. It becomes, accordingly, a vehicle for the *contemptus mundi* theme (with its classical and Christian variants) and for the Boethian *exhortatio ad astra.* (As such it may serve as a *suasoria* to the active or the contemplative life, to the pursuit of private or public virtue, to the study of theology or metaphysics — or perhaps mathematics and astronomy. In this way the apotheosis may overlap with a different though allied flight-motif — the ascent of the mind through contemplation.

In *Paradise Lost,* the flight-motif, like other heroic *topoi,* undergoes striking variations[3]. Instead of apotheosizing human virtue, it exposes the vanity of human merits. Instead of eulogizing the capacities of human reason, it emphasizes the limitations of man's intellect. From a symbol of heroic sapience it has become an image of mortal folly. The Elysium of the magnanimous hero and the divine philosopher has been transformed into a Limbo of Vanity, a Paradise of Fools. The ascent to the heavens has become closely identified with *hybris* — with vain ambition and sacrilegious presumption. The flight of the mind has become drunken elation, the intoxication of Satanic illusion.

In this epic of forbidden knowledge the motif of celestial laughter has undergone a comparable transformation. Though it is still associated with knowledge of the heavens, the laughter is now directed against the science of astronomy itself. In Lucan and Dante and Boethius, in Boccaccio and Chaucer, admiration of the stars had been coupled with contempt in the world. The hero's laughter had sprung primarily from his comparison of earth and heaven. In *Paradise Lost*, on the other hand, the study of the stars becomes an object of ridicule; the laughter is now attributed not to the liberated spirit of hero or philosopher, but to God Himself.[4] The joke is no longer on the "lowly wise" but on the ambitious sages who seek knowledge beyond their natural capacities, soliciting their "thoughts with matters hid" and endeavoring to *sapere in altum*. For the wise man's laughter from the vantage-point of the heavens, Milton has substituted divine laughter at the celestial speculations of the wise. For the *topos* of divine derision, moreover, he had Biblical authority; according to the Psalmist (ii. 4), "He that sitteth in the heavens shall laugh; the Lord shall have them in derision." Milton had already made use of this text earlier in *Paradise Lost,* to ridicule Satan's conspiracy. In the context of the dialogue on astronomy, it assumes a more complex significance. Besides stressing one of the major themes of the poem — the antithesis between intellectual temperance and intemperance, between the hunger for forbidden knowledge and contentment with a more modest diet of practical wisdom — Milton's image of divine laughter alters the basic values of the classical and medieval flight-tradition. The laugh is no longer on the world, but on the worldy-wise-man who pretends to scientific knowledge of the heavens.

Nevertheless, Milton's treatment of the ascent-motif in his epic is not always pejorative. In several significant passages it appears in its traditional (and favorable) light. In his allusion to "Translated Souls" and in Raphael's suggestion that Adam and Eve, after becoming more fully spiritualized, may eventually dwell in heavenly paradises the poet comes closer to the traditional apotheosis. However, the mortalist views expressed in his *Christian Doctrine* — the belief that the soul perishes with the body, to be resurrected at the Last Judgment — have inevitably undermined the pneumatological basis of the traditional flight-motif.

Though Milton could exploit this theme figuratively and allegorically, as in his Limbo of Vanity, he may have been reluctant to utilize it in a more literal sense.[5]

Raphael's suggestion to Adam, on the other hand, presented no theological difficulty, no overt or implicit conflict with Milton's mortalist views. Not only was it stated in conditional and hypothetical terms, but it applied specifically to man's unfallen state, underlining the Father's promise in Book VII:[6]

> ... there to dwell,
> Not here, till by degrees of merit rais'd
> They open to themselves at length the way
> Up hither, under long obedience tri'd,
> And Earth be chang'd to Heaven, and Heav'n to Earth,
> One Kingdom, Joy and Union without end.

Raphael's remark thus heightened the contrast between Adam's fallen and unfallen condition. Before his transgression, Adam possessed the ability to earn his exaltation to the skies through his own merits. After the Fall (as he would subsequently learn through Michael) he must sleep until the end of time; he could attain Heaven only through the imputed merits of Christ.

Milton's allusion to translated souls, in turn, rested on Biblical authority. Both Enoch and Elijah were believed to have escaped death. Enoch "walked with God: and he was not; for God took him" (Genesis v. 24). Similarly "the Lord would take up Elijah into heaven by a whirlwind" (II Kings ii. I). The fact that the latter's name bore a suggestive resemblance to that of Elysium might further accentuate the analogies and contrasts between heathen fable and Scriptural truth.

Finally, Milton could and did exploit another convention of the flight-motif in his epic—the metaphorical transport of the poetic imagination.[7] Inasmuch as this ascent was purely figurative, it presented no theological difficulties.

Though *Paradise Lost* retains several of the traditional features of the flight-motif, its variations are more significant and more impressive.

Since these should be viewed not only against the background of classical and medieval tradition, but also in the light of Milton's earlier poetry, let us turn first to the shorter poems and to *Comus*.

[I]

Milton's minor poems include several funeral elegies,[8] and in these he made ample use of classical or Christian conventions associated with the flight of the separated soul: its return to its native region among the stars, its contempt of the world, the Elysium-motif, and the theme of celestial laughter.

In "On the Death of a Fair Infant Dying of a Cough," Milton exploited the commonplaces of the soul's divine origin ("for something in thy face did shine Above mortality that show'd thou wast divine") and its reascent to its celestial abode, amplifying these themes with conventional speculations concerning the posthumous habitations of the "blest": Elysium, the sphere of the fixed stars, or the heaven beyond the *primum mobile*. Though he did not assign a specific location to the "Elysian fields" (and indeed expressed doubt as to their existence), they had traditionally been assigned to the lunar concave, the underworld, or the fortunate isles at the end of the earth. Having concluded his sixth stanza with an allusion to the soul's "flight," the poet devoted the seventh to a variation on the Platonic doctrine of the soul's return *ad comparem stellam*. Still later, he introduced another variation on an equally familiar commonplace—the comparison of earth and sky as a dual argument for contempt of the world and exhortation to heavenly felicity: "To scorn the sordid world, and unto Heav'n aspire."

In the Third Elegy, on the death of the Bishop of Winchester, the poet recalls the fate of translated heroes ("Heroum quos vidit ad aethera raptos"), dreaming of a Christian heaven ("lato . . . agro") reminiscent of Virgil's Elysian fields ("aeris in campis latis"). In the elegy on the Bishop of Ely, Death summons the souls of the blessed into light and air ("In lucem et auras"); attended by angels, the prelate is borne aloft to the stars ("Ad astra sublimis feror"). In an astral flight not dissimilar to those of Pompey, Scipio, and other heroic voyagers, the bishop soars above the sun, beholding the moon beneath his feet and passing successively through the planets ("Erraticorum siderum") and the Galaxy. Marvelling ("miratus") at his speed, he finally reaches the crystal and beryl palace of Olympus. This passage contains several verbal parallels with the flight-sequences we have traced elsewhere from Lucan through Dante to Boccaccio.[9]

The *Epitaphium Damonis* similarly concludes with an apotheosis. After ascending to the region of the stars ("ibis ad astra"), Damon dwells in the pure ether among gods and heroes:

> . . . purum colit aethera Damon,
> Aethera purus habet, pluvium pede reppulit arcum;
> Heroumque animas inter, divosque perennes,
> Aethereos haurit latices . . .

He has become, in fact, a sort of guardian daemon, capable of aiding the friend he had left behind on earth ("Dexter ades, placidusque fave").[10] Similar roles characterize other beatified souls in Milton's fun-

eral elegies. The fair infant can "best perform" her "office" of intercession in her new dwelling. Lycidas has become "the Genius of the
shore"—a tutelary daemon of the "perilous flood." Sabrina has become
a river-goddess, a guardian-deity of "ensnar'd virginity."

In their tutelary functions, these separated souls perform offices
that classical poets and philosophers had variously ascribed to heroes,
daemons, and gods and that Christianity had associated with angels
and saints. The tradition was sufficiently broad and complex for Milton to select at will the particular elements—classical or Christian,
heroic or daemonic, angelic or divine—that would best fit the context
of a particular poem. Like the souls of Hesiod's men of the golden race,
who had become "Daimones appointed by Zeus to be Watchers of
men",[11] the separated souls of Milton's early poetry have become
"guardians of men." Nevertheless, though some of them apparently
dwell on the earth, like Hesiod's daemons, as tutelary genii, others
inhabit the air or ether, like the heroes and daemons of neo-Platonic
and neo-Pythagorean pneumatology. Thus the Attendant Spirit, or
daemon, of *Comus* has his "mansion" in the purified regions of the air,
exercising his tutelary offices from the skies.

The anniversaries of the Gunpowder Plot afforded Milton an opportunity to combine allusions to Elijah's translation and to the soul's
return to its native stars as a source of epigrammatic wit. Guy Fawkes
had intended to send King James and his peers "ad astra caeli" in a fiery
chariot. Nevertheless, without such aid, the good monarch has returned to his kindred stars ("consortia . . . Astra").

Commonplaces of the apotheosis-tradition also occur frequently in
poems devoted to other topics than death or the imminent threat of
death. In the Fourth Elegy, to Thomas Young, Milton describes the
Protestant clergy as men who teach the way that leads after death to the
stars ("ad astra"). In "Il Penseroso," he desires to "unsphere" Plato's
spirit "to unfold What Worlds, or what vast Regions hold The immortal mind that hath forsook Her mansion in this fleshly nook: and of
those *Daemons*" who inhabit the four elements. His poem "On Time"
represents the soul as "Attir'd with Stars" after quitting "this Earthly
grossness." "Ad Patrem" refers to the "aethereos ortus, et semina caeli"
of the human mind and to the soul's return to its "patrium . . . Olym-
pum." In "Mansus," after praising the Marquis' friendships with Tasso
and Marino and expressing the wish for as loyal a friend, Milton paints
an imaginary picture of his own death and the posthumous honors
such a friend might bestow on his remains: urn-burial and perhaps a
portrait-bust garlanded with laurel and myrtle. From heaven, whither
its fiery virtue had brought it to a dwelling among the gods ("caelicolum
semotus in aethera divum"), the poet's spirit would look down upon
this scene with a smile of self-congratulation. In this passage we en-

counter further verbal parallels with the classical apotheosis. Like Lucan, Milton mentions the *ignea virtus* whereby the righteous soul returns to the regions of fiery ether. Like Lucan, he depicts the soul as looking down from heaven to observe the rites bestowed on its mortal remains. Like Lucan, he describes its posthumous laughter. But there the resemblance ends. Pompey's mirth reflects his contempt of the world; Milton's expresses his satisfaction with the honors posthumously accorded him. His fame will survive his death:

> . . . et tota mente serenùm
> Ridens purpureo suffundar lumine vultus,
> Et simul aethereo plaudam mihi laetus Olympo.

In the Fifth Elegy and "At a Vacation Exercise in the College," Milton employs the *topos* of the imaginative flight of the poet's mind, and in "Mansus" he alludes to the flight of fame. Though we must reluctantly pass over these and other motifs remotely connected with the conventions we have encountered in Lucan and Cicero and Boccaccio, they may serve to indicate the range and variety of Milton's pneumatological imagery. Whereas the concluding lines of the "Epitaphium Damonis" effectively combine Bacchic and Apocalyptic motifs, the sonnet on Mrs. Catharine Thomason makes exclusive use of Christian themes and images. In particular, the passage describing the flight of her "Works and Alms and . . . good Endeavor" (based on a text in the Apocalpyse)[12] introduces a theme that will receive very different elaboration in the *Limbo of Vanity*.

[II]

In *Comus* Milton employs many of the commonplaces of classical pneumatology and the apotheosis-tradition. In the first place, the Attendant Spirit's prologue and epilogue are studded with allusions to the Elysian fields. Besides his explicit mention of "*Elysian* dew," his references to "happy climes," "broad fields of the sky," and "liquid air" recall Virgil's Elysium, with its *laeta arva* and its *aeris . . . campis latis*. Though Virgil had apparently located his Elysium in the underworld, possibly in conformity to Orphic beliefs, Servius and other commentators had suggested that these lines might actually refer to the lunar concave, citing as confirmation Lucan's description of the abode of the heroes. The "Ocean" to which the Spirit flies and "the green earth's end" are likewise conventional sites of Elysium. To some of the "divine race of Heroes" or demigods, according to Hesiod, Zeus had given "a dwelling-place at the ends of the world, . . . in the Islands of the Blest, by the deep-flowing Okeanos . . ."[13] Nevertheless, the Attendant Spirit does not terminate his journey there, and Milton mentons these traditional Elysia apparently to reject them. The "corners of the Moon," on the other hand—like "the hollow round of *Cynthia's* seat" in the "Nativity Ode"—seem to denote the lunar concave. This is another traditional site of Elysium according to Servius' 'theologians', and in this region—beneath the stars and "Before the starry threshold of *Jove's* Court"—Milton's aerial daemon has his mansion:

> . . . where those immortal shapes
> Of bright aerial Spirits live inspher'd
> In Regions mild of calm and serene Air . . .

These aerial "Gardens . . . Of *Hesperus*" have sometimes been identified with the aerial islands of Plato's *Phaedo*;[14] and in Milton's allusion to "bright aërial Spirits" scholars have detected a contrast between aerial and ethereal beings. Milton does, in fact, consistently employ the term "aerial" in *Comus*, in contrast to his description of the "ethereal" abodes of the blessed in his Latin poems. Nevertheless, these terms are not mutually exclusive, and we cannot be sure that he intended to suggest a sharp distinction between air and ether. Like their classical predecessors, Renaissance natural philosophers did not always agree in their terminology for the various strata of the air. For some of them, the "Regions mild of calm and serene Air" would have meant the ether; and in fact the adjective "bright" preserves the literal sense of *aither* ("shining"). Moreover, some of these writers agreed with Lucan in distinguishing between the lower and higher ether. For these, the mansion of Milton's Attendant Spirit would be located in the lower ether, as contrasted with the higher regions of inflamed air.

Like the Elysium of the theologians and the abode of Lucan's heroes, the region of the Attendant Spirit extends to the lunar concave. Though Milton contrasts it with regions above the heavens ("Higher than the Sphery chime"), his prologue places its primary stress not on the distinction between air and ether, but on the contrast between heaven and earth. Like the classical pneumatologists he contrasts the spacious and luminous regions in the sky with "this dim spot" of earth, the purity and tranquility of the upper air with the turbulence and impurity of the lower atmosphere: "the smoke and stir" of earth, and "the rank vapors of this Sin-worn mold." Like Boethius, he emphasizes the "change" of the transitory sublunary world and the "low-thoughted care" of mortals who ignore their highest Good. As in the classical tradition, the contrast between earth and heaven accentuates the *contemptus mundi* theme.

Nevertheless, Milton has transformed several of the major commonplaces of this tradition, adapting them to the controlling images of his masque. Where Lucan and his contemporaries had stressed the fiery virtue (*ignea virtus*) whereby the soul naturally reascended after death to the regions of air and fire, Milton associates virtue with images that possess distinctly Christian overtones. It is the "Golden Key That opes the Palace of Eternity," and on its true servants it bestows an amaranthine "crown" of undying praise. The *sedes beatorum* of classical tradition, in turn, have become the "Sainted seats" of the just.

In *Comus,* as in the classical tradition, the soul must undergo purification before returning to the higher regions of the heavens. As a Protestant poet, however, Milton would not be inclined to favor Stoic and Neoplatonic notions of an aerial purgatory. The purification of the soul occurs, significantly, on earth and through moral trial. In *Comus,* as in *Areopagitica,* trial is by contraries, purifying the soul by bringing good and evil into clearcut opposition and eventual separation:

> Yea even that which mischief meant most harm
> Shall in the happy trial prove most glory.
> But evil on itself shall back recoil,
> And mix no more with goodness, when at last
> Gather'd like scum, and settl'd to itself,
> It shall be in eternal restless change
> Self-fed and self-consum'd; . . .

In the classical tradition, the soul might be purified even in this lifetime through philosophy. The love of wisdom, however, was more than an academic study; it was a way of life, a disciplined *askesis* in which the moral as well as the intellectual virtues were tested and exercised. Though (in the language of Neoplatonism) the Lady exhibits the virtues of a purified soul, she has achieved her catharsis not only through contemplation of the Platonic ideas or 'forms' but also through an act of moral decision, through *proairesis.*

In *Comus* the ascent-motif could have received dramatic emphasis through the use of machines. Milton made allowance for this possibility in his first stage direction ("The attendant Spirit descends or "enters"),[15] and it is conceivable that he envisaged a comparable ascent by "machine" at the end of the epilogue. Nevertheless, since we do not know how the masque was actually staged, we must rely primarily on verbal rather than visual imagery.

The Spirit's role as guardian ("I was dispatcht for their defense and guard") is the conventional office of a daemon or tutelary genius, and in assigning him a dwelling in the upper air or lower ether Milton has followed Neoplatonic tradition. The allusions to descent ("Swift as the Sparkle of a glancing Star I shoot from Heav'n") indirectly emphasize the ascent-motif. After completing his "task" the Spirit must, of course, reascend to his aerial mansion; and his protegés will ultimately climb to a higher position "Amongst the enthron'd gods on Sainted seats." The "pure Ambrosial weeds" and "sky robes" that he lays aside further emphasize the contrast between heaven and earth. In changing them for shepherd's weeds, he gives visual as well as verbal emphasis to this antithesis. Conceivably he may have resumed his original costume before delivering his epilogue. If so, he would have heightened the visual expression of the flight-motif. The traditional contrast between celestial light and earthly darkness likewise receives visual as well as verbal expression.

Though the prologue and epilogue allude respectively to the Spirit's descent from and reascent to his dwelling in the skies, both refer also to a further flight—the ascent of virtuous souls to the heavens. This celestial imagery is ironically counterpointed by Comus' stellar analogies:

> We that are of purer fire
> Imitate the Starry Choir

and by his application of the Elysium-motif to the sensual and prophane music of Circe and the Sirens:

> Who as they sung, would take the prison'd soul,
> And lap it in *Elysium;* . . .

The Lady's song to Echo introduces a further variation on the theme of celestial translation:

> Sweet Queen of Parley, Daughter of the Sphere,
> So mayst thou be translated to the skies,
> And give resounding grace to all Heav'n's Harmonies.

In *Comus* the flight-motif retains its conventional role as a topic of exhortation. In the prologue it is contrasted with the *contemptus mundi* theme; and in the epilogue the Spirit's description of his Elysian dwelling and the higher realm of "Celestial *Cupid*" and Psyche serves as a hortatory argument to persuade mortals to "follow" him to the heavens through the exercise and love of virtue: "to climb Higher than the Sphery chime . . ."

In *Paradise Lost* many of the same motifs will recur, but in different narrative contexts and in association with vice rather than virtue. The exhortation to "fly" will be a Satanic lure, and to "climb Higher" a sacrilegious ambition.

[III]

Classical arguments for the reascent of the soul represented a complex mixture of doctrines derived from several different sciences or pseudo-sciences: physics and cosmology and meteorology; psychology, pneumatology, and ethics; astrology, metaphysics, and astronomy. According to Aristotelian physics, the four elements sought their natural places by natural appetency. Fire and air moved upward by natural levity, earth and water downward by natural gravity.[16] For those philosophers who regarded the psyche as fire or air or both, the soul would naturally reascend to the regions of air or fire unless weighed down by earthly contagion. For the Platonists each soul must eventually return to its proper star. The theory of natural motion and natural place underlies the consolations of the Stoics and the speculations of the Neoplatonists. In the *Paradiso,* Beatrice explains the speed of Dante's flight through a Christian variation on classical physics. Heaven is man's natural place and his natural end, and his natural motion is heavenward.

In *Paradise Lost* these motifs undergo a sea-change. On two occasions Milton exploits the principle of levity to emphasize the fallen condition of man and angel, and to underscore the vanity of their ambition to regain heaven by their own exertions. In the case of the fallen angels, reliance on natural levity proves vain; and indeed their natural motion is no longer upward. In the case of fallen man, natural levity itself becomes a symbol of vanity.

In haranguing his troops, Satan suggests that they may reascend to heaven by their own endeavors:

> For who can yet believe, though after loss,
> That all these puissant Legions, whose exile
> Hath emptied Heav'n, shall fail to re-ascend
> Self-rais'd, and repossess thir native seat?

Subsequently, Moloch appeals to the principle of natural motion to demonstrate that the "ascent" will be "easy":

> . . . in our proper motion we ascend
> Up to our native seat: descent and fall
> To us is adverse.

In effect, he is arguing that as ethereal or fiery spirits the fallen angels must naturally reascend to the Empyrean. It is as natural for them to soar upward as for an earthly body to fall. Belial does not specifically refute this argument, but he sensibly condemns Moloch's strategy of revenge as vain.

If Moloch's argument is implicitly based on the natural motion of fire, Milton's "Limbo of Vanity" is erected on air:

> . . . store hereafter from the earth
> Up hither like Aereal vapors flew
> Of all things transitory and vain, when Sin
> With vanity had filled the works of men: . . .
> A violent cross wind from either Coast
> Blows them transverse ten thousand Leagues awry
> Into the devious Air; . . .
> The sport of Winds: . . .

In this passage scholars have detected the influence of Ariosto's *Orlando Furioso*, Dante's *Inferno*, and Chaucer's *House of Fame*, in addition to satire on the Church of Rome.[17] Theologically, it exemplifies "the vanity of human merits." Milton may also have had in mind Scriptural allusions to the ungodly as "the chaff which the wind driveth away" (Psalm i. 4). Primarily, however, his aerial symbolism centers on the commonplace of "empty air" (*aer vanus*) and on the principle of levity. Lacking solid merit, the works of unregenerate man are figuratively as light as air. The same principle underlies the ancient and medieval *psychostasia*, or "weighing of souls," where good and evil deeds, merits and demerits, are weighed against each other. It is significant that in the scale-episode at the end of Book IV Milton combines features of the *psychostasia*, the weighing of souls or lives, with those of the classical *kerostasia*, or weighing of fates;[18] Satan reads his "Lot" in the "celestial Sign" where he is "weigh'd, and shown how light, how weak" if he resists. In both instances lightness is associated with emptiness or vanity; and in both cases Milton exploits it for rhetorical "extenuation." In the scale-episode it diminishes the impression of Satanic strength so carefully built up over the first four books of the epic. In the "Limbo of Vanity" passage it minimizes or "extenuates" the pseudo-heroic exploits of the unregenerate.

Man's works and their reward are equally vain, and Milton's aerial symbolism emphasizes the emptiness of both. Worldly glory and fame, earthly honor and praise, are empty as air. Shakespeare's Falstaff had successfully utilized this commonplace for his own purposes,[19] and Milton does the same. Those who have sought "the praise of men, here find Fit retribution, empty as their deeds"; the reward of their vainglory is equally vain—empty air.

Like the classical pneumatologists, Milton has applied the concept of natural levity to the ascent of separated souls, but he has given it the pejorative meaning associated with lightness and vanity in Scripture and in the weighing-of-souls motif. In the same way he has treated other features of the apotheosis-tradition satirically. The ascent through the "Planets seven" and the higher spheres ends in comedy— an ecclesiastical raggle-taggle of fluttering "Cowls, Hoods and Habits . . ." Like the aerial abode of the heroes in Lucan's *Pharsalia*, the lunar Elysium of the Stoic sages, and the higher regions enjoyed by Neoplatonic philosophers, Milton's limbo is filled with heroes (the Biblical giants[20] and seekers after "Glory or lasting fame") and with philosophers (Empedocles and Cleombrotus); but their hopes are dismissed as "fond" and their exploits as "vain." In Christian doctrine heroic virtue had been re-defined as sanctity, and the saint had replaced the hero; but here the holiness of "Eremites and Friars" and "Pilgrims" (often regarded as heroes of the faith) is condemned as "painful Superstition and blind Zeal." The classical belief in an aerial Elysium where souls underwent purgation from earthly contagion is travestied, along with the Catholic doctrine of limbo, the veneration of relics, and papal indulgences, dispensations, and pardons. Cleombrotus' reward for his belief in 'Plato's Elysium' is a "Paradise of Fools" that nevertheless bears a striking resemblance to the lunar Elysium of Servius' 'theologians.'

In addition to these allusions to classical pneumatology, Milton's reference to the "final dissolution" of Nature's "unaccomplisht works" recalls the belief held by various Stoic philosophers[21] — that after its sojourn in the lunar concave, the soul is finally dissolved. This belief, in fact, antedates the Stoic philosophy; in the *Phaedo,* Socrates had scoffed at the childish fear "that when the soul leaves the body, the wind may really blow her away and scatter her . . ."[22]

Though Milton is aware of the classical tradition that assigned the souls of heroes to an Elysium in the lunar concave, he utilizes it primarily for contrast with his outer limbo. Its inhabitants are either heroes of true sanctity ("Translated Saints") or daemons ("middle Spirits . . . Betwixt th' Angelical and Human kind"), altogether different from the pseudo-heroes and false saints of the Paradise of Fools. Like the classical heroes and daemons, the latter have their dwelling in the air; but in its darkness and turbulence their celestial abode resembles the earth they left behind.

Though Milton alludes to "the neighboring Moon," his limbo is actually located at the farthest point in the skies from the lunar Elysium. Whereas the latter was traditionally situated in the concave of the heavens, Milton's Paradise of Fools is located on the "first convex," the outermost surface of the universe. In this respect it recalls Plato's *Phardrus,* where "the immortal souls . . . go out and stand upon the back of heaven, and the revolution of the spheres carries them round, and they behold the world beyond".[23] A similar doctrine occurs in Boethius' *Consolation:* "And when the thought hath don there inogh, he schal forleten the laste hevene, and he schal pressen and wenden on the bak of the swifte firmament, and he schal be makid parfit of the worschipful lyght of God."[24] Milton has apparently adapted this motif to the "Limbo of Vanity" episode; but, as with other features of the apotheosis-tradition, he has treated it pejoratively. The spirits who are "upwhirl'd aloft" and "Fly o'er the backside of the World" are presented as fools who receive the empty reward they have deserved.

In contrast to the light and serenity of the traditional aerial Elysium, Milton's limbo shares the darkness and turbulence of Chaos. Unlike Pompey's lunar concave, it is "Dark, waste, and wild," exposed to starless night and storms—"a windy Sea of Land." In thus consigning the vain "works of men" to the outer darkness, Milton is not only symbolizing their vanity, but emphasizing their worldly character. Unable to merit heaven, they cannot pass beyond the boundaries of "this round World." Figuratively and allegorically, they are brought to confusion, ultimately dissolving in the meteorological disturbances of Chaos. Like Mrs. Catharine Thomason, these spirits ascend to the skies, attended by their own works and endeavors; but they fall significantly short of heaven. Milton's variation on this motif accentuates the difference between these vainglorious worldings and "blessed" souls who have died "in the Lord" (Revelation xiv.13).

These variations on the conventions of the celestial ascent effectively emphasize the antithesis between true glory and vainglory and between true and false heroism. In classical and medieval tradition the astral flight had served the purposes of encomium; in Milton's travesty, on the other hand, it serves the end not of heroic glorification, but of comic reduction. Whereas the apotheosis-motif had extolled the merits of heroes and saints, Milton employs it to ridicule human ambition. For the aerial glory of heroes, he gives us the windy vain-glory enjoyed by pseudo-heroes. Instead of a celestial Elysium inhabited by wise men, he depicts a fool's paradise. Instead of the Christian heaven or the lunar purgatory, he has portrayed a gusty steppe haunted by phantasms and vain imaginations—a burlesque counterpart of the limbo of Christian tradition.

The analogy between Milton's "*Limbo* large and broad" and the broad and airy plains of Virgil's Elysium makes the divergences between them all the more forceful. The former is characterized by turbulence and darkness; the latter by serenity and light. Equally significant, however, are analogies and dissimilarities with the Christian limbo.

In this fool's paradise Milton has combined various features of the traditional limbo as well as different senses of the word itself. The term literally signified a surrounding border or edge, and in this sense it had been applied not only to regions on the border of Hell (the *limbus inferni*), but to the outer border of the astrolabe and to the zodiac itself.[25] In describing this region on the outermost edge of the cosmos as a "Limbo," Milton has not only retained the etymological meaning of this word, but has also fused several different associations and senses. He has combined its application to separated souls (the *limbus patrum* and *limbus infantium*) with the notion of the fool's paradise (*limbus fatuorum* or *paradisus stultorum*) and with the astronomical associations of *limbus*. The effectiveness of this scene results in large part from the conscious exploitation of ambiguities inherent in the notion of limbo. The varied and sometimes contradictory associations of this term enabled Milton to achieve novelty without altogether violating tradition. By combining traditional elements in a new and different way, he could achieve surprise—*meraviglia*—without entirely sacrificing probability.[26]

Though the reader would normally expect to find Limbo at the edge of Hades, its astronomical associations give support to Milton's innovation in treating it as the border not of Hell, but of the created universe.[27] Moreover, the *limbus patrum* was sometimes regarded as situated near heaven rather than in the underworld. The references to "Embryos" and "Idiots" seem deliberately reminiscent of the *limbus infantium* and the *limbus fatuorum;* but in selecting these particular details Milton has emphasized the vanity and the frustration of natural ends. Embryo and idiot alike represent the frustration of nature's endeavors; moreover, since both lack the power of rational decision, the notions of merit and reward are irrelevant. As a result of Adam's fall, Nature's works, like those of man, have become abortive and unnatural, monstrous and vain.

To the traditional limbo, theologians and poets had assigned various spirits who had not, in the strictest sense, merited either heaven or hell. Though Miton is not directly concerned with the latter question, he continues to associate limbo with a lack of the merits (in this case, the "imputed" merits of Christ, necessarily, in contrast to the vanity of man's own actions and deserts) essential for salvation. Finally, limbo also denoted a condition of oblivion or neglect. In this sense it is a fitting reward for those who have sought renown on earth and the praise of men. In Milton's windy limbo they achieve the oblivion that awaits all vain or useless things.

Like other heroic motifs, the features of the classical and Christian apotheosis have been transformed in this scene. Converting a symbol of glory into a symbol of vainglory, Milton has adapted a heroic convention to reinforce his critique of heroic tradition. The comic values of this scene result primarily from the poet's clever variations on heroic themes, exploiting the commonplaces of heroic praise for heroicomic effects. Topics that had conventionally "aggravated" or enhanced the theme of human merit now serve to "extenuate" it and to expose its vanity. Arguments that had traditionally served the end of praise now function as instruments of ridicule.

It is significant, finally, that Satan himself is the first spirit to ascend (or rather descend) to this region—a detail that may suggest the vanity of his own heroic enterprise and (like the stairs to heaven)[28] emphasize his "sad exclusion from the doors of Bliss."

[IV]

The classical ascent to the stars had been closely associated with the *contemptus mundi* theme. Filled with admiration for the magnitude and brilliance of the skies, the departed hero or the speculative philosopher learned to despise the dim and diminutive earth. In adapting this motif to the universe before Adam's fall, Milton had dissociated it from contempt of the world. Though he retains the commonplace of the globe-as-point, he employs this theme to emphasize the nobility rather than the significance of the earth. His archangel exploits this topic to encourage Adam to remain content with his present lot instead of seeking knowledge of loftier matters beyond his capacity—and to demonstrate the vanity rather than the desirability of astronomical speculation. The comparison with heaven serves to augment rather than minimize the theme of the world's magnificence; it underscores the beauty and excellence of the earth as part of the universal order. Instead of fostering disdain for the earth and contempt for terrestrial things, the downward glance through the spheres evokes admiration for the entire cosmos as the masterwork of a divine architect and musician—wonder at its proportions and its movements, and delight in its harmony.

In describing Satan's first glimpse of the created world, Milton applies the earth-as-point motif to the relative magnitude, not of the earth and stars, but of the entire cosmos in comparison with the Empyreal Heaven: "This pendant world, in bigness as a Star Of smallest Magnitude close by the Moon." The basic contrast in this scene is between the created universe and Chaos, between luminous order and the realm of confusion and night. The world is linked to heaven by a "golden Chain," and the comparison between them underscores the closeness of their relationship.

After ascending through Chaos to the storm-swept outer sphere, Satan achieves a world-view comparable to that of other cosmic voyagers. He beholds beneath him the panorama "Of all this World at once . . ." Like other voyagers, he experiences "wonder" (Milton compares this "sudden view" to the "godly prospect of some foreign land First seen" by a scout after a long journey through "dark and desert ways"), but the *contemptus mundi* theme is conspicuously absent. The downward glance from the skies arouses admiration for the entire cosmos, rather than contempt for the earth:

> Such wonder seiz'd, though after Heaven seen
> The Spirit malign, but much more envy seiz'd
> At sight of all this World beheld so fair.

Satan is keenly aware of the magnificence of the unfallen world. The comparison with heaven underscores their resemblance rather than their difference, and indeed it may result in giving preference to the earth. As the devil would subsequently exclaim, after a week's flight about the globe, the earth might actually be the more desirable habitation:

> O Earth, how like to Heav'n, if not preferr'd
> More justly, Seat worthier of Gods, as built

With second thoughts, reforming what was old!
For what God after better worse would build?
Terrestrial Heav'n, danc't round by other Heav'ns
That shine, yet bear thir bright officious Lamps,
Light above Light, for thee alone, as seems,
In thee concentring all thir precious beams
Of sacred influence: . . .

Such praise is far removed from the *contemptus mundi* expressed by Pompey and Scipio and Arcita.

In the dialogue on astronomy, Raphael similarly turns the comparison of heaven and earth into an argument for the latter's nobility. From the *topos* of the earth's small size, he draws conclusions very different from those we have encountered in Cicero and Chaucer and in Milton's *Comus*. In propounding his question, Adam argues from the *topoi* of nobility and the comparative brightness and magnitude of earth and sky. The earth seems a mere "spot, a grain, an Atom, with the Firmanent compar'd," and Adam marvels at Nature's extravagance. In creating "So many nobler Bodies" to traverse such "Spaces incomprehensible" merely to "officiate light Round this opac'ous Earth, this punctual spot," she has violated the principles of economy and the rule of parsimony.

In answering these doubts, Raphael argues that excellence depends neither on brilliance nor on size:

> . . . consider first, that Great
> Or Bright inferrs not Excellence: the Earth
> Though, in comparison of Heav'n, so small,
> Nor glistering, may of solid good contain
> More plenty than the Sun that barren shines . . .

In the classical tradition, the relative magnitude of earth and sky had served as a topic for dissuading man from earthly concerns and exhorting him to fix his mind on the heavens. Dame Philosophy had commended Boethius for his former astronomical pursuits, and in Seneca's opinion the felicity of separated souls largely consisted in contemplating the motions of the heavens. Raphael, on the other hand, converts this *topos* into a dehortative argument against astronomy. He employs it to dissuade his pupil from fruitless inquiry into the nature and operations of the heavens and to exhort him to fix his mind instead on earthly duties:

> . . . Heav'n is for thee too high
> To know what passes there; be lowly wise:
> Think only what concerns thee and thy being;
> Dream not of other Worlds, what Creatures there
> Live, in what state, condition or degree . . .

In placing the heavens so high above the earth, the Creator has deliberately concealed His ways from human sense:

> . . . that earthly sight,
> If it presume, might err in things too high
> And no advantage gain.

God has left the "Fabric of the Heav'n" to the disputes of man, in order "perhaps" to laugh at "thir quaint Opinions . . ."

In this scene the commonplaces of the apotheosis-tradition and the classical exhortation *ad astra* — the earth-as-point motif and the value of astronomical studies, the comparison between celestial and terrestrial concerns — have been adapted to strikingly different arguments and ends. They are designed to discourage ambition and the pursuit of forbidden knowledge, rather than to arouse contempt of the world.

[V]

In the temptation of Eve, the flight-motif serves as a Satanic lure. In "Assaying by his Devilish art to reach the Organs of her Fancy," he inspires her with the vain imagination of flight and the vain ambition to divinity:

> Taste this, and be henceforth among the gods
> Thyself a Goddess, not to Earth confin'd,
> But sometimes in the Air, as wee, sometimes
> Ascend to Heav'n, by merit thine, and see
> What life the Gods live there, and such live thou.

In her dream Eve ascends, not to stellar mansions or the upper regions of the air, but merely to the region of the clouds:

> . . . Forthwith up to the Clouds
> With him I flew, and underneath beheld
> The Earth outstretcht immense, a prospect wide
> And various: wond'ring at my flight and change
> To this high exaltation; . . .

Eve's apotheosis falls significantly short of the altitudes reached by Pompey and Arcita. Moreover, she is impressed by the magnitude of the earth rather than its insignificant size.

In relying on her own "merit" and the fruit of knowledge to ascend to the skies, Eve's imaginary apotheosis bears a significant resemblance to that of the classical philosopher. Dame Philosophy had shown her disciple the way to return to the heavens and, beyond the outermost sphere, to God Himself. Seneca had argued that philosophy could make a man equal to God (*par deo*), and Pseudo-Aquinas had endorsed this opinion. For Stoics and Neoplatonists alike, knowledge—

contemplation of heavenly things and purification through philosophy — would conduct the soul back to the skies. The character of Eve's dream, and Milton's pejorative adaptation of the ascent-motif in this and other passages, may reflect his critical attitude toward the exaggerated claims that had been made on behalf of philosophy. Nevertheless, they have also been conditioned, apparently, by the argument and subject-matter of *Paradise Lost*.

Satan had fallen through the ambition to "ascend" above his proper sphere. Lucifer had boasted (Isaiah XIV. 14), "I will ascend above the heights of the clouds; I will be like the most High." Since the Tempter himself had fallen through this desire, he infers not illogically that a similar appeal can be successful in seducing Eve. Accordingly he urges her to "Ascend to Heav'n" and to aspire to Godhead. The allusion to "Clouds" in this passage reinforces the parallel between the ambition whereby Satan fell self-tempted, and his appeal to ambition in his temptation of Eve.

Like Satan, mankind had also fallen through the desire for equality with God. Where Satan had sought to vie with Him in power and dominion, man had endeavored to rival Him in knowledge: "ye shall be as gods, knowing good and evil" (Genesis iii. 5). In the narrative context of *Paradise Lost*, the aspiration to superhuman knowledge, like the desire to ascend, might hold sinister implications; and Milton has developed these implications in his pejorative elaboration of both of these closely-related themes.[29]

Nevertheless, both desires — the desire to ascend to a higher state of being and the desire for knowledge — were in a sense natural to man and could be directed alternatively to good or evil. Man had been created for the heavens, though he must first earn his way thither by proving his merit; and the rational nature which distinguished him from beasts might naturally lead him to the knowledge of God: "for Heav'n Is as the Book of God before thee set, Wherein to read his wond'rous Works, and learn His Seasons, Hours, or Days . . ." In tempting man, Satan appeals to natural desires that in moderation could lead to virtue but could otherwise be abused through vicious excess.

It is essential to Milton's poetic strategy — both to his justification of God's providence and to the requirements of verisimilitude and probability — that mankind should transgress of his own free will and through natural impulses, that Adam and Eve should be impelled or motivated by natural desires capable of serving either good or evil. Yet it is also essential to the poet's theodicy that man should be warned in advance against the very temptations whereby he would subsequently fall. This, of course, is the purpose of Raphael's visit. The angel not only counsels Adam against one form of intemperance — excessive passion for his wife — but also against intemperance in knowledge —

excessive desire to know. In Satan's example he has portrayed the dire results of ambition and disobedience; and in the dialogue on astronomy he counsels his host against overweening curiosity into matters beyond human capacity. Raphael has demonstrated the limits as well as the proper objects of man's knowledge, and Adam has learned

> That not to know at large of things remote
> From use, obscure and subtle, but to know
> That which before us lies in daily life,
> Is the prime Wisdom; what is more, is fume,
> Or emptiness, or fond impertinence, . . .

Raphael does not overlook man's innate appetite for knowledge, nor does he ignore man's natural desire for a more spiritual condition. In his lecture on the great chain of being ("the scale of Nature set From centre to circumference, whereon In contemplation of created things By steps we may ascend to God"), the angel explains the procession of all things from God and their return to Him as an essential feature of the natural order:

> O *Adam*, one Almighty is, from whom
> All things proceed, and up to him return,
> If not deprav'd from good . . .
> But more refin'd, more spiritous, and pure,
> As nearer to him plac't or nearer tending
> Each in thir several active Spheres assign'd,
> Till body up to spirit work, in bounds
> Proportion'd to each kind.

Ascent is by degrees, and Raphael illustrates this principle through a vegetative simile adapted to Adam's limited knowledge and his experience as gardener. In accordance with the principle of progress by degrees, Adam and Eve may eventually "turn all to spirit, . . . and wing'd ascend Ethereal" or dwell at choice in earthly or celestial paradises. This exaltation is, however, contingent on their obedience, and they are not yet ready for it. In the meantime they should "enjoy . . . what happiness this happy state Can comprehend, incapable of more."

Like the poet's "warning voice", the angel's admonitions cannot prevent the Fall, but they nevertheless serve the divine purpose for which they were intended—"to render Man inexcusable . . ." Raphael has defined the conditions under which man can eventually ascend to a higher state. He has designated the proper objects of human knowledge. He has differentiated between the legitimate and illegitimate objects of human aspiration and inquiry. He has stressed the present limitations of man's condition as well as the opportunity for future progress. He has "largely . . . allay'd" Adam's thirst for knowledge, while reminding him that there remains much "surpassing human measure . . ." Though his warnings prove fruitless, the angel has performed his mission well. Adam is fully aware that in his present condition valid knowledge must necessarily be proportioned to his limited capacity and that he can ascend to the heavens only by degrees and upon the condition of obedience.

The contrast between legitimate and illicit ascent—between vaulting ambition and gradual elevation—had already received concrete expression in Book Three, where Milton had juxtaposed his description of the Limbo of Vanity with his account of the stairs to heaven. Having wandered over the dark surface of the outer sphere, Satan eventually decries "Ascending by degrees . . . a Structure high" terminating at the "Kingly Palace Gate" of heaven. Milton compares it to the ladder of Jacob's dream, with "Angels ascending and descending, bands of Guardians bright."

Through this image of gradual and legitimate ascent, Milton has brought into sharper focus the ambitious folly not only of fallen man but of Satan himself. A few lines earlier (through a literal "anticlimax") he had described the sudden reversal that frustrates the expectations of the vainglorious:

> . . . and now at foot
> Of Heav'n's ascent they lift thir Feet, when lo
> A violent cross wind from either Coast
> Blows them transverse . . .

The stairs themselves, in turn, serve as a bitter reminder of the ambition to ascend, whereby Satan has fallen. They have been "let down" either "to dare The Fiend by easy ascent" or to aggravate his exclusion.

Satan's journey from the "bare convex" of the world to the prelapsarian earth is, of course, the reverse of the conventional astral flight; he follows a course diametrically opposite to that of the apotheosized worthies of classical and Christian tradition and to that of the future inhabitants of the Limbo of Vanity. What is primarily significant, however, is not that he descends where they ascend, but that (like the direction of flight) many of the conventional values of the flight-tradition are reversed. The seat or *locus* of earthly vanities is not (for the moment at least) the earth itself but the outermost sphere of the heavens. The dark and turbid atmosphere belongs to this windy pseudo-Elysium or fool's paradise, not to the earth—not yet to the pure air of the unfallen world and the purer air of Paradise. The vanities of men will subsequently mount to this place—as the shades of classical worthies had mounted—through the principle of levity; but in the context of Milton's limbo this principle is no longer associated with purity of soul; instead, it has become an index of emptiness and insignificance. The locus of insignificance is no longer the minute earth, but (paradoxically) the convex of the highest of the spheres. Though Milton retains the imagery of air and the principle of local motion, he converts them into symbols of distributive and retributive justice; the worthless endeavors of fallen man ascend like aerial vapors to a region of stormy winds (an emblem of windy vanity) where they receive a reward as empty as themselves. The traditional *locus* of enduring glory and renown has become a place of oblivion. Elysium has become limbo.

Satan's journey ends with the earth—the starting point of the astral ascent of apotheosized mortals—but this is a yet unfallen world, worthy of admiration rather than contempt. It compares favorably with heaven itself; in contrast to the postlapsarian world, the *contemptus mundi* would be conspicuously inappropriate. In the temptation of Adam and Eve it will, in fact, become a sign of ingratitude for the gifts of God; and they will fall, not ascend, by scorning their (paradoxically) humble but exalted state and seeking an apotheosis, a premature ascent to heaven through their own presumed merits.

These reversals of the *topoi* of the flight-tradition in Satan's journey are consistent with the irony and ambiguity associated with the motifs of ascent and descent virtually throughout the poem. To ascend successfully one must be lowly wise; to bypass the "due steps" of ascent (to echo the language of *Comus*) is to invite abrupt downfall and sudden ruin. Man and angel alike fall through the ambitious aspiration for the attributes of divinity. Conversely, the Messiah is exalted through condescension and humiliation—a motif parodied in Satan's "foul descent" in undertaking a serpentine incarnation.

These variations on flight-conventions also serve, however, to reinforce the motifs of standing and falling, which are inherent in the very argument of the poem and recur, with further variations, throughout the epic. Moral concepts such as apostasy and constancy and changes in spiritual state—the state of innocence, the state of sin, the state of grace—receive additional emphasis through the physical elaboration of their literal etymologies. (The latter are derived, of course, from Greek and later roots meaning *stand*). The fall of the angels reinforces, through physical and senuous details, the significance of Satan's apostasy and the fall of man, thus providing an external analogy for an internal action. In the same way Milton adapts the motif of the temple-tower in *Paradise Regained* to emphasize, again in *physical* and *external* terms, the hero's moral constancy and a fundamental alteration in the spiritual state or condition of fallen man. Similarly, the ambitious desire for Godhead is brought into clearer focus through the imagery of physical ascent—such as Eve's demonic dream and imaginary flight.

Like his treatment of the ascent-motif, Milton's handling of the *contemptus mundi* theme was conditioned by the argument of his poem. In comparing earth and heaven, he stresses their resemblance rather than the differences between them. Satan suggests that earth may indeed be preferable to heaven, and Raphael argues that it may actually be nobler than the celestial spheres which minister to it. These variations of the conventional comparison between heaven and earth underscore the felicity of unfallen man and the changes that entered the world through sin. These alterations Milton himself would describe through such details as changes in climate and celestial influences, alterations in the dispositions of beasts and man, and the final destruction of the Earthly Paradise. Michael's survey of world history would further amplify this theme. In the "Limbo of Vanity" episode, moreover, the *contemptus mundi* theme had been ingeniously extended to the heavens themselves. Rendered vain by sin, the works of men and the "unaccomplisht works" of fallen nature find their condign habitation on the outermost sphere.

Milton introduces the *contemptus mundi* theme only in relation to the fallen world, and the difference is apparent in his treatment of "machining persons." Unlike the Attendant Spirit in *Comus*, Raphael does not fear that he will "soil" his clothes "With the rank vapors of this Sin-worn mold." Though he may accept Adam's allusion to the earth as "this punctual spot," he does not condemn it as "this *dim* spot," nor does he represent humanity as "Confin'd and pester'd in this pinfold here . . ." Far from exhorting his audience to "follow" him to the heavens, he urges Adam to be "lowly wise," contented with his present lot on earth. Whereas the Attendant Spirit had expressed the conventional disdain of the world, this attitude is altogether alien to Raphael.

Nevertheless, as *Comus* and *Paradise Lost* are separated both by generic distinctions and by an interval of thirty years, we should not overstress these differences between the attitudes of the aerial daemon and the sociable archangel. More relevant for the changes brought about by the Fall is the contrast between Raphael's "sociably mild" demeanor and Michael's "solemn and sublime" bearing. Adam may "confide" in the one, but he must meet the other "With reverence . . ." In Michael's prophecies he will encounter the commonplaces of the *contemptus mundi* theme so notably absent from Raphael's discourse: death and disease, violence and wantonness, persecution of the righteous by a world perverse:

> . . . so shall the World go on,
> To good malignant, to bad men benign,
> Under her own weight groaning, till the day
> Appear of respiration to the just,
> And vengeance to the wicked . . .

In place of the unfallen world that its Creator pronounced good and that aroused the admiration and envy of the devil himself, Michael portrays a "perverted World" that will end only with the Last Judgment.

Conclusion.

U nlike certain of his near-contemporaries, Milton never renounced the classical allusions that for generations had provided the traditional ornaments of poetry. Though he might on occasion disparage the tales of the *Metamorphoses* as superstitious fables, he continued to mine them for metaphors and similes, or to emulate them by elaborating his own substitute-myths. When he did brace himself to banish the "goodly . . . train of gods and goddesses,"[1] this was essentially a ritual gesture: an apotropaeic ceremony, introduced into the context of a re-enacted theomachy. Not infrequently he resorted to the archaic convention of the *pharmakos* or scapegoat; the principal divinities that he scourged into ignominious exile were monsters like Typhon and Dagon or brutish idols like Moloch, rather than the more amiable deities of Greece. When he did include the Olympians under his sentence of banishment, they were usually overshadowed by more sinister divinities of the ancient Middle East; his major emphasis generally fell less on the seductive graces of the Graeco-Roman pantheon than on the more repellent aspects of Oriental idol-worship.

Classical mythology owed its very considerable vogue in Renaissance Europe to the fact that it was no longer believed literally and might accordingly be enjoyed as a supreme fiction. Whatever its moral dangers, it was on the whole theologically innocuous, far less insidious than many of the philosophical doctrines of the ancients. With proper guidance a youth might enjoy its fables, while acquiring some knowledge of natural and moral philosophy easily and pleasantly through whatever allegorical interpretations his tutors or his handbook might make accessible. Maturer men might employ it as a medium for discourse. For these it might provide a variable, but intelligible vocabulary of symbols; a repository of motifs and images, exempla and commonplaces which might serve to reinforce a rhetorical argument; and a source for the ornaments of style.

On the other hand, its original associations with heathenism made it an easy target. Though the shrines of those gods of the Gentiles had long since been overturned, they had found at least a temporary refuge in the numerous mythographical and iconological manuals of the Renaissance and in Renaissance poetry and oratory. In that highly polemical age they were vulnerable to the attacks of moralists whose real objections were ultimately directed less against the religious content of the pagan myths than against their immorality and potentially corrupting influence on the young, or against their inutility. They were idle vanities, and reading them was a waste of valuable time that might well be devoted to more solid and profitable matter. The attack on pagan myth was, in many respects, essentially an attack on poetic fiction, ancient or modern, and must be assessed in the larger context of the quarrel of the arts. Poetry in general—and particularly its mythological ornaments—was still in large part subject to the objections that had been raised against it in the time of Plato, and that had been reiterated in various forms by late classical and medieval critics.

But the use of classical myth was also being challenged on essentially literary grounds. Since it was no longer credible (the idoloclasts argued), it must necessarily lack verisimilitude and probability; mythological allusions in contemporary poetry could only destroy the plausibility and efficacy of the poetic image. Representing the impossible and incredible instead of achieving a convincing likeness of the true or apparently true, how could the poet fulfill his traditional office? How could he create the lively and credible fiction that would simultaneously teach, move, and delight his reader? To certain critics the mythical ornaments of poetry seemed unfashionably obsolescent: an outworn garment of style that might best be passed on to a servant. The poet (they suggested) ought to seek new and original devices, fresh and ingenious inventions to adorn his discourse. Alternatively, he might be better advised to renounce ornamentation altogether, focusing his attention on matter rather than on manner and exploring the resources of the plain style. Others exhorted him to eschew fantasy for sound judgment, and fiction for solid truth, basing his art on the facts of natural or social history or of revealed religion. In particular the contrast between sacred and profane poetry engaged a number of leading poets and critics during this period: a contrast that accentuated the correlative antitheses between spiritual and secular themes and motifs, Biblical and pagan imagery, and divine and human inspiration.

Thus, in a congratulatory poem on Davenant's *Gondibert,* Abraham Cowley commended the author for eliminating the supernatural from his epic. Heroic poetry had hitherto seemed "like some fantastick *Fairy Land* . . .":

> *Gods, Devils, Nymphs, Witches* and *Gyants race,*
> And all but *Man* in *Mans chief work* had place.

Like "some *worthy Knight* with sacred Arms," Davenant had managed to "drive the *Monsters* thence, and end the *Charms.*" In another poem, an epicedium on the death of Richard Crashaw, Cowley praised the dead poet for restoring poetry from profane to sacred themes, leading the banished muses "home back to their *Holy Land*":

Still the old *Heathen Gods* in Numbers dwell,
The Heav'enliest thing on Earth still keeps up *Hell.*
Nor have we yet quite purg'd the *Christian Land;*
Still *Idols* here, like *Calves* at Bethel stand.
And though *Pans Death* long since all *Oracles* broke,
Yet still in Rhyme the Fiend *Apollo* spoke: . . .
What different faults corrupt our *Muses* thus?
Wanton as *Girles,* as *old Wives,* Fabulous!

In the preface to his *Poems* (1656), Cowley returned to the theme of sacred poetry.[3] He had designed his incomplete *Davideis* in twelve books "after the *Patern* of our Master *Virgil,*" and had intended to conclude its plot after the "examples of *Homer* and *Virgil,* whom we should do ill to forsake to imitate others . . . " In form and structure, then, he was following the poets of pagan antiquity; but his argument has been taken from Scripture—and he goes out of his way to extol "the *Dignity* of the *Matter*" he has chosen, based as it is on a Biblical theme: "When I consider this, and how many other bright and magnificent subjects of like nature the *Holy Scripture* affords and *proffers* . . . to *Poesie:* It is not without grief and indignation that I behold that *Divine Science* employing all her inexhaustible riches of *Wit* and *Eloquence*" in flattering great persons, in idolising foolish women, in scurrilous laughter, or at best "on the confused antiquated *Dreams* of senseless *Fables* and *Metamorphoses.*" Among all the holy things which "the *Devil* ever stole and alienated from the service of the *Deity,* . . . there is none that he so universally and so long usurpt as *Poetry.*" It is time, therefore, to "recover it out of the *Tyrants* hands, and to restore it to the *Kingdom of God,* who is the *Father* of it."

The reference to poetry as a "divine science,"[4] in this context is more than an echo of the Platonic commonplace—that poetry is a divinely inspired gift. The phrase itself had been traditionally applied to theology (though occasionally to metaphysics), and in transferring it to poetry Cowley has not only extolled the art itself. He has also adapted arguments conventional in late medieval and Renaissance defences of poetry—that it was formerly *prisca theologia,* that large sections of the Scriptures themselves were poetry, that poetry resembled mystical theology—to the cause of "divine" poetry: exhorting his contemporaries to select a Biblical theme.

Milton shared Cowley's views, on this subject at least, though he did not cite them. His own major achievement lay in the area of "divine poetry" (as his contemporaries would have called it); based as it is on sacred history and doctrine, his art is as intimately associated with the *divina scientia,* theology, as the celestial Muse Urania and her sister Celestial Wisdom. As with other poets of his century—Cowley and Crashaw, Donne and Herbert and Vaughan, and indeed Herrick—

there is a dichotomy in his *oeuvre* between the secular and the spiritual and it is significantly analogous at times to that between the Earthly and the Heavenly Man in his own poetry. But Milton can on occasion blur these distinctions; his secular verse is often more spiritual than worldly, and much of his minor poetry resists this kind of categorization.

The interrelationships between his classical and Biblical imagery also resist reduction to a single formula. In many instances it is the analogy which is predominant; in other cases Milton stresses the conflicts and discrepancies between them. His use of such images is conditioned almost inevitably by the genres in which he is writing, by his subject-matter or theme, by his literary models, and by his understanding of the principles of decorum. In his earlier Latin poems he is sometimes far more prodigal in his use of classical allusions than in some of his earlier English poems in the Spenserian or the Jonsonian tradition. Renaissance pastoral normally involved Sicilian or Arcadian allusions. Classical myth was virtually endemic in the masque. In his funeral elegies, whether Latin or English, Milton usually draws on both Biblical and classical imagery; but in several of his Italianate lyrics on religious themes his imagery is almost entirely Scriptural.

Like many other humanists of his period, he frequently treats the classical pantheon sympathetically. The religion of Greece and Rome provides similes for praising Adam and Eve and Samson, archangels and the divine persons of the Christian faith. Milton is quick to exploit analogies between the figments of Hellenic fable—the rebellion of the Titans, the fall of Vulcan, the garden of the Hesperides, the myth of Deucalion and Pyrrha—and the events of sacred history. On the other hand, he is equally quick to censure the errors of the Gentiles, to condemn the ancient myths as heathen fables, and to accentuate the contrast betwen true and false divinities: between the Judaeo-Christian God and the gods of paganism. On more than one occasion he stresses the cessation of the oracles and the rout of the pagan gods. This occurs (significantly) within the context of a theomachy; and it is equally significant that the poet places his greatest emphasis not so much on the classical divinities of Greece and Rome as on the more barbarous of the Gentile gods: the idols of the ancient Middle East, the rivals of Jehovah or the corrupters of His worshippers.

*   *   *

Although Biblical and classical tradition are apparently the major sources of Milton's imagery, they are, nevertheless, only two of many influences on his poetry; and it would be misleading to stress their interrelationships to the neglect of other sources of his images and comparisons: geographical and travel literature, natural history, astronomy, the new science.

While recognizing that Renaissance conceptions of these traditions often varied significantly from our own, we must also bear in mind that for Renaissance writers themselves their meaning and value were often variable and equivocal. That they might appear in very different perspectives to the poet, the natural philosopher, and the theologian. That the same author might see them in different lights—or deliberately place them in different lights in order to make his readers see them differently. That their shading, their coloring, even their shape, might vary with their poetic or polemical contexts, changing with the variable and shifting focus of the author's vision.

But "vision" is an ambiguous term; and the critic should not confuse the author's actual beliefs with the images he projects. What the poet sees himself, or thinks that he sees, may be one thing. What he tries to make his readers see is another matter.

By isolating and juxtaposing concepts like "the Biblical" and "the classical," moreover, the critic is apt to exaggerate either the analogies or the differences between them. As they are neither parallels nor logical contraries, treating them as a frame of reference for interpreting Renaissance art or literature can easily result in misinterpreting the works of art themselves and oversimplifying the categories or traditions the critic is applying to them. What is important, and significant, for the modern reader is not the way these diversities and similarities between the classical and the Scriptural appear to him and his own contemporaries, but how they appeared to the sixteenth- or seventeenth-century poet and to *his* contemporaries. And, more significantly, in what contexts, for what purposes, and by what poetic or rhetorical methods he heightens the correspondences or potential oppositions between them.

Thus in several respects the distinction "Biblical"—"classical" seems as potentially misleading for the student of Milton's poetry as the nineteenth-century antithesis between Milton the humanist and Milton the Puritan. Classical and Biblical values and motifs were so closely interwoven in Renaissance civilization that it did not necessarily require strenuous and systematic effort to reconcile them. The apparent reconciliations and accommodations which strike us perhaps as the achievements of this or that particular poet are frequently an inherited compromise rather than a new and hard-won solution. Conversely, the oppositions and antitheses that a writer may emphasize in bringing these traditions into confrontation may be less original than they appear to be—a legacy from dialectical battles fought long ago between partisans of Alithia and Pseustis. Again, the author's treatment of analogies or antitheses between the classical and the Scriptural generally varies with the immediate literary contexts of such allusions. If at one point he emphasizes the similarities and understresses the divergences between them—or reverses his emphasis elsewhere—the seeming inconsistencies are a response to the altered dramatic context in his own poetic fiction; he has varied his literary technique, not (necessarily) changed his own mind.

*   *   *

Neither mutually exclusive nor mutually compatible, the elements of the classical and Scriptural traditions coexisted in an uneasy truce, sometimes in a state of conflict, sometimes in temporary alliance. Interfused throughout Renaissance civilization—not unlike the hooked atoms of that aboriginal continuum, the void—the traditions themselves were still in a process of formation or re-formation, definition or re-definition. As structures and systems of meaning they still existed (to a significant degree) *in potentia*. The elements of these traditions were, in a sense, building-blocks; and diverse men might structure or restructure them quite differently. It remained the task of the individual, the group, the institution to sort them out, to separate or conjoin them, and to bring them into harmony or opposition. In varying literary contexts the same author might treat them variably, now stressing analogies and now emphasizing distinctions.

Just as the poetic and rhetorical exploitation of these traditions was often variable, their definition seems to have been flexible during the period of the sixteenth and seventeenth centuries. It would be dangerous, accordingly, to project twentieth-century conceptions of "the classical heritage," "the classical tradition"—or of their Biblical counterparts—retrospectively onto the thought and sensibility of the late Renaissance. In Milton's writings as in those of earlier periods—the *Commedia* of Dante, the *Ecloga Theoduli*, the Virgilian centos of still earlier Christian poets—the treatment of classical and Biblical images and motifs seem to have been largely conditioned by the organizational schema (or schemas) consciously selected by the author; by considerations of theme and genre, choice of models, the nature of his audience; by the techniques of persuasion and representation accessible to him and to his contemporaries; and by the kind of rhetorical objective (praise or blame, accusation or defense, exhortation or dehortation) he has committed himself to.

In short, the poet's presentation of tradition was, in a sense, a new and fresh creation: a restructuring and reconstitution of the tradition itself. However much it might reflect, consciously or unconsciously, the influence of predecessors, this redefinition was an original achievement, peculiar to the individual author or indeed to the individual work. The "real" meaning that Graeco-Roman antiquity and its heritage held for him is implicit in his own poetic structures; and it is sometimes hard for his later readers to distinguish his sense of tradition from the sense that he himself has, voluntarily or involuntarily, imposed upon the tradition—or to differentiate his idea of the tradition from the artificial restructuring of tradition in his own poetic fictions. If he does on occasion achieve a convincing redefinition of either or both traditions, harmonizing them or accentuating their divergences, this *concordia discors* is largely a literary achievement, relative to the specific poem.

A Renaissance poem was not a mirror held up to nature or to society, as some of its best writers professed it to be. Nor was it a reflection of the author's own mind and sensibility, or of a contemporary worldview, or of the spirit of an age, as critics of a later generation thought. It was rather a chrystallization of elements common to all of these—but selective, not all-inclusive—and the elements of what we call the classical and Scriptural traditions were among them. It possessed, moreover, inherent in its formal structures and scarcely isolable from them, an inner magnetic structure (so to speak) of "sympathies or antipathies" peculiar to itself. This pattern of relationships—between diverse and often conflicting values brought into temporary and perhaps unstable equilibrium—might be significant and valid within the context of the poem, but not *a fortiori* for the world beyond and without the poetic "heterocosm."

In this system of interlocking truths and apparent truths—of history and fiction and of philosophy and myth—the juxtaposition of the real and the fabulous might at one point result in discrediting the false; yet at another point the false might illustrate and lend vividness and verisimilitude to the true. Within the context of the poem the paradigmatic "seventeenth-century reader"—himself a fiction—might be willing to acknowledge and accept the ambiguities of the poetic image. The same fictional techniques (as he recognized) that made a lie seem credible might enhance the immediacy, if not the credibility, of truth. Yet by assimilating true and false to the level of *apparent* reality, to the status of poetic images or *eidola,* the same techniques might blur the essential distinctions between them. In the context of the poem the infinite could only be represented as finite, eternity in terms of time, the *invisibilia Dei* as though they were visible, and the spiritual as corporeal. Even in substituting Biblical history for pagan myth as heroic argument, and the Christian marvellous for the machinery of classical epic, the poet risked compromising the very realities that he was endeavoring to affirm: ruining (as Marvell feared the author of *Paradise Lost* might do) "The sacred Truths to Fable and old Song . . ."

Notes

Notes

Chapter One: *Sion and Helicon*

1. For the tension between classical and Christian elements in the works of Milton and his contemporaries, see Harold Roland Swardson, Jr., *Poetry and the Fountain of Light: Observations on the Conflict Between Christian and Classical Traditions in Seventeenth-Century Poetry*. For Milton's use of the Bible see James H. Sims, *The Bible in Milton's Epics* (Gainesville, Fla., 1962); and Burton O. Kurth, *Milton and Christian Heroism: Biblical Epic Themes and Forms in Seventeenth Century England* (Berkeley, 1959). For Milton's knowledge of patristic tradition and of medieval and Renaissance theological thought, and for the development of his own theological views, see John P. Pritchard, "The Fathers of the Church in the Hands of John Milton," *Classical Journal*, Vol. 33 (1937), pp. 79–87; C.A. Patrides, *Milton and the Christian Tradition* (Oxford, 1966); and *This Great Argument: a Study of Milton's De Doctrina Christiana as a Gloss upon Paradise Lost* (Princeton, 1962). For Milton's knowledge and use of rabbinical tradition, see Harris F. Fletcher, *Milton's Semitic Studies and Some Manifestations of Them in His Poetry* (Chicago, 1926) and *Milton's Rabbinical Readings* (Urbana, 1930; Harold Fisch, *Jerusalem and Albion: The Hebriac Factor in Seventeenth-Century Literature* (New York, 1964) and "Hebraic Style and Motifs in *Paradise Lost*," in *Language and Style in Milton*, ed. Ronald David Emma and John T. Showcross (New York, 1967), pp. 30–64. See also Kitty Cohen, *The Throne and the Chariot: Studies in Milton's Hebraism* (The Hague, 1975); Isabel Rivers, *Classical and Christian Ideas in English Renaissance Poetry: A Students' Guide* (London, 1979); Austin C. Dobbins, *Milton and the Book of Revelation: The Heavenly Cycle* (University, Alabama, 1975); Jonathan Howard Collett, "Characteristic Uses of Classical Mythology by Marvell and Milton," *DAI*, Vol. 31 (1971), 2871A; Thomas Augustus Brennan, "Idols and Idolatry in the Prose and Early Poetry of John Milton," *DAI*, Vol. 31 (1971), 2868A; Douglas Bush, *Pagan Myth and Christian Tradition in English Poetry* (Philadelphia, 1968); Michael Lieb, *Poetics of the Holy: A Reading of Paradise Lost* (Chapel Hill, 1981; Jason P. Rosenblatt, "A Revaluation of Milton's Indebtedness to Hebraica in *Paradise Lost*," *DAI*, Vol. 31 (1970) 368A.

2. The quotations from Milton's poetry in this chapter, as well as the English translations from his Latin poetry are derived from John Milton, *Paradise Regained, The Minor Poems, and Samson Agonistes* ed. Merritt Y. Hughes (Garden City, N.Y., 1937) and from John Milton, *Paradise Lost*, ed. Merritt Y. Hughes (New York, 1935). The first of these will be cited hereafter in this chapter as Hughes *(PR)* or *(MP)* or *(SA)*; and the second as Hughes *(PL)*. Unless otherwise specified, quotations from the prose are based on John Milton, *Complete Poems and Major Prose*, ed. Merritt Y. Hughes (New York, 1957); this will be cited hereafter in this chapter as *Major Prose*. For discussion of the probable sources of Milton's images, see the notes in the three editions by Hughes

listed above; the annotations on particular passages in Milton's Latin poems, minor English poetry, and *Paradise Regained* in *A Variorum Commentary on the Poems of John Milton*, gen. ed. Merritt Y. Hughes London and New York, 1970–), Vols. 1, 2, 4; the annotations in *The Poetical Works of John Milton*, ed. H.J. Todd, Second edition (London, 1809) and in *Paradise Lost*, ed. Thomas Newton (London, 1749 and *Paradise Regain'd . . . To Which is Added Samson Agonistes: and Poems upon Several Occasions* (London, 1752); relevant articles in *A Milton Encyclopedia*, gen. ed. William B. Hunter, Jr. (Lewisburg, Pa., 1978–80); and annotations in *Complete Prose Works of John Milton*, gen. ed. Don M. Wolfe (New Haven, 1953–1982).

3. Hughes (*MP*), p. 43n. See also *A Variorum Commentary*, Vol. 1. *The Latin and Greek Poems*, ed. Douglas Bush (New York and London, 1970).

4. Hughes (*MP*), pp. 47–49.

5. Hughes (*MP*), pp. 335–337.

6. Hughes (*MP*), pp. 83–93.

7. Hughes (*MP*), pp. 104–107.

8. Hughes (*MP*), pp. 60–69.

9. Hughes (*MP*), pp. 276–277.

10. Hughes (*MP*), p. 317.

11. Hughes (*MP*), pp. 304–307.

12. Hughes (*MP*), p. 299.

13. Among general studies of Milton's imagery see Theodore H. Banks, *Milton's Imagery* (New York, 1950), pp. 664–669. For typological imagery, see William G. Madsen, *From Shadowy Types to Truth: Studies in Milton's Symbolism* (New Haven and London, 1968); Hugh Reid MacCallum, "Milton and Figurative Interpretation of the Bible," *UTQ*, Vol. 31 (1962), pp. 397–415. For classical influence on Milton's poetry see Douglas Bush, *Mythology and the Renaissance Tradition in English Poetry* (Minneapolis and London, 1932); Davis P. Harding, *Milton and the Renaissance Ovid* (Urbana, 1946) and *The Club of Hercules: Studies in the Classical Background of Paradise Lost* (Urbana, 1962); Helga Spevack-Husmann, *The Mighty Pan: Miltons mythologische Vergleiche* (Münster, 1963). See also John A. Shawcross, "A Metaphoric Approach to Reading Milton," *BSUF*, Vol. 8 (1967), pp. 17–22; John A. Via, "Studies in the Imagery of Milton's Poetry and Prose to 1642," *DA* Vol. 29 (1968) 580A; Don Cameron Allen, *The Harmonious Vision: Studies in Milton's Poetry* (Baltimore, 1954): Patrick Grant, *Images and Ideas in Literature of the English Renaissance* (Amherst, 1979); Roland Mushat Frye, *Milton's Imagery and the Visual Arts: Iconographic Tradition in the Epic Poems* (Princeton, 1978); Joseph A. Galdon, S.J., *Typology and Seventeenth-Century Literature* (The Hague, 1975); Earl Miner (ed.), *Literary Uses of Religious Typology from the Late Middle Ages to the Present* (Princeton, 1977).

For other aspects of Milton's imagery see John C. Ulreich, Jr., "The Typological Structure of Milton's Imagery," *Milton Studies*, Vol. 5 (1973), pp. 67–85; Robert M. Adams, "Contra Hartman: Possible and Impossible Structures of Milton's Imagery," in *Seventeenth-Century Imagery: Essays on the Uses of Figurative Language from Donne to Farquhar*, ed. Earl Miner (Berkeley, 1971), pp. 25–47; Jonathan Goldberg, "*Virga Iesse*: Analogy, Typology, and Anagogy in a Miltonic Simile," *Milton Studies*, Vol. 5 (1973), pp. 177–190; Anny Crunelle, "Myth and Imagination in Milton's Images of Water," *Cahiers Elisabéthains*, Vol. 15 (1979), pp. 43–56; Julian Mason, "Milton Modifies a Metaphor: 'Veritas Filia Temporis,'" *Milton Quarterly*, Vol. 12 (1978), pp. 101–104. J. Pironon, "The Images of Woman in the Sonnets and Some Minor Poems of John Milton," *Cahiers Elisabéthains*, Vol. 18 (1980), pp. 43–52; C.M. George, "The Wolf Image in Milton," *ES*, Vol. 52 (1971), pp. 30–32; John C. Ulreich, "Typological Symbolism in Milton's Sonnett XXIII," *Milton Quarterly*, Vol. 8 (1974), pp. 7–10.

14. Cf. Thomas B. Stroup, *Religious Rite and Ceremony in Milton's Poetry* (Lexington, Kentucky, 1968).

15. The preceding line (54) is defective; John Heskin suggested an allusion to Mercy. For the textual problems associated with this passage, see Hughes (*MP*), p. 25n and *A Variorum Commentary*, Vol. 2, *The Minor English Poems*, ed. A.S.P. Woodhouse and Douglas Bush (New York and London, 1972).

16. See the study of this poem by Jackson I. Cope, "Fortunate Fall as Form in Milton's 'Fair Infant,'" *JEGP*, Vol. 63 (1964), pp. 660–674.

17. Among studies of *Lycidas* see James Holly Hanford, "The Pastoral Elegy and Milton's 'Lycidas,'" *PMLA*, Vol. 25 (1910), pp. 403–447; Rosemond Tuve, *Images and Themes in Five Poems by Milton* (Cambridge, Mass., 1957); Scott Elledge (ed.), *Milton's Lycidas: Edited to Serve as an Introduction to Criticism* (New York and London, 1966); Joseph Anthony Wittreich, Jr., *Visionary Poetics: Milton's Tradition and His Legacy* (San Marino, California, 1979); C.A. Patrides (ed.), *Milton's Lycidas: The Tradition and the Poem* (New York, 1961); Isabel G. MacCaffrey, "*Lycidas*: the Poet in a Landscape," in *The Lyric and Dramatic Milton*, ed. Joseph Summers (New York, 1965), pp. 65–92; Achsah Guibbory, "Natalis Comes and the Digression on Fame in Milton's 'Lycidas,'" *N&Q, n.s.*, Vol. 18 (1971), p. 292; J. Auffret, "Pagano-Christian Syncretism in *Lycidas*," *Anglia*, Vol. 87 (1969), pp. 26–38; Clay Hunt, *Lycidas and the Italian Critics* (New Haven, 1979); David S. Berkeley, "*Inwrought with Figures Dim*": *A Reading of Milton's "Lycidas"* (The Hague and Paris, 1974).

18. Hughes (*MP*), p. 285n.

19. Among studies of the Orpheus image in *Lycidas* and in other poems by Milton, see Caroline W. Mayerson, "The Orpheus Image in *Lycidas*," *PMLA*, Vol. 64 (1949), pp. 189–207; Elizabeth Sewell, *The Orphic Voice: Poetry and Natural History* (New Haven, 1960); Marilyn L. Williamson, "The Myth of Orpheus in 'L'Allegro' and 'Il Penseroso,'" *MLQ*, Vol. 32 (1971), pp. 377–386. In *Paradise Lost* (III, lines 15–20; VII, lines 30–39) Milton contrasts his Biblical and celestial muse with Calliope, the mother of Orpheus and muse of epic poetry, stressing parallels as well as differences between himself and the poet Orpheus in his art, his inspiration, and his personal danger. As theological poet, as supposed author of the Orphic Hymns, and as mythical visitor to the underworld, Orpheus would provide a classical counterpart to Milton's "divine" poetry on Judaeo-Christian themes. Similarly, mythographical interpretations of the power of Orpheus' singing over beasts and trees as allusions to the social function of the poet in moving and educating rude and savage men could serve as a pagan "type" (so to speak) for the social role of the English Christian poet seeking to employ his talents in works "doctrinal and exemplary to a nation."

20. See Wayne Shumaker, "Flowerets and Sounding Seas; A Study in the Affective Structure of *Lycidas*," *PMLA*, Vol. 66 (1951), pp. 485–494.

21. A recent study suggests that the final *consolatio*, bidding the mourning shepherds to cease their weeping as *Lycidas* is not truly dead but alive in Heaven, is delivered not in the *persona* of the uncouth swain, but in the *persona* of the Archangel Michael; see William G. Madsen, "The Voice of Michael in *Lycidas*," *SEL*, Vol. 3 (1963), pp. 1–7.

The emotional *peripeteia*, the sudden reversal "contrary to expectation" from the deepest despair to the reassurance of immortality is comparable to the change in tone in the concluding verses of Spenser's November Eclogue, where the antitheses between "buried body" and "blessed soul" and between earth and heaven are emphasized by the altered refrain: "O heavie herse, . . ., "O carefull verse"; "O happye herse, . . . O joyfull verse." In Milton's epicedium, however, the reversal is much more abrupt, and there is virtually no transition in this sudden alteration from doubt to faith.

22. See Robert Martin Adams, "Reading *Comus*," *MP*, Vol. 51 (1953), pp. 18–32.

23. Among studies of this entertainment, see John Malcolm Wallace, "Milton's *Arcades*," *JEGP*, Vol. 68 (1959), pp. 627–636, John Demaray, "'Arcades' as a Literary Entertainment," *PLL*, Vol. 8 (1972), pp. 15–26;

24. See James Holly Hanford and James G. Taaffe, *A Milton Handbook*, Fifth

Edition (New York, 1970), pp. 123-124. See also Nan C. Carpenter, "Milton and Music: Henry Lawes, Dante, and Casella," *English Literary Renaissance*, Vol. 2 (1972), pp. 237-242; and Willa McClung Evans, *Henry Lawes: Musician and Friend of Poets* (New York, 1966).

25. See D.T. Starnes, "The Figure Genius in the Renaissance," *Studies in the Renaissance*, Vol. 11 (1964), pp. 234-244.

26. For studies of Renaissance Platonism and Pythagoreanism and the correspondences between instrumental music and the harmony of the cosmos and the human microcosm, see S.K. Heninger, Jr., *Touches of Sweet Harmony: Pythagorean Cosmology and Renaissance Poetics* (San Marino, California, 1974); John Hollander, *The Untuning of the Sky: Ideas of Music in English Poetry, 1500-1700* (Princeton, 1961); Irene Samuel, *Plato and Milton* (Ithaca, 1947).

Both *Arcades* and *Comus* utilize imagery developed earlier in Milton's Second Prolusion, "On the Music of the Spheres." In this academic exercise Milton had alluded to Plato's myth of the celestial Sirens who "hold both gods and men fast bound by the wonder of their harmonious song." He had associated "that heavenly music" with the Hesiodic myth that "the Muses dance day and night before Jove's altar. . . ." (See Hughes, *Major Prose*, pp. 603n-604.) He had also suggested that Pythagoras, who "alone of mortals is said to have heard this harmony," may have been some "good genius or a denizen of the sky who perhaps was sent down by some ordinance of the gods to imbue the minds of men with divine knowledge and to recall them to righteousness"; see Hughes, *Major Prose*, pp. 603-604. As music tutor to the Egerton children, Lawes is, to a degree, assimilated to this idealized Pythagoras of the Second Prolusion. In *Arcades* he is the genius of the wood and harkens to the nightly music of the stars; in *Comus* he is a denizen of the skies, who dwells just below the stars and has been sent down from heaven to assist the favorites of Jove. The motif of chastity, central to *Comus*, is also enunciated in the Prolusion, where it is associated not only with the pure and temperate character of Pythagoras and with the music of the heavens, but also with the paradisal motif of the Golden Age. The imagery of this passage suggestively parallels that of the Nativity Ode: "If our hearts were as pure, as chaste, as snowy as Pythagoras' was, our ears would . . . be filled with that supremely lovely music of the wheeling stars. Then indeed all things would seem to return to the age of gold . . ., and we should enjoy the blessing of a peace that the gods themselves might envy"; see Hughes, *Major Prose*, p. 604.

27. See Angus Fletcher, *Allegory: The Theory of a Symbolic Mode* (Ithaca, 1964); Michael Murrin, *The Veil of Allegory: Some Notes Toward a Theory of Allegorical Rhetoric in the English Renaissance* (Chicago and London, 1969). Among recent studies of *Comus* see John S. Diekhoff (ed.), *A Maske at Ludlow: Essays on Milton's Comus* (Cleveland, 1968); John Demaray, *Milton and the Masque Tradition: The Early Poems, Arcades, and Comus* (Cambridge, Mass., 1968); John Reesing, *Milton's Poetic Art: A Mask, Lycidas, and Paradise Lost* (Cambridge, Mass., 1968); John Arthos, *On a Mask Presented at Ludlow-Castle by John Milton* (Ann Arbor, 1954); C.L. Barber, "A Mask Presented at Ludlow Castle: The Masque as a Masque," in *The Lyric and Dramatic Milton*, ed. Joseph H. Summers (New York and London, 1965), pp. 35-63; Sears Jayne, "The Subject of Milton's Ludlow *Mask*," *PMLA*, Vol. 74 (1959), pp. 533-543; Watson Kirkconnell, *Awake the Courteous Echo: The Themes and Prosody of Comus, Lycidas, and Paradise Regained in World Literature with Translations of the Major Analogues* (Toronto and Buffalo, 1973); Stephen Orgel, *The Jonsonian Masque* (Cambridge, Mass., 1965); Jack B. Oruch, "Imitation and Invention in the Sabrina Myths of Drayton and Milton," *Anglia*, Vol. 90 (1972), pp. 60-70; Philip D. Ortego, "Comus, Circe, and the Whole Bit," *University Review* (Kansas City, Mo.), Vol. 36 (1970), pp. 287-291; Daniel C. Colvin, "Milton's *Comus* and the Pattern of Human Temptation," *Christianity and Literature*, Vol. 27 (1978), pp. 8-17.

28. See Tuve, *Images and Themes*, pp. 114n–116; cf. pp. 130–134 on the Circe myth; cf. John Demaray, "Milton's Comus: The Sequel to a Masque of Circe," *HLQ*, Vol. 29 (1966), pp. 245–254; Merritt Y. Hughes, "Spenser's Acrasia and the Circe of the Renaissance," *JHI*, Vol. IV (1943), pp. 381–399.

29. Cf. Barber in Diekhoff, pp. 198, 203.

30. Cf. A.S.P. Woodhouse, "The Argument of Milton's *Comus*," *UTQ*, Vol. 11 (1941), pp. 46–71, and "*Comus* Once More," *UTQ*, Vol. 19 (1950), pp. 218–223; Sears Jayne, *op.cit.*; Tuve, *Images and Themes*.

31. R.M. Adams, *op.cit.*

32. Milton's Seventh Prolusion offers suggestive analogies with the themes and images of the Ludlow masque. The soul is "destined, after wandering for a time on earth in innocence and purity, like some celestial visitor, to fly upward to its native heaven, and return to its proper home and the land of its birth. . . . Contemplation is . . . the only means whereby the mind can set itself free from the support of the body and concentrate its powers for the unbelievable delight of participating in the life of the immortal gods." Though learning is "our leader and director in our quest for happiness," the "contemplative way which leads to all that is supremely desirable, can give us no taste of true happiness" without integrity and purity. The "heavenly powers of the mind" must be kept "clean and untainted from all filth and pollution . . ."; Hughes, *Major Prose*, pp. 623–627.

33. See Lily B. Campbell, *Divine Poetry and Drama in Sixteenth Century England* (Cambridge, Berkeley and Los Angeles, 1959).

34. Hughes (*MP*), p. 173.

35. Hughes (*MP*), p. 172. Among studies of the Nativity Hymn, see Arthur E. Barker, "The Pattern of Milton's *Nativity Ode*," *UTQ*, Vol. 10 (1941), pp. 167–181; Tuve, *Images and Themes*, pp. 37–52; D.C. Allen, *Harmonious Vision*, pp. 3–25, discusses the "conflict between Christian and pagan harmony" in this work. For the background of Milton's treatment of the flight of the Gentile gods, see C.A. Patrides, "The Cessation of the Oracles: The History of a Legend," *MLR*, Vol. 9 (1965), pp. 500–507. In the *Aeneid* (Book VIII) Evander's people chant verses in praise of Hercules' exploits, beginning with his strangling the serpents sent by Juno in his infancy, and subsequently celebrating his martial victories and his labors. See also the Homeric hymn to Hermes. See also Kathleen M. Swaim, "'Mighty Pan': Tradition and an Image in Milton's Nativity *Hymn*," *SP*, Vol. 68 (1971), pp. 484–495; Lawrence W. Hyman, "Christ's Nativity and the Pagan Deities," *Milton Studies*, Vol. 2 (1970), pp. 103–112; Lawrence W. Kingsley, "Mythic Dialectic in the Nativity Ode," *Milton Studies*, Vol. 4 (1972), pp. 163–176.

36. Hughes, *Major Prose*, p. 669.

37. Hughes (*MP*), pp. 157–158n.

38. See F.T. Prince, *The Italian Element in Milton's Verse* (Oxford, 1954), pp. 60–63. Prince also noted the influence of "the tradition of the canzone," on the Nativity Hymn, but ascribed the "Italianisms" in this and other youthful poems largely to Spenserian influence; pp. 60–61.

39. Prince, pp. 63–66. For Italian influences on *Lycidas* and the "wide deviations from the strict form of the *canzone*" in this poem, see pp. 71–88.

40. See Heninger, *Touches of Sweet Harmony* . . .; Hollander, *The Untuning of the Sky*. . . .

41. Hughes (*MP*), p. 616n. See also William Riley Parker, *Milton's Debt To Greek Tragedy in Samson Agonistes* (Baltimore and London, 1937).

42. See John M. Steadman, "Milton's Harapha and Goliath," *JEGP*, Vol. 60 (1961), pp. 786–795, and *Milton's Epic Characters* (Chapel Hill, 1968), pp. 177–193. Among major studies of this drama see F. Michael Krouse, *Milton's Samson and the Christian Tradition* (Princeton, 1949); Arnold Stein, *Heroic Knowledge: An Interpretation of*

Paradise Regained and Samson Agonistes (Minneapolis, 1957); Watson Kirkconnell, *That Invincible Samson: The Theme of Samson Agonistes in World Literature with Translations of the Major Analogues* (Toronto, 1964); Mary Ann Nevins Radzinowicz, *Toward Samson Agonistes: The Growth of Milton's Mind* (Princeton, 1978); Anthony Low, *The Blaze of Noon: A Reading of Samson Agonistes* (New York and London, 1974).

43. For the ship-woman and ship-tempest imagery in this drama, see G.M. Young, "Milton and Harrington," *TLS*, Jan. 9, 1937, p. 28; Barbara Kiefer Lewalski, "The Ship-Tempest Imagery in *Samson Agonistes*," *N&Q,n.s.*, Vol. 6 (1959), pp. 372–373. Among other studies of the imagery of *Samson Agonistes*, see Lee Sheridan Cox, "Structural and Thematic Imagery in *Samson Agonistes* and *Paradise Regained*," *DA*, Vol. 23 (1963), 4342 (Indiana); John Carey, "Sea, Snake, Flower, and Flame in *Samson Agonistes*," *MLR*, Vol. 62 (1967), pp. 395–399; B. Eugene McCarthy, "Metaphor and Plot in *Samson Agonistes*," *Milton Quarterly* Vol. 6 (1972), pp. 86–92; J.J. M. Tobin, "*Samson* and Sea-Imagery Again," *ELN*, Vol. 15 (1977), pp. 23–27; Duncan Robertson, "Metaphor in *Samson Agonistes*," *UTQ*, Vol. 38 (1969), pp. 319–338; Samuel S. Stollman, "Samson's 'Sunny Locks the Laws': An Hebraic Metaphor," *SCN*, Vol. 26, No. v (1968), Item 3.

44. Hughes, (*SA*), p. 549n.

45. Hughes, (*SA*), p. 564n.

46. See Lee Sheridan Cox, "The 'Ev'ning Dragon' in *Samson Agonistes*: A Reappraisal," *MLN*, Vol. 76 (1961), pp. 577–584; Edward W. Tayler, "Milton's Firedrake," *Milton Quarterly*, Vol. 6 (1972), pp. 7–10; Lynn V. Sadler, "Typological Imagery in *Samson Agonistes*: Noon and the Dragon," *ELH*, Vol. 37 (1970), pp. 195–210; Samuel S. Stollman, "Samson as 'Dragon' and a Scriptural Tradition," *ELN*, Vol. 7 (1970), pp. 186–189.

47. For discussion of the phoenix symbol in this drama, see Roger B. Wilkenfeld, "Act and Emblem: The Conclusion of *Samson Agonistes*," *ELH*, Vol. 32 (1965), pp. 160–168; Albert R. Cirillo, "Time, Light, and the Phoenix: The Design of *Samson Agonistes*," in *Calm of Mind . . .*, ed. Joseph Anthony Wittreich, Jr. (Cleveland and London, 1971), pp. 209–233; Anthony Low, "The Phoenix and the Sun in *Samson Agonistes*," *Milton Studies*, Vol. 14 (1980), pp. 219–23.

48. See Ralph Nash, "Chivalric Themes in *Samson Agonistes*," in *Studies in Honor of John Wilcox*, ed. A Doyle Wallace and Woodburn O. Ross (Detroit, 1958), pp. 23–38; George R. Waggoner, "The Challenge to Single Combat in *Samson Agonistes*," *PQ*, Vol. 39 (1960), pp. 82–92.

49. For discussion of the hyaena-metaphor in this scene, see Robert A. Van Kluyve, "Out, Out, Hyaena," *American Notes & Queries*, Vol. 1 (1963), pp. 99–101; J.J.M. Tobin, "A Note on Dalila as 'Hyaena,'" *Milton Quarterly*, Vol. 11 (1977), pp. 89–91. Cf. the Hebrew words *tsabó' a* (hyena), *tsabú' a* (color or paint). The same word *tsabó' a* can signify "painted" or "colored" and "hypocritical."

49[a]. For discussion of similar imagery in Homeric and Virgilian epic, see Bernard Knox, "The Serpent and the Flame: The Imagery of the Second Book of the *Aeneid*," in *Virgil: A Collection of Critical Essays*, ed. Steele Commager (Englewood Cliffs, N.J., 1966), pp. 124–142; Cedric H. Whitman, *Homer and the Heroic Tradition* (New York, 1965), pp. 128–153. When the exhausted Odysseus prepares for sleep, covering himself with leaves in the Phaeacian thicket, he is compared to "a spark hidden under ashes"; see Whitman, p. 120; *Odyssey* V, 486 ff. As Hector awaits Achilles for their final combat, he is compared to a poisonous serpent waiting by its hole to attack some passerby (*Iliad* XXII. 93 ff.). In an omen prophesying the failure of the Trojan attack on the Greek ships, the two sides are symbolically represented by an eagle and a serpent (*Iliad* XII. 200 ff.). Similes comparing the Greek or Trojan heroes to blazing flame recur throughout the *Iliad* (XI. 155 ff., 595; XIII. 330 ff., 673 ff., 687 ff.; XIV. 394 ff.; XV. 604 ff.; XVIII. 88 ff., 366 ff., 735 ff.; XVII 1 ff., 203 ff.; XIX. 475 ff.; XX. 370 ff., 422 ff., 490 ff.; XXI, 11 ff.).

Fire imagery is associated with both Turnus and Aeneas, as well as with other warriors in Virgil's epic (cf. Books X, XI, XII); although Virgil frequently employs it in the Homeric manner to heighten the heroic values in his battle-scenes, he sometimes treats it pejoratively, as with Dido's passion for Aeneas (Book IV) and the rage with which the Fury Allecto inspires Turnus and the Latin queen Amata (Book VII). In Aeneas' account of the fall of Troy, the Greek warrior Pyrrhus in his flashing armor is likened to a serpent that has just sloughed off its old skin and now glistens in its new (Book II).

49[b]. In the *Odyssey* the imminent destruction of the suitors is foreshadowed through omens of birds of prey and the slaughter of lesser birds and barnyard fowl. When two eagles fly over the Ithacan assembly, the omen is interpreted as a warning of the doom awaiting the suitors when Odysseus returns (II, 146 ff.). At the palace of Menelaus an eagle flies to the right of Telemachus' chariot carrying a tame goose snatched from the yard (XV, 160 ff.); this too is explained as an omen of Odysseus' revenge. A further sign, a hawk tearing a pigeon, receives the same interpretation (XV, 525 ff. XVII, 150 ff.). Subsequently Penelope dreams that an eagle, swooping down from the mountains, slays her domestic geese, identifying himself afterwards as Odysseus and the slaughtered geese as the suitors (XIX, 535 ff.). In the revenge-scene itself, as Odysseus and his son and two loyal retainers fall upon the suitors, they are compared to mountain vultures attacking smaller birds (XXII, 302 ff.). For discussion of this imagery, see Anne Amory, "The Reunion of Odysseus and Penelope," in Charles H. Taylor, Jr. (ed.), *Essays on the Odyssey* . . . (Bloomington, Indiana, 1965), pp. 109–110; *The Odyssey*, tr. Robert Fitzgerald (Garden City, NLY., 1963), pp. 479–483. Fitzgerald challenges the conventional interpretation of *aigypioi* (XXII, 302) as "vultures," arguing that Homer "meant a bird like a hawk or an eagle, a killer, a threat to geese, a hunter of small birds in general."

Conversely, while the suitors are plotting against Telemachus' life, they behold a similar but inauspicious omen; an eagle carrying a pigeon flies over them on the *left* side (XX, 240 ff.).

At the very end of the *Odyssey* there is a final reprise of this motif; as Odysseus attacks the relatives of the dead suitors. As they flee in panic, he falls upon them like an eagle (XXIV. 547 ff.); but further slaughter is averted by a sign from Zeus: a thunderbolt that falls at Athene's feet.

Similes based on birds of prey recur in the *Iliad*, but without the careful patterning that Fitzgerald perceives in the eagle similes of the *Odyssey*. Achilles runs with the speed of an eagle (XXI. 251 ff.). When Menelaus looks for Nestor's son Antilochus to carry the news of Patroclus' death back to Achilles, he is compared to the eagle—the most sharp-sighted of creatures—which suddenly spots a hare and plunges to seize him (XVII. 673 ff.). This aspect of Homer's eagle-simile would have interested Milton, as it would be ironically relevant to the paradox of Samson's exterior blindness and inner vision ("blind of sight," but "With inward eyes illuminated"). When Hector strikes at Achilles with his sword, he is likened to an eagle swooping down upon some lamb or hare (XXII, 306 ff.); and when he attacks one of the Greek ships, intending to set it afire, he is compared to an eagle plunging down upon feeding geese or cranes or swans (XV. 688 ff.). (Cf. the translations of the *Iliad* and *Odyssey* by Richmond Lattimore.) Similes based on falcons are not uncommon in the *Iliad*. The younger Greek warriors flee before Aeneas and Hector like daws or starlings before a hawk (XVII. 755 ff.). Patroclus resembles a flying hawk scattering daws and starlings before him (XVI. 582 ff.). And Artemis herself flees from Hera like a pigeon from a hawk (XXI, 491 ff.).

The imagery of "cloudless thunder" and "lightning" (*SA*, lines 1696, 1283–1286) is associated with heroes as well as with Zeus. Thus Idomeneus is compared to a thunderbolt that Zeus has hurled as a divine omen to men (*Iliad* XVII, 240 ff.). Virgil likens Aeneas to a bolt of lightning (*Aeneid*, Book XII).

Virgil makes occasional use of the imagery of birds of prey. Turnus seizes the young warrior Helenor as an eagle swoops up to the heavens with a swan or rabbit (Book IX). Camilla pounces on her foe like a hawk seizing a dove (Book XI). In a good omen announcing the safe arrival of the Trojan ships at Carthage, twelve swans that an eagle had scattered appear to be alighting on land (Book I).

See Viktor Pöschl, *The Art of Vergil: Image and Symbol in the Aeneid*, tr. Gerda Seligson (Ann Arbor, Michigan, 1966).

49ᶜ. Samson was sometimes regarded as an Old Testament type of Christ; and both as deliverer of God's people and as the agent of divine wrath and justice, his actions in the Philistine theatre might suggest analogies with the Last Judgment. See F. Michael Krouse, *Milton's Samson and the Christian Tradition* (Princeton, 1949). All four of the images in the Semichorus have traditional Christian connotations in addition to their classical associations; and one might recall the flame and eagle imagery associated with the Messianic advent and destruction of the rebellious angels in Raphael's account of the war in Heaven (*PL* VI, lines 762–766):

. . . at his right hand Victory
Sat Eagle-wing'd, beside him hung his Bow
And Quiver with three-bolted Thunder stor'd,
And from about him fierce Effusion roll'd
Of smoke and bickering flame, and sparkles dire. . . .

50. See Barbara Kiefer Lewalski, *Milton's Brief Epic: The Genre, Meaning and Art of Paradise Regained* (Providence and London, 1966); Louis L. Martz, *The Paradise Within: Studies in Vaughan, Traherne, and Milton* (New Haven and London, 1964); *A Variorum Commentary*, Vol. 4, *Paradise Regained*, ed. Walter MacKellar (New York and London, 1975). Among other studies of this brief epic and its images and themes, see Louis L. Martz, "*Paradise Regained*: The Meditative Combat," *ELH*, Vol. xxx 1960), pp. 223–247; Northrop Frye, "The Typology of *Paradise Regained*," *MP*, Vol. 53 (1956), pp. 227–238; Merritt Y. Hughes, "The Christ of *Paradise Regained* and the Renaissance Heroic Tradition," *SP*, Vol. 35 (1938), pp. 254–277; Lee Sheridan Cox, "Food-word Imagery in *Paradise Regained*," *ELH*, Vol. 28 (1961), pp. 225–243; Cooper R. Mackin, "Aural Imagery as Miltonic Metaphor: The Temptation Scenes of *Paradise Lost* and *Paradise Regained*," in *Explorations in Literature*, ed. Rima Drell Reck (Baton Rouge, 1966), pp. 32–42; D.C. Allen, *Harmonious Vision*, pp. 110–124; Arnold Stein, *Heroic Knowledge*, pp. 3–134; Jacques Blondel, *Le paradis reconquis* (Paris, 1955); Michael Fixler, "The Unclean Meats of the Mosaic Law and the Banquet Scene in *Paradise Regained*," *MLN*, Vol. 70 (1955), pp. 573–577; Elizabeth M. Pope, *Paradise Regained: The Tradition and the Poem* (Baltimore, 1947); Herbert H. Petit, "The Second Eve in *Paradise Regained*," *Papers of the Michigan Academy of Science, Arts and Letters*, Vol. 44 (1959), pp. 365–369; Robert E. Reiter, "In Adam's Room: A Study of the Adamic Typology of Christ in *Paradise Regained*," *DA*, Vol. 25 (1964), 3581–3582 (Univ. Michigan); Balachandra Rajan, "Jerusalem and Athens: The Temptation of Learning in *Paradise Regained*," in *Th' Upright Heart and Pure*, ed. Amadeus P. Fiore, O.F.M. (Pittsburgh and Louvain, 1967), pp. 61–74. Kirkconnell, *Awake the Courteous Echo*: Balachandra Rajan, *The Lofty Rhyme: A Study of Milton's Major Poetry* (London and Coral Gables, Florida, 1970); Louis L. Martz, *Poet of Exile: A Study of Milton's Poetry* (New Haven, 1980); Irene Samuel, "The Regaining of Paradise," in Balachandra Rajan (ed.), *The Prison and the Pinnacle* (Toronto and Buffalo, 1973), pp. 111–134; W.N. Knight, "To Enter Lists with God': Transformation

of Spenserian Chivalric Conventions in *Paradise Regained*," *Costerus*, Vol. 2 (1972), pp. 83–108; Robert A. Stein, "The Sources and Implications of the Jobean Analogies in *Paradise Regained*," *Anglia*, Vol. 86 (1970), pp. 323–333; Gayle E. Wilson, "Emblems in Paradise Regained," *Milton Quarterly*, Vol. 6 (1972), pp. 77–78; Robert A. Stein, "Eloquence as Power: Another Dimension of the Hercules Simile, *Paradise Regained*, IV, 562–8," *Milton Quarterly*, Vol. 4 (1970), pp. 22–24; Kathleen M. Swaim, "Hercules, Antaeus, and Prometheus: A Study of the Climactic Epic Similes in *Paradise Regained*," *SEL*, Vol. 18 (1978), pp. 137–153.

50[a]. This image of the rock withstanding the rage of the sea occurs also in classical epic. While his people are clamoring for war against the Trojans, King Latinus stands firm, like a rock in the sea, steadfast against the shock of the waves (*Aeneid*, Book VII). When Etruscans and Trojans attack Mezentius, he stands firm and immovable, like a cliff or promontory exposed to the violence of wind and sea (Book X). In the context of Milton's temptation-drama, this conventional image of constancy acquires additional meaning through the typological associations of the rock with Christ and His church, and of the sea with the world (cf. the aphorism *mundus mare*). The rock-simile in this passage points forward to the later image likening Christ's kingdom to a rock that will shatter all earthly monarchies. Though this image is based on Scripture, it also has analogues in classical heroic poetry. Hector is compared to a boulder crashing down from a rock-face and wreaking destruction below (*Iliad* XIII, 136 ff.); and Virgil applies a similar image to Turnus (*Aeneid*, Book XII). Cf. Daniel ii. 31–45; Matthew xxi. 42–44; Ephesians ii. 20–22; 1 Peter ii. 4–9.

51. Hughes (*PR*), p. 508n.

52. Hughes (*PR*), p. 484n.

53. Among studies of the identity-motif in this poem and its relation to the question of how much Satan knows about the true nature of his adversary, how much the Christ of *Paradise Regained* already knows about his own nature and his divine mission already (*before* the temptation-ordeal), and how much he learns during the course of this testing, see George McMurry Muldrow, "An Irony in *Paradise Regained*," *Papers on Language and Literature*, Vol. 3 (1967), pp. 377–380; Lawrence J. Nieman, The Nature of the Tempations in *Paradise Regained* Books I and II," *University Review* (Kansas City), Vol. 34 (1967), pp. 133–139; Irene Samuel, "The Regaining of Paradise"; Sheila Dana Dwight, "Satan's Motivations: A Reinterpretation of Milton's *Paradise Regained*," *DAI*, Vol. 38 (1977), p. 276A.

This motif is, in fact, closely linked with that of heroic wisdom and "heroic knowledge" with the allied themes of spiritual combat and spiritual kingship and with the image of recovered Paradise: the Paradise within. Moreover (though the devil does not realize it), it follows logically from the temptation of Athens: the bait of Greek learning and wisdom. "Know thy foes," wrote Donne in his Third Satire," The foul Devill . . . would allow/ Thee faine, his whole Realme to be quit. . . ." The world is "a withered and worne strumpet. . . ." The last of this triad of mortal enemies is the flesh; see Charles M. Coffin (ed.), *The Complete Poetry and Selected Prose of John Donne* (New York, 1952), pp. 96–97. "Know thyself," declared the Greek; and in the opinion of many this much-admired aphorism seemed more divine than human. It could be regarded as the epitome of Greek wisdom; yet in the temptation of Athens the Greek philosophers are accused of being "Ignorant of themselves," and even more ignorant of God. As spiritual king, ruling within the soul of man, the hero of this epic restores to the human soul its original liberty, its self-command; the original dominion of right reason over the appetites and passions, and the submission of right reason itself to the will of God. This inner obedience is comparable to that state of inner justice (or righteousness) that Tasso describes in the Allegory to his epic *Jerusalem Delivered*. A state of inner harmony and peace, appropriately symbolized by the figure of a Paradise within.

See Martz, *The Paradise Within*; Patrick Cullen, *Infernal Triad: the Flesh, the World, and the Devil in Spenser and Milton* (Princeton, N.J., 1975).

54. See Dante Alighieri, *La Divina Commedia*, ed. Natalino Sapegno, Vol. 3 (Firenze, 1967). Subsequently, as Beatrice gazes at the gryphon (the "twofold beast") and the poet fixes his own gaze on her eyes, he beholds now the attributes of one nature, now of another (xxxi. lines 118–123): "Come in lo specchio sol, non altrimenti/ la doppia fiera dentro vi raggiava,/ or con altri, or con altri reggimenti." Sapegno glosses this passage (p. 356) as a reference to the consideration of Christ as true man and true God. Cf. *Purgatorio* xxxii, line 47, 'l' animal binato"; line 96, "biforme fera." At the conclusion of the *Paradiso* (xxxiii, lines 127–132) the poet contemplates simultaneously the mysteries of the Incarnation and the Trinity. The second of the three symbolic circles which he beholds in his vision seems to bear a human likeness: "mi parve pinta della nostra effige. . . ." See Sapegno, Vol. 3 (Firenze, 1971).

55. See Irene Samuel, *Dante and Milton: The Commedia and Paradise Lost* (Ithaca, 1966).

56. See Frank Kermode, "Milton's Hero," *RES,ns*, Vol. 4 (1953), pp. 317–330; Michael Fixler, *Milton and the Kingdoms of God* (Evanston, 1964); Hughes, "The Christ of *Paradise Regained* and the Renaissance Heroic Tradition"; John M. Steadman, *Milton's Epic Characters: Image and Idol* (Chapel Hill, 1968), pp. 65–66, 125n.; Howard Schultz, *Milton and Forbidden Knowledge* (New York, 1955).

57. See Nieman, "The Nature of the Temptations. . . ."

57[a]. For discussion of the motif of self-knowledge and self-discovery in the *Odyssey*, the identity-motif, the theme of testing, and the disguise and false autobiographies of the hero, see George E. Dimock, Jr., "The Name of Odysseus," in *Essays on the Odyssey . . .*, ed. Taylor, pp. 54–72; Anne Amory, "The Reunion of Odysseus and Penelope," in *idem*, pp. 100–121; Charles Rowan Beye, *The Iliad, the Odyssey, and the Epic Tradition* (Garden City, N.Y., 1966), pp. 180–188; Cedric H. Whitman, *Homer and the Epic Tradition*, pp. 300–303; W.B. Stanford, *The Ulysses Theme . . .* Second Edition (Ann Arbor, Michigan, 1968), pp. 8–24.

57[b]. See Stanford, pp. 90–158, 281–323. Contrasting the "Autolycan element" in Odysseus' character and career with Athene's influence (pp. 24–42), Stanford emphasizes the range and variety of post-Homeric attitudes toward the Ithacan. On the one hand, he becomes a philosopher's ideal: "the ideal *homo viator*," the "type of the Stoic Citizen of the World," a "Choice pattern of the manly and the wise," a man "unconquered by labours, scorning pleasures, victorious in all lands" (pp. 121, 123, 125, 264n.). Yet he is also excoriated as the "nefarious liar"; and epithets applied to him in classical Latin poetry represent him as *fallax, fictor, infidus, subdolus, varius* (pp. 22, 286n.). He is also described as *artifex scelerum, commentor fraudis, inventor scelerum, machinator fraudis*. Several of these epithets anticipate those that Milton bestows on the anti-hero of *Paradise Lost* and *Paradise Regained*: "subtle Fiend" (*PL* II, line 815; *PR* I, line 465); "false dissembler (*PL* III, line 681); "fraudulent Impostor" (III, line 692); "Artificer of fraud" (IV, line 121).

Similar epithets had been applied to Satan and the serpent of Eden (John viii. 44; Genesis iii. 1). Milton might endow his devil with Odyssean traits in both epics while maintaining the traditional decorum of both characters.

57[c]. See Beye, pp. 165, 188; Stanford, p. 3. Etymologically *polytropos* suggests "of many turns," according to Stanford; and in the opinion of modern scholars Homer used this epithet in the sense of "one who has been turned in many ways, much-travelled, widely experienced . . .," deliberately placing it in the opening line of his epic to emphasize "the poem's main theme; . . . Odysseus's many wanderings and adventures before he regained his kingdom." In the late fifth century B.C. the "detractors" of Odysseus apparently interpreted the word "pejoratively in an ethical sense as 'often changing one's character, hence unstable, unprincipled, unscrupulous.'" Odysseus was sometimes compared (sometimes favorably, but usually pejoratively) to the polypus— and later to the chameleon—on the basis of their "protective changes of colour"; Stanford, pp. 91, 99, 259, 261. In defending Homer's hero the proto-Cynic philosopher Antisthenes maintained that, instead of referring to character, the word "simply denotes Odysseus' skill in adapting his figures of speech ('tropes') to his hearers at any particular time." Livius Andronicus translated *polytropos* as *versutus* "the man of turns"). To Roger Ascham it signified "'skilfull in many mens manners and facions . . .'"; and to George Chapman it meant one "'whose genius . . . turns through many and various ways towards the truth"; Stanford, pp. 99, 129, 315–316.

The word *sophos*, frequently applied to Odysseus, could signify "clever, skilled in technique' as well as 'wise,'" while the Latin *sapiens* might range in meaning from "'having common sense' to 'being a philosopher'". Stanford, pp. 109, 265n. For interpretations of similar epithets associated with Odysseus (*polymechanos, polymetis, polyplokos*, etc.), see Stanford, pp. 255, 259, 261, 299.

57[d]. See Louis L. Martz, "*Paradise Regained*: The Meditative Combat," *ELH*, Vol. 27 (1960), pp. 223–247.

57[e]. See Stanford, p. 184.

57[f]. See Stanford, p. 117.

58. Cf. C.H. Herford, *Dante and Milton* (Manchester, 1924).

59. Cf. A.J.A Waldock, *Paradise Lost and Its Critics* (Cambridge, 1956). For discussion of the Satanist controversy, see Hughes, *Complete Poems and Major Prose*, pp. 177–179; Milton Miller, "*Paradise Lost*: The Double Standard," *UTQ*, Vol. 20 (1951), pp. 183–199; Merritt Y. Hughes, "Satan and the 'Myth' of the Tyrant," in *Ten Perspectives on Milton* (New Haven and London, 1965), pp. 165–195; Calvin Huckabay, "The Satanist Controversy of the Nineteenth Century, "*Studies in English Literature* ed., Waldo F. McNeir (Baton Rouge, 1962), pp. 197–210.

Among studies of classical and Biblical elements in *Paradise Lost*, see Anne Bowers Long, "The Relations Between Classical and Biblical Allusions in Milton's Later Poems," *DA* Vol. 28 (1968), #5022-A; Edward L. Herbst, "Classical Mythology in *Paradise Lost*," *Classical Philology*, Vol. 29 (1934), pp. 147–148; Purvis E. Boyette, "Milton's Eve and the Neoplatonic Graces," *Renaissance Quarterly*, Vol. 20 (1967), pp. 341–344; Lawrence A. Sasek, "Satan and the Epic Hero: Classical and Christian Tradition" (Harvard Univ. diss., 1953); Coleman O. Parsons, "The Classical and Humanist Context of *Paradise Lost*, II, 495–505," *JHI*, Vol. 29 (1968), pp. 33–52; William R. Herman, "Heroism and *Paradise Lost*," *College English*, Vol. 21 (1959), pp. 13–17; Allen R. Benham, "Things Unattempted Yet in Prose or Rime," *MLQ*, Vol. 14 (1953), pp. 341–347; Jacques Blondel, *Milton, poète de la Bible dans le Paradis perdu* (Paris, 1959); J.M. Evans, *Paradise Lost and the Genesis Tradition* (Oxford, 1968); Nathaniel Venable David, Jr., "Biblical Proof Texts and Their Epic Contexts in *Paradise Lost*," *DAI*, Vol. 49 (1980), 4040A; Albert C. Labriola, "The Titans and the Giants: *Paradise Lost* and the Tradition of the Renaissance Ovid," *Milton Quarterly*, Vol. 12 (1978), pp. 9–16; Holly Jackson, "Ovid's *Metamorphoses* and Milton's *Paradise Lost*: The Pattern of Allusions," *DAI*, Vol. 36 (1975), 3653A; Rajan, *The Lofty Rhyme* . . .; Martz, *Poet of Exile* . . .; Michael Lieb, *Poetics of the Holy: A Reading of Paradise Lost* (Chapel Hill, 1981); Elizabeth J. Vessels, "A Mythic Light on Eve: The Function of Mythological Allusion in Defining Her Character and Role in the Epic Action of *Paradise Lost*," *DAI*, Vol. 33 (1973), 3605A; Joseph E. Duncan, *Milton's Earthly Paradise: A Historical Study of Eden* (Minneapolis, 1972); U. Milo Kaufmann, *Paradise in the Age of Milton* (Victoria, B.C., 1978); Margaret Jennings, "Typological Dialectic in Milton's Major Poems," *BSUF*, Vol. 17, No. 2 (1976), pp. 16–22; Kitty Cohen, *The Throne and the Chariot* . . .; Edward W. Tayler, *Milton's*

Poetry: Its Development in Time (Pittsburgh, 1979); *Milton and the Art of Sacred Song*, ed. J. Max Patrick and Roger H. Sundell (Madison, 1979); A.S. P. Woodhouse, *The Heavenly Muse: A Preface to Milton*, ed. Hugh MacCallum (Toronto and Buffalo, 1972); Francis Charles Blessington, *Paradise Lost and the Classical Epic* (Boston, 1979); Joan Webber, *Milton and His Epic Tradition* (Seattle, 1979); Arnold Stein, *The Art of Presence: The Poet and Paradise Lost* (Berkeley, 1977); Frederick Plotkin, *Milton's Inward Jerusalem: Paradise and the Ways of Knowing* (The Hague, 1971); Northrop Frye, *The Return of Eden: Five Essays on Milton's Epics* (Toronto, 1975); D.M. Rosenberg, *Oaten Reeds and Trumpets: Pastoral and Epic in Virgil, Spenser, and Milton* (Lewisburg, Pa., 1981); Thomas E. Maresca, *Three English Epics: Studies of Troilus and Criseyde, The Faerie Queene, and Paradise Lost* (Lincoln, Neb., 1979).

60. See James Holly Hanford, "The Temptation Motive in Milton," *SP*, Vol. 15 (1918), pp. 176–194; for the theme of spiritual combat in the Book of Job and its significance for *Paradise Regained*, see Lewalski, *Milton's Brief Epic* and Northrop Frye, "The Typology of *Paradise Regained*"; Clifford Davidson, "The Dialectic of Temptation," *BSUF*, Vol. 8 (1967), pp. 11–16.

61. See John M. Steadman, "The Idea of Satan as the Hero of *Paradise Lost*," *Proceedings of the American Philosophical Society*, Vol. 120, No. 4 (August, 1976), pp. 253–294.

62. See Rosalie L. Colie, *The Resources of Kind: Genre-Theory in the Renaissance*, ed. Barbara K. Lewalski (Berkeley, Los Angeles, London, 1973).

63. Cf. Robert M. Boltwood, "Turnus and Satan as Epic Villains," *Classical Journal*, Vol. 47 (1952), pp. 183–186.

64. See Michael J. Lieb, *Poetics of the Holy. . . .*

65. For the concepts of the "Christian poet," "divine poetry," and the "Christian muse" during the Renaissance, see Lily B. Campbell, "The Christian Muse," *Huntington Library Bulletin*, No. 8 (1935), pp. 29–70; Campbell, *Divine Poetry and Drama . . .*; William G. Riggs, *The Christian Poet in Paradise Lost* (Berkeley, 1972); Barbara Kiefer Lewalski, *Protestant Poetics and the Seventeenth-Century Religious Lyric* (Princeton, 1979); John Spencer Hill, *John Milton, Poet, Priest, and Prophet: A Study of Divine Vocation in Milton's Poetry and Prose* (Totowa, N.J., 1979).

66. See Thomas Greene, *The Descent from Heaven: A Study in Epic Continuity* (New Haven, 1963); Mason Hammond, "Concilia Deorum from Homer through Milton," *SP*, Vol. 30 (1933), pp. 1–16; Edward S. Le Comte, "Milton's Infernal Council and Mantuan," *PMLA*, Vol. 69 (1954), pp. 979–983; Watson Kirkconnell, *The Celestial Cycle: the Theme of Paradise Lost in World Literature, with Translations of the Major Analogues* (Toronto, 1952); Merritt Y. Hughes, "Devils to Adore for Deities," in *Studies in Honor of Dewitt T. Starnes*, ed. Thomas P. Harrison *et al.* (Austin, Texas, 1967), pp. 241–258; John R. Knott, Jr., "The Visit of Raphael: *Paradise Lost*, Book V," *PQ*, Vol. 47 (1968), pp. 36–42; William B. Hunter, Jr., "Prophet Dreams and Visions in *Paradise Lost*," *MLQ*, Vol. 9 (1948), pp. 277–285; Barbara Kiefer Lewalski, "Structure and the Symbolism of Vision in Michael's Prophecy, *Paradise Lost*, Books XI–XII," *PQ*, Vol. 42 (1963), pp. 25–35.

67. Among studies of the epic simile in Milton's poetry, see Christopher Waldo Grose, "The Rhetoric of the Miltonic Simile," *DA*, Vol. 27 (1966), #1785-A; James Whaler, "The Miltonic Simile," *PMLA*, Vol. 46 (1931), pp. 1034–1074 and "Animal Simile in *Paradise Lost*," *PMLA*, Vol. 45 (1932), pp. 534–553; Warren D. Anderson, "Notes on the Simile in Homer and His Successors," *Classical Journal*, Vol. 53 (1957), pp. 127–133; Davis P. Harding, "Milton's Bee-Simile," *JEGP*, Vol. 60 (1961), pp. 664–669; Claes Schaar, "Vida, Ramsay, and Milton's Bees," *English Studies*, Vol. 46 (1965), pp. 417–418; Kingsley Widmer, "The Iconography of Renunciation: The Miltonic Simile," *ELH*, Vol. 25 (1958), pp. 258–269; John F. Huntley, "The Ecology and

Anatomy of Criticism: Milton's Sonnet 19 and the Bee-Simile in *Paradise Lost*, I.
768–76," *JAAC*, Vol. 24 (1966), pp. 383–391; Roger Ioan Stephens Jones, "The Epic
Simile in *Paradise Lost*," (B. Litt thesis, Oxford, 1967); Philip Hobsbaum, "The
Criticism of Milton's Epic Similes," *Studia Neophilologica*, Vol. 36 (1964), pp. 220–
231; George G. Loane, "A Simile of Milton," *N&Q*, Vol. 175 (1938), pp. 434–435;
James C. Keet, "The Plateaus of Correspondence: A Critical Interpretation of the Epic
Similes of *Paradise Lost*," *DAI*, Vol. 39 (1970), 2971A; R.D. Bedford, "Similes of
Unlikeness in *Paradise Lost*," *Essays in Criticism* (Oxford), Vol. 25 (1975), pp.
179–196. John Edward Gorecki, "Milton's Similitudes for Satan and Traditional Impli-
cations of Their Imagery," *Milton Quarterly*, Vol. 10 (1975), pp. 101–108; James P.
Holoka, "'Thick as Autumnal Leaves': The Structure and Generic Potentials of an Epic
Simile," *Milton Quarterly*, Vol. 10 (1976), pp. 78–83; Linda Gregerson, "The Limbs
of Truth: Milton's Use of Simile in *Paradise Lost*," *Milton Studies*, Vol. 14 (1980), pp.
135–152; John H. Swift, "Similes of disguise and the Reader of *Paradise Lost*," *South
Atlantic Quarterly*, Vol. 79 (1980), pp. 425–435; John T. Shawcross, "The Simile of
Satan as a Comet . . .," *Milton Quarterly*, Vol. 6 (1972), p. 5; Jerry L. Mills, "Satan as
Cormorant . . .," *N&Q,n.s.*, Vol. 17 (1970), pp. 414–415.

C.M. Bowra compares the comet-similes of Virgil and Milton (*Aeneid* X, 272–[75]
PL, II, lines 707–711). These suggest a further analogy between Satan and Aeneas.
Similar imagery occurs in the *Iliad*; and in likening Mulciber to a falling star (*PL* II, line
745) and Satan to the Morning star (V, line 708), Milton assimilates Biblical symbols to
classical imagery. Cf. Revelation viii. 10; ix, 1; Isaiah xiv. 12–14; Jude 13. Hector
shines like a baleful star among dark clouds (*Iliad* XI. 61 ff.), and Achilles like the
baleful Dog-star in Orion (*Iliad* XXII. 25 ff.). Achilles' helmet shines like a star, and
his spear gleams like Hesperus (*Iliad* XIX, 380 ff.; XXII, 317 ff.). Even as his glory
wanes, the devil shines "Star-bright" in the darkness of Hell (*PL* X, line 45). For
discussion of comparisons of the hero to a star, see Cedric H. Whitman, *Homer and the
Heroic Tradition*, pp. 142–144. In comparing Aeneas in his shining armor to the baleful
Dog-star Sirius and to a comet, Virgil is following Homer's example, just as Milton is
following both of these classical poets.

Like Satan's shield, the shield of Achilles shines like the moon (*Iliad* XIX. 371 ff.); in
the *Aeneid* lunar similes sometimes occur in sinister contexts, as in Virgil's description
of the underworld (Book VI).

Milton's simile likening the fallen angels to fallen leaves has numerous parallels in the
epic tradition. Homer had compared the generations of mortal men to leaves (*Iliad* VI.
145 ff.; XXI. 461 ff.); and Bowra has traced the "comparison of spirits in the underworld
to fallen leaves" from Bacchylides through Virgil and Dante and Tasso to Milton. See
C.M. Bowra, *From Virgil to Milton* (London and New York, 1965), pp. 229, 240–241.

68. See Merritt Y. Hughes, "Satan and the Myth of the Tyrant," in *Ten Perspectives
on Milton* (New Haven and London, 1965), pp. 165–195.

69. In Boiardo's *Orlando Innamorato* (Book II, Canto 13) the fay Alcina kidnaps
Duke Astolfo by luring him onto a seeming islet in order to show him a siren. This
"isoletta" is actually a whale under the sorceress' command; and it bears him out to sea
and ultimately to her own domain. In Ariosto's *Orlando Furioso* (Canto 6) Astolfo, now
metamorphosed into a myrtle tree, relates this episode to Rogero; cf. *Ariosto's Orlando
Furioso* (Selections), tr. Sir John Harington, ed. Rudolf Gottfried (Bloomington, Indiana, 1963), pp. 138–139:

> Among the rest that were too long to count
> We saw the fish that men balena call;
> Twelve yards above the water did amount
> His mighty back, the monster is so tall;
> And for it stood so still, we made account

It had been land, but were deceived all;
We were deceived, well I may rue the while;
It was so huge we thought it was an isle.

70. See Joseph Anthony Wittreich, Jr., "The Crown of Eloquence: The Figure of the Orator in Milton's Prose," in Michael Lieb and John T. Shawcross (eds.), *Achievements of the Left Hand: Essays on the Prose of John Milton* (Amherst, 1974), pp. 3–54.

71. Hughes (*PL*), p. 10n.; see also Hughes, "Myself Am Hell," in *Ten Perspectives on Milton* (New Haven and London, 1965), pp. 136–164. Tartarus has Biblical as well as classical associations; God casts the angels who sinned into Tartarus (2 Peter ii. 4).

72. See the discussions of Pharaonic imagery by Harold Fisch, "Hebraic Style and Motifs in *Paradise Lost*," in *Language and Style in Milton*, pp. 30–64; and John T. Shawcross, "*Paradise Lost* and the Theme of Exodus," *Milton Studies*, Vol. 2 (1970), pp. 3–26.

73. For Milton's adaptations of apocalyptic imagery and motifs, see Michael Fixler, "The Apocalypse within *Paradise Lost*," in Thomas Kranidas (ed.), *New Essays on Paradise Lost* (Berkeley, Los Angeles, and London, 1971), pp. 131–178; Austin C. Dobbins, *Milton and the Book of Revelation: The Heavenly Cycle* (University, Alabama, 1975); Leland Ryken, "Milton and the Apocalyptic," *HLQ*, Vol. 31 (1978), pp. 223–238, and *The Apocalyptic Vision in Paradise Lost* (Ithaca, 1970).

74. See Joseph H. Summers, *The Muse's Method: An Introduction to Paradise Lost* (New York, 1968), pp. 32–70; Arlene A. Swidler, "Milton's *Paradise Lost*, II, 866–870," *The Explicator* Vol. 17, No. 6 (1959), item 41; William B. Hunter, Jr., "The Heresies of Satan," in *Th' Upright Heart and Pure*, ed. Amadeus P. Fiore, O.F.M. (Pittsburgh and Louvain, 1967), pp. 25–34; Ernest Schanzer, "Milton's Hell Revisited," *UTQ*, Vol. 24 (1955), pp. 135–145; Hughes, "Myself Am Hell," *Ten Perspectives*, p. 137. For parodic allusion to the meeting between Diomedes and Glaucos in this episode, see John Eugene Seaman, "Homeric Parody at the Gates of Milton's Hell," *MLR*, Vol. 62 (1967), pp. 212–213.

75. See E.M.W. Tillyard, "The Causeway from Hell to the World in the Tenth Book of *Paradise Lost*," *SP*, Vol. 38 (1941), pp. 266–270; Simon Trefman, "A Note on the Bridge of Chaos in *Paradise Lost* and Matthew XVI," *Seventeenth-Century News*, 20 (1963), item 204.

76. See Walter C. Curry, "Milton's Chaos and Old Night," *JEGP*, Vol. 46 (1947), pp. 38–52; E.E. Slaughter, "Milton's Demogorgon," *PQ*, Vol. 10 (1931), pp. 310–312; Hughes (*PL*), p. 73n. observes that Demogorgon "first entered literature" in a scholium to Statius' *Thebaid* and emphasizes the influence of Boccaccio's mythographical treatise on Renaissance conceptions of this god of the abyss; cf. Harris F. Fletcher, "Milton's Demogorgon—Prolusion I and *Paradise Lost*, II, 960–5," *JEGP*, Vol. 57 (1958), pp. 684–689.

77. See Merritt Y. Hughes, "Milton's Limbo of Vanity," in *Th' Upright Heart and Pure*, pp. 7–24; Frank L. Huntley, "A Justification of Milton's Paradise of Fools . . .," *ELH*, Vol. 21 (1954), pp. 107–113; Esmond L. Marilla, "Milton's Paradise of Fools," *English Studies*, Vol. 42 (1961), pp. 159–164; Berta Moritz-Siebeck, "Der Limbus-Passus in Milton's *Paradise Lost* . . .," *Anglia*, Vol. 79 (1962), pp. 153–176; Norma Philips, "Milton's Limbo of Vanity and Dante's Vestibule," *ELN*, Vol. 3 (1966), pp. 177–182; Bruce P. Baker, "Ironic Contrast in Milton's Paradise of Fools," *N&Q,n.s.*, Vol. 13 (1966), p. 378.

78. See C.A. Patrides, "Renaissance Interpretations of Jacob's Ladder," *Theologische Zeitschrift*, Vol. 18 (1962), pp. 411–418; for interpretations of the "golden Chain" of the *Iliad*, see Hughes (*PL*), p. 76n. See also Harry F. Robins, "Milton's Golden Chain," *MLN*, Vol. 69 (1954), p. 76.

79. See George W. Whiting, "The Golden Compasses in *Paradise Lost*," *N&Q*,

Vol. 172 (1937), pp. 294–295. Among other studies of the imagery of *Paradise Lost*, see Christine Brooke-Rose, "Metaphor in *Paradise Lost*: A Grammatical Analysis," in *Language and Style in Milton*, pp. 252–303; Jackson I. Cope, *The Metaphoric Structure of Paradise Lost* (Baltimore, 1962); Ann Gossman, "The Use of the Tree of Life in *Paradise Lost*," *JEGP*, Vol. 65 (1966), pp. 680–687; Isabel G. MacCaffrey, *Paradise Lost as Myth* (Cambridge, Mass., 1959); Clifford Davidson, "Sceptre and Keys as Visual Images in *Paradise Lost*," *Dalhousie Review*, Vol. 48 (1968–69), pp. 539–549; George E. Miller, "'Images of Matter': Narrative Manipulation in Book VI of *Paradise Lost*," *Ariel: A Review of International English Literature*, Vol. 11, No. 1 (1980), pp. 5–13; Ann Gossman, "The Ring Pattern: Image, Structure, and Theme in *Paradise Lost*," *SP*, Vol. 68 (1971), pp. 326–339.

80. Cf. *Purgatorio*, xxxii, line 22, "quella milizia del celeste regno. . . ." See Irene Samuel, *Dante and Milton*. . . .

81. See Kester Svendsen, "Milton's Chariot of Paternal Deity . . .," *N&Q*, Vol. 193 (1948), p. 339; John T. Shawcross, "The Son in His Ascendance: A Reading of *Paradise Lost*," *MLQ*, Vol. 27 (1966), pp. 388–401; Kitty Cohen, *The Throne and the Chariot*. . . .

82. Hughes (*PL*), p. 212n.; J.H. Adamson, "The War in Heaven: Milton's Version of the Merkabah," *JEGP*, Vol. 57 (1958), pp. 690–703. In Raphael's description of the Son ("Gloomy as Night") Hughes finds an analogy with Hector (*Iliad* XII, 462 ff.) Herakles also advances like night in the first Nekyia in the *Odyssey* (XI. 605 ff.).

83. Cf. the "two-handed engine" of *Lycidas* (line 130); see Maurice Kelley, "*Lycidas*: The Two-Handed Engine," *N&Q*, Vol. 181 (1941), p. 273; John M. Steadman, "Milton's Two Handed Engine and Jehan Gerard," *N&Q,n.s.*, Vol. 3 (1956), pp. 249–250 and "Milton's Two-Handed Engine," *N&Q,n.s.*, Vol. 7 (1960), p. 237. See also Kathleen M. Swaim, "Retributive Justice in *Lycidas*: The Two-Handed Engine," *Milton Studies*, Vol. 2 (1970), pp. 119–129; A.M. Gibbs, "'That Two-Handed Engine' and Some Renaissance Emblems," *RES*, Vol. 31 (1980), pp. 178–183; W. Arthur Turner, "The Quest of the Mysterious Engine," *Milton Quarterly*, Vol. 13 (1979), pp. 17–20.

For epic prototypes of the vaunts and sarcasms of the battling angels, compare the vauntings of Deiphobos over the slain Hypsenor, of Idomeneus over the slain Alkathoös, and of Patroclus over the dead Kebriones (*Iliad* XIII. 410 ff., 445 ff.; XVI 739 ff.). Hector taunts the dying Patroclus, and Achilles the dying Hector (XVI. 825 ff.; XXII, 330 ff.). In the *Odyssey* the herdsman Philoitios sarcastically taunts his own victim Ktesippos (XXII, 285 ff.). Compare *Aeneid* (Book X) for the vaunts of Aeneas over his enemies.

84. For the names of Milton's angels and their background in Biblical, rabbinical, or occult tradition, see Robert H. West, *Milton and the Angels* (Athens, Georgia, 1955). Compare the following passage from Virgil's *Aeneid* (X, 747–749):

Caedicus Alcathoum obtruncat, Sacrator Hydaspen
Partheniumque Rapo et praedurum viribus Orsen,
Messapus Cloniumque Lycaoniumque Erichaeten.

Commenting on the "faint ghostly figures behind the resounding names," Bowra observed that "Such a passage bears no relation to experience and is purely literary"; C.M. Bowra *From Virgil to Milton* (London and New york, 1965), p. 39.

85. See, *inter alia*, Arnold Stein, "Milton's War in Heaven—An Extended Metaphor," *ELH*, Vol. 18 (1951), pp. 201–22; Stella Revard, "Milton's Critique of Heroic Warfare in *Paradise Lost* V and VI," *SEL*, Vol. 7 (1967), pp. 119–139), and *The War in Heaven: Paradise Lost and the Tradition of Satan's Rebellion* (Ithaca, 1980). Grant McColley, "Milton's Battle in Heaven and Rupert of Saint Heribert," *Spectator* Vol. 16 (1941), pp. 230–235; J.H. Adamson, "The War in Heaven: Milton's Version of

the Merkabah"; J.B. Broadbent, *Some Graver Subject: An Essay on Paradise Lost* (London, 1960); Allan H. Gilbert, "A Parallel between Milton and Boiardo," *Italica*, Vol. 20 (1943), pp. 132–134; Priscilla P. St. George, "Psychomachia in Books V and VI of *Paradise Lost*," *MLQ*, Vol. 27 (1966), pp. 185–196; Dick Taylor, Jr., "The Battle in Heaven in *Paradise Lost*," *TSE*, Vol. 3 (1952), pp. 69–92; Everett H. Emerson, "Milton's War in Heaven: Some Problems," *MLN*, Vol. 69 (1954), pp. 399–402.

86. Hughes (*PL*), p. 200n; see also Kirkconnell, *The Celestial Cycle*; Harold H. Scudder, "Satan's Artillery," *N&Q*, Vol. 195 (1950), pp. 334–347; John M. Steadman, "Islamic Tradition and 'That Divelish Engin,'" *History of Ideas News Letter*, 4 (1958), pp. 39–41.

87. See Merritt Y. Hughes, "Satan Now Dragon Grown (*Paradise Lost*, X, 529," *Etudes Anglaises*, Vol. 20 (1967), pp. 356–369.

88. See John M. Steadman, "Leviathan and Renaissance Etymology," *JHI*, Vol. 28 (1967), pp. 575–576. Milton had already exploited the symbolic Satan-Leviathan analogy, traditional in patristic and medieval exegesis, in an earlier simile likening the Archfiend to a whale. In this scene, on the other hand, he may be elaborating the serpentine imagery associated in Renaissance etymologies of the Hebrew word. For some lexicographers, it meant either "society" or "prince", or both. There is a remote possibility that Milton is obliquely alluding to the paradigm of absolute monarchy, with (perhaps) a side-glance, or a side-swipe, at the political theories of Hobbes.

89. Irene Samuel, *Dante and Milton*, pp. 105–116; cf. Raymond Tschumi, "The Evolution of Myths from Dante to Milton," in *English Studies Today*, Fourth Series, ed. Ilva Cellini and Giorgio Melchiori (Roma, 1966), pp. 237–254.

90. See Marjorie Hope Nicolson, "Milton and the Telescope," *ELH*, Vol. 2 (1935), pp. 1–32.

91. Hughes (*PL*), p. 104. Robert West observes that when Milton "lists the four chief angels—Michael, Gabriel, Raphael, Uriel—he has not only availed himself of the four principal names of good angels that the canonical and apocryphal books provide, but has of necessity touched the vast Jewish tradition that binds four together, as the major angels corresponding to the elements, the directions, the seasons, and to various nations and days and months and other things invisibly swayed by God's messengers"; *Milton and the Angels*, p. 152. Cornelius Agrippa regarded these four angels as the rulers respectively of east, north, west, and south; p. 68. For discussion of the more obscure names among Milton's angels, see West, pp. 152–156.

92. For discussion of Milton's use of natural science and for his allusions to alchemy, see Kester Svendsen, *Milton and Science* (Cambridge, Mass., 1956). See also Allen G. Debus and Robert P. Multhauf, *Alchemy and Chemistry in the Seventeenth Century* (Los Angeles, 1966).

93. Hanford and Taaffe, *A Milton Handbook*, Fifth Edition, pp. 152–153.

94. Hughes (*PL*), p. 146.

94a. See S.K. Heninger, Jr., *Touches of Sweet Harmony*. . . .

94b. For the contrast between the festal decorum of Heaven and the pastoral decorum of the rural repast that Adam and Eve share with Raphael, see John R. Knott, Jr., "The Visit of Raphael: *Paradise Lost*, Book V," *PQ*, Vol. 47 (1968), pp. 36–42; see also Thomas Kranidas, *The Fierce Equation: A Study of Milton's Decorum* (The Hague, 1965); and Knott, *Milton's Pastoral Vision: An Approach to Paradise Lost* (Chicago, 1971).

94c. See Michael J. Lieb, *Poetics of the Holy*. . . . In *Considerations Touching the Likeliest Means to Remove Hirelings Out of the Church*, Milton takes the priesthood of Aaron as a type of a "better reality," citing I Peter ii. 5; "that priesthood is in us now real, which in him was but a shadow." See Hughes, *Complete Poems and Major Prose*, p. 860; cf. p. 861 on Christ as "our high priest and king."

95. See Robert R. Cawley, *Milton and the Literature of Travel* (Princeton, 1951).

96. *The Complete Works of Joshuah Sylvester*, ed. Alexander B. Grosart, repr. (New York, 1967), Vol. I, p. 100. To Satan the stars seem other worlds, or happy isles like "those *Hesperian* Gardens fam'd of old . . ." (*PL* III, lines 567–570). In the epilogue to *Comus*, the Hesperian gardens are located "Up in the broad fields of the sky . . ." (lines 979–983). For alternative locations of Elysium and the Fortunate Isles, see John M. Steadman, *Disembodied Laughter* . . . (Berkeley, Los Angeles, London, 1972), pp. 21–41. See DeWitt T. Starnes, "The Hesperian Gardens in Milton," *UTSE*, Vol. 31 (1952), pp. 42–51; A. Bartlett Giamatti, *The Earthly Paradise and the Renaissance Epic* (Princeton, 1966).

96[a]. In the context of the imminent ruin of Eve through tasting the forbidden fruit—and of Adam's ruin through her persuasions—the allusions to Alcinoüs and Solomon acquire sinister overtones. Solomon's foreign wives (who included Pharaoh's daughter) "turned his heart after other gods . . . And Solomon did evil in the sight of the Lord . . .," adoring Ashtoreth and Chemosh and Molech (1 Kings xi. 1–13). Milton had formerly considered writing a drama on this subject; the alternative titles "Salomon Gynaecocratumenus" or "Thysiazusae" or "Idolomargus" stress the interconnection between the monarch's uxoriousness and his idolatry, his subjection to his alien wives and his worship of alien gods. Before seducing Adam into partaking of the forbidden fruit, Eve will have already fallen into idolatry herself; and uxorious Adam like Solomon will be "fondly overcome with Female charm" (IX, line 999).

Milton had alluded to Alcinoüs' garden earlier (V, line 341) in the context of the fruits that Eve was gathering for the meal that she and Adam were to share with their angelic guest. The fruit that she will shortly gather and share with Adam will alienate them from such celestial intimacy. In addition to this ironic counterpointing of two rural repasts linked through allusions to the same Phaeacian garden, there is an ominous analogy between the fate of the Phaeacians and that of Adam and Eve themselves. In the opening lines of book IX (lines 1–13) Milton had stressed the loss of man's friendship and "familiar" conversation with Heaven. Instead of intimacy with "God or Angel Guest" there will be estrangement; and, on the part of an alienated Heaven, "Anger and just rebuke, and judgment giv'n. . . ." The Phaeacians had enjoyed a similar intimacy with the gods until they aroused Poseidon's anger and incurred his revenge. The Phaeacians are very close to the gods (Alcinoüs informs his own visitor and guest, the hero Odysseus), either visiting the islanders singly or in company, attending their sacrifices and sharing in their feasts (VII, 186 ff.). But there is a prophecy that they will provoke the wrath of Poseidon and that the god will wreck one of their home-bound ships and hide their city under a mountain (VIII, 555 ff.) Part of the prophecy is fulfilled, when Poseidon turns the ship to stone; but for the moment the remaining threat is averted (XIII, 125 ff.). Cf. *Odyssey* V. 34 ff. and VI. 201 ff. on the Phaeacians' nearness and dearness to the gods.

97. See Erwin Panofsky, *Idea: A Concept in Art Theory*, tr. Joseph J.S. Peake (Columbia, S.C., 1968), pp. 74, 80, on mannerism and Lomazzo's championship of "the idea of the *figura serpentinata*. . . ." Cf. Roy Daniells, *Milton, Mannerism and Baroque* (Toronto, 1963).

98. Hughes (*PS*), p. 181n.

99. See Don Cameron Allen, "Milton's Amarant," *MLN*, Vol. 72 (1957), pp. 256–258.

The Greek adjective *amarantos* literally means "unfading" or "everlasting" or "imperishable" and is apparently derived from the prefix *a* (not) and the adjective *marantos* (fading or corruptible). The form *amaranth* appears to be a corruption, formed by association with words like *polyanthus* containing a word for flower (*anthos*). The Latin noun is *amarantus*. In Greek the word *amarantos* occurs both as an adjective and as a substantive (*to amaranton*); and it provides the basis for another adjective *amarantinos*.

In Latin and Greek herbal literature, and sometimes in classical poetry, *amarantos* (or its Latin equivalent) designated a plant (or plants) belonging to an unidentified species. Examples have been noted in Dioscorides, Columella, Pliny, Pseudo-Apuleius, Ovid, Lygdamus, and other authors.

Classical writers sometimes applied this adjective (*amarantos*, in the sense of unfading or unwithering) to a flower, a grassy meadow, or the like. The Septuagint applied it to wisdom (*sophia*, in the Book of Wisdom vi. 12). In early Christian literature it was often associated with eternal life or eternal bliss. In 1 Peter i. 4 it was linked with *klēronomia* ("unfading inheritance"); and in 1 Peter v. 4 it designated an eternal crown of glory: "ton amarantinon tēs doxēs stephanon. A similar reference to an "unfading" crown of amarant (*amarantos stephanos*) occurs in the writings of Philostratus the Sophist (*Heroicus*). The *Apocalypse of Peter* similarly refers to *amaranta anthē*, i.e. "*Unfading flowers* (as they bloom in the next world). . . ." Arndt and Gingrich also find possible allusions to "straw-flowers" ("everlastings") and to "a wreath of amarantus" in early Christian literature.

Allusions to amarant (or amaranth) either as an imaginary flower or as a genus of plants that includes Prince's Feather and Love-lies-bleeding appear in English herbals, in the poetry of Spenser (*FQ*, III. vi. 45) and *PL* III, line 553). The word was also used to denote a purple color like "that of the foliage of *Amarantus*." Renaissance herbals also mention an *Amaranthus Luteus*, or yellow amaranth.

In associating it with Heaven (and temporarily with the Earthly Paradise) as a symbol of eternal life and eternal joy, Milton primarily had in mind its New Testament connotations. Yet, in the context of his allusion elsewhere to the Ethiopian Mount Amara (a traditional seat of the Earthly Paradise, though Milton rejects this identification in favor of the Mesopotamian site), there may be an etymological pun involving Mount Amara and the Greek *anthos*, in Milton's use of the amaranth-motif.

See *A New English Dictionary*, *s.v. amarant(h)*; H.G. Liddell and R. Scott, *A Greek-English Lexicon*, New Edition, rev. H.S. Jones (Oxford, 1925), *s.v. amarantos*; C.T. Lewis and C. Short, *A Latin Dictionary* (Oxford, 1907), *s.v. amarantus*; W.F. Arndt and F. Wilbur Gingrich, *A Greek-English Lexicon of the New Testament and Other Early Christian Literature* (Chicago and Cambridge, 1957), *s.v. amarantinos* and *amarantos*; *Thesaurus Linguae Latinae* (Teubner: Lipsiae, 1900), *s.v. amarantus*.

100. C.M. Bowra, *From Virgil to Milton* (London and New York, 1965), p. 41.

101. See Joseph Anthony Mazzeo, "A Critique of Some Modern Theories of Metaphysical Poetry," *MP*, Vol. 50 (1952), pp. 88–92; "A Seventeenth-Century Theory of Metaphysical Poetry," *RR*, Vol. 42 (1951), pp. 245–255; "Metaphysical Poetry and the Poetic of Correspondences," *JHI*, Vol. 14 (1953), pp. 221–234.

102. See Thomas P. Roche, Jr., *The Kindly Flame* (Princeton, 1964), pp. 3–31.

103. See Robert McNulty (ed.), *Ludovico Ariosto's Orlando Furioso Translated . . . By Sir John Harington* (Oxford, 1972), pp. xxxvii–xxxviii; Graham Hough, *A Preface to the Faerie Queene* (New York, 1963), p. 119; Rudolf Gottfried (ed.), *Ariosto's Orlando Furioso* (Selections), tr. Sir John Harington (Bloomington, Indiana, 1963), p. 305; John M. Steadman, *The Lamb and the Elephant: Ideal Imitation and the Context of Renaissance Allegory* (San Marino, California, 1974), p. 101.

104. Madsen regards the symbolism of *Paradise Lost* as "typological rather than Platonic": see "Earth the Shadow of Heaven . . ." and *From Shadowy Types to Truth*; see also Michael Lieb, *Poetics of the Holy. . . .*

105. Among studies of the last two books of *Paradise Lost*, see Barbara Kiefer Lewalski, "Structure and the Symbolism of Vision in Michael's Prophecy, *Paradise Lost*, Books XI–XII," *PQ*, Vol. 42 (1963), pp. 25–35; Berta Moritz-Siebeck, *Untersuchungen zu Milton's Paradise Lost: Interpretation der beiden Schlussbücher; Quellen und Forschungen zur Sprach- und Kulturgeschichte der German'schen Völker*, Neue Folge, 12 (Berlin, 1963); Balachandra Rajan, "*Paradise Lost*: The Hill of History,"

HLQ, Vol. 31 (1967), pp. 43–63; F.T. Prince, "On the Last Two Books of *Paradise Lost*," *Essays and Studies by Members of the English Association*, Vol. 11 (1958), pp. 38–52; George Williamson, "The Education of Adam," *MP*, Vol. 61 (1963), pp. 96–109; Lawrence A. Sasek, "The Drama of *Paradise Lost*, Books XI and XII," *Studies in English Renaissance Literature*, ed. Waldo F. McNeir (Baton Rouge, 1962), pp. 181–196; H.R. MacCallum, "Milton and Sacred History: Books XI and XII of *Paradise Lost*," *Essays in English Literature . . . Presented to A.S.P. Woodhouse* (Toronto, 1964), pp. 149–168.

105[a]. See William Haller, *The Rise of Puritanism . . .* (New York, 1938); Arthur E. Barker, *Milton and the Puritan Dilemma, 1641–1660* (Toronto and London, 1956); Don M. Wolfe, *Milton in the Puritan Revolution* (New York and London, 1941); Michael Fixler, *Milton and the Kingdoms of God* (Evanston, 1964); Christopher Hill, *Milton and the English Revolution* (London, 1977; New York, 1978); Hugh M. Richmond, *The Christian Revolutionary: John Milton* (Berkeley and Los Angeles, 1974).

As scholars have long recognized, much of the imagery in this episode is based on Biblical allusions to the second advent. Milton's hero approaches (*PL* VI, line 767) "Attended with ten thousand thousand Saints. . . ." This is an echo of the prophecy attributed to Enoch (Jude, verses 14–15): "Behold, the Lord cometh with ten thousands of his saints,/ To execute judgment upon all, and to convince all that are ungodly among them of all their ungodly deeds. . . ." Milton's comparison of the rebel angels to "a Heard/ Of Goats or timerous flock" (VI, lines 856–857) is likewise based on a Biblical reference to the Last Judgment (Matthew xxv. 31–46): "When the Son of man shall come in his glory, and all the holy angels with him, then shall he sit upon the throne of his glory./ And before him shall be gathered all the nations; and he shall separate them one from another, as a shepherd divideth his sheep from the goats./ And he shall set the sheep on his right hand, but the goats on the left. . . . And these shall go away into everlasting punishment, but the righteous into life eternal."

105[b]. These "heavenly things"—often represented through the imagery of the earthly—are the archetypes of the latter, just as the original tabernacle at Sinai and the sacred objects within had been modelled on a pattern divinely revealed on the mountain (Exodus xxv. 9, 40; xxvi. 30, xxvii. 8) and just as the form and pattern of an ideal temple had been divinely revealed to Ezekiel (chapter 43). See Michael Lieb, *Poetics of the Holy . . .*; William Madsen, "Earth the Shadow of Heaven" and *From Shadowy Types to Truth*; Joseph Anthony Wittreich, Jr., *Visionary Poetics . . .*; For other instances of "heavenly things" still invisible and hidden, to be manifested on earth in future history, compare the revelation to Ezra by the angel Uriel in 2 Esdras vii. 26–38. Prophesying the Messiah's advent and future judgment, the angel predicts that the city (i.e. Zion) now invisible shall appear in the future, and the country now concealed be made visible.

The ambiguous temporal references of the war in Heaven, which in Raphael's account is represented as past history yet which foreshadows the events of the last days, including the Second Advent and the Last Judgment, are analogous to the ambiguities that generations of commentators had found in the Apocalypse itself. Some had interpreted its account of the war in heaven between Michael and Satan and their angelic legions as a record of the original revolt of the angels prior to the creation of the world or during the first week of the creation). Others regarded it as a prophecy of future history. Thus in *A Treatise of Angels* (London, 1613), John Salkeld observed that other theologians had based their estimate of the number of fallen angels on the Apocalypse, where the dragon drags one third of the stars down with him. In Salkeld's view, however, the Apocalypse was plainly referring not to the original rebellion, but to the last fight before the Last Judgment; see Robert H. West, *Milton and the Angels* (Athens, Georgia, 1955), pp. 48–49.

106. The alternation of evening and morning in Heaven provides an archetypal pattern

for the vicissitudes of evening and morning on earth during the successive six days of the creation (cf. Genesis i. 5, 8, 13, 19, 23, 31). These grateful vicissitudes in the material universe precede the creation of the sun, which did not take place until the fourth day. In Milton's "materialistic angelology" one critic has found the basis for a closer correspondence between the earthly and the heavenly than most of the poet's contemporaries (she suggests) might have believed. Another critic maintains that as Milton's audience we ourselves are "the subjects of the true poems we read"; the "Platonic or 'accommodative' shadow of substantial Heaven itself." See Virginia R. Mollenkott, "A Note on Milton's Materialistic Angelology," *Seventeenth-Century News*, 22, No. 1)(1964), item 9; John S. Lawry, *The Shadow of Heaven: Matter and Stance in Milton's Poetry* (Ithaca, 1968), pp. v–vi. In *Milton and the Angels* (pp. 45–46, 53–55), Robert H. West discusses the opinions of seventeenth-century Englishmen (John Salkeld, Henry Lawrence, Isaac Ambrose) concerning the materiality of the angels. As he notes, various earlier theologians had held the "idea that the angels are corporeal compared with God and spiritual compared with man. . . ."

107. See Roche, *The Kindly Flame*; S.K. Heninger, *Touches of Sweet Harmony*. . . .

108. See Anne Davidson Ferry, *Milton's Epic Voice: The Narrator in Paradise Lost* (Cambridge, Mass., 1963); Joseph Anthony Wittreich, Jr., *Visionary Poetics* . . .; Wittreich (ed.), *Milton and the Line of Vision*; William W. Kerrigan, *The Prophetic Milton* (Charlottesville, 1974); Michael J. Lieb, *Poetics of the Holy* . . .; Merritt Y. Hughes, "Milton and the Symbol of Light," *SEL*, Vol. 4 (1964), pp. 3–20; William B. Hunter, Jr., "Holy Light in *Paradise Lost*," *Rice Institute Pamphlet*, 46 (1960), pp. 1–14 and "The Meaning of Holy Light in *Paradise Lost* III," *MLN*, Vol. 74 (1959), pp. 589–592; Albert R. Cirillo, "Noon-Midnight and the Temporal Structure of *Paradise Lost*," *ELH*, Vol. 29 (1962), pp. 372–395; A.B. Chambers, Wisdom at One Entrance Quite Shut Out: *Paradise Lost*, III, 1–55," *PQ*, Vol. 42 (1963), pp. 114–119.

108[a]. See Christopher Waldo Grose, "Some Uses of Sensuous Immediacy in *Paradise Lost*," *HLQ*, Vol. 31 (1968), pp. 211–222.

109. See Stanley Eugene Fish, *Surprised by Sin: the Reader in Paradise Lost* (London and New York, 1967); Anne Davidson Ferry, *Milton's Epic Voice*. . . .

110. Hanford and Taaffe, *A Milton Handbook*, Fifth Edition, p. 152. In this "Third Draft" Adam and Eve have already fallen when they first appear (Act 4). Similarly in the Fourth Draft they make their first entrance after their seduction by the serpent; appearing "confusedly, covered with leaves." In the cancelled First Draft, they are simply listed "with the serpent" among the *dramatis personae*. Since they are immediately preceded in the list by Lucifer, and immediately followed by Conscience, they are (in all likelihood) already fallen; see pp. 151–153.

111. See Stanley Stewart, *The Enclosed Garden. The Tradition and the Image* (Madison, Wisconsin, and London, 1966).

112. See John S. Coolidge, "Great Things and Small: The Virgilian Progression," *Comparative Literature* (1965), pp. 1–23; cf. *PL* II, lines 921–922; VI, lines 310–311; *PR* IV, lines 563–564.

113. For Milton's techniques of accommodation and his use of the inexpressibility-*topos*, cf. *PL* VI, lines 296–301 (". . . for fight/ Unspeakable; for who, though with the tongue/ Of Angels, can relate, or to what things/ Liken on Earth conspicuous, that may lift/ Human imagination to such highth/ Of Godlike Power: for likest Gods they seem'd . . ."); *PL* VI, lines 893–894 ("Thus measuring things in Heav'n by things on Earth/ At thy request . . ."); *PL* VII, lines 176–179: ("Immediate are the Acts of God, more swift/ Than time or motion, but to human ears/Cannot without process of speech be told,/ So told as earthly notion can receive." See C.A. Patrides, "*Paradise Lost* and the Theory of Accommodation," *TSLL*, Vol. 5 (1963), pp. 58–63.

Appendix: *Sion and Helicon*

1. Among studies of the imagery of Milton's prose, see Stanley E. Fish, "Reasons that Imply Themselves: Imagery, Argument, and the Reader in Milton's *Reason of Church-Government*," in *Seventeenth-Century Imagery: Essays on the Uses of Figurative Language from Donne to Farquhar*, ed. Earl Miner (Berkeley, 1971), pp. 25–47; Timothy J. O'Keefe, "The Imaginal Structure of John Milton's *Eikonoklastes*," *BSUF*, Vol. 11 (1971), pp. 33–45; Timothy J. O'Keefe, "The Function and Pattern of Imagery in Milton's Prose, 1641–1649," *DA*, Vol. 28 (1968), 4642A; Edgar F. Daniels, "Samson in *Areopagitica*," *N‡Q, n.s.*, Vol. 11 (1962), pp. 92–93; John X. Evans, "Imagery as Argument in Milton's *Areopagitica*," *TSLL*, Vol. 8 (1966), pp. 189–205; Harris Francis Fletcher, "The Use of the Bible in Milton's Prose (Urbana, 1929).

Chapter Two: *Milton's Urania and the Renaissance Tradition*

1. Torquato Tasso, *Jerusalem Delivered*, tr. Edward Fairfax, ed. John Charles Nelson (Capricorn Books: New York, n.d.), p. 1.

2. Torquato Tasso, *La Gerusalemme Liberata*, ed. Piero Nardi (Edizioni Scholastiche Mondadori: Verona, 1968), p. 54.

3. Tasso, *Gerusalemme Liberata*, ed. Nardi, p. 54.

4. See Lily B. Campbell, *Divine Poetry and Drama in Sixteenth-Century* (Cambridge, Berkeley and Los Angeles, 1959) and "The Christian Muse," *Huntington Library Bulletin*, No. 8 (1935), pp. 29–70. Among significant studies see Merritt Y. Hughes, "Milton and the Symbol of Light," *SEL*, Vol. 4 (1964), pp. 1–33; William B. Hunter, Jr., "Milton's Urania," *SEL*, Vol. 4 (1964), pp. 35–42; Jackson I. Cope, "Milton's Muse in *Paradise Lost*," *MP*, Vol. 55 (1957), pp. 6–10; John T. Shawcross, "The Metaphor of Inspiration in *Paradise Lost*," in *Th' Upright Heart and Pure*, ed. Amadeus P. Fiere, O.F.M. (Pittsburgh, 1967), pp. 75–85; James Holly Hanford, "That Shepherd Who First Taught the Chosen Seed": A Note on Milton's Mosaic Inspiration," *UTQ*, Vol. 8 (1939), pp. 403–419.

5. Among recent studies see also, Stella P. Revard, "Milton's Muse and the Daughters of Memory," *English Literary Renaissance*, Vol. i (1979), pp. 432–44; Margaret M. Byard, "Divine Wisdom-Urania," *Milton Quarterly*, Vol. 12 (1978), pp. 134–137; George W. Nitchie, "Milton and his Muses," *ELH*, Vol. 44 (1977), pp. 75–84; Walter Leo Schindler, "Voice and Crisis: The Pattern of Invocation in Milton's Poetry," *DAI*, Vol. 39 (1978), 1600A; Lois W. Parker, "The Muse of *Paradise Lost*: The Holy Spirit," *DAI*, Vol. 31 (1971), 5371A; Francelia Butler, "The Holy Spirit and Odors in *Paradise Lost*," *Milton Newsletter*, Vol. 3 (1969), pp. 65–69; Mark L. Gnerro, "Marian Typology and Milton's Heavenly Muse," *Proceedings of the PMR Conference: Annual Publication of the Patristic, Mediaeval and Renaissance Conference*, Vol. 2 (1977), pp. 39–48; James H. Sims, "The Epic Narrator's Mortal Voice in Camões and Milton. Calíope, Me Ensina, O Spirit . . . Instruct Me," *Revue de Littérature Comparée*, Vol. 51 (1977), pp. 374–384. Cf. Hunter, "Milton's Urania"; Campbell, *Divine Poetry . . .*; Hughes, "Milton and the Symbol of Light," Professor Campbell detects the influence of DuBartas' poem *L' Uranie* on Spenser's hymns of Heavenly Love and of Heavenly Beauty. She also reminds us that Ficino had identified Heavenly Beauty with Sapience and that he had personified Heavenly Beauty as Venus Urania (p. 90). In the *Symposium*, Plato had distinguished two Aphrodites and two Loves (or Erotes). The elder Aphrodite is "of no mother born, but daughter of Heaven, whence we name her Heavenly [Ourania]; while the younger was the child of Zeus and Dione, and her we call Popular [Pandemos]." But Plato also contrasts the Heavenly Muse (Urania), from whom the noble and heavenly love springs, with the muse

Polyhymnia, from whom springs the popular love. "kai houtos estin ho kalos, ho ouranios, ho tēs Ouranias mousēs Eros: ho de Polymnias ho pandēmos . . ."; "this is the noble, the Heavenly Love, sprung from the Heavenly Muse. But the Popular Love comes from the Queen of Various Song. . . ." See *Plato*, Vol. 5 (*Symposium*), tr. W.R.M. Lamb (Loeb Classics: London and New York, 1925), pp. 109, 128–129.

6. *Purgatorio*, Canto 29, lines 37–42: "Or convien che Elicona per me versi,/ e Urania m' aiuti col suo coro/ forti cose a pensar mettere in versi." See Dante Alighieri, *La Divinia Commedia*, ed. Natalino Sapegno, Vol. II (Firenze, 1967), p. 326. Sapegno identifies Urania as the muse who represents the knowledge ("scienza") of supernatural things.

7. *Paradiso*, Canto 2, lines 7–9. See Dante Alighieri, *La Divina Commedia*, ed. Natalino Sapegno, Vol. III (Firenze, 1971), p. 19.

8. William Alabaster, Sonnet #1, in *The Meditative Poem: An Anthology of Seventeenth-Century Verse*, ed. Louis L. Martz (Garden City, N.Y., 1963), p. 53.

9. Campbell, *Divine Poetry . . .*, pp. 87–91.

10. See *Teares*, lines 1–2, 481–534; Spenser, *Poetical Works*, ed. J.C. Smith and E. de Selincourt (London, New York, Toronto, 1965), pp. 480, 485.

11. Campbell, *Divine Poetry . . .*, pp. 1–5, 75–99; see "Urania, or the Heavenly Muse," in *The Complete Works of Joshua Sylvester*, ed. Alexander B. Grosart, repr. (New York, 1967), Vol. II, pp. 3–7.

12. Campbell, *Divine Poetry . . .*, p. 97.

13. Sylvester, ed. Grosart, Vol. I, pp. 19, 27, 40, 52, 61, 72.

14. Spenser, *Poetical Works*, ed. Smith and de Selincourt, p. 596.

15. See Hughes, "Milton and the Symbol of Light" for discussion of J.B. Broadbent's interpretation of this passage.

16. Torquato Tasso, *Il Mondo Creato*, ed. Giorgio Petrocchi (Firenze, 1951), pp. 3–5; "Primo Giorno," lines 1–77.

17. Sylvester, ed. Grosart, Vol. I, p. 89.

18. Sylvester, ed. Grosart, Vol. I, p. 114.

19. Professor Campbell cites examples in the works of James I, Samuel Austin, Barnabe Barnes, and other poets. As she also notes, Jefferson B. Fletcher had identified Spenser's Sapience, in the Hymn of Heavenly Beautie, with the Holy Ghost; see *Divine Poetry . . .*, pp. 91, 137–138.

20. See Maurice Kelley, "Milton and the Third Person of the Trinity," *SP*, Vol. 32 (1935), pp. 221–134, and *This Great Argument . . .* (Princeton, 1941); William B. Hunter, Jr., "Milton's Urania"; John Milton, *Complete Poems and Major Prose*, ed. Merritt Y. Hughes (New York, 1957), pp. 964–973; Milton, *The Christian Doctrine*, Book I, Chapter 6.

21. Milton's discussion of the texts most closely associated with the Spirit invoked in *PL* (I, lines 17–22) and *PR* (I, lines 8–10, 80–85) is of interest. Though he observes that "many both of the ancient and modern interpreters" explain Genesis i. 2 in terms of the Father's power and virtue—and particularly the "divine breath or influence by which every thing is created and nourished"—Milton himself interprets it as an apparent "reference to the Son through whom the Father is so often said to have created all things." But he still entertains doubts about the meaning of this passage; and in the following chapter (on the creation of the world) he glosses "*the Spirit of God*" in this text as "his divine power, rather than any person. . . . unless indeed that Spirit were Christ. . . ."

Again, he takes the text introducing Christ's temptation in the wilderness (Luke iv. 1: "And Jesus, being full of the Holy Ghost, returned from the Jordan, and was led by the Spirit into the wilderness") as a reference to "the power of the Father" rather "than of the Holy Spirit itself. . . ." Similarly (Milton suggests) "the Spirit descended upon

Christ at his baptism, not so much in his own name, as in virtue of a mission from the
Father, and as a symbol and minister of the divine power. . . . The descent therefore and
appearance of the Holy Spirit in the likeness of a dove, seems to have been nothing more
than a representation of the ineffable affection of the Father for the Son, communicated
by the Holy Spirit under the appropriate image of a dove, and accompanied by a voice
from heaven declaratory of that affection" (cf. Matthew iii. 16; Mark i. 10; Luke iii. 22;
John i. 32–33).

In commenting on the texts (1 Corinthians iii. 16, vi, 19; 2 Corinthians vi. 16), "*the
temple of God . . . the temple of the Holy Ghost*," Milton maintains that "it is not
because the spirit alone, but because the Father also and the Son *make their abode with
us*, that we are called *the temple of God*." In interpreting this metaphor, Milton also cites
Ephesians ii. 22. (See Hughes, *Complete Poems and Major Prose*, pp. 965–967, 969,
975.) Milton's comment on the Wisdom of Proverbs viii, moreover, may be relevant to
the opening lines of *PL* Book VII (lines 1–12); It is not, in his opinion, "the Son of God
who is there introduced as the speaker, but a poetical personification of wisdom, as in
Job xxviii. 20–27 . . ."; Hughes, pp. 974–975.

In relating the act of creation later in his epic (*PL* VII, lines 234–239) Milton
describes the Spirit of God in terms similar to those he has employed in the invocation of
Book I: "His brooding wings the Spirit of God outspred/ And vital vertue infus'd, and
vital warmth. . . ." Earlier allusions to the Spirit in this episode apparently associate this
Spirit with the power and virtue of the Father (VII, lines 163–167):

And thou my Word, Begotten Son, by thee
This I perform, speak thou, and be it don:
My overshadowing Spirit and might with thee
I send along, ride forth, and bid the Deep
Within appointed bounds be Heav'n and Earth. . . .

The Son issues forth in "Paternal Glorie"—"Girt with Omnipotence" and crowned
with the radiance of "Majestie Divine, Sapience and Love/ Immense," while "all his
Father in him shon"—and the gates of Heaven open "to let forth/ The King of Glorie in
his powerful Word/ And Spirit coming to create new Worlds" (VII, lines 192–220).
Similarly, the Father transfuses His "Vertue and Grace/ Immense" into the Son before
sending Him to expel the rebellious angels, "Mightiest in (his) Fathers might" and
mounted in the "Chariot of Paternal Deitie, . . . It self instinct with Spirit. . . ." (VI,
lines 703–753). Cf. also the angelic hymn in Book III of *Paradise Lost* (lines 383–395):
"on thee/ Impresst the effulgence of his Glorie abides,/ Transfus'd on thee his ample
Spirit rests."

22. Cf. 1 Corinthians vi. 19, "Know ye not that your body is the temple of the Holy
Ghost who is in you, whom ye have of God . . .?"; 2 Corinthians vi. 16, "For ye are the
temple of the living God; as God hath said, I will dwell in them, and walk in them. . . ."
See the discussion of these texts in *The Christian Doctrine* (Hughes, p. 969). Cf. the
metaphor of the body as a tabernacle in 2 Corinthians v. 1–7 and 2 Peter i. 13.

23. Hebrews viii. 8–10; cf. ix. 11, 24; x. 15–16; Jeremiah xxxi. 33. In *The Christian
Doctrine*, Book I, Chapter 15, Milton associates these texts with the "inward law and
spiritual power" whereby Christ as divine king governs and preserves the Church.

24. In *The Christian Doctrine*, Book I, Chapter 6, Milton applies these (and similar)
texts explicitly to the Holy Ghost; see Hughes, p. 967. Since he regarded the Father and
the Son as indwelling within the "temple" of the heart, along with the Holy Spirit, and
since the Spirit proceeds from both Father and Son, these allusions to the Spirit of Truth
as an inward oracle, indwelling within all believers as his "living Temples, built by
Faith to stand," are not incompatible with the view that the power invoked in the opening
lines of *Paradise Lost* is God the Father, from whom the gift of the Spirit (and of its
attendant gifts) proceeds.

25. If his readers were likely to interpret Urania as a figurative allusion to the Holy Spirit, they might similarly take the reference to her converse with "Eternal wisdom . . .,/ Wisdom thy Sister, . . . In presence of th' Almightie Father-- (*PL* VII, lines 8–12) as a symbolic allusion to the Son of God. In Hebrews the Son had been described in terms analogous to those applied to the divine Wisdom of the Old Testament (cf. Hebrew i. 3 and Wisdom of Solomon vii. 25–26). The Wisdom of Proverbs viii had sometimes been interpreted as an allusion to the Son as Logos, though Milton himself (as we have seen) questions this identification in his theological treatise. As she was, in his opinion, possibly a "poetical personification of wisdom," he may similarly have intended his heavenly muse to serve as a poetical personification of the Father's virtue and power (or of some other divine attribute) rather than as a symbol for either Father, Son, or Holy Spirit. (See Kelley, *This Great Argument* and "Milton and the Third Person of the Trinity.")

26. Campbell, *Divine Poetry* . . ., p. 97; see DuBartas, *La Judit*. The invocations to the "true God" in *La Sepmaine* are usually correlated with the subject matter and scene of the particular day's work that he is describing, and he may exploit both classical and Biblical allusions in addressing the Deity. On one occasion he invokes God the Father as "true *Neptune*"; on another he addresses his invocation to the "Pure Spirit that rapt'st above the firmest Sphear,/ In fiery Coach, thy faithfull Messenger . . ."; Sylvester, Vol. I, pp. 20, 52.

27. *The Christian Doctrine*, Book I, Chapter 1; Hughes, p. 903. Milton adds that "Under the definition of CHRIST are also comprehended Moses and the Prophets, who were his forerunners and the Apostles whom he sent"; Hughes, p. 903. In his chapter on the Holy Spirit, Milton insists that "Christ alone . . . is, properly speaking, and in a primary sense, the Word of God, and the Prophet of the Church . . ."; Hughes, p. 966. On the basis of this passage, along with Milton's interpretation of Genesis i. 2, one might conceivably find support for associating the Spirit invoked in *Paradise Lost* (Book I) with the Son of God. Milton has, however, left the object of his invocations in perhaps deliberate obscurity.

Cf. *A Treatise of Civil Power* . . ., in Hughes, pp. 840–841, on the authority of the holy scripture "from without us," and "within us . . . the illumination of the Holy Spirit so interpreting that scripture as warrantable only to ourselves, and to such whose consciences we can so persuade. . . ." Every "true Christian able to give a reason of his faith, hath the word of God before him, the promised Holy Spirit, and the mind of Christ within him. . . ."

28. See *Boccaccio on Poetry*, tr. Charles G. Osgood (Indianapolis and New York, 1956), pp. 149n., 160n–161n.

28ᵃ. See Philip Sidney, *An Apologie for Poetrie*, in *English Literary Criticism: The Renaissance*, ed. O.B. Hardison, Jr. (New York, 1963), pp. 102–103.

28ᵇ. Echoes of Hesiod are frequent in Milton's poetry, and there are further allusions to Hesiod's works in Milton's First Prolusion and other prose compositions. As Douglas Bush has observed, Charles Grosvenor Osgood regarded Homer, Hesiod, Vergil, and Ovid as the four poets from whom Milton "certainly derived more help than from any others"; see Osgood, *The Classical Mythology of Milton's English Poems* (New York, 1900); Douglas Bush, *Mythology and the Renaissance Tradition in English Poetry*, New Revised Edition (New York, 1963), p. 261. See also the notes in *A Variorum Commentary* . . ., Vols. 1, 2, 4; and in Hughes, *Complete Poems and Major Prose*. The frequent "imitations" of Hesiod and other classical poets serve at times not only to evoke the classical tradition but also to undercut it; by accommodating images and motifs from Hesiod's *Theogony* or *Works and Days* to his Biblical subject, Milton can suggest the superiority of his own account of the origins of things, based on the authority of the Scriptural revelation, to Hesiod's fables.

29. Cf. Saint Augustine, *On Christian Doctrine*, tr. D.W. Robertson, Jr. (Indianapolis and New York, 1958), pp. x, 118–124, 132–138 on the union of wisdom and eloquence; see also Jerrold E. Seigel, *Rhetoric and Philosophy in Renaissance Humanism: The Union of Eloquence and Wisdom, Petrarch to Valla* (Princeton, 1938); John M. Steadman, *The Lamb and the Elephant* . . .(San Marino, California, 1974), pp. 19, 126, 181; cf. *Paradise Regained*, Book IV, lines 334–364.

30. Among recent studies, see Joseph Anthony Wittreich, Jr., *Visionary Poetics* . . .; *Milton and the Line of Vision*, ed. J.A. Wittreich, Jr.; William W. Kerrigan, *The Prophetic Milton*; Michael Lieb, *Poetics of the Holy* . . .;Christopher Hill, *Milton and the English Revolution* (London, 1977; New York, 1978); John Spencer Hill, *John Milton, Poet, Priest, and Prophet: A Study of Divine Vocation in Milton's Poetry and Prose* (Totowa, N.J., 1979).

31. Cf. William Haller, *The Rise of Puritanism* . . . (New York, 1957), pp. 262–263 on enthusiam and separatism in seventeenth-century England.

32. Cf. Barnabe Barnes' address to his Christian Reader in *A Divine Centurie of Spirituall Sonnets* (Campbell, *Divine Poetry* . . ., p. 137) on "the secret fire of immortall Enthusiasme" and the power of "divine rage and sacred instinct. . . ." Barnes exhorts his reader to "refine and illuminate his numerous Muses with the most sacred splendour of the Holy Ghost. . . ."

33. Abraham Cowley, "Preface to *Poems*," in *English Literary Criticism: The Renaissance*, ed. O.B. Hardison, Jr. (New York, 1963), p. 328.

34. Spenser, *Poetical Works*, ed. Smith and de Selincourt, p. 456. (Greek transliterated.)

35. Philip Sidney, *An Apologie for Poetrie*, in Hardison, p. 134. In the peroration to his defense, Sidney recalls many of the standard arguments concerning the nobility, antiquity, and divinity of poetry, but playfully and perhaps ironically. He conjures his readers to laugh no more "at the name of Poets . . .; but to beleeve, with *Aristotle*, that they were the auncient Treasurers of the Grecians Divinity. To beleeve, with *Bembus*, that they were first bringers in of all civilitie . . . To beleeve, with *Clauserus*, . . . that it pleased the heavenly Deitie, by *Hesiod* and *Homer*, under the vayle of fables, to give us all knowledge, Logick, Rhetorick, Philosophy, naturall and morall. . . . To beleeve, with *Landin*, that they are so beloved of the Gods that whatsoever they write proceeds of a divine fury"; pp. 145–146.

36. George Puttenham, *The Arte of English Poesie*, in Hardison, pp. 148, 150–153. In *The Governor* Sir Thomas Elyot declares that in antiquity poetry was so highly esteemed that "all wisdom was supposed to be therein included and poetry was the first philosophy that ever was known. . . . Yea . . . in poets was supposed to be science mystical and inspired, and therefore in Latin they were called *vates*, which word signifyeth as much as prophets. And therefore Tully in his *Tusculan Questions* supposeth than a poet cannot abundantly express verses sufficient and complete, or that his eloquence may flow without labor words well sounding and plenteous, without celestial instinction, which is also by Plato ratified." See *Literary Criticism: Plato to Dryden*, ed. Allan H. Gilbert (Detroit, 1962), pp. 237–238.

37. Ben Jonson, *Timber, or Discoveries*, in Hardison, pp. 280–281. Castelvetro observes that Aristotle did not believe that "poetry was a special gift of God bestowed on one man rather than on another, as is the gift of prophecy," and that he undoubtedly intended (though he did not openly say so) "to refute the opinion that some attribute to Plato, that poetry is infused into men through divine madness. This opinion had its origin and source in the ignorance of the common people and has been increased and favored by the vainglory of the poets. . . . It is wrong then to attribute to Plato this opinion of the *furor* infused into the poets," and when Plato mentions it he is surely jesting; Castelvetro, *The Poetics of Aristotle Translated and Annotated*, in Gilbert, pp.

310–311. Cf. Gilbert, p. 502, for Tasso's view that the poet "speaks more loftily in his own person and discourses as though with another tongue, like one who feigns to be rapt out of himself by divine inspiration. . . ."

38. *The Reason of Church-Government*, in *Complete Poems and Major Prose*, ed. Hughes, pp. 669–671.

39. Edward Phillips, "The Preface to *Theatrum Poetarum*, in *Literary Criticism* . . ., ed. Hughes, p. 667.

40. *Boccaccio on Poetry*, ed. Osgood, pp. 22, 37, 39. Boccaccio subsequently reiterates his belief that "this science of poetry has ever streamed forth from the bosom of God"; p. 41. He makes a similar reference to Philosophy (p. 33), "messenger from the very bosom of God, mistress of all knowledge." Osgood suggests that the "ancestress" of Boccaccio's personification of Philosophy in this passage is Wisdom in Proverbs ix and Book of Wisdom vii ff.; he also cites Wisdom vii. 25 and ix. 2, 3, 9, 11; (See Osgood, p. 153n.)

41. Osgood, p. 46; cf. p. 42. On the invention of poetry by the Hebrews, see pp. 160n.–161n. Like Eusebius and John of Salisbury, Boccaccio considers the possibility that "Moses and Musaeus were one and the same"; pp. 46, 163n. He also cites Aristotle's view "that the first poets were theologians"; pp. 46, 163n. (cf. *Metaphysics*). Cf. Milton's remarks on the Hebrew origins of poetry and music and the argument that "rather *Greece* from us these Arts derived" in *Paradise Regained* IV, lines 331–342. For Albertino Mussato's defense of poetry as a "divine art" because "it deals with gods and things celestial, because those who follow it are *vates*, because it comes from God. . . . because Moses used it to praise God and bring his people out of slavery" see Osgood, pp. xli n.–xlii n. In *The Life of Dante* Boccaccio argues that poetry is theology and that "theology is none other than the poetry of God"; see Gilbert, pp. 208–211.

George Chapman represents Wisdom in terms which (as Douglas Bush observes) "recall some famous utterances of Milton's, with a difference": Wisdom visits "only those who approach her 'with invocation, fasting, watching; yea, not without having drops of their souls like an heavenly familiar'"; Bush, *Mythology and the Renaissance Tradition* . . ., p. 207.

42. Much earlier, in "At a Vacation Exercise . . .," Milton had invoked his "native Language," and after describing the imaginary poetic flights he would prefer to undertake into the heavens, through the spheres of fire and air to the sea to the arcana of Nature and heroic themes, he recalls his "wandering Muse" to the immediate task in hand: the academic playlet on the predicaments. Professing his desire to employ his native tongue "in some graver subject," such as "may make thee search thy coffers round,/ Before thou cloath my fancy in fit sound," he hopes some day to exercise his imagination and poetic skills in viewing the realms of the gods and the secrets of nature/ (lines 29–58):

> Such where the deep transported mind may soare
> Above the wheeling poles, and at Heav'ns dore
> Look in, and see each blissful Deitie. . . .
> Then sing of secret things that came to pass
> When Beldam Nature in her cradle was;
> And last of Kings and Queens and *Hero's* old
> Such as the wise Demodocus once told. . . .
> But fie my wandering Muse how thou dost stray!
> Expectance calls thee now another way. . . .

In Demodocus Milton recognized, so early, the image of the inspired bard taught by the muse. Later his own blindness would give additional point to the analogy. For in the *Odyssey* Demodocus had been described as a favorite of the Muse, who had rendered him both good and evil, granting him the gift of song but bereaving him of sight (VIII, 43–82).

43. For interpretations of the ascent to Heaven and descent to Hell in poetic fiction as metaphors for the contemplation of good and evil and their respective rewards (and for alternative interpretations of these motifs), see D.W. Robertson, Jr., *A Preface to Chaucer* (Princeton, 1962); Thomas E. Maresca, *Three English Epics: Studies of Troilus and Criseyde, The Faerie Queene, and Paradise Lost* (Lincoln, Nebraska, 1979); Michael Murrin, *The Allegorical Epic: Essays in Its Rise and Decline* (Chicago, 1980).

44. For DuBartas' imagery of flight or descent in the company of his Muse, according to his varying subject matter, see Sylvester, ed. Grosart, Vol. I, pp. 40, 52, 154, etc. The treatment of the metaphors of poetic inspiration and visionary flight by a less gifted poet offers points of comparison as well as contrast with Milton's treatment of similar motifs; and there are in fact occasional verbal parallels between the two poets. In "The Third Day of the First Weeke," the poet and his Muse descend from the Heavens to the earth (lines 12–23):

> My sacred Muse, that lately soaréd high,
> Amongst the glistring Circles of the Sky, . . .
> Commanding all the Winds and sulph'ry Storms,
> The lightning Flashes, and the hideous Forms
> Seen in the Aire; with language meetly brave
> Whilom discours'd upon a Theme so grave:
> But, *This-Day*, flagging lowly by the *Ground*,
> Shee seems constrain'd to keep a lowly sound;
> Or if, sometimes, she somewhat raise her voice,
> The sound is drown'd with the rough Ocean's noyse.

In "The Fourth Day of the First Weeke" he ascends again into the skies to contemplate the courses of the planets (lines 12–27):

> Pure Spirit that rapt'st above the firmest Sphear,
> In fiery Coach, thy faithful Messenger,
> Who, smiting *Jordan* with his pleighted Cloak,
> Did yerst divide the Waters with the stroke:
> O! take me up; that far from Earth, I may
> From Sphear to Sphear, see th' azure Heav'ns *To-Day*.
> Be thou my Coach-man, and now Cheek by Joule
> With *Phoebus'* Chariot let my Chariot roule;
> Drive on my Coach by *Mars* flaming Coach.
> *Saturn* and *Luna* let my wheels approach:
> That, having learn'd of their Fire-breathing Horses,
> Their course, their light, their labor, and their forces;
> My Muse may sing in sacred Eloquence,
> To Vertue's Friends, their vertuous Excellence:
> And, with the Load-stone of my conquering Verse,
> Above the Poles attract the most perverse.

In "The Columnes" ("The Fourth Part of the Second Day of the II. Weeke"), DuBartas proposes "to treat of the Mathematickes," and accordingly "imploreth especiall assistance in handling so high and difficult a Subject"—a theme that requires divine inspiration (lines 12–31; see also marginal gloss):

> If ever (Lord) the purest of my Soule
> In *sacred Rage* were rapt above the Pole:
> If ever, by thy Spirit my spirit inspir'd,
> Offred thee Layes that learnéd *France* admir's,
> Father of light, Fountain of learnéd Art,
> Now, now (or never) purge my purest part:
> Now quintessence my Soule and now advance
> My care-free Powrs in some celestiall Transe:

That (purg'd from Passion) thy divine addresse
May guide me through Heav'n's glistering Palaces:
Where (happily) my dear URANIA's grace,
And her fair Sisters I may all imbrace:
And (the melodious *Sirens* of the Sphears,
Charming my senses in those sweets of theirs)
So ravishéd, I may at rest contemple
The Starry Arches of thy stately Temple:
Unto this end, that as (at first) from thee
Our Grand-sires learn'd Heav'ns Course and Quality;
Thou now maist prompt me some more lofty Song,
As to this lofty Subject doth belong.

In adapting the classical invocation-formula and the imagery of poetic inspiration and visionary flight to the changing subject matter and shifting locales of the six-days' works, DuBartas tends at times to reduce the principle of decorum to the method of a geographical or astronomical handbook or a traveller's guidebook: a cosmic Baedeker or Murray's Guide. The flights of the imagination become half-whimsical excusions into the heavens or under the sea, or backwards and forwards in time. The Muse herself not only serves as conductor and tour-guide, but provides appropriate transportation. DuBartas would surely have equipped her with rocket and bathysphere and time-machine, if such inventions had been available to him. On one occasion he asks divine aid to enable him to plunge into the depths of the sea and inspect the fishes at first hand. In contrast to these mannerist raptures, and DuBartas' extended ascents or descents with his Muse, one may compare Milton's analogous, but far less artificial accommodation of his visionary flight to his subject matter (*PL* VII, lines 21–24), even in a passage where he seems to have consciously echoed Sylvester's version of *La Sepmaine*:

Half yet remaines unsung, but narrower bound
Within the visible Diurnal Spheare;
Standing on Earth, not rapt above the Pole,
More safe I Sing with mortal voice. . . .

45. See Anne Davidson Ferry, *Milton's Epic Voice: The Narrator in Paradise Lost* (Cambridge, Mass., 1963); William W. Kerrigan, *The Prophetic Milton*; Joseph Anthony Wittreich, Jr., *Visionary Poetics . . .*; Michael Lieb, *Poetics of the Holy . . .*; John Spencer Hill, *John Milton, Poet, Prophet, and Priest. . . .*

Chapter Three: *Urania: "Meaning" and "Name"*

1. Lily Bess Campbell, "The Christian Muse", *Huntington Library Bulletin*, VIII (October, 1935), pp. 29–70; *idem, Divine Poetry and Drama in Sixteenth-Century England* (Berkeley and Los Angeles, 1959). The author stresses the point that "it is the subject matter of the poem or drama that makes it divine poetry or drama" (*ibid.*, p. 5).

2. *Complete Prose Works of John Milton*, I (New Haven, 1953), p. 815.

3. Cf. Joseph Addison, in *Milton Criticism*, ed. James Thorpe (London, 1956), p. 23.

4. Cf. Milton's "Ad Patrem", line 17 ("vatis opus divinum . . . carmen") and Horace's *Ars Poetica*, line 400 ("divinis vatibus"); see also Allen H. Gilbert, *Literary Criticism from Plato to Dryden* (New York, 1940), pp. 458, 500, on Sidney's belief in the poet's "divine fury", Landino's view that "the divine spirit" fills the poet with "divine thoughts", and Tasso's opinion that the great poet is "called divine for no other reason but that, because he resembles in his work the supreme architect, he comes to participate in his divinity".

5. Milton, *Prose Works*, I, p. 813.

6. *Ibid.*, p. 815.

7. William J. Grace, "Orthodoxy and Aesthetic Method in *Paradise Lost* and the *Divine Comedy*", *"Comparative Literature*, I (1949), pp. 174, 176.

8. Campbell, *HLB*, pp. 43–44.

9. D. T. Starnes and E. W. Talbert, *Classical Myth and Legend in Renaissance Dictionaries* (Chapel Hill, 1955), p. 264.

10. Macrobius, *Commentary on the Dream of Scipio*, tr. William Harris Stahl (New York, 1952), p. 194.

11. Cora E. Lutz (ed.), *Johannis Scotti Annotationes in Marcianum* (Cambridge, Mass., 1939), pp. 30, 170.

12. *Practica Musice Franchini Gafori Laudensis* (Mediolani, 1496); *Theorica Musice Franchini Gafuri Laudensis* (Mediolani, 1492).

13. *Geofredi Linocerii Vivariensis Mythologiae Musarum Libellus*, in *Natalis Comitis Mythologiae* (Geneva, 1641); cf. *Plutarch's Moralia*, IX, tr. E. L. Minar, F. H. Sandbach, and W. C. Helmbold (Cambridge, Mass., and London, 1961), p. 283, "let us then similarly place one of the Muses in the heavens, and suppose her concern to be with the heavenly bodies"; 282, "kai hēmeis homoiōs men tithōmen en ouranoi kai peri ta ourania mian tōn Mousōn" [Greek transliterated]. Cf. *Plutarchi Chaeronensis omnium quae exstant operum tomus secundus . . . Gulielmo Xylandro interprete* (Lutetiae Parisiorum, 1624), p. 777," . . . sicut, inquam, Plato nominibus tanquan vestigiis deorum se facultates putat invenire: ita nos quoque similiter imponamus coelo & rebus coelestibus, Uraniam Musam quae à coelo nomen habet."

14. H. N. Fowler (tr.), *Plato*, VI (Loeb Classical Library, London and New York, 1926), p. 49; cf. *Omnia divini Platonis opera tralatione Marsilii Ficini, emendatione, et ad Graecum codicem collatione Simonis Grynaei . . . repurgata* (Lugduni, 1548), p. 215, "Est autem is [Kronos] ouranou, id est, coeli filius, ut fertur. Quippe aspectus ad supera merito *ourania* vocatur, quasi *horō*sa ta anō. Unde affirmant . . . ij qui de rebus sublimibus agunt, puram mentem adesse, & ouranoi iure nomen impositum."

15. See Starnes and Talbert, p. 264.

16. Henricus Stephanus, *Thesaurus linguae Graecae* ([Genevae,] 1572), *s.v. Ouranios*.

17. Cf. Plato, *The Republic*, tr. Paul Shorey, II (Loeb Classical Library, London and Cambridge, Mass., 1935), p. 181, "this study [astronomy] certainly compels the soul to look upward [anankazei psychen eis to ano horan] and leads it away from things here to those higher things." Cf. Ficino, p. 424, "Nam cuique patere existimo hanc animi oculos ad superiora dirigere, & hinc illuc ipsum perducere." (Greek transliterated henceforth.)

18. Robertus Stephanus, *Thesaurus linguae Latinae* (Basileae, 1576–1578), *s.v. Urania*, cf. *Ambrosii Calepini Bergomatis lexicon adauctum et recognitum denuo* (Haganoae, 1526), *s.v. Urania*, "uranos vero dicitur quasi oranos, ut inquit Amb. lib. Hex. ab *horao*, quod sit visui pervium & minime densum, ut est aqua & terra."

19. Giovanni Boccaccio, *Genealogie Deorum Gentilium Libri*, ed. Vincenzo Romano, II (Bari, 1951), 541; *idem, Il Comento alla Divina Commedia*, ed. Domenico Guerri, I (Bari, 1918), pp. 201–202; cf. *Enarrationes allegoricae fabularum Fulgentij Placiadis* (Venetiis, [c. 1500]), f. 11, "Octava Urania .i. caelestis post diiudicationem .n. etiam eligis quid dicas, quid despuas. eligere .n. utile caducumque despuere caeleste ingenium est."

20. Linocier, *op.cit.*

21. *Della piu che novissima Iconologia di Cesare Ripa Perugino . . . ampliata dal Sig. Cav. Gio. Zaratino Castellini Romano* (Padova, 1630), p. 505.

22. Lutz, p. 65.

23. *Iconologia . . . van Cesare Ripa*, tr. D. Pietersz Pers (Amstelredam, 1644), p. 340.

24. See Starnes and Talbert, p. 264, "quasi coelestium rerum cantu, vel a cantus divinitate."

25. H. Stephanus, *s.v. Ouranios*. Johannes Scapula's *Lexicon Graeco-Latinum Novum* (Basileae, 1615) gives a similar variety of meanings for *ouranios* and *ourania*, and lists several etymologies of *Ouranos:* "Ab *horos* derivat Aristot. de mundo: quum inquit "ouranion etymos kaloumen apo tou horon einai ton ano. Alij ab *horao* deducunt, quod sit visui pervium." Ficino suggests (p. 210) that the name Coelius may signify God himself, his fecundity, the soul of the sphere of fixed stars, or an "aspectum ad superiora".

26. Ripa, p. 505.

27. *Ibid.*, pp. 576–578.

28. Campbell, *HLB,* p. 69.

29. Starnes and Talbert, p. 263.

30. See *Textus Bibliae cum . . . Nicolai de Lyra postilla* (Lugduni, 1528–1529) for the comparison of Wisdom's sport (Proverbs viii. 30–31) to a *ludus pilae*.

31. Macrobius, p. 194.

32. Lutz, p. 3.

33. Boccaccio, *Comento,* p. 200; *idem, Genealogie,* pp. 539–540.

34. H. Stephanus, *s.v. Mao*.

35. Calepine, *s.v. Musa; Bibliotheca Eliotae* (London, 1548), *s.v. Musa;* Francis Holyoke, *Dictionarium Etymologicum Latinum* (London, 1633), *s.v. Musa;* [Guillaume Morel,] *Verborum Latinorum cum Graecis Anglicisque coniunctorum . . . commentarij* (Londini, 1583), *s.v. Musa; Thomae Thomasii Dictionarium* (Cantabrigiae, 1596), *s.v. Musa;* cf. *Lexicon Graeco-Latinum Novum . . . Joannis Scapulae, s.v. Mousa,* "Musa, dea cantus", "Aliquando accipitur pro ipso cantu".

36. Macrobius, pp. 193–194.

37. Lutz, p. 30.

38. Boccaccio, *Comento,* p. 200; cf. . . . *Genealogie,* p. 539, "eas equiparans octo sperarum celi cantibus, nonam volens omnium celorum modulationum esse concentum". Cf. Ficino, p. 117, "Musas, sphaerarum mundi animas".

39. Conti, p. 770.

40. [V. Cartari,] *The Fountaine of Ancient Fiction,* tr. Richard Linche (London, 1959), p. 36.

41. *Iulii Caesaris Scaligeri . . . Poetices libri septem* ([Lyons,] 1561), p. 4.

42. Boccaccio, *Comento,* p. 200; cf. *Genealogie,* p. 540; Fulgentius, f. 10.

43. *Pub. Ovidii Nasonis Heroides* (Venetiis, 1542), f. lxxxi.

44. Lutz, p. 134.

45. Boccaccio, *Comento,* p. 202; *Genealogie,* p. 539.

46. *Dictionarium Historicum geographicum Poeticum, Authore Carolo Stephano* (Oxonii, 1671), *s.v. Musa.*

47. *Conti, pp. 762, 764.*

48. *Plato, VI, pp. 79–81.* For the association of the Muses with the humanities and liberal arts, cf. Boccaccio, *Genealogie,* p. 540, "Nos vero novem Musas doctrine atque scientie dicimus modos"; R. Stephanus, "Musae, pro Humanitate, doctrina, & literis accipiuntur . . . Quin & Philosophicas disputationes appellat Musas mansuetiores, & pro quacunque doctrina Musam ponit"; C. Stephanus, "Musarum autem nomine omnes artes liberales continentur; quippe quae ab iis inventae creditae sunt"; "humanitatem, & literas"; "studii seu disciplinae"; H. Stephanus, "Non tam vero cantus, quam etiam bonarum literarum praesides eaedem credebantur: item & humanitatis"; Conti, p. 764, "Callimachus tamen in quodam epigrammate, non solum Musas poeticam facultatem, sed omnia scriptionum disciplinarumque genera invenisse scribit sed quid unaquaeque invenerit, ita patefecit"; Scapula, "Bonarum etiam litterarum praesides eaedem credebantur & humanitatis."

49. H. G. Liddell and R. Scott, *A Greek-English Lexicon*, revised H. S. Jones (Oxford, 1925), *s.v. mosis*.

50. *P.L.*, LXXXII, col. 163. Among the MS readings are *mōsai* (col. 163n) and *masai* (Charles G. Osgood (ed.), *Boccaccio on Poetry* [Princeton, 1930], p. 159).

51. Boccaccio, *Comento*, p. 199; *Genealogie*, p. 539.

52. Cassiodorus Senator, *An Introduction to Divine and Human Readings*, tr. Leslie Webber Jones (New York, 1946), p. 189. Variants are *mosthai, masai, masteuein* (p. 189n.). Cf. *P.L.*, LXX, col. 1208, "Quae musae ipsae appellatae sunt *apo tou masenein* id est a quaerendo, quod per ipsas . . . vis carminum et vocis modulatio quaeretur." Cf. Scapula, "Suid. & Eust. à *maō (quaero)* derivant: quoniam est *pasēs paideias aitia:* quod etymon sequitur & Plato in Cratylo"; *Photii Myriobiblon, sive bibliotheca*, tr. Andreas Schottus Antverpianus (Rothomagie, 1653), col. 1582, suggests several alternative etymologies with essentially the same meaning: "Musam alij derivant à *maiousan tina*, id est, *investigatricem:* doctrina enim Musarum nihil à mysteriis discrepat. Alij à *maasai* derivant. Quaerere enim Dores dicunt *mō*. Et tertia persona *mōtai* extat apud Epicharmum. *mōntai* apud Euphronionem & *mōmenai* participium apud Sophoclem. Aptius igitur est Musam sic dici, tanquam inventricem omnium disciplinarum existimatam. *maiesthai* Homerus quoque pro *quaerere* dixit, & *maian* illam dicimus, quae consulit Medicum de abscondito."

53. Calepine, *s.v. Musa*.

54. *Fabularum Ovidii Interpretatio, Ethica, Physica, et Historica, tradita . . . a Georgio Sabinio* (Cantabrigiae, 1584), p. 185.

55. Scaliger, p. 3.

56. *P.G.*, XXI, cols. 108–109.

57. Scaliger, p. 3.

58. Ripa, p. 503, Cf. Scapula, "Euseb. vero *para to myein*, significante *didaskein & paideuein*.

59. *P.L.*, LXIX. cols., 643–644. Cf. Scapula, "Plutarch autem in lib. *peri philadelph*, ait *mousas* vocatas quasi *homou di' eunoian aei kai philadelphian ousas:* alij quasi *homoiousas* dictas volunt, quòd uno nexu omnes disciplinae teneantur, atque fiat *enkyklopaideia;* Stobaeus, p. 476, "Musas nominatas aiunt quasi *homou ousas*, id est, simul degentes propter sororiam animorum coniunctionem."

60. Cartari, p. 36.

61. See James Strong, *A Concise Dictionary of the Words in the Hebrew Bible* (New York, 1890), No. 4561.

62. Conti, p. 771.

63. *The Holie Bible faithfully translated into English* (Douai, 1609), notes on the Psalms.

64. Scaliger, p. 3.

65. A. W. Verity (ed.), *Paradise Lost*, II (Cambridge, 1929), p. 431.

66. Lutz, p. 134.

67. Cartari, p. 36.

68. See notes on the Psalms in the Douai Bible.

Chapter Four: *Urania: Wisdom and Spiritual Exegesis*

1. *Complete Prose Works of John Milton II*, ed. Ernest Sirluck (New Haven, 1959), pp. 596–597.

2. Cf. D. Pietersz Pers (tr.), *Iconologia . . . van Cesare Ripa* (Amstelredam, 1644), p. 340, where Urania is interpreted as "Hemel-Sangh".

3. Cf. David Masson (ed.), *The Poetical Works of John Milton*, III (London, 1874), p. 210; A. W. Verity (ed.), *Paradise Lost*, II (Cambridge, 1929), p. 530.

4. Harris Francis Fletcher, *Milton's Rabbinical Readings* (Urbana, 1930), pp. 110–

112; for criticism of this interpretation, see Maurice Kelley, *This Great Argument* (Princeton, 1941), pp. 109–118; *idem.* "Milton and the Third Person of the Trinity," *SP*, XXXII (1935), pp. 221–234.

5. W. Gesenius, E. Robinson, and F. Brown (eds.), *A Hebrew and English Lexicon of the Old Testament* (Boston and New York, 1928), p. 315, describe this form as "pl[ural] abst[ract: emph[atic]." *The Interpreter's Bible*, IV (New York, 1955), p. 789, suggests, however that "The Hebrew form *hokhmôth*, found here and in 9:1; 14:1; 24:7; Ps. 49:4 (Heb.), is probably not a feminine plural but an abstract singular corresponding to the Phoenician form of the word."

6. *Biblia Hebraica. Eorundem Latina Interpretatio Xantis Pagnini Lucensis, Recenter Benedicti Ariae Montani Hispal. & quorundam aliorum collatio studio, ad Hebraicam dictionem diligentissime expensa* (Antverpiae, 1584), p. 55.

7. *Testamenti Veteris Biblia Sacra . . . Latini recens ex Hebraco facti, brevibusque Scholiis illustrati ab Immanuele Tremellio & Francisco Junio* (Londini, 1593).

8. *Johannis Piscatoris Commentariorum in omnes libros veteris testamenti*, III (Herbornae Nassoviorum, 1644), p. 339.

9. [Peter Muffet], *A Commentarie upon the whole booke of the Proverbs of Salomon* (London, 1596), p. 13.

10. Kelley, p. 117n; *The Works of John Milton*, XV (Columbia Edition, New York, 1933), p. 13.

11. See Leah Jonas. *The Divine Science: The Aesthetic of Some Representative Seventeenth-Century English Poets* (New York, 1940), pp. 5, 165; J. E. Spingarn (ed.), *Critical Essays of the Seventeenth-Century*, II (Oxford, 1908), p. 88.

12. Muffet, pp. 13–14.

13. Michael Iermin, *Paraphrasticall Meditations, by way of commentarie, upon the whole booke of the Proverbs of Solomon* (London, 1638), pp. 15–16.

14. *Lexicon Heptaglotton . . . Authore Edmundo Castello*, II (Londini, 1686), cols. 1222–1223, *s.v.* hakham: "*Sapuit, sapiens fuit*, Certam rerum tam divinarum, quam humanarum cognitionem, et scientiam, significat doctrinam, s. peritiam quamconque: Hinc quaelibet Ars, s. Facultas, Hebr. dicitur hokhmoth et cujuslibet artis peritus, hakham Prov.23.15 & 9.12"; in Rabbinical Hebrew the work hokmoth ("Sapientia") can be applied to a variety of arts and sciences, including theology, astronomy, and music: "1 Scientia Divinitatis, Theologia, Metaphysica, 2 Naturalis physica, 3, Dispositionis astrorum, Astronomia . . . 5, Modulationis, Musica," etc. Cf. *Schindleri Lexicon . . . In Epitomen redactum a G.A.* (Londini, 1635), p. 148, hokmoth . . . hicma sapientia, peritia, . . . scientia, ars"; hakham . . . hacim sapiens, peritus, doctus, eruditus, artifex. *Arab.* artista, . . . studiosus, auditor." [Hebrew transliterated.]

15. *Natalis Comitis Mythologiae* (Geneva, 1641), pp. 764, 771–772.

16. *Dictionarium Historicum Geographicum, Poeticum, Authore Carolo Stephano* (Oxonii, 1671), *s.v. Musa*. Cf. *Danielis Heinsii Aristarchus Sacer, sive ad Nonni in Johannem Metaphrasin Contextus* (Lugduni Batavorum, 1627).

17. See *Interpreter's Bible*, IV, p. 781, "*Instruction:* The root meaning of the word *mûsar* is 'discipline,' 'chastisement.' Here, in parallelism with *wisdom*, it means the result of training, the instruction received from submitting oneself to the teaching of the wise men." For Muffet (p. 3), "*instruction . . .* is a vertue consisting in the right using of wisedom, whereby through the Lords working and schooling, the heart and life of men is reformed." For Robert Cleaver (*A Briefe Explanation of the whole Booke of the Proverbs of Salomon* [London, 1615], p. 2), "*instruction*" is "the meanes whereby wisedome is to be obtained, as doctrine, exhortation, reprehension, &c." Michael Cope (*A Godly . . . Exposition uppon the Proverbes of Solomon*, tr. Marcelline Outred [London, 1580] fol. 2) stresses the heavenly character of this instruction: "Whereby wee shoulde knowe what to doe and what to eschue, for to live in this present worlde

soberly, righteously, and religiously: the which instruction is not onely in woordes, but also in temptations and afflictions. Whereuppon it followeth that Solomon beeing on earth, spake not earthly, but heavenly: for wee can have no instruction, unlesse God speake to us from Heaven, as Moses doeth shewe it very well. Out of Heaven hee made thee heare his voyce to instruct thee, &c"; cf. Deut. viii.I and iv. 46. For definitions of *Musar,* see Gesenius, *s.v. yasar* ("admonish," "instruct," "discipline") and *musar* ("discipline, . . . chastening, correction"); James Strong, *A Concise Dictionary of the Words in the Hebrew Bible,* in *The Exhaustive Concordance of the Bible* (New York, 1890), Nos. 4561, 3256; Castellus, cols. 1622–1625, "Castigatio, disciplina, eruditio"; Schindler, *s.v. yasar* ("Per Metaphoram, *yasar* castigavit, erudivit, instituit"; "Nom *musar* et *mosar* castigatio, disciplina, punitio, increpatio"). For other examples in Proverbs, see Gesenius, *loc. cit.* [Hebrew transliterated.]

18. Gesenius, pp. 965–966; cf. Schindler, col. 505; Castellus, col. 3731.

19. *Ambrosii Calepini Bergomatis Lexicon* (Haganoae, 1526), *s.v. ludo;* cf. Robertus Stephanus, *Thesaurus Linguae Latinae* (Basileae, 1576–1578), *s.v. ludo.*

20. [Sir Thomas Elyot,] *Bibliotheca Eliotae* (London, 1548), *s.v. ludo.*

21. Thomas Cooper, *Thesaurus Linguae Romanae & Britannicae* (Londini, 1584), *s.v. ludo; Thomae Thomasii Dictionarium* (Cantabrigiae, 1596), *s.v. ludo;* [Guillaume Morel,] *Verborum Latinorum cum Graecis Anglicisque coniunctorum . . . Commentarij* (Londini, 1583), *s.v. ludo;* Francis Holy-Oke, *Riders Dictionarie* (London, 1633), *s.v. ludo.*

22. *Milton, Complete Prose Works,* II, p. 597.

23. Fletcher, p. 113.

24. *Ibid.,* p. 113.

25. See Pagninus, *Biblia Hebraica,* on Proverbs viii.

26. *Hebraica Biblia latina planeque nova Sebast. Munsteri tralatione . . . adiectis insuper è Rabbinorum comentarijs annotationibus* (Basileae, 1534), fol. 640.

27. Piscator, III, p. 354.

28. Jermin, p. 172.

29. *Textus bibliae cum Glossa Ordinaria, Nicolai de Lyra postilla* (Lugduni, 1528–1529).

30. Piscator, III, p. 354.

31. Cleaver, p. 139.

32. Gesenius, pp. 965–966. Cf. Tremellius, fols. 28, 35, 36, 75. In the Authorized Version of these texts the verb is consistently translated as "play."

33. *Biblia Hebraica,* p. 69; cf. pp. 88 ("ludebant coram Domino," "ludam ad facies Domini"), 182 ("ludentes ad facies Dei").

34. Piscator, II, 201; cf. II, pp. 157 ("Respondebant autem mulieres illae ludentes"), 201 (*"Gestivi*] Vel, lusi"), III, pp. 403 (*"Prae laetitia gestiebant.*] Heb. Ludebant"), 406 (*"Gestientem.*] Heb. Ludentem").

35. The text is usually interpreted in terms of familiarity, common habitation, and "converse"—a reading which is retained in Milton's allusion to the sisterhood of Urania and Wisdom. Cf. Cleaver, p. 113: "Say unto Wisedome, Thou art my sister . . . hee attributeth a person to Wisedome, and requireth that there bee such inward friendship and familiaritie betwixt us and her, as if she were our sister, and neerest kinswoman. It is a pleasing thing to brothers and sisters . . . to live together in one house . . . And thus conversant and familiar ought we to be with Wisedome"; Muffet, pp. 88–89, "The love between brethren, sisters, and kinsfolk is verie naturall, and againe their familiaritie verie great . . . In like sort then, we are not to be strangers in the word, but we must be daylie conversant therein"; Cope, fol. 98, "For as much as we have neither wisedome nor knowledge, but so much as the Word of God doeth print in our hearts, and that it pleaseth him to give us; we ought to understand that Solomon would have us like unto the

blessed man: so doing, wisdom should be as our sister, & understanding should be familiar unto us . . ."

36. Milton, *Complete Prose Works,* I, ed. Don M. Wolfe (New Haven, 1953), p. 820.

37. Cf. *At a Solemn Musick,* line 2.

38. John Milton, *Private Correspondence and Academic Exercises,* tr. Phyllis B. Tillyard (Cambridge, 1932), p. 64; John Mitford (ed.), *The Works of John Milton,* VII (London, 1851), p. 422.

39. Milton, *Works,* I, p. 26. A. W. Verrall, *Lectures on Dryden* (Cambridge, 1914), p. 194, finds in "both Milton and Dryden" the "theory . . . that the world was created, and is held together, by harmony . . ."

40. Milton, *Works,* I, p. 63.

41. *Ibid.,* p. 65.

42. Tillyard, p. 65.

43. Cf. the Vulgate version (xi. 21), "sed omnia in mensura, et numero, et pondere disposuisti."

44. John Peter, *Artificial Versifying,* Second Edition (London, 1678).

45. See the *Theorica Musice Franchini Gafuri Laudensis* (Mediolani, 1492), Bk. I, chap. 2, 3, and 4.

46. For Milton's angelology, see Robert H. West, *Milton and the Angels* (Athens, Ga., 1955).

47. Milton, *Works,* II, pp. 33, 101.

48. *Practica Musice Franchini Gafuri Laudensis* (Mediolani, 1496).

49. *Theorica Musice,* Bk. I, chap. 1.

50. Cf. Conti pp. 769–771; Macrobius, *Commentary on the Dream of Scipio,* tr. William Harris Stahl (New York, 1952), p. 194.

51. *Theorica Musice,* Bk. I, chap. 1.

52. *Della piu che novissima Iconologia di Cesare Ripa Perugino . . . Ampliata dal Sig. Cav. Gio. Zaratino Castellini Romano* (Padova, 1630), p. 505.

53. *Ibid.,* p. 578; cf. the stellar symbolism in an alternative description of "Poesia," pp. 576–577.

54. See Tremellius on Job xxxviii.7; cf. the Genevan version of *The Bible* (Edinburgh, 1579) on the same text, "Meaning, the Angels"; *Sacra Biblia ad LXX. Interpretum Fidem Diligentissime Tralata* (Basileae, 1526), "Laudaverunt me voce magna omnes angeli mei."

55. *Job Expounded by Theodore Beza* (Cambridge, 1593?).

56. Piscator, p. 94.

57. The relationship between the invocations of Books I and VII of *Paradise Lost* will be considered in a separate study. For Urania's traditional role as the "Christian Muse" in Renaissance "divine poetry," see Lily Bess Campbell, "The Christian Muse," *HLB,* VIII (1935), pp. 29–70; *idem, Divine Poetry and Drama in Sixteenth-Century England* (Berkeley, Calif., 1959). For recent studies of Milton's Muse and prologues, see John S. Diekhoff, "The Function of the Prologues in *Paradise Lost,*" *PMLA,* LVII (1942), pp. 697–704; Jackson I. Cope, "Milton's Muse in *Paradise Lost,*" *MP,* LV (1957), pp. 6–10; G. W. Whiting and A. Gossman, "Siloa's Brook, the Pool of Siloam, and Milton's Muse," *SP,* LVIII (1961), pp. 193–205. For Milton's knowledge of Renaissance dictionaries, see D. T. Starnes and E. W. Talbert, *Classical Myth and Legend in Renaissance Dictionaries* (Chapel Hill, 1955), pp. 226–339.

Chapter Five: *Urania: "Spirit" and "Muse"*

1. Its position in the sentence would normally indicate that 'chiefly' is associated with 'Thou' and that Milton is stressing the distinction between his Muse and a higher power,

the Spirit of God. Alternative possibilities would, however, be fairly consistent with the complex syntax of Milton's epic style. If one assumes that 'chiefly' modifies 'instruct', then it would apparently involve a contrast between the two imperatives ('sing' in line 6 and 'instruct me' in line 19) rather than a distinction between the Spirit and the Muse. There would, however, be little point in emphasizing the difference between instruction and singing, and it is more likely that 'chiefly' modifies 'prefer' and stresses the contrast between the favorite haunts of the supernatural power (or powers) the poet is invoking. Whereas the Heavenly Muse delights in such sacred mountains or brooks as Horeb, Sion, and Siloa, the Spirit prefers, before all temples, the 'upright heart and pure'.

2. J. H. Hanford, *A Milton Handbook* (New York, 1946), p. 194; *idem, John Milton, Englishman* (New York, 1949), pp. 211–212.

3. G. W. Whiting and A. Gossman, 'Siloa's Brook, the Pool of Siloam, and Milton's Muse,' *SP,* 58 (1961), p. 202.

4. Lily Bess Campbell, 'The Christian Muse,' *HLQ,* 8 (1935), p. 69. Professor Kelley has shown that, as 'the *De doctrina* forbids invocation of the Third Person' of the trinity, it is unlikely that Milton is involving the Holy Spirit. Instead, he apparently 'turned for inspiration and knowledge not to what he considered a subordinate figure but rather to the Father himself—the very fountainhead of all wisdom and enlightenment.' See Maurice Kelley, *This Great Argument* (Princeton, 1941), pp. 109–118; *idem,* 'Milton and the Third Person of the Trinity,' *SP,* 32 (1935), pp. 221–234.

5. David Masson (ed.), *The Poetical Works of John Milton,* III (London, 1874), p. 114.

6. A. W. Verity (ed.), *Paradise Lost,* II (Cambridge, 1929), pp. 368, 370.

7. Masson, p. 114.

8. William J. Grace, 'Orthodoxy and Aesthetic Method in *Paradise Lost* and the *Divine Comedy,*' *Comparative Literature,* 1 (1949), pp. 174, 176.

9. Don M. Wolfe (ed.), *Complete Prose Works of John Milton,* I (New Haven, 1953), pp. 820–821; cf. Ida Langdon, *Milton's Theory of Poetry and Fine Art* (New Haven, 1924), pp. 271–273.

10. *PL,* VII, 12; cf. *Iconologia . . . van Cesare Ripa, tr.* D. Pietersz Pers (Amstelredam, 1644), p. 340, 'Urania. *Hemel-Sangh.*'

11. *Natalis Comitis Mythologiae* (Geneva, 1641), p. 769.

12. See Ralph W. Condee, 'The Formalized Openings of Milton's Epic Poems,' *JEGP,* 50 (1951), pp. 502–508.

Chapter Six: *Darkness Visible The Quality of Hellfire*

1. L. C. Martin (ed.), *The Poetical Works of Robert Herrick* (Oxford, 1956), 387, "Hell-fire." Cf. A. W. Verity (ed.), *Paradise Lost,* II (Cambridge, 1936), 372.

2. See my note, "John Collop and the Flames without Light," *N&Q, n. s.,* II (1955), 582–3.

3. *The Poems of John Donne,* ed. Sir H.J.C. Grierson (London, 1945), 118.

4. David Masson (ed.), *The Poetical Works of John Milton,* III (London, 1890), 385.

5. Martin, 576; Walter W. Skeat (ed.), *Notes to the Canterbury Tales, The Complete Works of Geoffrey Chaucer,* Second Edition (Oxford, 1900), 452. Among additional studies of this motif and related aspects of Milton's Hell, see Douglas Chambers, "Darkness Visible," in *Familiar Colloquy: Essays Presented to Arthur Edward Barker,* ed. Patricia Brückmann (Ontario, 1978), pp. 163–178; Katharine M. Morsberger, "Darkness Visible: Imagination and Evil in *Paradise Lost,*" *Odyssey: A Journal of the Humanities,* Vol. 3, No. 1 (1978), pp. 3–12; Edgar F. Daniels, "Thomas Adams and Darkness Visible . . . ," *N & Q, n.s.,* Vol. 6 (1959), pp. 369–370; Ann Gossman, "Milton, Plutarch, and Darkness Visible," *N & Q, n.s.,* Vol. 8 (1961), pp. 182–183; Ants Oras, "Darkness Visible: Notes on Milton's Descriptive Procedures in

Paradise Lost," in *All These to Teach,* ed. Robert A. Bryan et al. (Gainesville, Florida, 1965), pp. 130–143; Joseph E. Duncan, "Milton's Four-in-One Hell," *HLQ,* Vol. 20 (1957), pp. 127–136; John P. Cutts, "The Miserific Vision: A Study of Some of the Basic Structural Imagery of *Paradise Lost,"* *EM,* Vol. 14 (1963), pp. 57–72.

6. *Sancti . . . Basilii Magni . . . Opera Omnia,* II, Pt. 2 (Paris, 1618), 118; Migne, *P.G.,* XXXII (Paris, 1857) 1297–1300: "Eita barathron bathy, kai skotos adiexodeuton, kai pyr alampes en toi skotei, ten men kaustiken dynamin echon, to de phos apheiremenon." (Greek transliterated.) Basil's belief that the heaviest penalty of Hell was disgrace and shame provides an interesting parallel to the humiliation of Satan and his colleagues in Book X of *Paradise Lost.* (All italics are mine with two exceptions: 1) texts from Scripture, and 2) quotations from Thomas Aquinas and Bonaventura.)

7. Basil, *Opera,* II, Pt. 2, 119; cf. *P.G.,* XXXII, *loc. cit.:* "Tote to pyr hetoimasmenon eis kolasin toi diaboloi kai tois angelois autou diakoptetai tei phonei tou Kyriou: hina epeide dyo eisin en toi pyri dynameis, he te kaustike kai he photistike, to men drimy kai kolastikon tou pyros tois axiois tes kauseos prosapomeinei, to de photistikon autou kai lampron tei phaidroteti ton euphrainomenon apoklerothei: hos alampes einai to pyr tes kolaseos, akauston de to tes anapauseos apomeinai. Kai me amphiballe. En gar tais ton bebiomenon hemin antapodosesi, tou pyros he physis diairethesetai: kai to men phos, eis apolausin tois dikaiois: to de tes kauseos odyneron, tois kolazomenois apotachthesetai." (Greek transliterated.)

8. Migne, *P.G.,* XLVII (Paris, 1863), 289. "Ti an tis, eipoi ta apo tou skotous deimata tais hemeterais enginomena psychias? hosper gar ouk estin analotikon ekeino to pyr, houtos oude photistikon: oude gar an skotos en." (Greek transliterated.)

9. Migne, *P.G.,* XXX (Paris, 1857), 925: ". . . Deus volens famulum suum mirifica visione convertere, sic apposuit rubo flammam, ut solam vim claritudinis ejus, deposita torriditate, monstraret. Sicut et psalmus testatur dicens: *Vox Domini intercidentis flammam ignis (Psal.* xxviii, 7). Unde etiam in retributionibus delictorum quae in vita contraximus, ratio quaedam nos secretior docet *partiendam ignis esse naturam: cujus lux ad illuminandos deputabitur justos, ardor autem ad concremandos proficiet peccatores."* Cf. Migne, *P.L.,* LIII (Paris, 1865), 923.

10. In the Authorized Version, *Genesis* 1:14.

11. Migne, *P.L.,* XIV (Paris, 1845), 192. Both paragraphs are from the *Hexaemeron.*

12. Migne, *P.L.,* LXXV (Paris, 1849), 912–4. Cf. 914: ". . . flamma comburit, sed nequaquam tenebras discutit . . ."

13. *Ibid.,* 915.

14. *Ibid.,* 916. "Ecce quae maneat damnatos poena cognovimus; et instruente nos sacro eloquio, quantus in damnatione ignis, quanta in igne obscuritas, quantusque in obscuritate pavor sit, nullatenus ambigimus" (*ibid.,* 916).

15. Migne, *P.L.,* CXIII (Paris, 1852), 787.

16. Migne, *P.L.,* CXVIII (Paris, 1852), 952–6.

17. *Ibid.,* 956.

18. *Ibid.,* 956–7.

19. Migne, *P.L.,* CLXVIII (Paris, 1854), 1015.

20. *Divi Thomae Aquinatis . . . in librum B. Iob expositio* (Romae, 1562), 145. Cf. *B. Alberti Magni . . . Commentarii in Iob,* ed. Melchoir Weiss (Friburgi Brisgoviae, 1904), 153: "*et nullus ordo,* quia etiam qualitates elementales ibi ordinem suum non servant. Unde Gregorius: 'Flamma, quae hic urit et illuminat, ibi ruit et obscurat.' Ps (XXVIII, 7): 'Vox Domini intercidentis flammam ignis.' Basilius dicit super illud: Quia ustivum ignis mittitur ad inferos, illuminativum autem ad superos."

21. Part III (Supplement), Question 97, Article 4. The *"Summa Theologica" of St. Thomas Aquinas,* tr. Fathers of the English Dominican Province (London, 1922), 172–3.

22. See III (Suppl.), Q. 74, A. 6, "Whether that fire will engulf the wicked?": ". . . so too will it be with the fire of that conflagration, as Basil says in Ps. xxviii. 7, *The voice of the Lord divideth the flames of fire*, because whatever fire contains of burning heat and gross matter will go down into hell for the punishment of the wicked, and whatever is subtle and lightsome will remain above for the glory of the elect." *Ibid.* (London, 1921), 166.

23. Q. 97, A. 4. *Ibid.* (London, 1922), 172.

24. *Ibid.*, 173.

25. *Ibid.*, 173.

26. Job 18:5.

27. *S. Bonaventurae Opera Omnia*, ed. PP. Collegii a S. Bonaventura (Ad Clasar Aquas [Quarracchi], 1889), IV, 925.

28. *Ibid.*, 925.

29. Book IV, Distinction 44, Part 2, Article 2: "Ad illud quod obiicitur de luciditate, dicendum, quod ignis tres sunt species, scilicet *lux, flamma*, et *carbo*, et istae species materiales; et quamvis in omnibus his salvetur natura lucis tamen minime est in materia terrestri, et *maxime terrestris* parum habet de luce et multum resolubilis est in fumositatem; et in tali materia, utpote in sulphure et pice, ignis potius est tenebrosus quam lucidus, quia magis visum impedit, quam adiuvet. Et per hanc modum imaginari possumus ignem infernalem et ad hoc adiuvari auctoritate Scripturae. Dicitur enim Apocalypsis decimo quarto: *Cruciabuntur igne et sulphure;* item, Isaiae trigesimo quarto: *Dies ultionis Domini* etc.; et post: *Convertentur torrentes eius in picem, et humus eius in sulphur''* (*ibid.*, 927).

30. III (Suppl.), Q. 97, A. 6. ". . . It belongs to the nature of this fire of ours to give light. But the fire of hell gives no light, hence the saying of Job xviii. 5: *Shall not the light of the wicked be extinguished? . . . I answer that . . .* the fire of hell is of the same species as the fire we have so far as the nature of fire is concerned . . . To give light does not belong to fire according to any mode of existence, since in its own matter it gives no light; wherefore it does not shine in its own sphere according to the philosophers: and in like manner in certain foreign matters it does not shine, as when it is in an opaque earthly substance such as sulphur. The same happens also when its brightness is obscured by thick smoke. Wherefore that the fire of hell gives no light is not sufficient proof of its being of a different species." *Op. cit.*, 178–9.

31. Richard Rolle de Hampole, *The Pricke of Conscience (Stimulus Conscientiae)*, ed. Richard Morris (Berlin, 1863), 184, See Skeat, 451–2.

32. Rolle, 186.

33. Ibid., 253.

34. Skeat (ed.), *The Canterbury Tales: Text*, Second Edition (Oxford, 1900) 575–7.

35. Ibid., 579.

36. "Phone Kyriou diakoptontos phloga pyros." (Greek transliterated.) Cf. Authorized Version, Psalm 29:7, "The voice of the Lord divideth the flames of fire." See *Homilia in Psalmum XXVIII, Opera*, I (Paris, 1618), 176: "Intercidit enim ignis flammam secundum historiam trium Puerorum apud Babylonem, quando caminus supra cubitos xlix. sese effuderat, eosque qui circumstabant, ambussit omnes. E diverso eadem flamma Dei praecepto intercisa in se recepit spirantem auram, nempe perquàm iucundissimam respirationem atque refrigerationem pueris tribuens veluti sub unius alicuius arboris peramabili umbra, tranquillo ac requieto in stato constitutis. Facta est (inquit) flamma, veluti spiritus roris suavi spirans sibilo. Longè est admirabilius ignis naturam intercidi, quàm mare rubrum in partes dividi. Attamen domini vox ignis continenter sibi cohaerescentem atque unitam naturam intercidit. Quanquam igitur indivisibilis & insecabilis humanis sensibus videatur ignis, verumtamen ad praeceptum domini interciditur ac dividitur. Existimo autem quòd ignis ad supplicium diabolo & angelis eius paratus domini voce interciditur. Quoniam duo sunt in igne potissima,

ustiva vis & illustratoria. Vis prior ignis acerrima quidem ad poenas irrogandas, reposita est his qui ustione sunt digni. Altera nempe splendiflui sui luminis diffusiva velut sortitò succedet iis, qui claritate perfruituri sunt gaudia perennis. Vox itaque domini intercidentis flammam ignis ac dividentis, ita ut obscurus quidem sit ignis supplicij, vi verò comburendi careat lux illa refocillationis." Cf. Migne, P.G., XXIX (Paris, 1857), 297: "Oimai de, hoti to pyr to hetoimasmenon eis kolasin toi diaboloi kai tois angelois autou diakoptetai tei phonei tou Kyriou: hina, epeide dyo eisin en toi pyri dynameis, he te kaustike kai he photistike, to men drimy kai kolastikon tou pyros tois axiois tes kauseos prosapomeinei, to de photistikon autou kai lampron tei phaidroteti ton euphrainomenon apoklerothei. Phone oun Kyriou diakoptontos phloga pyros kai merizontos, hos alampes men einia to pyr tes kolaseos, akauston de to phos tes anapauseos apomeinai." (Greek transliterated.) Cf. page 3, footnote 1, supra.

37. See Homilia VI in Hexaemeron, Opera, I, 71: "Nam & ignis vim ustivam ab eius splendore tu quidem ipse separare minimè vales: Deus autem volens famulum suum reddere sibi attentiorem illo admirabili spectaculo, in rubum ignem splendore solùm agentem, otiosam autem flagrandi urendique facultatem habentem immisit, ut & Psaltes testatur: Vox Domini, dicendo, intercidentis flammam ignis. Unde arcana quaedam doctrina nos docet, cum pro iis, quare in vita gessimus, mercedes nobis retribuentur, naturam ignis in haec distributum iri: Lux sanè iustis in perennem & peramoenam fruitionem cedet: è diverso supplicio addicendis seorsim attribuetur vis ustiva." Cf. Migne, P.G., XXIX, 121:
"Epei kai soi ten kaustiken dynamin tou pyros apo tes lamprotetos chorisai amechanon: ho de Theos, paradoxoi theamati ton heautou theraponta epistrepsai boulomenos, pyr epetheke tei batoi apo mones tes lamprotetos energoun, ten de tou kaiein dynamin scholazousan echon. Hos kai ho Psalmoidos martyrei legon: Phone Kyriou diakoptontos phloga pyros. Hothen kai en tais ton bebiomenon hemin antapodosesi logos tis hemas en aporrhetoi paideusi, diairethesesthai tou pyros ten physin, kai to men phos eis apolausin tois dikaiois, to de tes kauseos odyneron tois kolazomenois apotachthesesthai." (Greek transliterated.)

38. "Deute, tekna, akousate mou: phobon Kyriou didaxo hymas." (Greek transliterated.) Cf. Authorized Version, Psalm 34:11, "Come, ye children, hearken unto me: I will teach you the fear of the Lord." See Homilia in Psalmum XXXIII, Opera, I, 225: "Deinde eos qui multa perperam in vita admiserunt, horrendi quidam ac tristes circunstabunt Angeli . . . Subin[de] conspicient barathrum in imum patens, tenebras impermeabiles quidem illas, ignemque obscurum, urendi quidem in tenebris vim habentem, luce verò destitutem." Cf. Migne, P.G., XXIX, 372: "Eita barathron bathy, kai skotos adiexodeuton, kai pyr alampes, entoi skotei ten men kaustiken dynamin echon, to de phengos apheiremenon." (Greek transliterated.)

39. "Kai estai to phos, tou Israel eis pyr." (Greek transliterated.) Cf. Authorized Version, Isaiah 10:17, "And the light of Israel shall be for a fire, and his Holy One for a flame: and it shall burn and devour his throns and his briers in one day . . ." See Enarratio in Esaiam, Opera, I, 1052: "Cúmque operatoriae vires ignis duae sint potissimùm, illustrativa & adustiva: prior quidem perquam suavis & amoena, ob id sanè est & apprimè gratiosa, splendor ignis persistet ut ipsum Israël illustret, suaque claritate circunfundat, amarulenta autem afflictio & aegritudo animi in superbum distribuetur, ut ipsum incendat, & per adustionem absque consolatione afflictioni tradat. Et sanctificabit eam in igne flagranti, & comedet quasi foenum sylvam. Pandit hic naturam ignis. Quia lustrativus est & purgatorius: sanctificabit enim ipsum quasi in igne ardenti." Cf. Migne, P.G., XXX (Paris, 1857), 544: "Estai gar, phesi to phos tou Israel eis pyr. Kai dyo energeion ouson peri to pyr, tes te photistikes kai tes kaustikes . . ." (Greek transliterated.)

40. Ioannis Merceri . . . Commentarij in librum Iob (Geneva, 1573), 42. Mercerus commented on Job. 10:22 as follows: "Nostri theologizantes ad infernum, ubi confusio

& horror, perpetuae tenebrae, luctus & stridor dentium, quasi sibi ob oculos haec Iob proposuerit. Liceat quidem delatione ita *theologizein* [Greek transliterated]. Verùm simpliciter Iob ad mortem & sepulchrum respexit." Cf. *Iob Petri Merlini Commentariis Illustratus* (Geneva, 1599), 74–5. The subject of Job 10:22, Merlinus agreed, was "sepulchri conditio." "Inepti sunt ergo qui hic inferni & damnatorum conditionem describi putant . . ."

41. Ioannes Ferus, *Iobi Historiae . . . Explicatio* (Coloniae, 1571), 255: "Quartò nullus in inferno ordo est . . . Mortis proprietas est, hominem interficere, ignis natura sua non ardet tantum, vero etiam splendet. In damnatis verò neutrum horum naturam suam retinet. Mors eos non interimit, licet perpetuò moriantur. Ignis urit quidem, & cruciat, sed nihil illis splendoris adfert. Ad huc modum nullus est ordo in inferno." Cf. Ioannes de Pineda, *Commentariorum in Iob Libri Tredecim* (Coloniae Agrippinae, 1600), I, 406: "*Ubi nullus ordo . . .* An etiam naturalis rerum ordo ibi in versus esse videtur, cum ignis non luceat . . . ?" *Ibid.*, 411: "Nullus praeterea ulla in re ordo sed incredibilis confusio . . . ; ut etiam ignis, qui natura sua lucidus est, quasi perturbata natura, obscuritatem potiùs, quam splendorem eo in loco afferat."

42. Torquato Tasso, *Discorsi del Poema Eroico, Prose,* ed. Francesco Flora (Milan, 1935), 333–4, 360–3.

43. *P.L.,* LXXV, 916.

44. *Opera,* I, 176.

45. Ibid., 71.

46. *P.L.,* XIV, 192.

47. *Verity,* 372.

48. By describing Hell as a flaming "Furnace" Milton may have intended to suggest the contrast between the predicament of the evil angels and the situation of the "three children" in the fiery furnace of Babylon. For the latter God miraculously divided the dual properties of flame, so that they remained unharmed by the heat of the fire. For the devils, on the other hand, he performed a similar miracle, with precisely the opposite effect. By suggesting the contrast between the two episodes, Milton could emphasize the antithetical rewards and punishments of the just and unjust.

49. Cf. also Jude, verse 6. "And the angels who kept not their first estate, but left their own habitation, he hath reserved in everlasting chains under darkness unto the judgment of the great day." In Revelation xx. 13, Satan is "cast . . . into the bottomless pit"; and in Revelation xx. 10 he is "cast into the lake of fire and brimstone," to "be tormented day and night forever and ever." Cf. also Matthew xxv. 41 ("everlasting fire, prepared for the devil and his angels."

50. See Stanley Eugene Fish, "Discovery as Form in *Paradise Lost*," in *New Essays on Paradise Lost,* ed. Thomas Kranidas (Berkeley, Los Angeles, and London, 1971), pp. 1–14.

51. See John P. Cutts, "The Miserific Vision: A Study of Some of the Basic Structural Imagery of *Paradise Lost*," *EM,* Vol. 14 (1963), pp. 57–72.

52. See Howard Schultz, *Milton and Forbidden Knowledge* (New York, 1955).

53. 2 Thessalonians ii. 10–12; cf. Romans i. 21–28; Ephesians iv. 18.

54. The optical illusions associated with Satan's temptations, along with imagery drawn from the science of optics (mirages, apparitions of battles and argosies in the clouds, telescopes and microscopes), are an integral part of the larger pattern of illusion (including self-deception as well as beguiling others) which Milton associates with the fallen angels. The infernal wonders and *mirabilia* whereby the "juggling" fiends change their shape or size at will—now larger than giants, now smaller than tiniest elves—belong to the same art of illusion as the art of the lying magician or the sophistic orator. It involves the art of deliberate magnification or diminution comparable to the skills of the sophistic rhetorician, who knows how to make the small appear great (or vice versa) and the worse the better reason.

55. For Milton's views on the creation and fall of the angels, the special government of good and evil angels, the four degrees of death, and the final judgment passed on the evil angels, see *The Christian Doctrine,* Book I, Chapters 7, 9, 12, 13, 33. The knowledge of the fallen angels "is great, but such as tends rather to aggravate than diminish their misery; so that they utterly despair of their salvation"; *The Prose Works of John Milton,* Vol. IV, *A Treatise on Christian Doctrine,* tr. Charles R. Sumner (London, 1870), p. 219. Arguing that "Hell appears to be situated beyond the limits of this universe," Milton cites Matthew viii. 12 on "outer darkness" and Luke xvi. 26 on the "great gulf" between the blessed and the damned: pp. 490–491.

The forbidden tree was "called the tree of knowledge of good and evil from the event; for since Adam tasted it, we not only know evil, but we know good only by means of evil"; p. 221. In Milton's representation of the punishment inflicted on Satan and his angels in Book X of *Paradise Lost,* the image of the knowledge of evil, based on the symbol of the forbidden fruit, has apparently been combined with the image of death as the punishment for sin, and the Pauline metaphor concerning the "motions of sins" which "bring forth fruit unto death" (Romans vii. 5). The first degree of death includes all evils "which lead to death, and which . . . came into the world immediately upon the fall of man . . . ." Spiritual death consists in the "loss of divine grace, and . . . of innate righteousness," and it affects both mind and will. It involves first "the obscuration to a great extent of that right reason which enabled man to discern the chief good, and in which consisted . . . the life of the understanding"; and secondly the "deprivation of righteousness and liberty to do good," and (conversely) a "slavish subjection to sin and the devil, which constitutes . . . the death of the will"; pp. 263–265.

After the third degree of death (the death of the body; pp. 268–286) there follows "eternal death, or the punishment of the damned." This consists "partly in the loss of the chief good, namely, the favour and protection of God, and the beatific vision of his presence, which is commonly called the punishment of loss; and partly in eternal torment, which is called the punishment of sense"; pp. 488–489.

In *Milton and the Angels,* p. 47, Robert H. West discusses John Salkeld's views on the subject of angelic knowledge.

56. In this scene Milton portrays the experience of extreme evil and misery through gustatory imagery, just as in the scenes in Heaven he has represented the fruition of the Supreme Good and highest felicity through the imagery of "Angels Food" and "rubied Nectar" (*PL,* lines 630–638) and just as he has portrayed man's intimate converse with Heaven before the fall through the imagery of a shared repast and an afterluncheon dialogue. In much the same way Christ's recovery of Paradise for mankind at the end of his temptation-ordeal is celebrated by a divine banquet served by ministering angels and including food and drink from the tree and fountain of life. Milton had utilized similar imagery earlier in *Epitaphium Damonis,* in portraying Damon's (i.e. Diodati's) fruition of eternal life and joy: "AEthereos haurit latices & gaudia potat/ Ore Sacro" (lines 206–207). Whereas the elect angels quaff immortality and joy in the presence of the Deity, partaking of the "copious" bounty of divine fulness (plenitude or pleroma) without danger of satiety or surfeit, the fallen angels chew the ashes of remorse as part of their penance, symbolically tasting death, greedily engorging but starving with famine.

Chapter Seven: *Eyelids of the Morn*

1. See David Masson (ed.), The Poetical Works of John Milton III (London, 1874), p. 447; A. W. Verity (ed.), Comus and Lycidas (Cambridge, 1898), p. 130; M. Y. Hughes (ed.), Milton . . . Minor Poems (New York, 1937), p. 286; H. A. Todd (ed.), The Poetical Works of John Milton, V (London, 1801), pp. 18–19. Cf. The Bible (London, 1613) on Job iii. 9, "Heb. the eye lids of the morning." Hughes (p. 386 notes a

further parallel to Milton's metaphor in Henry More's *Psychozoia*, Canto I, stanza 24. See also the notes by A.S.P. Woodhouse and Douglas Bush in *A Variorum Commentary on the Poems of John Milton*, gen. ed. Merritt Y. Hughes, Vol. 2, *The Minor English Poems* (New York and London, 1972).

2. The Bible (London, 1613), Job xli. 18. In some versions of Job this text is numbered as 9 or (more rarely) as 10.

3. William Gesenius, Edward Robinson, and Francis Brown (eds.), A Hebrew and English Lexicon of the Old Testament (Boston and New York, 1928), translate this phrase as *"eyelids of dawn*, break of dawn." Cf. Gesenius and Robinson (Boston, 1860), *"the eye-lashes of the dawn*, for the rays of the morning sun. . . . Better, '*aphapayim* (Hebrew transliterated) for the eyelids with the eyelashes as a whole, like Lat. *palpebrae*. . . . In these passages—Job. iii.9, xli.10] the allusion is specially to *the eyelashes*, as a figure to represent the first rays of dawn; so too the Arabic."

4. Ibid., s.v. *'uph* (Hebrew transliterated) cf. James Strong, A Concise Dictionary of the Words in the Hebrew Bible (New York, 1890).

5. Schindleri Lexicon Pentaglotton . . . In Epitomen redactum à G.A. (Londini, 1635).

6. Lexicon Heptaglotton, . . . Authore Edmundo Castello, II (Londini, 1686).

7. Olympiodori Alexandrini in Beatum Job (P.G., XCIII, cols. 60, 444); Sacra Biblia ad LXX. interpretum fidem diligentissime tralata (Basileae, 1526). Olympiodorus (col. 60) explains the allusion in Job iii. 9 alternatively as the morning star or the sun, "Me idoi heōsphoron anatellonta, toutesti, ton heōthinon astera, e kai ton helion." (Greek transliterated.)

8. Cf. Biblia. Breves in eadem Annotationes, ex doctiss. interpretationibus, & Hebraeorum commentariis (Parisiis, 1532). The Glossa Ordinaria explains this figure literally as the last hours of the night and allegorically as a reference to the worldy-wise (Textus bibliae cum Glossa ordinaria, Nicolai de Lyra postilla [Lugduni, 1528–1529]): "Palpebras diluculi extremas horas noctis accipimus: in quibus quasi nox oculos aperit dum venturae lucis iam initia ostendit. Prudentes igitur saeculi maliciae antichristi perversis consilijs inhaerentes quasi palpebrae sunt diluculi: quia fidem quam in christo inveniunt, quasi errorem noctis asserunt: & venerationem antichristi veram esse mane pollicentur." According to Lyranus' commentary, the phrase "Ortum surgentis aurorae" (Job iii. 9) refers literally to the "signum aurorae surgentis quae praecedit lucem solis," while the eyelid-image in Job xli tropologically signifies the devil's false revelations: "Oculi eius ut palpebrae diluculi. Per oculos eius designantur revelationes falsae quas tanquam veras recipiunt prophetae diaboli & hoc significantur per palpebras diluculi."

9. Biblia Hebraica. Eorundem Latina Interpretatio Xantis Pagnini Lucensis, Recenter Benedicti Ariae Montani Hispal. & quorundam aliorum collatio studio, ad hebraicam dictionem . . . expensa (Antverpiae, 1584).

10. Leo Juda (tr.), Biblia Sacrosancta Testamenti Veteris & Novi, è sacra Hebraeorum lingua . . . translata (Tiguri, 1544).

11. Biblia Interprete Sebastiano Castalione . . . In recenti hac translatione . . . expressam Hebraeae atque Graecae sententiae Veteris ac Novi Testamenti veritatem (Basileae, 1551).

12. Hebraica Biblia, Latina planeque nova Sebast. Munsteri tralatione (Basileae, 1534).

13. Testamenti Veteris Biblia sacra, . . . latine recens ex hebraeo facti, brevibusque scholiis illustrati ab Immanuele Tremellio & Francisco Junio (Londini, 1593).

14. Iohannis Piscatoris Commentariorum in Omnes Libros Veteris Testamenti, III (Herbornae Nassoviorum, 1644). Piscator's commentaries on the Old and New Testaments had been previously published between 1601 and 1616.

15. The implication of swiftness and the analogy between eyelashes and solar rays are

as appropriate in the Latin text as in the Hebrew. Like the Hebrew noun *'ap'appáyim,* the Latin *palpebrae* could signify both eyelids and eyelashes, and its etymology had been traced by Renaissance lexicographers to the verb *palpitare.* Cf. Ambrosii Calepini Bergomatis Lexicon (Haganoae, 1526); Robert Stephanus, Thesaurus Linguae Latinae (Basileae, 1576); Thomas Cooper, Thesaurus Linguae Romanae & Britannicae (Londini, 1584).

16. Iobus, sive de patientia liber Poetica Metaphrasi explicatus, Authore Abrahamo Aurelio (Londini, 1632).

17. The Holy Bible, tr. John Wycliffe and his Followers, ed. Rev. Josiah Forshall and Sir Frederic Madden (Oxford, 1850); cf. N.E.D., x.v. Eyelid.

18. The Bible (Edinburgh, 1579).

19. The Holy Bible (London, 1584).

20. Arthur Golding (tr.), Sermons of Master Iohn Calvin, upon the Booke of Iob (London, 1574).

21. Iob Expounded by Theodore Beza . . . Faithfully translated out of Latine into English (Cambridge, 1593?).

22. Iosuah Sylvester, *Iob Triumphant,* in *DuBartas His Divine Weekes and Workes* (London, 1641).

23. The Matthew, Coverdale, Taverner, and "Great" Bibles agree in rendering the two passages as "the rysynge up of the fayre morning" (Job iii) and "hys eyes lyke the mornynge shyne" (Job xli). See The Bible in Englyshe (London, 1541); The Bible . . . translated into Englische by Thomas Mathewe (London, 1549); The Whole Bible . . . Faythfully Translated into Englyshe by Miles Coverdale (Zurich, 1550); The Byble, . . . faithfully set furth according to the Coppy of Thomas Matthews translacion (London, 1551); cf. T. H. Darlow and H. F. Moule, Historical Catalogue of the Printed Editions of Holy Scripture in the Library of the British and Foreign Bible Society (London, 1903).

24. The Holie Bible faithfully translated into English, out of the authentical Latin. Diligently conferred with the Hebrew, Greeke, and other Editions in divers languages . . . By the English College of Doway (Doway, 1609), "the rysing of the appearing morning" (Job iii), "his eies as the twinklings of the morning" (Job xli). Revised editions of the Douai version alter this reading to "the rising of the dawning of the day" and "his eyes like the eye-lids of the morning"; see The Holy Bible, translated . . . and first published by the English College at Doway, Anno 1609. Newly revised, and corrected (Philadelphia, 1790).

25. La Bible, qui est Toute la sainte Escriture, à savoir le vieil & nouveau Testament (Lyon, 1561).

26. La Bible qui est toute la saincte escriture du Vieil & du Nouveau Testament . . . Le tout reveu & conferé sur les textes Hebrieux & Grecs par les Pasteurs & Professeurs de l'Eglise de Geneve (Geneve, 1588).

27. La Biblia que es, los sacros libros del vieio & nuevo Testamento. Traslade en Español (Basilea, 1569).

28. Biblia: das ist: Die gantze Heilige Schrifft: Deudsch Auffs new zugericht. D. Mart. Luth. (Wittemberg, 1545).

29. Den Bybel Dat is de boecken der heyligher Schriftuer/uytten oirspornckelijcken Hebreuschen ende Grieckschen ghetrouwelick verduytschet (Schotlandt/by Danswiuck, 1598).

30. La Bibbia, cioè i libri del vecchio e del nuovo testamento: nuovamente traslatati in lingua Italiana, da Giovanni Diodati . . . (Geneva, 1607), "le palpebre dell'alba . . . maniera di parlar figurato: per loqual significa que' primi chiarori che si veggono allo spuntar dell'alba" (Job iii.9); "alle palpebre dell'alba . . . . c. sono cosi grandi, rosseggianti, e lucenti, che risplendono da lungi, come l'alba" (Job xli. 18). Cf. Pious Annotations upon the Holy Bible . . . by the Reverend . . . Iohn Diodati (London, 1643), "*The dawning of*] the Italian, *the eye lids of* or the first appearing of day light: a poeticall

terme" (Job iii. 9), *"the eye lids of]* like unto the dawning of the day" (Job xli. 18).

31. Cf. Todd, V, p. 18; Sophocle, I, ed. A. Dain and tr. P. Mazon (Paris, 1955), p. 77,

> . . . o chryseas
> hameras blepharon . . .
> (Greek transliterated.)

Though Mazon (p. 76) translates this passage as "oeil du jour doré" (*"eye* of golden day") rather than as "eye-lid," the word *blepharon* (Greek transliterated.) like the Hebrew noun *'ap 'ap*) may support both interpretations. Cf. H. G. Liddell, R. Scott, and H. S. Jones, A Greek-English Lexicon (Oxford, 1925), s.v. *blepharon.* (Greek transliterated.) Robertus Stephanus (s.v. Palpebrae) cites *blephara* and *blepharides* (Greek transliterated) as the Greek equivalents of *palpebrae;* and Henricus Stephanus, Thesaurus Graecae Linguae (Genevae, 1572), defines BLEPHARON (Greek transliterated) as "Palpebra, . . . i. Pellis oculis obducta & hos tegens, quae & *kalymma* (Greek transliterated) vocatur . . . Etymolog. dictum vult hoc vocabulum quasi *tou blepontos pharos."* (Greek transliterated.) On the other hand, Thomas Watson (Sophoclis Antigone, Londini, 1581, p. 19) translates Sophocles' phrase as "O aurata tandem emicas/ Claritas diei."

32. Cf. Todd, V, pp. 18–19; Thomas Middleton, A Game at Chesse, ed. R. C. Bald (Cambridge, 1929), pp. 55–56; Christopher Marlowe, The Jew of Malta, ed. H. S. Bennett (London, 1931), p. 74; Geoffrey Bullough (ed.), Philosophical Poems of Henry More (Manchester, 1931), p. 19; The Poems . . . of Richard Crashaw, ed. L. C. Martin (Oxford, 1927), pp. 125, 151. For later parallels in the works of Tennyson and Bayard Taylor, see Verity, p. 130, and N.E.D., s.v. Eyelid.

33. De Bybel (Leyden, By de Weduwe van Joannes Elzevier, 1663).

34. La sainte Bible, qui contient le Vieux et le Nouveau Testament, Edition nouvelle, faite sur la Version de Geneve, reveue, & corrigée; Enrichie outre les anciennes Notes, de toutes celle de la Bible Flamande, de la plupart de M. Diodati, & de beaucoup d'autres (Amsterdam, Chez Louys & Daniel Elzevier, 1669).

35. Cf. Liddell and Scott, s.v. *Blepharon* (Greek transliterated), "of the curtain of darkness at nightfall, *nuktos aphenges B.* (Greek transliterated.) E[uripides] *Ph[oenissae]* 543."

36. Verity, p. 159

37. Todd, pp. 18–19.

38. N.E.D., s.v. Glimmer.

Chapter Eight: *Haemony: Etymology and Allegory*

1. See Edward S. LeComte, "New Light on the 'Haemony' Passage in *Comus,"PQ,* XXI (1942), 284–285.

2. Robert M. Adams, *Ikon: John Milton and the Modern Critics* (Ithaca, N.Y., 1955), p. 18.

3. John Arthos, *On a Mask Presented at Ludlow-Castle by John Milton* (Ann Arbor, Mich., 1954), pp. 44–45. Among numerous studies of Milton's herb, see John Arthos, "Milton's Haemony and Virgil's Amellus," *N&Q,n.s.,* Vol. 1 (1961), p. 172; James Holly Hanford, "Haemony . . . ," *TLS,* Nov. 3, 1932, p. 815; T. P. Harrison, Jr.; "The Haemony Passage in Comus Again," *PQ,* Vol. 22 (1943), pp. 251–254; Edward S. LeComte, "New Light on the Haemony Passage in *Comus,"PQ* Vol. 21 (1942), pp. 283–298; Sara R. Watson, "An Interpretation of Milton's Haemony," *N&Q,* Vol. 178 (1940), pp. 260–261 and "Moly in Drayton and Milton," *N&Q,* Vol. 176 (1939), pp. 243–44; Sacvan Bercovitch, "Milton's Haemony: Knowledge and Belief," *HLQ,* Vol. 33 (1970), pp. 351–359; J. Karl Franson, "An Anglo-Saxon Etymology for Milton's Haemony," *American Notes & Queries,* Vol. 14 (1975), pp. 18–19; John D. Ulreich,

Jr., "'A Bright Golden Flow'r': Haemony as a Symbol of Transformation," *SEL*, Vol. 47 (1977), pp. 119–128; Charlotte Otten, "Homer's Moly and Milton's Rue," *HLQ*, Vol. 33 (1970), pp. 361–372 and "Milton's Haemony," *English Literary Renaissance*, Vol. 5 (1975), pp. 81–95.

4. *Orlando Innamorato, Composto gia del Sig. Matteo Maria Bojardo . . . , ed ora rifatto . . . da M. Francesco Berni* (Fiorenza, 1725), pp. 55, 126–127, 172.

5. *Orlando Furioso di M. Lodovico Ariosto* (Venetia, 1603), pp. 61, 70.

6. Ibid., pp. 32, 51.

7. Giangiorgio Trissino, *L'Italia Liberata da' Goti* (Orleans, 1787), I, 91–146; cf. Merritt Y. Hughes, "Spenser's Acrasia and the Circe of the Renaissance," *JHI*, IV (1943), 381–399; D. C. Allen, *The Harmonious Vision* (Baltimore, Md., 1954), p. 33.

8. Torquato Tasso, *Jerusalem Delivered*, tr. Edward Fairfax, ed. Henry Morley (London, 1890), pp. 439–442.

9. *Eustathii Archiepiscopi Thessalonicensis Commentarii ad Homeri Odysseam*, I (Lipsiae, 1825), 381, "hōs ek molou d esti kakopatheias perigignomenēn (Greek transliterated henceforth.) Cf. LeComte, p. 287.

10. *A Lexicon Abridged from Liddell and Scott's Greek-English Lexicon* (Oxford, 1926), x.v. *haimos*. The chief merit of this derivation is the parallel with the "prickles" on Milton's herb. The usual definition of this word, however, is *drymos (copse, thicket); see A Greek-English Lexicon*, ed. H. G. Liddell and R. Scott, rev. Sir H. W. Jones (Oxford, 1953), s.v. *haimos, drymos.* Cf. *Hesychii Alexandrini Lexicon*, ed. Kurt Latte, I (Hauniae, 1953), "*Haimoi: drymoi*"; G. Budaeus, *Lexicon Graeco-Latinum* (Ex off. Jo Crispini, 1554), "*haimos*, . . . nemus, arbustum"; Henricus Stephanus, *Thesaurus Graecae Linguae* (Paris, 1572), I, "*Haimos*, Locus arboribus densus aut fructibus, Dumus"; IV, "*Haimoi*, . . . Saltus, locus arborosus." Another possible derivation is *Haimion*, which Stephanus defines as *Hostia*, the animal slain in sacrifice—an allusion which would reinforce LeComte's conception of haemony as a symbol of Christ's blood and Coleridge's sacramental interpretation.

11. A. W. Verity (ed.), *Comus* (Cambridge, 1953), p. 91.

12. Sarah Ruth Watson, "An Interpretation of Milton's 'Haemony'," *N&Q*, CLXXVIII (1940), 260.

13. Actually the river Haemon is not in Arcadia, but lies east of Chaeronea in Boeotia. The closest verbal link between Haemony and Arcadia seems to be *Haimoniai*, an old city allegedly founded by *Haimon* and situated between Megalopolis and Asea in Arcadia. Spenser may have had the latter in mind, but his reference to "grassie bancks" suggests that his *Haemony* may be a river—possibly a symbol for the Thames. See Georg Wissowa and Wilhelm Kroll (eds.), *Paulys Real-Encyclopädie der classischen Altertumswissenschaft* (Stuttgart, 1912), s.v. *Haimon, Haimonia, Haimoniae*. Cf. Budaeus, x.v. *haimōn*, "haemon fluvius qui & *Thermōdon*."

14. John Milton, *The Minor Poems*, ed. Merritt Y. Hughes (New York, 1937), p. 251n.

15. Wissowa, s.v. *Haimonia;* cf. Hesychius, "*Haimonia: hē Thessalia. kai hē Ephesos*"; Budaeus, "Haimonia . . . , Thessalia & Ephesus."

16. Wissowa, s.v. *Haimos;* cf. Budaeus, "*Haimos* . . . , Haemus, mons Thraciae."

17. Verity, p. 91.

18. "Elegia Secunda," l. 7; cf. LeComte, p. 285. For the parallel with Ovid's *Metamorphoses*, VII. 264, see Hughes's note, *Minor Poems*, p. 34n.

19. *The Prose Works of John Milton*, IV (London, 1883), 328–331.

20. *Le Metamorfosi di Ovidio, Ridotte da Gio. Andrea dall' Anguillara in ottava rima* (Venetia, 1587), fol. 98.

21. *Natalis Comitis Mythologiae* (Francofurti, 1584), pp. 587–590, 599–600.

22. Ibid., p. 589.

23. LeComte, p. 285.

24. Ibid., p. 288n.; Arthos, pp. 72–73.

25. *A New English Dictionary* (Oxford, 1901), s.v. *Haemony;* Le Comte, pp. 285–286.

26. *Nova Iconologia di Cesare Ripa Perugino* (Padova, 1618), p. 74; "Pietà" is similarly described (p. 412) as "vestita di rosso . . . , perche e compagna, e sorella della Carità, allaquale conviene questo colore."

27. Liddell and Scott, rev. Jones, s.v. *haimonios;* cf. G. Kaibe (ed.), *Athenaei Naucratitae Dipnosophistarum Libri XV,* I (Lipsiae, 1887), 177, "Ton d' en Paroi tei nesoi—diaphora gar kantautha ginetai syka ta kaloumena para tois Pariois haimonia, tauta onta tois Lydiois kaloumenois, aper dia to erythrodes kai tes prosegorias tautes etychen—Archilochos mnemoneuei legon houtos: ea Paron kai syka keina ka thalassion bion." Cf. C. D. Yonge (trans.), *The Deipnosophists or Banquet of the Learned of Athenaeus,* I (London, 1854), 127.

28. Eustathius, II (1826). 326. "The ancients frequently explain this as a species of fig, also called *haimonia* (blood-red) on the island of Paros because of its red color."

29. Stephanus, I, s.v. *Haimonia syka.* "*Haimonia syka* (the blood-red fig), a species of fig on the island of Paros, so called because of its red color, as Athenaeus declares in Book III and as Eustathius states after him. When these declare that the fig is thus named because of its redness, they suggest that its name was derived from *haima* (blood), just as if they had said *dia to haimatoeides chroma,* because of its bloody color. In the same passage Athenaeus writes that this species is also called Lydian."

30. *Omnia Andrea Alciati . . . Emblemata: Cum commentariis . . . per Claudium Minoem Divionensem* (Antverpiae, 1581), p. 424, "Purpureus color pudoris indicium"; Ripa, pp. 554–556, "Vergogna Honesta . . . vestasi di rosso, . . . essendo questo colore proprio della vergogna, bellisimo in donzelle, & garzoni per inditio della modestia loro . . . , e Menandro solea dire *Omnis erubescens probus esse mihi videtur.* Ogni huomo che s'arrosisce, mi pare buono, siche il colore rosso molto conviensi alla figura della vergogna."

31. LeComte, pp. 285–287; Budaeus, '*haimon* . . . , cruentus."

32. LeComte, pp. 289–290.

33. Ibid., pp. 290–297; see Adams, pp. 11–17, for a criticism of this interpretation.

34. Wissowa, s.v. *Moly.*

35. *N.E.D.,* s.v. *Haemony;* LeComte, pp. 285–286.

36. *Eustathii Episcopi Thessalonicensis Commentarii ad Homeri Iliadem,* I (Lipsiae, 1827), [Book V], v. 49 ff. "He says that Scamandrios fell by the hand of Menelaos and was *theres haimona* (skilled in hunting), that is to say *epistemona* (wise), a good hunter, excelling in archery, whom Artemis herself had taught. . . . *Haimon* signifies *daimon* or indeed *daemon* (knowing)."

37. Hesychius, s.v. *haimona;* cf. *Apollonii Sophistae Lexicon Homericum,* ed. I. Bekker (Berolini, 1833), p. 14. "*haimona epistemona, empeiron:* '*haimona theres.*'"

38. Thomas Gaisford (ed.), *Etymologicon Magnum* (Oxonii, 1848), s.v. *Haimon.* "daio (to know) is *gignosco* (to know) or *manthano* (to learn). From this word are derived the terms *daskalos* and *didaskalos* (teacher) and *daialos;* and, by repetition of the *d,* the word *daidalos,* i.e., *epistemon* (wise); and *daimon,* or *autodidaktos* (self-taught); and, by aphaeresis of the *d, haimon* (skilled)."

39. Budaeus, s.v. *haimon.* "*Haimon* is the same as *epistemon* (wise), *empeiros* (knowing), i.e., *peritus* (skilled). This word is derived from *daimon* by dropping a letter."

40. Stephanus, IV, s.v. *Haimon.* "*Haimon* is believed to have been derived by aphaeresis of the letter *d* from *daimon,* signifying *daemon* (knowing), *gnarus* (experienced), *peritus* (skilled). Hesychius also explains *haimona* as *epistemona* (wise), *em-*

peiron (knowing), with reference to the phrase *haimona theres* (skilled in hunting) in Homer's *Iliad,* Book V, verse 49." For Milton's knowledge of Renaissance dictionaries, see D. T. Starnes and E. W. Talbert, *Classical Myth and Learning in Renaissance Dictionaries* (Chapel Hill, N.C., 1955).

41. LeComte, pp. 285–286.

42. J. H. Hanford, "Haemony *(Comus* 616–648)," *TLS,* 3 Nov. 1932, p. 815; idem, *A Milton Handbook,* Fourth Edition (New York, 1947), p. 160; idem, *John Milton, Englishman* (London, 1950), p. 83; Sears Jayne, "The Subject of Milton's Ludlow *Mash,*" *PMLA,* LXXIV (1959), 540.

43. Cf. Adams, pp. 14–15; LeComte, p. 287; Frances A. Yates, *The French Academies of the Sixteenth Century* (London 1947), pp. 244–245; Alciati, p. 628, "Id figmentum non rarò intelligitur de virtute omnique eruditione, ad quam primus aditus arduus est ac sudoris plenus, sed suavissimus omnium fructus"; Apollonius, p. 114, s.v. *moly,* "Kleanthes de ho philosophos allegorikos phesi delousthai ton logon, di' hou molyontai hai hormai kai ta pathe." Professor Stanford observes that in Cleanthes' opinion "*moly* was etymologically connected with the verb *molynein* 'to soften' and represented the reasoning faculty 'by which the impulses and passions are softened.'" In his *Homeric Allegories* Heracleitus had interpreted the herb *moly* as "an emblem of intelligence," the god Hermes as "the rational intelligence," and the enchantress Circe as "the allurement of strange vices . . ."; W. B. Stanford, *The Ulysses Theme . . . ,* Second Edition (Ann Arbor, Michigan, 1968), pp. 126–127.

44. LeComte (p. 285n.) observes that "grammarians associate the word [*haimon* with '*daemon,*'" but does not cite any definitions except those of Liddell and Scott, who define the former term as "perhaps eager" and the latter as *skillful.*

45. *Plato,* VI (Loeb Classical Library, London, 1926), 55.

46. Dardi Bembo (tr.), *Commento di Ierocle Filosofo sopra i Versi di Pitagora detti d'Oro* (Venetia, 1604), pp. 22, 25.

47. Budaeus, s.v. *Daimōn.*"

48. Stephanus, I, s.v. "*Daēmōn, Daimōn.*"

49. Eustathius, *Comment. ad Iliadem,* v. 49 ff.; cf. Alexander Politus (tr.), *Eustathius in Homerum, Graece, et Latine* III, (Florentiae, 1735), 1120.

50. Cf. Luke xi.49; I Cor. i.21–24; Eph. iii.10; James iii.17.

51. Hanford, *John Milton, Englishman,* p. 76.

52. John Smith, *Select Discourses* (London, 1660), pp. 164–165; cf. I Cor. xiii.9–12.

53. Cf. *Minor Poems,* pp. 341 ("Lady, that in the prime," etc.), 466 ("Hard are the ways of truth"); *Hamlet,* I. iii.

54. Cf. *Minor Poems,* p. 341; Dante Alighieri, *Inferno,* Canto II, 1. 105.

55. With these interpretations of Haemony in terms of Christian theology one might compare Saint Augustine's use of the image of Christian "medicine" in his theological treatise *On Christian Doctrine:* ". . . so the medicine of Wisdom by taking on humanity is accommodated to our wounds, healing some by contraries and some by similar things . . . Thus the Wisdom of God, setting out to cure men, applied Himself to cure them, being at once the Physician and the Medicine . . . Instruction will reveal many other examples of Christian medicine operating either by contraries or by similar things. . . ." Saint Augustine, *On Christian Doctrine,* tr. D. W. Robertson, Jr. (Indianapolis and New York, 1958), pp. 14–15.

Appendix: *Haemony: Etymology and Allegory*

1. *Comus,* lines 636–7.

2. For the views of Coleridge and John A. Hines, see Edward S. LeComte, "New Light on the 'Haemony' Passage in *Comus,*" *PQ,* XXI (1942), 288n.

3. *Ibid.*, 297.

4. *Gulielmi Budaei . . . Lucubrationes Variae* (Basileae, 1557), 206.

Chapter Nine: *Dalila, Ulysses, and Renaissance Allegorical Tradition*

1. Cf. Milton, *Paradise Regained, The Minor Poems, and Samson Agonistes*, ed. Merritt Y. Hughes (New York, 1937), pp. 433–4, 582; Douglas Bush, *English Literature in the Earlier Seventeenth Century* (Oxford, 1945), p. 394. Among recent studies of Dalila and Milton's Samson, see Stephanie A. Fisher, "Circean Fatal Women in Milton's Poetry: Milton's Concept of Renaissance Women," *DAI*, Vol. 32 (1971), 2639A; J.J.M. Tobin, "A Note on Dalila as 'Hyaena,'" *Milton Quarterly*, Vol. 11 (1977), pp. 89–91; John B. Mason, "Multiple Perspectives in *Samson Agonistes:* Critical Attitudes toward Dalila," *Milton Studies*, Vol. 10 (1977), pp. 22–33; Paul F. Reichardt, "Milton's Samson and the Iconography of Worldly Vice," *Studies in Iconography*, Vol. 5 (1979), pp. 135–145; Thomas Kranidas, "Dalila's Role in *Samson Agonistes*," *SEL*, Vol. 6 (1966), pp. 125–137.

2. Cf. *Natalis Comitis Mythologiae* (Frankfurt, 1584), pp. 760–1; *Omnia Andreae Alciati V. C. Emblemata: Cum Commentariis . . . Per Claudium Minoem Divionensem* (Antwerp, 1581), pp. 411–12.

3. Cf. 410–11: 'But fou! effeminacy held me yok't Her Bond-slave.'

4. Alciati, pp. 284–7. Cf. p. 285: 'Circe meretrix, quos sibi amore turpi devinxit. . . . Cui sententiae subscribit Palladas lib. 1. Graecor. epigr. . . . *Nam meretrix quondam perniciosa fuit.'*

5. *Ibid.*, pp. 410–16. Cf. Conti, p. 763; 'At Dorion in libro de Piscibus formosas quasdam meretriculas fuisse Sirenas scribit in litore habitantes, quae suavitate harmoniae ad se navigantes allicerent.'

6. Alciati, pp. 285–7.

7. *Ibid.* pp. 411–16.

8. Conti, pp. 575, 763–4. Cf. Giuseppe Horologgi's 'Annotationi' in *Le Metamorfosi di Ovidio, Ridotte da Gio. Andrea dall' Anguillara in ottava rima* (Venice, 1587), pp. 188–9: 'Circe che trasforma gl'huomini in fiere, e in sassi, è quella fiera passion naturale, che chiamano Amore. . . . I compagni di Ulisse trasformati da Circe in Porci, significano gli huomini che si lasciano vincere dalla libidine divenire come Porci.'

9. Conti, p. 763; Alciati, p. 412.

10. Conti, p. 764.

11. Alciati, pp. 412, 415.

12. *Ibid.* pp. 410–11.

13. Conti, p. 757.

14. Alciati, p. 413.

15. Conti, p. 763. Cf. Horologgi, p. 68: 'Le sirene . . . trasformate in *mostri* marini, sono secondo Palefatto le *meretrici, le quali per la loro infame libidine, si possono dire veramente mostri;* e i nomi loro ci danno lume delle loro *arti;* Perche Partheno voce greca, significa vergine, onde le meretrici . . . si fingono, per coglierli . . . donzelle, overo femine caste, con tenere gli occhi bassi, arrossire à ogni parola . . . : usano queste & altre simili *arti per coglierli nelle loro reti,* e farsi maggiormente amare, e desiderare. l'altra si chiama Leucosia, che vuol dire bianco, figurato per la purità dell'animo, *finta accortamente dalle Meretrici per coprire l'arte . . .* la terza è detta Ligia, che s'interpreta *giro, e viene à significare i lacci, le Reti, e le prigioni, nelle quali tengono gli infelici innamorati.'* The italicized words and phrases have close parallels in Milton's representation of Dalila. Cf. Alciati, p. 414: 'Ligia, non à ligando, ut putant nonnulli, neque ab illiciendo, sed à Graeco *ligeion* (Greek transliterated), quod canorum sonat: aut *ligeos* (Greek transliterated), dulciter, quod ad sermonis & colloquii refertur illicium.' Cf. the numerous allusions in *Samson Agonistes* to sensual snares (trains, toils,

gins, etc.; lines 230, 409, 532–533, 931–933), erotic servitude or captivity (lines 410–419, 808, 945, 950, 1040–1043), sorcery (lines 819, 934–937), and deceptive rhetoric (lines 402–405, 901).

16. Horologgi, p. 68.

17. Alciati, p. 414.

18. Francesco Berni, *Orlando Innamorato . . . dal Sig. Matteo Bojardo* (Florence, 1725), pp. 37, 214. See also Merritt Y. Hughes, 'Spenser's Acrasia and the Circe of the Renaissance', *J.H.I.* iv (1943), 381–99. In Boiardo's text (Book I, Canto VI) Orlando sees a painting of the story of Circe (Circella) in the enchanted garden of the sorceress Dragontina; *Orlando Innamorato*, ed. Aldo Scaglione (Torino, 1963), Vol. I, p. 309. The sorceress is depicted so "vivamente" that the viewer seems to hear her speak ("par che oda parlare"). Cf. *ibid.*, Vol. II, pp. 219–220, for the account of Alcina's fishing. The name of Boiardo's sorceress recalls that of the halcyon or kingfisher (*alcione*). Cf. the similar account of Alcina's fishing in *Orlando Furioso* (Canto VI):

> E senza rete e senza amo traea
> Tutti li pesci al lito, che volea.
>
> * * *
>
> Alcina i pesci uscir facea de l'acque
> Con semplici parole e puri incanti.

Ludovico Ariosto, *Orlando Furioso*, ed. Enrico Bianchi (Firenze, 1948), pp. 124–125.

19. Alciati, p. 286. For the fish-and-net image, see also Emblem no. 75 (In amatores meretricum), pp. 281–3.

20. Arnold Stein, *Heroic Knowledge: An Interpretation of Paradise Regained and Samson Agonistes* (Minneapolis, 1957), p. 205.

21. Conti, pp. 576–7.

22. Alciati, pp. 284–7.

23. Seneca adapted the myth of Ulysses and the Sirens to the prudence which enables a man to "escape the Siren voices of pleasure . . .", and Roger Ascham utilized the same imagery to emphasize the moral perils that might confront the English traveller in Italy. The visitor might fall "into the lap of some wanton and dalying Dame Calypso: and so suffer the danger of many a deadlie Denne, not so full of perils to destroy the body, as, full of vayne pleasures, to poyson the mynde. Some Sirene shall sing him a song, sweete in tune, but sownding in the ende, to his utter destruction . . . Some *Circes* shall make him, of a plaine English man, a right Italian"; W. B. Stanford, *The Ulysses Theme . . .* , Second Edition (Ann Arbor, 1968), pp. 125, 184.

Thus the Circe myth, as reinterpreted by Renaissance mythographers or imitated and adapted by various Renaissance poets (Ariosto, Spenser, Tasso) offered parallels to Samson's relations with his Philistine concubine: sensual folly and intemperance in the first instance, with consequent degradation to conditions worse than those of a beast. Such analogies, however, would link Samson rather with Circe's victims than with the wise Ulysses. Insofar as Samson affords an example of "heroic knowledge" (in Professor Stein's phrase) it is in qualities that associate him with Renaissance idealizations of Homer's hero: in his eventual triumph both over himself and over the powerful enchantress, in his bitterly-acquired self-knowledge, in his endurance in successive trials that test and confirm his heroic magnanimity and his fortitude of mind.

Nevertheless, Dalila's temptation, proposing as it does a life of idleness, and sensual pleasure, recalls not only the blandishments of Homer's sorceress but also the promises whereby Pleasure or Vice, in the legend of Hercules at the Crossroads, attempts to entice the youthful hero from the laborious path of Virtue. Yet, as Milton well knew, there were also Scriptural analogies both for the crossroads motif and for the thematic opposition between wisdom (*sapientia*) and the harlot or *meretrix*. This antithesis had received elaborate development in the Book of Proverbs, and the imagery describing the lethal flattery of the *meretrix* bears at times significant resemblances to Milton's image of Dalila. Wisdom herself stands at the crossroads (Proverbs iii. 2), calling to the passerby; and throughout the book she is repeatedly contrasted with the harlot, "the strange woman . . . who flattereth with her words" and whose "house inclineth unto death . . ." (ii. 16–19). Dalila's "bait of honied words" and "sting/ Discover'd in the end" (*SA*, lines 997–998, 1066) are likewise reminiscent of the imagery of Proverbs (v. 3–5): "For the lips of a strange woman drop as an honeycomb, and her mouth is smoother than oil,/ But her end is bitter as wormwood, sharp as a two-edged sword./ Her feet go down to death . . ." Cf. also Proverbs vii. 7–23; ix. 13–18; xxii. 14; xxiii. 27–28.

Chapter Ten: *Eve's Dream and the Conventions of Witchcraft*

1. William B. Hunter, Jr., "Eve's Demonic Dream," *ELH*, XIII (1946), 256–265; cf. *idem*, "Prophetic Dreams and Visions in *Paradise Lost*," *MLQ*, IX (1948), 277–288. Among recent studies relevant to this episode, see Manfred Weidhorn, *Dreams in Seventeenth-Century Literature* (The Hague, 1970); Linda Draper Henson, "The Witch in Eve: Milton's Use of Witchcraft in *Paradise Lost*," in *Milton Reconsidered: Essays in Honor of Arthur E. Barker*, ed. John Karl (Salzburg, 1976), pp. 122–134; Donald R. Howard, "Flying Through Space: Chaucer and Milton," in *Milton and the Line of Vision*, ed. Joseph A. Wittreich, Jr. (Madison, 1975), pp. 3–23.

2. Cf. Reginald Scot, *The Discoveries of Witchcraft*, ed. Montague Summers (London, 1930), 14, 19, 23, 25, 28, 33; Francesco Maria Guazzo, *Compendium Maleficarum*, tr. E. A. Ashwin, ed. Montague Summers (London, 1929), 33–50, "Whether Witches Are Really Transported from Place to Place to their Nightly Assemblies"; Jacob Sprenger and Henricus Institoris, *Malleus Maleficarum*, tr. Montague Summers (London, 1928), 104–109, "How they are Transported from Place to Place"; R. Trevor Davies, *Four Centuries of Witch Beliefs* (London, 1947), 25, 29, 97; Wallace Notestein, *A History of Witchcraft in England from 1558 to 1718* (Washington, 1911), 97–98; Robert Burton, *The Anatomy of Melancholy*, ed. Floyd Dell and Paul Jordan-Smith (New York, 1927), 177; George Lyman Kittredge, *Witchcraft in Old and New England* (Cambridge, Mass., 1929), 29, 243–244, 269–274, 564–565; Henry Charles Lea, *Materials towards a History of Witchcraft*, ed. Arthur C. Howland (Philadelphia, 1939), *passim*.

3. For Richard Bernard's allusion to "the Devilish Art of Witchcraft," see Davies, 137.

4. For the toad as familiar, see Davies, 67, 105, 116; Lea, 1374, 1438; Notestein, 36, 161.

5. *Johannis Wieri de praestigiis daemonum, et incantationibus ac veneficijs libri V, Tertia editione aucti* (Basileae, 1566), 224–225. Cf. the chapters, "De melancholicorum depravata imaginatione," 228ff., and "De phantasia, & quomodo vitiatur," 231ff.

6. *Ibid.*, 225–226. Cf. Davies, 98, for Richard Bernard's belief that Satan seduces more women than men to witchcraft as a result of his initial success with Eve. (Translations mine, except when otherwise indicated.)

7. "Eve's flight "up to the Clouds" is thus analogous both with Satan's ascent "above the height of the clouds" and with the conventional witch's imaginary flight "in aerem usque ad nubes." In Eve's flight, there is another traditional element particularly appropriate for a dream centering on the tree of forbidden knowledge—the aerial journey as a symbol of intellectual contemplation. See F. Cumont, "Le mysticisme astral dans l'antiquité," *Bulletin*, Académie Royale de Belgique, 4th series (1909), 258ff., 278ff.; cf my article, "Chaucer's Eagle: A Contemplative Symbol," *PMLA*, LXXV (1960), 153–159.

8. The problem of demonic transportation was broader than that of the witch's flight, and writers who rejected the latter as a delusion might nevertheless recognize the devil's

power to transport persons or objects through the air. One of the texts most commonly cited in support of this doctrine was the Biblical account of Christ's temptation (Matthew iv. 5, 8; Luke iii. 5, 9), where the devil takes Jesus into a high mountain and also sets him on a pinnacle of the temple at Jerusalem. Weyer discusses the point in his chapter, *"An & quomodo & quando corpora per aerem deferre diabolus possit"* (Wierus, 247ff.), observing that theologians disagree in their interpretation of the episode on the temple-tower: "Indeed theologians disagree on this point, as to whether Christ was carried off and snatched away by the devil or merely led, so that he himself climbed thither on foot." Cf. Lea, *passim*. In *Paradise Regain'd* Milton treats this as a power specifically granted to Satan for the occasion: (III, 251–252), "With that (such power was giv'n him then) he took The Son of God up to a Mountain high"; IV, 541ff., "So saying he caught him up, and without wing Of *Hippogrif* bore through the Air sublime Over the Wilderness and o'er the Plain; . . . There on the highest Pinacle he set The Son of God . . . ." For the *Canon Episcopi* and Pseudo-Augustine's *Liber de Spiritu et Anima*, see Lea, 178–181; Kittredge, 244–245.

9. Wierus, 239.

10. *Ibid.*, 245–246.

11. *Ibid.*, 246, ". . . because afterwards [Ponzinibio] mentions that those women testify that they ride at night on beasts and travel through many lands. And he declares that most are deceived in this opinion, believing that there is anything of deity and divinity beyond the one God. Hence he enjoins . . . that all these things should be regarded as false and that such phantasms are imposed on men's minds not by a divine but by an evil spirit. And he gives the reason in the text, 'for Satan himself is transformed into an angel of light.' When Satan overcomes the mind of any woman and subjugates her to himself through infidelity, he immediately transforms himself into the appearances and likenesses of different persons and leads the captive mind astray, deluding it with dreams and showing it both glad and sorrowful objects and known and unknown persons."

12. *Ibid.*, 342, 684.

13. Cf. Sprenger, 3, 7; Lea, 189–109, 197; Kittredge, 246.

14. Lea, 183–185.

15. *Ibid.*, 131–175, "And thus deceive the five senses by the phantasms that they receive. Hence many people in their folly believe that there are witches who wander at night with Dame Habonde." Cf. the variant version in *Le Roman de la Rose*, ed. Ernest Langlois, Vol. IV (Paris, 1922), 228–229, "Qui les cinc sens ainsinc deceit/Par les fantosmes qu'el receit."

16. J. Huizinga, *The Waning of the Middle Ages*, tr. F. Hopman (London, 1927), 219, "As long as I live I shall not believe That a woman can bodily Travel through the air like blackbird or thrush. . . . When the poor woman lies in her bed, In order to sleep and to rest there, The enemy who never lies down to sleep Comes and remains by her side. Then to call up illusions Before her he can so subtly, That she thinks she does or proposes to do What she only dreams."

17. Lea, 1919.

18. *Ibid.*, 191–192.

19. Kittredge, 248.

20. *Ibid.*, 249–250.

21. Davies, 60.

22. *Ibid.*, 62.

23. *Ibid.*, 68.

24. There is a certain propriety in investing the temptation to disobedience with the conventions of witchcraft. In discussing *inobedientia* in the *De Doctrina Christiana* (Columbia Edition, Bk. II, Ch. 3), Milton quotes 1 Samuel xv. 23 as a prooftext, "rebellion is as the sin of witchcraft, and stubbornness is an iniquity and idolatry."

25. See Lea, 260, 271, 276, 284, 291, 297, 302, 348, 354–6, 377–80, 400–2, 413–14.

26. Davies, 170–172.

27. Kester Svendsen, *Milton and Science* (Cambridge, Mass., 1956), 74–75.

28. Howard Schultz, *Milton and Forbidden Knowledge* (New York, 1955), 46–47; see *The Works of John Milton* (Columbia Edition), XVII, 148–150.

Chapter Eleven: *Paradise Lost and the Apotheosis Tradition*

1. Though the apotheosis should not be confused with other flight-motifs—such as the metaphorical ascent of the mind through contemplation of celestial objects, the flight of the imagination in dream-visions and in poetic or prophetic rapture, the flight of fame and metaphorical elevation to the skies through praise and renown—it frequently absorbs these motifs; and poets often combine them in a single work. In Renaissance art and literature, as in classical antiquity, the apotheosis became a standard convention of the rhetoric of encomium; and few poets or painters cared to restrict it to its original sense of actual deification, the transformation of a mortal into a god. In antiquity the term had been broadened to include daimons and heroes; commentators on Lucan refer to Pompey's apotheosis, though he actually takes his place among the shades of demigods and heroes, not among the Olympians. Apollo and Artemis were literally apotheosized; they became divinities without tasting death; Keats would portray the former as shrieking at the dawn of celestial glory. On the other hand, Hercules had to undergo death before achieving deification. His status remained curiously equivocal, for he ranked not only among the gods of Olympus but also among the heroic shades of the underworld. A poet might literally deify Julius Caesar (as did Virgil and Ovid), for Caesar had in fact been accorded posthumous honors as a deity. Similarly, a later emperor of Rome might legitimately jest, on the point of death, about "becoming a god." Nevertheless, in the Renaissance as in late antiquity, writers and artists tended to extend the conventions of the apotheosis beyond their original meaning, transferring them to virtually any person whom the poet or painter might delight to honor. They could apply not only to mortals who had actually become deities or had been translated to Elysium without experiencing death, but to almost any separated soul considered worthy of praise.

In the Christian era the original significance of the term was extended still further to include the glorification of the saints and the resurrection of the just; and the conventions of the classical apotheosis were similarly extended not only to princes of the church and state but to persons in private life. Milton did not hesitate to eulogize Edward King and Charles Diodati in language reminiscent of Virgil's apotheosis of Caesar. In his epic on the Fall, however, where man and angel alike transgress through desire for divinity, he found it poetically expedient to exploit (often for ironic effect) the original sense of the term.

No created being could legitimately aspire to divinity through his own merits. Nevertheless, there was one sense in which (in accordance with theological conceptions of *deificatio* or *theosis*) man might ultimately become "deified"—i.e. through the fullness of God in Christ. In the *Christian Doctrine* Milton significantly interprets the translation of Enoch and Elijah as types of the perfect glorification of the righteous. This will consist (he explains) in "eternal life and perfect happiness, arising chiefly from the divine vision." Moreover, upon the resurrection of the dead the living themselves "shall be caught up together with them in the clouds, to meet the Lord in the air . . ." (I Thess. iv. 15–18); *The Prose Works of John Milton* (Bohn Library: London, 1870), Vol. IV, pp. 475, 481, 491. Deification (or apotheosis in the *literal* sense) is possible only in the sense in which "Christ has received his fulness from God" and "in which we shall receive our fulness from Christ"—and the sense in which "God shall be All in All"; cf. *Prose Works,* Vol. IV, p. 143; *Paradise Lost,* Book III, line 341.

For the extension of the original meaning of apotheosis ('"transformation into a god") to the glorification and exaltation of the saints or (still more loosely) to the resurrection and release from earthly life, see *NED, s.v. apotheosis.* For the concept of deification in Christian theology, see *NED, s.v.* deification; and *Encyclopaedia of Religion and Ethics,* ed. James Hastings, *s.v.* Soteriology, and *s.v.* Deification. In Christian theology the "condition under which salvation viewed as deification is obtained by men is necessarily union with Christ—i.e. oneness is being with His divine being."

2. For studies of this tradition, see Morton W. Bloomfield, *The Seven Deadly Sins, An Introduction to the History of a Concept, with Special Reference to Medieval English Literature* (Lansing, Mich., 1952); Franz Cumont, *Astrology and Religion Among the Greeks and Romans* (New York and London, 1912); Cumont, *After Life in Roman Paganism* (New Haven, 1922); Martin P. Nilsson, *Greek Piety,* tr. Herbert Jennings Rose (New York, 1969); and John M. Steadman, *Disembodied Laughter: Troilus and the Apotheosis Tradition* (Berkeley, Los Angeles, London, 1972) pp. 6–8 and *passim.*

3. Among studies of Milton's astronomy and cosmology, see Grant McColley, "The Seventeenth-Century Doctrine of the Plurality of Worlds," *Annals of Science,* Vol. I (1936), pp. 385–430; idem, "The Astronomy of *Paradise Lost,*" *SP,* Vol. XXXIV (1937), pp. 209–247; idem, "Milton's Dialogue on Astronomy: The Principal Immediate Sources," *PMLA,* Vol. LII (1937), pp. 728–762; Kester Svendsen, *Milton and Science* (Cambridge, Mass., 1956); Arthur O. Lovejoy, "Milton's Dialogue on Astronomy," in *Reason and the Imagination: Studies in the History of Ideas,* ed. J. A. Mazzeo (New York, 1962), pp. 129–142; Walter Clyde Curry, *Milton's Ontology, Cosmogony and Physics* (Lexington, Kentucky, 1957); Harry F. Robins, "That Unnecessary Shell of Milton's World," *Studies in Honor of T. W. Baldwin,* ed. Don C. Allen (Urbana, 1958), pp. 211–219; Thomas N. Orchard, *The Astronomy of Milton's Paradise Lost,* Revised Edition (London, 1913).

4. On the motif of divine laughter, cf. Donald Maurice Rosenberg, "Milton and the Laughter of God," diss., Wayne State University, 1966.

5. In contrast to Milton's minor poems, neither of his epics makes unqualified use of the conventions of the Christian apotheosis. Though this omission may be significant, one should not (without further evidence) assume that it results altogether from his theological beliefs. The genre and arguments of both poems may have been largely responsible. Although the motif of the soul's celestial glorification was not uncommon in Christian epic, it was virtually unavoidable in Christian funeral elegy. The arguments of Milton's epics are concerned, on the other hand, with events preceding the death of the first Adam in one instance, and prior to the death and resurrection of the second Adam in the other case. In contrast to the earlier funeral poems there would be no real need to portray the soul's ascent in either of these heroic poems.

6. Quotations from Milton's poetry are based on John Milton, *Complete Poems and Major Prose,* ed. Merritt Y. Hughes (New York, 1957).

7. Cf. the flight of the poetic imagination in Milton's Fifth Elegy and his "At a Vacation Exercise."

8. For the apotheosis-motif as an element in the *consolatio,* see Michael West, "The *Consolatio* in Milton's Funeral Elegies," *HLQ,* Vol. XXXIV (1971), pp. 233–249.

9. Cf. the motif of the flight of fame in *Mansus.* The Echo-song in *Comus,* with its suggestion that Echo be translated to the skies is also reminiscent of the traditional flight of fame.

10. Hughes, pp. 138–139. Like the apotheosis of Lycidas (Edward King), who has become "the Genius of the shore" and the tutelary guardian of "all that wander in that perilous flood"—a role comparable to that of the elemental daimons of classical

tradition—the apotheosis of Damon (Charles Diodati) is a pastoral convention, recalling Virgil's apotheosis of Daphnis (Julius Caesar) in the Fifth Eclogue; cf. James Holly Hanford, *John Milton, Poet and Humanist,* ed. John S. Deikhoff (Cleveland, 1966), pp. 140–141; Hughes, p. 125 n. Mingling Christian and classical eschatology, both of Milton's pastoral elegies summon the dead shepherd to the mystic marriage of the Lamb (Revelation xix). Classical decorum appears, however, to be more consistently observed in the later elegy. Both poems, in fact, allude to the communion of saints; nevertheless, whereas *Lycidas* explicitly calls them "Saints," the *Epitaphium Damonis* refers, in accordance with the *maniera antica,* to the fellowship of "the souls of heroes and the immortal gods." In this poem, as in *Comus,* Milton exploits one of the commonplaces of Neoplatonic pneumatology—the correlation between pure ether and the purified soul—and converts it to the praise of virginity. "Damon dwells in the pure aether, the aether which he is pure enough to possess." The emphasis on "holy simplicity" and "unsullied virtue" ("Sanctaque simplicitas, . . . candida virtus") as the qualities which have entitled him to this ethereal dwelling belongs to the same tradition. Traditionally the soul recovers the primitive simplicity of its true nature in proportion to its separation from earthly contagion and the grossness of matter.

For Pythagorean discussions of gods, daimons, and heroes and for the Hesiodic tradition that men of the golden race became daimons and guardians of mankind, see *Disembodied Laughter,* pp. 21, 28–29 and *Milton's Epic Characters,* pp. 324–326.

11. Erwin Rohde, *Psyche,* tr. W. B. Hillis (New York, 1966), Vol. I, p. 73.

12. Cf. Revelation xiv. 13, "And I heard a voice from heaven saying unto me, Write, Blessed are the dead which die in the Lord from henceforth: Yea, saith the Spirit, that they may rest from their labours; and their works do follow them." Cf. the motif of *vain* alms and *vain* endeavors in Ariosto's *Orlando Furioso.*

13. Rohde, Vol. I, p. 74. For discussion of the representation of Elysium in classical and Renaissance literature, see also A. Bartlett Giamatti, *The Earthly Paradise and the Renaissance Epic (Princeton, 1966).*

14. *The Works of Plato,* tr. B. Jowett (New York, *n.d.*), Vol. III, p. 262, "islands which the air flows round." Cf. C. S. Lewis, "Above the Smoke and Stir," *TLS* (July 14, 1945), p. 311; B. A. Wright, *TLS* August 4, 1945), p. 367; Robert Eisler, *TLS* (September 22, 1945), p. 451; Lewis, *TLS* (September 29, 1945), p. 463; Wright, *TLS* (October 27, 1945), p. 511. Cf. John Arthos, "The Realms of Being in the Epilogue of *Comus,*" *MLN,* Vol. LXXVI (1961), pp. 321–324. On the garden of Eden and Elysium, cf. DeWitt T. Starnes, "The Hesperian Gardens in Milton," *University of Texas Studies in English,* Vol. XXXI (1952), pp. 42–51; cf. Robert Burton, *The Anatomy of Melancholy* (London, 1837), Vol. I, p. 159, on "Platos Elysian fields."

15. The Trinity Manuscript of *A Maske* alludes merely to "A Guardian spirit, or Daemon" and does not specify his mode of entrance. According to the Bridgewater version *"a guardian spiritt or demon descendes or enters."* In the 1645 edition of Milton's *Poems, "The attendant Spirit descends or enters."*

16. For the principles of levity and gravity and their relations to the theory of motion, see Aristotle, *On the Heavens* in *The Basic Works of Aristotle,* ed. Richard McKeon (New York, 1941), pp. 454–466. "The consideration of these questions is a proper part of the theory of movement, since we call things heavy and light because they have the power of being moved naturally in a certain way . . . There are things whose constant nature it is to move away from the centre, while others constantly move towards the centre; and of these movements that which is away from the centre I call upward movement and that which is towards it I call downward movement . . . By absolutely light, then, we mean that which moves upward or to the extremity, and by absolutely heavy that which moves downward or to the centre. By lighter or relatively light we mean that one, of two bodies endowed with weight and equal in bulk, which is exceeded by the other in the speed of its natural downward movement." Thus fire is absolutely

light, and earth absolutely heavy; but the lightness or heaviness of air and water is relative.

17. For studies of Milton's Limbo of Vanity, see Bruce P. Baker, "Ironic Contrast in Milton's Paradise of Fools," *Notes and Queries*, n.s., Vol. XIII (1966), p. 378; William J. Grace, "Notes on Robert Burton and John Milton," *SP*, Vol. LII (1955), pp. 578–591; Joseph Horrell, "Milton, Limbo, and Suicide," *RES*, Vol. XVIII (1942), pp. 413–427; Merritt Y. Hughes, "Milton's Limbo of Vanity," in *Th' Upright Heart and Pure*, ed. Amadeus P. Fiore, O.F.M. (Pittsburgh, 1967), pp. 7–24; Frank L. Huntley, "A Justification of Milton's Paradise of Fools," *ELH*, Vol. XXI (1954), pp. 107–113; Esmond L. Marilla, "Milton's Paradise of Fools," *English Studies*, Vol. XLII (1961), pp. 159–264; Berta Moritz-Siebeck, "Der Limbus-Passus in Milton's *Paradise Lost*," *Anglia*, Vol. LXXIX (1962), pp. 153–176; Norma Phillips, "Milton's Limbo of Vanity and Dante's Vestibule," *ELN*, Vol. III (1966), pp. 177–182; Irene Samuel: *Dante and Milton: the Commedia and Paradise Lost* (Ithaca, 1966), pp. 85–93; Julian Ziegler, "Two Notes on J. T. Williams' Words into Images in Chaucer's *House of Fame*," *MLN*, Vol. LXIV (1949), pp. 73–76; Hughes, *Complete Poems*, p. 269 n.

Though these parallels are not close, they nevertheless share the motifs of fame, vanity, and merit or demerit; some or all of them have been in Milton's mind, though one can hardly regard them as sources. Chaucer's *House of Fame* is, in some respects, a burlesque encomium of the goddess, just as Milton's Limbo of Vanity represents, to some extent, a burlesque apotheosis. Both poems utilize the imagery of wind and air to emphasize the vanity of fame ("the praise of men")—a Boethian as well as a Biblical commonplace—and both involve the issue of merit. Ariosto's moon serves as a mirror for the follies and vanities of men. Here (in a passage that Milton quotes in *Of Reformation* from Harington's translation) Astolfo perceives "A mightie masse of things straungely confused, / Things that on earth were lost or were abused." The crowns and scepters of Assyrian and Greek monarchs are now a hill of bladders, representing (according to Harington's gloss) the "Pride of Princes and vanitie of their titles." Here too are "Gifts given to Princes in hope of reward," "false flatteries," "fond loves," "Favorites rewards," "Great mens promises," great cities overthrown by treachery, "Alms and charitable deeds done to late," the Donation of Constantine, the beauty of women, and the lost wits of men. Though Ariosto denies the presence of folly (*pazzia*) since that remains with us on earth, Harington correctly observes that "All those things that he faynes to have been showed *Astolfo* in the circle of the Moone are but similitudes and likeness of such follies as he that will marke them well shall easely discerne." The principal analogies between the *Orlando Furioso* and Milton's Paradise of Fools are thematic—their common emphasis on human follies and vain endeavors. Though Ariosto's episode also includes an allegory of time and fame, its point is the power of poetry to bestow enduring glory and to preserve the names of great men from inevitable oblivion. The allegory culminates in a temple of fame where historians and poets preserve the names of their patrons "in cleare fame and good report" and in St. John's fiery denunciation of the failure to reward contemporary writers. Amply rewarded for the volume he had written in his Master's praise, he loves writers well and is indignant at their wrongs. Ariosto's treatment of fame and oblivion has little in common with Milton's; see *Lodovico Ariosto's Orlando Furioso Translated . . . by Sir John Harington*, ed. Robert McNulty (Oxford, 1972), pp. 396 to 403.

The inhabitants of Dante's Limbo (*Inferno*, IV) do not lack merit; they lack baptism. Dante's description of the virtuous pagans and the Noble Castle is "reminiscent of Virgil's Elysian fields." The privileged position that they, and certain Moslems, occupy among the souls in Limbo is (Sapegno suggests) Dante's own invention, "che non trova riscontro nei teologi medievali"; see *La Divina Commedia di Dante Alighieri*, ed. C. H. Grandgent, Revised Edition (Boston, New York, 1933), pp. 36–37; Dante

Alighieri, *La Divina Commedia*, ed. Natalino Sapegno, Vol. I (Firenze, 1955), p. 42 n. The inhabitants of the Antinferno, on the other hand, who have merited neither praise nor blame, remain without fame in the world and are excluded from both Heaven and Hell, whirling forever in the dark air "come la rena quando turbo spira"; Sapegno, pp. 30–33.

Milton's Limbo of Vanity contains elements reminiscent of all of these (and other) parallels; but the analogy is not close, and he has radically transformed whatever details or themes he may have borrowed from them.

18. For a comparison of Milton's treatment of the scales motif with Homeric and Virgilian examples and for Milton's adaptation of "those Biblical balances in which Belshazzar was weighed and founding wanting" (*Daniel*, v. 27), see Dennis H. Burden, *The Logical Epic: A Study of the Argument of Paradise Lost* (London, 1967), pp. 28–31. In the encounter between Satan and Gabriel in *Paradise Lost* the scales-motif, introduced in a martial context like the classical *kerostasia* and *psychostasia*, resembles the medieval *psychostasia* insofar as it involves a clearcut opposition between good and evil. For the classical *kerostasia* see Books VIII and XXII of the *Iliad* and Book XII of the *Aeneid*. Here the fate of the Greeks is weighed against that of the Trojans, the fate of Hector against that of Achilles, and the fate of Turnus against that of Aeneas. In all three instances the heavier scale presages defeat and death. In Book Two of the *Posthomerica* of Quintus Smyrnaeus (a work well known to Milton), the fates (Keres) indicate the outcome of battle, without the actual introduction of the scales-motif. See Quintus Smyrnaeus, *The Fall of Troy,* tr. Arthur S. Way (London and New York, 1913), p. 105, "And now amongst the Blessed bitter feud / Had broken out; but by behest of Zeus / The twin Fates suddenly stood beside these twain, / One dark—her shadow fell on Memnon's heart; / One bright—her radience haloed Peleus' son."

For a discussion of *kerostasia* and *psychostasia*, see Jane Harrison, *Prolegomena to the Study of Greek Religion* (New York, 1955), pp. 183–187. In the *Iliad* the sinking scale denotes the loser; in Aeschylus' lost *Psychostasis*, as in *Paradise Lost*, it designates the victor. Cf. *NED, s.v.* psychostasy, "A weighing of souls; in *Anc. Mythol.* supposed to take place during a combat, the combatant having the lighter soul being slain." See also Emile Mâle, *The Gothic Image: Religious Art in France of the Thirteenth Century*, tr. Dora Nussey (New York, 1958), pp. 376–377 and Fig. 186. In medieval representations of the Last Judgment, St. Michael holds the scales in which sins are weighed against good actions. Citing parallels in the writings of St. Augustine and St. John Chrysostom and in the ancient beliefs of India and Egypt, Mâle observes that the metaphor of the weighing of good and evil, "constantly used by writers and preachers in the Middle Ages, struck the popular imagination, and was realised in art." See also Mâle, p. 32, on the application of the imagery of "chaff before the wind" to the fate of sinners in medieval Scriptural allegory.

Karl Künstle, *Ikonographie der christlichen Kunst* (Freiburg im Breisgau, 1928), Vol. I, pp. 249–250, argues that (contrary to the widespread opinion of iconographers), the angel bearing the scales for the weighing of good against evil deeds at the Last Judgment should not be identified with St. Michael. "Michael ist der *Seelenführer* und *Paradieswächter*, aber nicht der *Seelenwäger*."

19. *Henry IV* Part One, Act VI, Scene I, "What is honour? A word. What is that word honour? Air. A trim reckoning! . . . Honour is a mere scutcheon . . ."

20. For the Biblical giants as types of secular heroism, see *Milton's Epic Characters*, pp. 177–193.

21. For discussion of classical pneumatology, see E. Vernon Arnold, *Roman Stoicism* (Cambridge, 1911); Thomas Whittaker, *The Neo-Platonists*, Second *Edition* (Cambridge, 1928); *Disembodied Laughter*, passim.

22. Jowett, Vol. III, p. 214; cf. pp. 219, 224.

23. *Ibid.,* Vol. III, p. 405.

24. Boethius, Book IV, Meter I; *The Complete Works of Geoffrey Chaucer,* ed. F. N. Robinson (Cambridge, Mass., 1933), pp. 419–420.

25. Lewis and Short, *s.v.* limbus. Like Milton's limbo of vanity, both the theological and astronomical definitions of this term retain the original sense of "border." Cf. *NED, s.v.* limbo, limbus: "A region supposed to exist on the border of Hell as the abode of the just who died before Christ's coming and of unbaptized infants." For the astronomical senses of this term, see Alfred Hoare, *An Italian Dictionary,* second edition (Cambridge, 1925), *s.v.* limbo, "limb, edge of a celestial body" or "outer circle of an astrolabe"; and ibid., *s.v.* lembo, "border edge," "limb, graduated edge of the circle of an instrument or (*astr.*) edge of a heavenly body." *NED* cites Milton's *Apology for Smectymnuus* for an early instance of the use of the term *limbo* as "Any unfavourable place or condition, likened to Limbo; *esp.* a condition of neglect or oblivion to which persons or things are consigned when regarded as outworn, useless, or absurd." See also Derek J. Price, ed. *The Equatorie of the Planetis* (Cambridge, 1955), passim, on the astronomical sense of limbus.

26. For the probable and the marvellous in Aristotelian and Renaissance critical theory, see John M. Steadman, *Milton's Epic Characters: Image and Idol* (Chapel Hill, 1968), p. 299 and passim.

27. Among recent studies of ascent and descent imagery in Milton's poetry, see Jackson I. Cope, *The Metaphoric Structure of Paradise Lost* (Baltimore, 1962); Anne Davidson Ferry, *Milton's Epic Voice: The Narrator in Paradise Lost* (Cambridge, Mass., 1963).

28. Cf. Mâle, p. 105, on virtue as a ladder linking earth to heaven and on Honorius of Autun's moral interpretation of Jacob's ladder as a *scala* of fifteen virtues.

29. Cf. Howard Schultz, *Milton and Forbidden Knowledge* (New York, 1955). For the analogy between Eve's illusion of flight and the delusions of witches under demonic influence see John M. Steadman, "Eve's Dream and the Conventions of Witchcraft," *JHI,* Vol. XXVI (1965), pp. 567–574.

Conclusion

1. Cf. Thomas Carew, "An Elegy upon the Death of Doctor Donne," in *Seventeenth-Century English Poetry,* ed. Shawcross and Emma, pp. 258–259.

1a. Abraham Cowley, "To Sir *William Davenant* Upon his two first Books of *Condibert,* finished before his voyage to *America,*" in *The Anchor Anthology of Seventeenth-Century Verse,* Vol. 2, ed. Richard S. Sylvester (Garden City, N.Y., 1969), pp. 590–591.

2. "On the Death of Mr. Crashaw," in *ibid.,* pp. 594–595.

3. *English Literary Criticism: the Renaissance,* ed. O. B. Hardison, Jr. (New York, 1963), pp. 327–329.

4. Cf. Leah Jonas, *Divine Science: The Aesthetic of Some Representative Seventeenth-Century English Poets* (New York, 1940).

Index of Names

Aaron, 27, 43, 61, 63, 214
Adams, R. M., 13, 142
Addison, Joseph, 89
Aeschylus, 1, 19
Agrippa, Cornelius, 214
Alabaster, William, 74
Albertus Magnus, St., 234
Alciabides, 4
Alciati, Andrea, 155, 156, 157, 243, 244, 245
Alexander the Great, 4, 26, 27, 54
Ambrose, Isaac, 218
Ambrose, St., 91, 121, 123, 128, 227
Andrewes, Lancelot, Bp. of Winchester, 3, 171
Andronicus, Livius, 209
Anguillara, Giovanni Andrea dell', 157
Anselmus, Georgius, 110, 111
Apollinaris of Alexandria, 70
Apollonius of Rhodes, 23, 39, 244
Ariosto, Lodovico, 11, 29-30, 38, 41, 45, 59, 86, 142, 143, 144, 150, 178, 211-12, 246, 251, 252
Aristotle, 4, 33, 70, 72, 176, 223, 224, 228, 251
Arthos, John, 142, 144
Ascensius. See Badius Ascensius, Jodocus
Ascham, Roger, 209, 246
Athenaeus, 72, 147, 148, 243
Augustine, St., 31, 83, 126, 162, 244, 253
Aurelius, Abraham, 138
Austin, Samuel, 220

Bacon, Francis, 62, 165
Badius Ascensius, Jodocus, 95
Barber, C. L., 13
Barnes, Barnabe, 220, 223
Baroni, Leonora, 5-6
Bartas, Guillaume de Saluste, sieur du, 14, 17, 23, 37, 51, 75, 76, 77, 78, 81, 86, 87, 89, 219, 222, 225, 226
Basil the Great, St., 121, 122, 123, 124, 125, 126-27, 127-28, 234, 235, 236
Ben Gerson, 103
Benvenuto da Imola, 74
Bernard, Richard, 247
Berni, Francesco, 142, 144
Bèze, Théodore de (Beza), 112, 138

Boccaccio, Giovanni, 82, 85, 86, 91, 94, 95, 96, 168, 169, 171, 173, 212, 224, 228
Boethius, 168, 169, 174, 179, 183, 252
Boiardo, M. M., 28, 142, 158, 211, 246
Bonaventura, St., 125-26
Bowra, C. M., 56, 211, 213
Bruno, Giordano, 59
Budé, Guillaume, 149, 150, 152, 153, 242, 243
Burden, Dennis H., 253
Bush, Douglas, 222, 224

Caesar, Augustus, 70
Caesar, Julius, 27, 249, 251
Calderini, Domizio, 95
Calepinus, Ambrosius, 90, 92, 94, 96, 97, 98, 106, 227
Callimachus, 15, 228
Calvin, John, 138
Campbell, Lily Bess, 75, 81, 88, 89, 115, 119, 219, 220, 223
Cartari, Vincenzo, 95, 98, 101
Cassiodorus, 96, 98, 229
Castell, Edmund, 136, 230, 231
Castellio, Sebastian (Castalio), 137
Castelvetro, Lodovico, 223
Chapman, George, 35, 209, 224
Chaucer, Geoffrey, 86, 121, 126, 127, 128, 168, 169, 178, 183, 252
Chrysippus, 70
Cicero, 70, 71, 92, 173, 183, 223
Cleanthes, 244
Cleaver, Robert, 106, 107, 230, 231
Cleombrotus, 41, 178, 179
Coleridge, Samuel Taylor, 146
Collop, John, 121
Columbus, Christopher, 53
Columella, 216
Comes, Natalis. See Conti, Natale
Conti, Natale, 89, 95, 96, 99, 105, 118, 144, 145, 146, 155, 156, 157, 158-59, 228, 245
Cooper, Thomas, 106
Cope, Michael, 230, 231
Cornutus, 96
Coverdale, Miles, 240
Cowley, Abraham, 84, 191-92
Crashaw, Richard, 15, 191, 192
Curius (M. Curius Dentatus), 27
Cyrus, 70